HANZI

THE LISTENING SOCIETY

A Metamodern Guide to Politics
Book One

METAMODERNA

First Edition, 2017

ISBN 978-87-999739-0-3

Metamoderna ApS | www.metamoderna.org

Our mission, in a nutshell, is thus:

To unite the many struggles
of the exploited bodies of the poor
with the struggles of the lost,
suffering souls of the rich world.
And to expand that struggle
to sustainability across time and space.
And to expand that solidarity
to fathom the vast suffering
and multiplicity of perspectives
of the animal realm in its entirety.
And to deepen the struggle
until it is reborn as play.

CONTENTS

PROLOGUE

> "Yeah, yeah, I get it, I get it. There's this talk about something called 'political metamodernism'. It is said to be a new ideology replacing and outcompeting liberal democracy and capitalism as we know them. Quietly, its proponents suggest, it is all but completely trashing socialism, liberalism, conservatism and ecologism, each on its own terms, leaving many people's feelings hurt in the process. Political metamodernism has the capacity to gradually, but profoundly, change the lives of countless millions of people for the better, by cultivating a deeper kind of welfare system and economy—propelling us towards a saner, kindlier world. The welfare system part of this is called **the listening society**. All of this is said to slowly but surely be growing out of the cultural and economic development of the most progressive and advanced societies in the world, like the Nordic countries. And to understand and ally oneself with the listening society is both very useful to oneself and a service to mankind and all the other suffering animals. And it comes with certain risks, like all potent things do... But is it *real*?"

You have it all backwards, my friend. In a way, "is it real" is the dumbest question you can ask, if you quite understand what reality is. Reality is much more than the facts of the matter. The *real* reality resides at the crossroads of fact and fiction. It is born precisely at the point where our imaginations, the stories we tell ourselves, meet the facts of the world and put them into context. Political metamodernism becomes real by the rebellious act of telling a good story, a story that will both haunt and reward its listener.

The mix in this book is mostly fact and some dabs of fiction—meaning that I use emotions, dreams, aphorisms, mental images and some qualified guesses. I play with language and with the relationship with you, the reader.

But other than that, your summary was okay. Political metamodernism is the single most powerful ideology in existence in the world today and you would have to be an idiot not to want to learn about it. Whether you like it or not, whether you are for it or against it, you had better pay attention.

By the way, if the word "ideology" gives you the creeps, feel free to exchange it for "way of thinking and feeling about society", which is something that we all undeniably have—even you.

This book is about you; your own intellectual and emotional development, as well as your place and status in the world. But it is also about society and relationships, about other humans and animals, about how a deeper sociological understanding of the world can help you serve compassionately, and why this is so.

Mixing fact and fiction is of course what children and the insane do. But upon closer inspection, it becomes clear that everybody does it. The question is only how consciously and productively it is done. I use dabs of "fiction" to make this book come alive as a political and cultural current of change. The difference between this approach and drier, more traditionally academic books on social science is that, in this book, the fictional part is owned up to. We take Hanzi's role as an intellectual less seriously—and we take the necessarily fictional part of reality much more seriously. That is how the facts serve us best, with a spoonful of fictional sugar. But make no mistake; the bitter medicine must go down. And it does work.

Most political intellectuals, from Nancy Frazer to Milton Friedman, from Noam Chomsky to Arne Næss, put on these silly garbs to try to look serious and scientific, while they are all still emotionally invested in their ideas and have tearful (fictional) stories about what makes their own perspective the right one and themselves into the humble hero and servant of truth. I am hereby taking off that silly mask. And so should you, frankly. But *how* do you throw off the mask? By admitting that you are wearing it—and then using it more deliberately.

I am just going to tell the story straight and let you play with it. Because that's where the action is. That's where we change the world for real. Along the way we can have a beautiful, albeit dangerous, adventure. Politics, just like life itself, is always an experiment. We have to take risks. We have to be vulnerable to make a deeper impact for better or worse, to truly make a difference that makes a difference.

Political Metamodernism Is the Future

So I want to tell you about something that I call **political metamodernism.** It is a new perspective on politics. It changes not only how we do politics, but also what the role of politics in society is in the first place—and of course, it sets new goals for what we want to achieve in society, and it provides explanations for why.

Very basically, political metamodernism tries to bring about the society that comes *after*, and goes *beyond*, what we usually think of as "modern society". Take a modern country today, like Sweden, and consider how different it is today—politically, socially and economically—from a century ago. And how very different its citizens are. Where did all the hackers, yoga people and feminist vegans come from, for one thing?

The Social Democrats of the early 20th century had an ideology—a vision, an idea of what the future welfare society might look like. In large parts, that society has successfully materialized. But since a few decades, we have no such visions or goals—even as the world is changing more rapidly than ever and the technological possibilities are much greater than before. **So where are the major political visions?**

Seriously. Where are they? The Left works only to maintain the welfare state, the Greens to maintain the sustainability of our current civilization, the libertarian Right to boost economic growth and the nationalist or conservative Right seeks to maintain the old nation state in the face of immigration and globalization. All of these movements and ideologies are stuck in the mindset of party politics that evolved from industrial society, with its classes and issues. None of them actually offer us anything new, or anything that might substantially improve our lives in a way that would compare to the building of the modern liberal democracy with a market economy and welfare state. What is the equivalent of this system in the society of the future, a society we know is globalized, digitalized and postindustrial? **In which direction can and should our society evolve?** Is that an unreasonable question? I don't think it is. I think it's deeply unsettling that we, as humanity, are not having that conversation.

This is where political metamodernism comes in. Political metamodernism tries to achieve a society that is as different from today as today's Sweden is from Sweden in 1900. Everything is going to be different. For good or bad, people are going to vote differently, educate differently, work differently, live and travel differently—even love and socialize differently. We will have different ideas about the world and our place in it. Just being alive will feel different.

So the aim of political metamodernism is to take us from one "modern" stage of societal development (liberal democracy, party politics, capitalism, welfare state) to the next "metamodern" stage of development. It is aiming to outcompete liberal democracy as a political system, outcompete all of the political parties and their ideologies, outcompete capitalism as an economic system, and outcompete and replace our current welfare system. There. Did I get your attention?

Political metamodernism is built around *one* central insight. **The king's road to a good future society is *personal development* and *psych-***

ological growth. And humans develop much better if you fulfill their innermost psychological needs. So we're looking for a "deeper" society; a civilization more socially apt, emotionally intelligent and existentially mature.

There are three different parts of political metamodernism:

- **The Listening Society**—which is the welfare of the future, a welfare that includes the emotional needs and supports the psychological growth of all citizens. A society in which everyone is seen and heard (rather than manipulated and subjected to surveillance, which are the degenerate siblings of being seen and heard).
- **Co-Development**—which is a kind of political thinking that works across parties, works to keep ego-issues and emotional investments and biased opinions in check, and seeks to improve the general climate of political discourse: "I develop if you develop. Even if we don't agree, we come closer to the truth if we create better dialogues and raise the standards for how we treat one another."
- **The Nordic Ideology**—this is my name for the political structure that would support the long-term creation of the listening society and make room for co-development. It is called the Nordic ideology because its early sprouts are cropping up in and around Scandinavia. It includes a vision of six new forms of politics, all of which work together to profoundly recreate society. A large part of this has to do with how to defend citizens from new sources of oppression that can emerge as a side-effect of a "deeper" society. These new forms of oppression are generally of a more subtle and more psychological kind than what we have seen in the 20th century.

So these three things taken together are what I call political metamodernism. This book focuses mainly on the listening society, and explains how we as humans develop and grow psychologically. The idea is that there is an intimate connection between understanding how humans grow and evolve—intellectually, cognitively and emotionally—and how good or bad society is going to be. **Hence, it should—or must—become a top political priority to support the psychological development of all citizens.**

The next book, titled *Nordic Ideology*, is going to tackle the issues of how societies develop, how the new political system works, and how it's going to beat today's system of liberal democracy.

I have increasingly come to believe that political metamodernism is exceedingly useful for addressing society's ailments, such as:

- the multifaceted ecological crisis;
- the instability of the economy;
- the excessive global inequalities;
- the widespread anxiety, or "alienation", that modern people harbor;
- the challenges of global migration;
- the transition to a postindustrial, robotized and digitalized economy;
- and the challenges of transnational governance.

In other words—I believe it can productively address the major problems of late modern society. The listening society is the bridge that can take us, in a few generations, from the modern world, to a metamodern society.

So basically, a metamodern society is defined as one which has "solved" the problems of modern society, much like modern society "solved" the problems of pre-industrial, traditional society (dramatically reducing poverty, disease, wars, serfdom, slavery and misuse of monarchical power).

Because metamodern thinking encapsulates much of the logic of our current day and age, it is also useful for you as an individual person—especially if you have political ambitions. We will get to that.

Who Is Hanzi Freinacht?

If you are like other human animals, your social brain follows the logic of rhetoric, set out so many centuries ago by Aristotle. This means that for you to be affected by the rational arguments of this book, the *logos*—indeed, for you to at all be capable of taking into account what I am saying—your emotions must be engaged (*pathos*). And, which is the point here, you must also have a relationship to me, the writer: my *ethos*. And within that realm, you probably want to know three things:

- If I am sticking to reality or if there are serious delusions present;
- if I am morally good or evil; if I am "on your side", and
- if I am intelligent, potent, competent; if my words really do matter.

So who is this "the great Hanzi Freinacht", the contender who dares to even try to tell us about the next major ideology to outcompete and replace liberal democracy and capitalism? Much of the answer depends on you, dear reader. With which voice are you sub-vocalizing these words? If you think of Disney's *The Lion King*, is my voice heard as the booming, reliable and goodhearted lion king himself? Or is it the squeaky, mean and rebellious voice of those strange Nazi hyenas, greedily waiting for their turn to grab the meat? Or am I perhaps the malicious, composed voice of the king's conspiring brother? Is it the insolent brat, the aged master, or the enlightened academic, that you hear?

I am a social scientist and political philosopher, with a background in sociology. Within academia I have particularly been interested in criminological issues such as field studies of the police force and the role of ethnicity within the judicial system. My main mentor has been an eccentric but fascinating psychologist-mathematician at Harvard University, called Michael Lamport Commons, the originator of the Model of Hierarchical Complexity (MHC). The MHC is a potent psychological theory that we will discuss in this book (chapters 8 and 9). The genius of Commons' work, and its profound applicability to so many issues in nature, science and society, saturate large parts of the ideas presented here.

On a more personal note I can say this. During most of my adult life I have been followed by a sense of tragedy, a subtle but pervasive sadness that seems to lie in the background; mellow, solemn, still. Everyday events and encounters usually don't connect to it. I'll be optimistic and upbeat or casual. But it seems central to me, in life goals, aspirations and choices. I believe that this sense is shared by many people. When I bring it up or allude to it I often notice that the gaze of the other person freezes for a moment, how your eyes soften a bit. Perhaps there is a sense of recognition.

This sadness may be rooted in my personal life experience, in the (not very unusual) contradictions and adversities that I have lived by. Coming of age was for me to a large extent a process of making peace with this sadness—and a deeper, fundamental anxiety that came with it. It was a long, painful, existential and—dare I say—spiritual journey. And in that process I paradoxically found what appears to be a sustainable source of happiness and meaning. The aching heart itself became the main engine of my life's work. In its mature form, that solemn sadness extended. It became a sense of the tragedy of the world, of the suffering of others, and perhaps even more, an awareness of beauty lost, of potentials that never materialize.

This is a rather cerebral book, an intellectual work. I argue about ideas and concepts in order to state my case and to develop the perspective that I want to share with you. But, my friend, do know that I write this from a subtle longing of the heart. I wish to find paths for society to be genuinely better, as a felt experience for real human beings and other animals. I have come to believe that such paths not only do exist, but that they are increasingly at a competitive advantage to the forms of politics and economy that we know today; that they make sense. I also believe that these paths go through you, the reader. But the road is both difficult and dangerous, which I will return to throughout this book and the next.

Maybe I am mistaken about such paths existing. But at the least I want to share these thoughts with you and see where it leads. I can only hope that someone, somewhere, listens and understands. And, according to my emotional and intellectual capabilities, I will listen to you as well.

Writing this book, I live alone in a house in the French speaking part of the Swiss Alps. I am borrowing it from a wealthy man and his family—I believe he is a billionaire, but I didn't ask. This man is a self-made ex-banker, physicist and philosophical explorer, who for some time has been a supporter of my ideas. Nowadays I call him a good friend. It is true that I live away from family, friends and lovers. But every word of this book is written in quiet peace, overlooking a majestic mountain top, soft green populated valleys and a complex horizon of rugged cliffs that cut against the most often light blue skies. The house is large and wooden, a so-called *chalet*, with very tall windows letting in the view and the light. I don't meet people for weeks and months on end.

I keep a tight schedule: three hours of meditation per day, one hour of physical exercise, half a day's study and half a day's writing. I eat vegan, with much nuts and berries, and take B12 and omega-3 supplements. Sometimes I walk in the mountains alone, daydreaming or speaking passages of the book out loud to myself. Living here, I usually don't even think about family life, hot men, sex with students, weed or LSD—except as societal concerns.[1] The house also has a sauna and a big Jacuzzi by a wide window with a mountain view. In the bubble bath, only the buzzing flies keep me company. And the philosophers. And the ideas. And the determined struggle for a deep, effective change in society.

So is Hanzi good or bad? I am not quite sure. Sometimes people call Hanzi Freinacht a gambler, playing with his own life, with too dangerous ideas, with the future of society. Others go as far as calling me a charlatan, an imposter or poser, an intellectual con-artist. I ask too great questions, speak with too great certainty, express myself much too vividly and seductively about too grand issues. Surely I can be up to no good?

I don't pretend to promise you only good intentions. But it is my unshakable conviction that in risky times, it takes a gambler to place the highest and safest bets. And in the most confused of discourses, only a charlatan can speak the truth.

Readers of Bronze, Silver and Gold

It is also my conviction that this book, if its ideas spread, will cause deep suffering and confusion to a lot of kind and intelligent people, in so many, so delicate and devious ways.

Perhaps I am flattering myself that such an impact could be made by my writings. But after all, I suppose, writing is never a humble thing to do, taking up monologue for hours on end; speaking, speaking with no interruption or reply. And when you speak about society, especially with analytical rigor, you sometimes hurt people. Presumptuous or not, I believe that is a correct assessment of this text.

Yet it is without a shred of moral doubt that I go ahead to write and publish. A true writer, on important topics, can hold no illusions of intellectual and social innocence. Thoughts and perspectives are so important that they are worth every bit of the harm caused to others.

The harm caused has to do with developmental psychology as we shall discuss further in the chapters of the second part of this book. Writing this book is something of a vulgar act, like showing too sexually explicit images to a small child. Some—or most—people are just not ready to receive the messages herein. Neither are most societies, social groups or settings.

But it is not the young who are most threatened by my perspectives. It is not their minds that are scandalized. My ideal reader is about ten years old. She is talented but doesn't fit in that well at school. She doesn't always do what parents and teachers tell her. And she lives and breathes the digital age. When she grows up she will be idealistic and questioning, and she will sense that something is profoundly wrong with society. When she enters university or otherwise develops a worldview of her own, she will find that the education offered, the answers of parents, teachers, media and leaders are all lacking. They somehow miss the point. They don't see her reality, the new reality. And then there is Hanzi Freinacht, who puts words to her experience, who connects the dots. She looks into the mirror and realizes that she is the creator of an entirely new society.

Another source of harm is the inevitable misuse of the perspectives. Philosophers, sociologists and economists—even physicists and mystics—have all been misinterpreted, their works perverted and misused. They have thereby caused direct or indirect harm and confusion. So will no doubt the political metamodernism suggested in these pages. And as with the work of all thinkers, my work, if it catches on, is destined to be positive in some ways and harmful in others. That's just the dialectical nature of life.

On a more personal and intimate level, people put up psychological barriers to protect themselves from the pain of sharp ideas that challenge their convictions and emotional investments. The most common defense mechanism is of course to simply put down the book, ignore it and forget about it. Other options available are ridicule, semi-deliberate misunderstandings of its message, or picking out a detail to argue against while forgetting the big picture—or why not sub-vocalizing with that mean hyena voice again?

I welcome you to use all of these strategies. Over the years I have seen so much pain associated with wrestling the metamodern perspective. People get obsessed, they resist, they rage, they condemn, they belittle, they self-censor and find reasons to feel terribly affronted. I acknowledge that this is because my theories deeply insult the prevailing moral intuitions that people have. I spit straight in the face of their political identities, both on the Left and Right, from anarchists to conservatives. It is the solemn duty of the philosopher to piss on all that you hold dear and sacred, to show you that your gods are false.

And how could it be any different? To genuinely develop society you must put forward challenging ideas, ideas that reveal today's society—even our most idealistic progressives—as unethical, unkind, primitive, hypocritical and judgmental. The best is an enemy of the good, as Voltaire wrote. I am attacking your time, your society and your way of life. If the book is too much for you, you are under no obligation to finish it or to learn and understand its core ideas.

And of course, I welcome you as an intellectual and spiritual adversary. To the dialectically inclined political philosopher, followers are made of bronze, informed critics of silver and spiritual adversaries of molten gold. Uninformed critics, however, are only the dirt on my boots and rolled-up sleeves. And then there's a fair share of fool's gold, too, unfortunately.

But most of all I am looking for resourceful and imaginative co-creators—people for whom the whole social" hierarchy (am I better than Hanzi or vice versa?) and "good or bad" issues matter less. These are people who know when to follow, when to criticize and when to revolt and take the lead. They are children who love to play. They don't care about academic titles, or bourgeois "success", or whether you stick to the writing rules of their favorite literary genre. They recognize the tune I am playing, join in the dance, and playfully re-create society and reality.

All said and done, remember that you are in charge, not me. I am just dead letters on a piece of paper or a screen. You are co-creating this by reading. You can cut me up, rearrange me, quote me, ignore me, interpret me and put pieces of me into places I couldn't dream of. The reader, not the writer, has the power. So welcome, co-creator, I am at your mercy.

As a certain Zarathustra spake:

> "Companions the creator seeks, not corpses, not herds and believers. Fellow creators the creator seeks—those who write new values on new tablets. Companions the creator seeks, and fellow harvesters; for everything about him is ripe for the harvest."

Introduction

WHAT WE MUST ACHIEVE

What do we need to achieve with this book? You are to learn about a political and social theory, which, if enough people understand it, can and will dramatically improve the lives of coming generations. And spare humanity and the other animals from oceans of suffering and degradation. This is what I contend.

What you are reading is nothing else than the warrior's code to changing the world—something we are in dire need of, given the vast challenges ahead. And the worlds of mice and men are *political* worlds. Politics means games for power. Power matters in all aspects of life. Who makes the calls? Who is considered morally pure and sexy? Who gets to be smart and respectable, or to be the cool, romantic rebel? Who gets to be the kind, wise woman and who gets to be the boring old hag? Who gets the cards stacked against them in a fight they cannot win? What ideas rule the world and creep deep into our minds and dreams, constituting and structuring everyday reality? These, my friend, are the questions of politics in its true sense.

So. Metamodern politics is the issue of the hour. What does that mean? Let us begin by asking *you* a few questions. Now, I want to reveal to you your own ignorance. I understand that this may be a harsh slap to your pretty little face—not at all a nice thing to do. But Hanzi Freinacht is not nice. He is right. And that is something else entirely. Now I am staring you straight in the eye and slowly asking you:

- First question: What is human development?
- Second question: What is the development of society?
- Third question: What is freedom?

The less intellectually gifted readers are by now conjuring up ways to get out of the stranglehold:

> "Who says there is such a thing as human development at all? I, for one, am so humble and appreciative of others, especially children, cute animals and indigenous cultures, that I don't at all *care* about development. And who says freedom is so important in the first place? I mean, a good person like

> myself, lives for dignity and the duty to serve others, not to run around trying to be 'free', whatever that means."

The problem with this response is that you are taking yourself much too seriously, and the very real suffering of other humans and animals much too lightly. Let me demonstrate.

Let's say you are so "intellectually open" and "morally evolved" that you don't care about human development. Then you don't mind your own kid being starved, her body growth stunted, her brain development impaired and her mind and emotions scarred for life. I mean because, after all, who are *you* to make that value judgment about human development? Maybe a stunted life is better. Bingo.

Oh, and you are so humble that you don't think societies develop. They just change, and you can't say which one is better. So now, I am going to make you a slave at my colony, a cotton plantation. You will live in poverty and have your family killed if you resist. What's that? You think that is barbaric? Wait a minute! I thought you were above such petty developmental models of social reality? Hmm, I don't particularly like you *implying* that today's society is "more developed" than 18th century America. The arrogance!

And by the way, you are to live in North Korea and have a death penalty commandment to muster all emotions you can to be *deeply in love* with Kim Yong Un, for the rest of your life. And remember, he sees you when you're sleeping. Because, after all, what *is* freedom? I mean, how *dare* you try to tell me that loving the supreme leader is not freedom in its most sublime expression? Just look at those cheeks, and that uniform, and that hair-do! How dare you?

So—if this was your reaction, you are intellectually and emotionally fooling yourself, something we shall get back to. You absolutely *do* care about these things and it is intellectually and morally indefensible not to—even if you may have good reasons to prefer other words than "freedom" and "development". In fact, you care about them quite passionately, and you are probably more willing to die for them than any patriot ever was for his nation, any revolutionary for her cause.

More intellectually honest and emotionally mature readers are instead trying to actually answer the questions: "Uhhm, you mean like, just now? Off the top of my head, just like that?"—Yes, just now. Off the top of your head. I mean like this: What is the capital of France? Paris. How many fingers do you have? Ten (probably). What is freedom?

Some of you may have partial answers but I think it is safe to admit that you don't have very clear, detailed or satisfying ones. Responding to these questions doesn't come very naturally, even if you are an academic with a PhD in philosophy. Think about it. We have these three things we care so passionately about that we would maybe even give our lives for them. And yet, you don't know what the hell you are talking about.

This book (and its sequel) cures you of that ailment. After having read this book, you will have a much more advanced insight into psychological and societal development.

In the next book you will also gain a clear and original understanding of elemental political concepts such as freedom and equality. You will actually know what you are talking about. Unless, of course, your mind starts playing Jedi tricks on you again, and you revert to your intellectual dishonesty by avoiding understanding. Fundamentally, you will be cured of two very serious kinds of intellectual blindness:

- **Developmental blindness**—meaning that you *consistently fail* to see the developmental stages of human beings, animals and societies.
- **Inner dimensions blindness**—meaning that you *consistently fail* to take into account the subjective dimensions of life and how they fundamentally shape society and reality

There are other forms of blindness that are somehow touched upon in this book, but these two are the most central ones. Unfortunately, such blindness is very prevalent in today's society and no less in the scientific communities.

Beyond that, this book offers a rather unique perspective on life, society and existence, useful in all walks of life.

This Book and the Next

So here's a rough sketch of the book. After this introductory chapter the book unfolds in two major parts.

- **The first part** explains the basics of metamodern politics. You have one chapter describing how the whole political spectrum has changed (and why) and another chapter that presents the great crisis-revolution that is our contemporary period. A third chapter discusses some examples of what the listening society is, and the following chapter discusses how and why it is possible in practice. The fifth chapter presents new political practices, such as how "the process oriented political party" works. And the sixth, final one discusses the metamodern political philosophy.

- **The second part** describes what human psychological development is. It has eleven chapters. One introduces the topic and all the following ones discuss vital aspects of what it means for a human being to develop: Two chapters are devoted to smarts, two to learning, two to well-being, two to wisdom and two to putting it all together into what I call the theory of "effective value memes". Again and again I have found that before people understand this part—why development matters—everything else I teach about metamodern politics seems to magically evaporate. It just won't stick, no matter how smart or educated the audience. I have tried with a room full of Harvard professors (they were lawyers and psychiatrists) but to no avail. The most trivial metamodern insight seems to be completely incomprehensible. However, once people come out of their "developmental blindness" the rest seems to come quite naturally. But does this mean that we have to study stages of how "developed" different adult humans are? Yes. That is exactly what it means.

Then there is one last chapter that takes stock of the whole book. In *Nordic Ideology* we will discuss how society as a whole develops through stages. We will also present six new forms of politics that are necessary to create a metamodern society, how metamodernism beats the existing ideologies (socialism, liberalism, etc.), and how it relates to the "dangerous dreams" of the 20th century: the utopian and totalitarian movements like communism, fascism and New Age. Only this time, totalitarianism—despite what our historical experience tells us—is not unambiguously evil. Long story.

These are dangerous books, admittedly. But I believe they are necessary, given that we live in what can reasonably be described as interesting times.

To sum it up, you could say that this book will change your life—and the next book will change the world. Or actually you will, once you've read both of them.

Metamodernism: The Philosophical Engine

So what is this word "metamodernism" that I keep using? It is a kind of philosophy, a view of the world. It is quite different from what we are generally taught in school, even at universities. It is different from the general "modern" worldview.

A lot of people think that philosophy is a certain activity: that you write books about it, or listen to radio shows, daydream or discuss with friends. But philosophy is more than that—it is:

- How you view the world (ontology, "what is really real" and epistemology, "how to know stuff");
- and your place in it (your idea of a "self"),
- and what is right and wrong (ethics or ideology).

So everybody has a philosophy. When someone prays, or doesn't pray, or saves money, or helps a stranger, or works to end animal slavery, all of these things are rooted in the philosophy of that person (as well as in her psychological and cognitive development, as we shall see).

This book is not about philosophy, but about politics, society and psychological development. But it is written *as an expression of* what I call metamodern philosophy. Metamodern thinking is the *engine* that runs this book. **We need to talk about society—from a metamodern perspective.** That's what we're doing in this book. The point is where the car is going, so to speak, not how the engine works. We're doing a "show it, don't tell it" so that you can see how fruitful and powerful metamodern thinking can be.

Just to say a few words about metamodernism—the term has been taken from two Dutch art scholars (Timotheus Vermeulen and Robin van der Akker), who popularized the word. They claim to see some new trends within the arts, and they hold that these trends seem to combine irony and sarcasm with sincerity and vulnerability. I will deepen this theme throughout the book.

So Vermeulen, van der Akker and others think of metamodernism as a kind of cultural "phase", a kind of fashion or spirit of arts and culture that has been showing up more often lately. The way I use the word "metamodernism", builds upon their understanding, but I add two more meanings. The first meaning is that metamodernism is a kind of philosophy, a kind of engine for your mind. The second meaning is that **metamodernism is a developmental stage**. I work with the idea that we, as humanity, can advance to a metamodern stage of development.

If you want to look inside the engine, and get a brief overview of the metamodern philosophy, **there is an appendix at the end of this book**. There you will find a more academic and detailed discussion of metamodernism as cultural phase and as philosophy. You can see the engine from which Hanzi thinks and writes. It is meant only for readers of gold and for philosophical co-creators. Reading the appendix is not necessary for understanding the rest of this book and its main ideas.

Academic Heresy

In academia, there is a certain phantom of the opera—at least within the social sciences and humanities: the phantom of narcissism. The often so dry, repetitive seminars and timid scholarly discussions seem to whisper of vague but intimate promises: ascension, immortality, passion and prophesy.

Because each academic researcher is modeled on the great, mythologized intellectuals of past, we can all pretend to be like them, without even having to present empirical findings or significant advances (which is at least partly different in medicine or physics). All we need to do is to display a certain arrogant, "learned" demeanor and we can reap the rewards of feeling extraordinary and talented. By acting very sure of ourselves, and employing rich jargon, we can put up poses of unfalsifiable brilliance and aspire for dazzling moral conviction. But such extravagances are only possible at the expense of our poor colleagues, who have to put up with us, getting less speaking time, attention and recognition in the process.

This phantom is thus something that must be contained in the everyday interactions and social games at the universities—lest the academic social order become quite dysfunctional, full of conflicts, with little real work being done. "So I didn't finish the paper on time? Hah! Neither did Wittgenstein!" Just imagine the chaos if people could get away with that stuff.

The chief means to keeping the phantom of narcissism under the table is to subscribe to (and hold one another accountable to) certain norms and virtues. These are increasingly prevalent within academic life, at least at surface level: humility and honest working camaraderie, and respecting only solid results, such as peer reviewed articles and acquired research grants. It is as though academics subtly nudge one another to take on a humbler role—the professional researcher rather than the intellectual prophet. And there are good reasons for this priority.

But under some circumstances, such humility is not advisable, and one has more to gain from venturing outside the halls of academic virtue. Academic writing is not always the best form to present ideas, or indeed, to develop new ones. There is even sociological research to support that claim: Academia is more suitable for small, incremental advances in ground research and most ground-breaking innovation occurs in other sectors.[2]

If you want to present a new overarching perspective, like in this book, you may have to break with academia and its norms altogether. You may have to perform the darkest rituals, commit the gravest heresies, in order to invoke forbidden phantoms: Farewell respectability (I never loved you), hello new truths, welcome new perspectives.

I come from academia, so I know roughly what the philosophers, legal scholars, economists, sociologists, political scientists, anthropologists, historians and psychologists are up to. And none of them can offer you the understanding you get in this book. You cannot get it from the brilliant neo-Marxists, not the impressively data-driven, digitalized complexity economists, not the ecology and sustainability-oriented economists, not the animal rights theorists, not the chaos theory researchers at the Santa Fe Institute, not the postmaterialists (as in the philosophical school) and "new materialists", posthumanists, transhumanists, postconstructivists, speculative realists, cybersemioticians, enactivists and neurophenomenologists, or even from the other metamodernists who work with cultural theory and art. Excuse all the difficult words; it's just to get the academics off their high donkeys.

If you are an intellectual, you likely have one or two favorite thinkers. And, what's more, you often use your understanding of these thinkers to say to yourself about others that they "don't really get it". But does your favorite thinker put you, the reader, "above and beyond" this book?

Not so, unless you are reading this farther into the future. He or she cannot save you—not Gilles Deleuze, not Alain Badiou, Slavoj Žižek, Karen Barad, Roy Bhaskar, Quentin Meillassoux, Ken Wilber, Susanne Cook-Greuter, Otto Scharmer, David Graeber, Stephen Wolfram, Manuel DeLanda, Nick Bostrom, Peter Sloterdijk, Paul Tillich, Murray Bookchin, Roberto Unger, André Gorz, Victor Frankl, Alan Watts, Fritjof Capra, Buckminister Fuller, Christopher Alexander or their respective followers. Excuse the name-dropping (and the high proportion of men).

And mainstream sociology or social science will certainly not suffice: poststructuralism, Foucauldian thought, queer theory à la Judith Butler, postcolonialism, discourse analysis, critical theory, Habermasian theory, intersectionality, world-systems theory, Luhmann's systems theory, Mertonian "middle range theory", Bourdieu's tradition, network theory, rational choice, mathematical sociology, ethnomethodology, social constructivism or interactionism. Excuse the term-dropping.

And no psychoanalyst or Nobel Prize winning economist will do, not even the not-yet prize winning theoreticians of the peer-to-peer and sharing economies.

Nor can you get the same understanding from any of the political leaders, business executives, neuroscientists, physicists, behavioral biologists, logicians, cosmologists, spiritual gurus, Zen masters or even Bruce Lee. None of them have an encompassing enough picture of political life to give you the answers that you get in this book and its sequel.

All of these things will get you somewhere along the way, but none of them contain a metamodern understanding of politics. You'll just have to study this text in order to get the hang of political metamodernism. No small claim, admittedly. But then again, all those people are good at other things. And I am sure you are too. And I am the great Hanzi Freinacht. That's just life, another reality you have to deal with, here at the auspicious crossroads of fact and fiction.

I owe a lot to many of the mentioned ones, most of whom are considerably more significant than my own work. But the point I want to make here is that *I am subsumed by none of them.* I am not plowing any of their fields; I am claiming a new one. You cannot replace reading my work with any of them. Your favorite philosopher won't save you, even if it's Charles Sanders Peirce himself. In fact, I hereby challenge you to find one source in the world that says anything resembling the overall message of this book and its sequel. You, the contemporary reader, cannot.

And, of course, in this beautiful transpersonal world where everybody is entangled with everything, in a gazillion hypercomplex ways, Hanzi Freinacht couldn't even exist without the inspiring and groundbreaking works of pretty much all of the above. Just as I cannot exist without you, the reader. You are co-creating me through the brave act of reading a stranger's words.

The Reader Rebels

What else must we achieve with this book? You are to be equipped with a multidimensional political-psychological-developmental map of our time. You will see some fundamental dynamics of how society and its citizens are evolving, in which directions, and how different kinds of people fit into that map. And, yes, that includes yourself.

For most readers, unavoidably, this is a disappointing read—yet another reason to try to ignore and resist the text. After all, you are less likely to inhabit a super-flattering part of the map. Few people do. But that is okay. And, as we shall discuss, there are other aspects of life that are more important. However, you are probably still better off being aware of the map, so that you can successfully navigate the world. Especially if you are someone with considerable power in society. I can only hope that you use it for good ends. Now let's go on to introducing the book.

> "Hang on a minute; I am still mad at you for insulting me a few pages ago. And then you even had the nerve to brag, right after putting me down. You are such a pretentious bastard."

Oh, really? If this is the case, you may have been upset while you read the last few pages, thereby missing some very important points. You should probably put down the book, go take a long, hard look in the mirror, get over yourself, and re-read the last section. You know, you can't actually have a fight with me. I'm dead text at your disposal, remember?

> "Don't tell me what to do. These are my feelings. I read this book mainly because of how it makes me feel. And you are making me *feel* bad, so maybe I'm just going to dump you. I hate you already Hanzi. I can see what a false, manipulative, rotten apple you really are, and I will reveal it."

Frankly, my dear, I don't give a damn about your feelings. Listen, we are trying to achieve something here: To substantially contribute to sparing a vast number of people and other animals from oceans of suffering and degradation. If you want to do this, you are going to have to start taking responsibility as a reader and stop having arguments with a piece of text. Again, remember, *you* are doing this. You are the creator.

Now, if you were not provoked by these academic heresies—wonderful. You might be one of the worthier readers, an emotionally stable and imaginative co-creator of our time.

And don't worry, you'll get to rebel. But you need to do it at the right time, with the right clues, for the right cause.

Your Predictable Objections

Is this an empirical work, a work of solid science? Some chapters, or parts of chapters, are well backed with empirical findings, such as the ones on cognitive development (chapters 8 and 9). There are many peer reviewed articles used, together with some other sources, like the writings of reporters, scholars and philosophers. Of course, peer reviewed articles can themselves be criticized for their methodologies, interpretations of results and the like. I use high quality articles and skip sketchier ones.[3] And I avoid using references as best I can—you will find a minimum number of sources, just enough so that you can easily find out more about each topic and check my claims. However, I sometimes write sub-discussions in the endnotes. For more advanced or interested readers, you will find many answers there. If you just want to get the hang of the book's main message, you can skip past them.

Other parts of the book are based on arguments and generalizations that you must weigh and consider with your own rational and emotional faculties, much like the arguments of other social theorists. You see, politics is continuous not only with the ritualized forms of knowledge that we call "science", but perhaps even more with the "common sense" of everyday life. Social theory is where science and common sense meet, where you discipline your mind and use the best scientific findings you can come across—but you still have to build upon your common sense in order to make assumptions about society, politics and social reality.

Think about it. Did anybody ever "prove", by means of scientific method, that human rights are good? Did they prove that liberal, representative democracy—with capitalism, courts, prisons, schools and a welfare state—is the best form of governance and economy? Did they prove that feminism is good or bad, or that we should care about the happiness and suffering of the other animals? That English is a good language to communicate with? Not really. People have made good or bad arguments for or against these things, and sometimes such arguments are supported by various empirical findings, but they cannot be "proven" in any strict sense of the word.

The people on the political Left keep saying that they have science on their side, with so much evidence of the great ills that inequality brings and of the glorious benefits of welfare. The people on the Right, in turn, have so much evidence that their pro-market policies give us lower unemployment and higher economic growth—and thereby greater social stability and human happiness. The Greens have clear evidence that the whole shebang is crashing either way, and that we should probably stop destroying the environment. Libertarians have plenty of sociological evidence of the benefits of de-criminalized narcotics. Conservatives have plenty of medical evidence to the contrary. Take immigration into Western countries as another example—mountains of empirical findings seem to support arguments both for restrictive and liberal policies.

Much more than we realize it, science is a whore dressed up as queen, a jester posing as king. We don't recognize how easily it is bought and sold and how often it makes fools of us before the whole royal court. Somehow, you are always on the side of science, or so you believe. Yet, strangely, so many intelligent and educated people seem to have opinions differing from your own, even when science herself clearly says that you are correct. They must all be deluding themselves, mustn't they?

People who desperately want to know "if this is science", in matters of social theory, philosophy and existence, have lived their lives in childlike ignorance of the vast continents that constitute the philosophy of science and the sociology of knowledge—not to mention the very fruitful discipline of metaphysics and the now growing field of cognitive psychology (which also has considerable bearing on how we should view science). Unfortunately, likely because of serious flaws in our educational systems, this includes so many highly educated and talented people. Somehow, despite all the key understandings that our civilization has unraveled during the last century, showing that knowledge is contextual beyond anything we might previously have imagined, people persist in the driest scientific naivety. They are ruled by a jester and a whore.

Science is a very powerful method—or set of methods—for understanding the world. But real human beings, participating in all manner of everyday situations, base their worldviews and political opinions on much more than science. Simply because we damn well have to. We, including the scientists, have common sense understandings about society, the world and ourselves. We each have our own "social theory", which is continuous with our "common sense" and philosophical outlook, loaded to the brim with emotions and unrecognized assumptions. Much of this book is devoted to mapping such common sense—and to developing it.

Your own social theory, dear reader, can be more or less formally stated, more or less complex, more or less ridden with contradictions and logical loopholes, and it can build on different forms of scientific findings. Such findings can in turn be taken from more or less fruitful branches of science; they can be more or less reliable, more or less relevant to the matter at hand, and your interpretation of them can be more or less perverse.

So, to be very clear, if you are like most people, you have been overestimating your own "scientificness" to a preposterous extent. And if I want to propose a social theory, my measure of success is not whether or not I have "solid proof", but simply whether or not I am less mistaken, perverted and uninformed than you are. **If my mode of thinking is *less wrong* than yours, my social theory is valuable.** Even if there are problems inherent in my perspective (which is unavoidably the case) there is no "scientific" default perspective to which you can revert and feel secure in your worldview. Your secure "rational worldview" is a lie that you have been telling yourself—for emotional reasons, more often than analytical ones.

And to spell this out with even cruder clarity, here is my claim: If you call yourself a socialist, you are ridiculously outdated; if you think that you are a careful, no-bullshit conservative, you are deluding yourself; if you are a free market libertarian, you live on the moon; if you are an idealistic Green... you might be on your way, but you have yet to understand some of the most crucial aspects of social and political life.

None of these positions can be proven or disproven, but they can be criticized from other positions that are more complex, more scientifically informed, more comprehensive, nuanced and coherent—and less wrong.

More Predictable Objections

Next I would like to discuss three different "double-binds" that readers can use to protect themselves from understanding this text. A double-bind is a term for an "unsolvable dilemma" that has a nasty emotional undercurrent to it. Examples are "don't obey me!" (bad parent) or "you must love me out of your own free will!" (bad deity). This term was coined by the polymath biologist Gregory Bateson, back in the day in an attempt to explain the causes of schizophrenia. Of course, this explanation has not stood the test of time, if we consider recent and more evidence-based psychiatry (and our overall understanding of schizophrenia has since changed considerably). But the term caught on, primarily because of its usefulness in other psychological and sociological matters.

Very few people are wicked enough to consciously apply double-binds to others. Yet it sometimes happens, perhaps because we feel pressured or confused. When I, earlier in my career, presented more conventional research, such as the findings from police ethnography, nobody would use double-binds or the like. People would be ideal listeners. The moment that I try to convey metamodern thoughts, however, double-binds start occurring with an almost frightening predictability. The mental resistance that people harbor towards metamodernism is immense. Thereby, the psychological tricks that people use to quickly brush it aside show up at every corner.

The double-bind works simply by holding the presented ideas to impossible standards, ones that your currently accepted views couldn't match either. You present a "damned if you do, damned if you don't", usually without realizing that you are doing it. Your mind can then quickly rush to a critical standpoint and feel justified in denouncing the new idea that threatens your *status quo*. Part of this is necessary—with so much implausible information around these days, we do need quick ways to get rid of the worst of it. But if you let your inner inquisition and thought-police control your input at a too early stage, you are bound to miss goldmines and hidden treasures with jewels you couldn't dream of. There will be vast horizons that just never open, and you will remain simple-minded.

The more radical the new idea, the more painful it is to accommodate. When fundamental modes of thought are challenged—such as your very sense of self, your sense of reality and your basic ethics—your mind starts playing tricks on you. You are tempted to use self-deceit to get out of the uncomfortable situation, so that you can promptly return to more familiar territories. Most people simply don't have the self-knowledge and meta-cognition to catch themselves doing this, not even psychologists and long-term meditators. So to help you bust your own bullshit while you read the rest of the book (and, later on, solemnly bust the bullshit of others), here are three double-binds that people often employ.

"Specifics please": The first double-bind we can call "specifics please". It means that you feel irritated towards someone—like Hanzi—who insists on going on and on about philosophy, science and perspectives. "Yes, yes" you say to yourself, "but what does all of this amount to? What are the *specifics*, in concrete reality? Just cut the crap and tell me what it is! I'm a matter-of-fact person, you see." Suddenly you feel less threatened, having taken the initiative, cutting to the chase. Now Hanzi is up against the wall, and you are off the hook when it comes to dealing with all those difficult new ideas. If you do get specifics before you see the context within which these become meaningful, they appear counter-intuitive and you can rush to a falsifying conclusion. Or you can start arguing about details, thereby shielding yourself from the new overarching perspective. Ah, what a relief! But if the speaker *does* begin from the specifics, you throw a sly smirk and say "Oh, here is a naive one, who thinks that you can just change things in society without knowing the greater context." The specifics are a slippery slope; you can always ask for more until it becomes incomprehensible or until the speaker runs out of knowledge about technical details. Effectively, you have locked out any possibility of learning anything new. Congratulations.

"The humble seeker": The second double-bind is "the humble seeker". The humble seeker thrives in ambiguity, in questions rather than answers, in cracks in the puzzle, in exceptions rather than rules, in minute details and relations, in subtle whispers and the non-obvious. Or so he tells himself. Here's the humanities student, the posthumanist, the Nietzschean, the Deleuzian, the Foucauldian, Derrida-fans or even just Heidegger people, cultural theorists and some deep ecologists or Taoists. They are offended by the certainty of the speaker, and by the very fact that her thoughts *can* be systematized, organized and lead to concrete conclusions. These consider themselves to be of a subtler and nobler breed, being humbler, more dynamic and open towards the paradoxical mysteries of the world. The problem, which makes this into a double-bind, is that you have in effect precluded all system building and concrete suggestions, all overarching maps and all simple underlying rules that could elegantly explicate the complex emergence of the universe. You try to force the speaker into your way of thinking and speaking, by relying on a concealed hierarchical system of your own. Your system looks like this: All "open, subtle thinkers" are morally and intellectually superior to all "rigid system builders", and thereby all system builders have false conclusions. Of course, this is very convenient for you, since if the system builder is *not* rigorous and systematic, you can brush the speaker off for that reason instead.

"Spiritual purity": A third double-bind, used by another kind of people, is "spiritual purity". Here you attack and degrade the speaker because she is not spiritual enough, because she "thinks too much" or "tries to force her intellect upon the world". The problem with this is of course that the speaker can never prove her spiritual value to you (this being a subjective quality). You force upon her your own vague definitions of what you "sense" in her. This means that you feel empowered and superior to her and morally entitled to cut past her message, to stop listening to her. If she insists on trying to explain her point, you view it as further evidence of your own superiority. If she follows your lead and stops trying to think so much, you also take it as proof of your own spiritual superiority and that you thereby had nothing to learn from her in the first place. Indeed, *she* must listen to *you*, in order to attain the "spiritual purity" that you think that you already have. This last double-bind is by far the nastiest one.

It should also be noted that the second and the third double-binds can be combined into an especially mean concoction called "organic growth", where you consider yourself wiser than the speaker because she does not let things "grow organically". Of course, there *can* be wisdom in such advice, but the call for "organic growth" is often used as a double-bind method to pacify those of differing opinions and agendas other than one's own. All to protect yourself from the pain of being seriously challenged.

Ours is a world full of self-deceit, my friend. But it is at the same time a world full of sincere truth seeking, scientific progress and curios late night conversations about the nature of reality and existence. If you are anything like myself and most other people, you harbor both these sides within; truth seeking and self-deceit. **When you make objections while reading this book, try not to deceive yourself in the process; try not to protect yourself from actually understanding.**

If you think that I am too gender biased (like when I spoke of science as a "whore", as if there were nothing gender-politically problematic about it), or that I focus too little on race/ethnicity, or speak too little about ecology or animal rights or spiritual union with Gaia, or that I mention the banking system too little, or if I am too Eurocentric or anthropocentric, or you just don't like me much, by all means, do criticize me. But do not turn it into an excuse for closing down your own process of learning and development. I am certain that you can improve upon the ideas presented here with your own perspective, knowledge and experience—once you understand the pattern that connects. Up until that point, your critique is very likely fool's gold.

Psycho-Active Literature

What people don't understand is that all ideas have a certain psychology—or a set of psychologies, depending on contexts (this is perhaps best captured in the French philosopher Gilles Deleuze's notion of the *rhizome*).

It is a general prejudice we have, based on unreflectively held Platonic ideas and Cartesian divisions of reality, that ideas are somehow *pure form*, that they don't need feelings, embodiments, dramatic performances and personalities to be real. But nothing could be farther from the truth. From the poetic crystal clarity of mathematics, to the dense, solemn vengefulness of communism and the fresh, sprinkling hope of environmentalism, all great ideas come with lived moods, visions and rituals.

Metamodern ideas are no different; they arrive at the scene with a certain form of audacity, bordering on aristocratic arrogance. There is an existential tinge, a kind of adventurous but gentle sense of vastness that grips the heart and mind of the afflicted. You see complex patterns unfolding in the strangest dance, universality in every event, open horizons, and a depth—as if everyday phenomena became astronomical mysteries revealed by the Hubble telescope. There is a sense of connectedness, but in a universal and impersonal way.

The progress of metamodern ideas is faced with so many challenges and impediments. Although some of the ideas may be intellectually demanding, this is not the main obstacle to their successful communication. **The main obstacles to understanding these ideas are psychological ones: allergic emotional overreactions, prejudices, investments in beliefs, envy, fear, confusion and self-deceit.**

Like a psycho-active drug, I have written this book to engage your emotions as well as your mind. I am conveying something that lies outside of the normal channels that we have available for communicating with one another. So I have to break all the rules of the established genres: Being too academic for a novelist, too concrete for a philosopher, too vulgar and careless for an academic, too rational for a mystic—and just too arrogant, harsh and mean to be a normal "concerned citizen".

I suppose I am saying, I expect you to read this book with anger at my insolence, disgust at my bad taste and contempt towards my disproportionate ambitions. But I know that you will be affected by the ideas—indeed, *infected* by their viral DNA—even if you don't want to afford me the pleasure. And I know that you will be enriched and empowered in the process.

So that is why I write with this "cocky and evil" style. If you want to be Freudian about it and delve deep into guesses about my childhood, go ahead, have a double. It's on the house.

You see, the most interesting part is that it doesn't even matter that I tell you how I am pushing your psycho-active buttons. *It still works*, much like perfume, obvious flirtation or make-up. And if it doesn't work, you will just be outcompeted, in many subtle ways, by the people it did work on—the ones who managed to pick up the useful piece of "cultural code" that I am offering.

I am not relating to you as an individual person with one, whole, non-contradictory free will, separate from my own. Rather, I relate to you as what Deleuze called a **dividual**, full of different parts, of different voices and drives working in different contexts. You are not only the rider of the elephant, your conscious and rational mind, but also the elephant itself, full of contradictory urges, ambitions, dreams, fears, doubts and hunger. To convey my message, I must sometimes speak to your rational mind, sometimes to the elephant itself, and sometimes to the relationship between the two.

And you are even the very path that the elephant tramples, a path that other people have cut by teaching you this language, these values and habits. I sometimes write to other people than you specifically, and then take up your thread again. Sometimes I speak to others *through* you, *beyond* you as an individual person.

I relate to you **transpersonally**, meaning that I meet you not as one single, rational individual, but as the cross-section of the beautiful and terrifying depths of your inner life and the conflicts and potentials inherent in the social, economic and cultural fabric of the digitalizing world. I speak to you as a thinker and seeker like myself, who is also sensing soul,[4] and who is also society itself in all of its multitudes. To treat you with the deepest respect is not to pretend that you are only your rational mind, but to speak to the totality of your transpersonal existence. You are, fundamentally, the world-soul itself; and you are simultaneously speaking and listening as you read these words. Future readers will understand this better than contemporary ones.

This intimate, transpersonal way of co-creating the world builds upon the acknowledgement that I exist within you, and that you exist within me—in a paradoxical hall of mirrors. It is an inescapable conclusion. **The hall of mirrors replaces the notion of you being one, single individual reader, who reads this one, single atom of a writer.** Instead, you create Hanzi just as Hanzi creates you. In this ironic game, we can play with our identities, with who we are, who we want to become, what we seek to create, with reality itself and with what we must achieve.

Sincere Irony

This leads us to a first, simple definition of metamodernism. The psychoactive literature of this book only works because I am being ironic. You see, the distance-creating irony and sarcasm are what allow me to be perfectly honest and genuine with you, to be absurdly sincere and thereby ridiculously vulnerable.

Metamodernism is the marriage of extreme irony with a deep, unyielding sincerity. These two sides are in superposition to one another. The sincerity makes the irony much more effective, because it becomes genuinely ambiguous; the irony, because it is all-encompassing, creates room for an unapologetic, even religious, sincerity of emotions, hopes and aspirations.

Without the irony and the sarcasm, my sincerity would simply be too much; it would awaken severe suspicions, and for good reason too. There are so many goblin gurus who will tell you that they offer truth and enlightenment, but end up fooling you and fucking your wife.

I begin by telling you that I'm going to fool you and fuck your wife, make her come like Vesuvius, just to get your attention, and only then do I reveal what this is actually about: universal solidarity with all sentient beings, from all perspectives. But if I would have said that right away, it would have bored you, made you suspicious—or both. It is here, in the deepest irony, that we can find the most pristine, pure sincerity in our struggle for a better world. It is only here that the madness stops for a while, allowing us a moment of peace and clarity.

To "be a metamodernist" is to apply oneself to sincerity with religious fervor, while keeping an ironic smile at one's own self-importance; to be as sincere as the poet William Blake or the newly sanctified Mother Teresa—and as ambiguous and sarcastic as the worst of internet trolls.

That is how the metamodern aristocracy gains mastery over the world, which is what we must achieve.

I take it you understand I am being ironic.

PART ONE

The New Political Landscape

Chapter 1

HOW POLITICS CHANGED

What does a political revolution look like these days? The Arab Spring. The Chinese growth wonder. The rise of tentative social democracy across Latin America. The food price riots across the world. The Occupy movement. The struggling Burmese restoration of democracy. The Kurdish rebirth. The Orange Revolution of Ukraine. The global climate movement. The rise of Greek Syriza—ah, the genuine Left back on track!

At each scene the world media and political scientists flock as eager onlookers (and semi-deliberate co-creators of the events)—this, *this* is where it happens, the historical moment, where it all changes. Or so we think. But somehow, the news always seems to fade and the promised revolutions never materialize beyond their initial fireworks. Intellectuals are groping for "visions" and "goals", but they cannot seem to find them. They can't find visions because they don't know where to look, and what analytical instruments to use when trying. They look with a telescope but have not yet invented the microscope.

Of course, we have some rapid changes of economic circumstances, food supplies, communications and technology. None of this should be neglected. And there are some toppled regimes and rude street brawls here and there. But how satisfying are the changes in, say, Egypt, where the new NATO-supported dictatorship still captures, tortures and kills dissidents—albeit nowadays often members of the Muslim Brotherhood?[5]

If we speak of *authentic* revolutions in the terms of Karl Marx, meaning rapid developmental changes in the social relations and the logic by which society functions and is governed—none of the mentioned examples seem to satisfy. The abolishment of Apartheid and the fall of the Berlin Wall reaffirmed the dominant world-system: liberal capitalism with representative democracy and a strong undercurrent of accelerating economic and cultural globalization (and its discontents).

But the revolution is here. It is happening right now, with greater force and efficiency than the French Revolution and American War of Independence (albeit with less drama). And just as irrevocably.

It is occurring—much more in line with Marx's ideas—where the world-system is most culturally and economically developed. And development has gone the farthest, by quite a margin, in some rather quiet corners of the world. The goldilocks conditions for revolution are to be found at just the right distance from the financial and industrial world centers, in a place where everything functions and runs smoothly: in Scandinavia. In the Nordic countries we are beginning to see clear patterns of metamodern politics at play.

'Somewhat vaguer tendencies can be observed in a few other countries, most notably the Netherlands, Switzerland and New Zealand, and interesting trends can be spotted here and there in other developed parts of the world. But within the larger central economies, including the newly emerging Asian metropolises, we are still far away from the landscapes of metamodern politics.

The metamodern political revolution goes under the radar of global media—and academia—because it happens so inconspicuously, so gradually. And, moreover, the Scandinavians themselves lack any conception of the profound global changes that are beginning to take place in their own backyards, changes in many ways effected by their own doings.

Whereas small minorities within these countries have hunches or a general sense of direction, there is (at the time of writing) nowhere in the world a movement properly informed by an explicit and clear metamodern ideology. But metamodernism's fingerprint is unmistakably there. Key players within key movements will have a formal theory of their playing field once they have read and understood this book and its sequel *Nordic Ideology*.

So, revolution in Scandinavia? There are no bloody birth pangs, no rolling heads or riots worth mentioning, certainly no coups. In the Nordic countries you will at the most find some burning cars in the *banlieus*, some racist violence here and there and the occasional ritual clash between the far Left and the police—but nothing resembling a revolution, not even close. Where exactly is this new revolution?

Oh, but you have it all backwards, again. The Nordic countries are extremely ordered societies, even today under the pressures of globalization and immigration. **It is within the framework of this *extreme level of order*—and the far progression of the dynamics inherent to modern society—that the revolution occurs.**[6] Deep changes of the social, economic, political and behavioral structures are happening at an accelerating pace, because this is the only place in the world that runs smoothly enough to allow it. From deep within the struts and beams of society you can hear it: Crack! Snap! Click! We just passed a critical threshold.

Our hypothetically held gods pause for a moment.[7]

The Most Progressive Countries in the World

Political "progressivity" is a rather strange notion. The idea presupposes that there can be a certain form of "historical progression", a goal or at least direction towards which humanity can and should evolve. It presupposes, furthermore, that there is a "background space" with preset measures and markings in it, denoting both directionality and distance of social development.

Some different possible meanings of "progressive" should thereby be mentioned before we go on. When people use the word in different contexts, progressivity can mean:

- That one favors values that have appeared recently over values that have existed a longer time.
- That one is invested in the ideas and political opinions that happen to become ratified by people in the future—thereby the future "shows that you were right".
- That one is eager to see change in society and thereby is willing to take risks and experiment with new social forms.
- That one is simply leftwing—and the more leftwing, the more progressive.
- That one is simply good, instead of bad (conservative) or evil (regressive, reactionary).

None of these meanings quite capture the idea of the Nordic countries being "progressive". We are not really speaking of progression through historical time—and certainly not a determined progression.

So, what do we mean? Let's take a few examples. In Sweden, all parties discuss sustainability issues much more than almost anywhere in the world. This country also accepts more refugees than other European countries (at least until it reached an administrative limit in 2015), shows lower levels of explicit xenophobia in the surveys, gives more money to foreign aid development, is more digitalized, has lower crime[8] rates and corruption, lower income inequality (at least until recently) higher standards of living, higher levels of reported happiness, and greater gender equality (Sweden has the only significant feminist party in the world and an explicitly feminist foreign policy). The country generally supports free trade and manages to have relatively little red tape on enterprise despite its high taxes and strong labor rights. People live longer, at better health, with better teeth, with greater trust for other people and the authorities. People are more secularized than in almost any other country. Kids who grow up there nowadays often start working seriously only at around 30, after having travelled the world, studied (paid for by government), played computer games and gone to music festivals. Gender equality is much better, with liberal, permissive expressions of sexuality as a result. When the girls select guys, they go less after the hyper-masculine and socio-economically dominant ones than is the case in other countries.

Sweden is by no means, and never has been, the socialist semi-utopia it was sometimes portrayed as. There is unemployment, social tensions of all sorts and plenty of human and animal misery. Issues of racism, exclusion and poverty are at every corner. Police, nurses and teachers feel undervalued and protest at waning real wages, sometimes to the point of leaving their jobs. But overall, the country has some qualities that make it a good example for understanding what general cultural progression might look like.

Sweden is a tiny part of the economic system of some seven billion people that today spans the globe, constituting circa 1/700th of the world's population. It has a favorable position within that system, where it has been able to combine relative wealth with relative equality and stability for a considerable period of time. There is nothing within the "Swedish soul", nothing inherent to their "Swedish model" *Folkhemmet* ("The People's Home", a welfare system which in fact resembles other European countries much more than people generally realize), or about the country's natural resources, that explains this progression. When Mary Wollstonecraft, the English mother of first wave feminism, travelled Sweden in 1796, she wrote in her famous *Letters Written in Sweden, Norway, and Denmark* about the appallingly low status of women in these societies, how barbaric it all seemed. Until the early 1700s, the Swedes were arguably the most blood-thirsty, warmongering people in Europe. Only in 1865 did the country transition from an estate system with nobility, church, bourgeoisie and peasantry to a bicameral parliamentary system (which has since been replaced by a single chamber).

Sweden had relatively few industries and a poor population, with major migrations to America in the 19th century and widespread poverty well into the early 20th century. The comparatively small bourgeois class could not gain the same political influence as in France and Germany, and worker parties established social democracy—an alliance between poor, relatively conservative workers and progressive intellectuals (supported by the peasant party). In exchange for representing their economic interests, the intellectuals imposed their more cosmopolitan values upon the workers by use of the institutions of the industrial nation state: schooling, mass media and the bureaucracy. This system was supplemented with a few "popular movements" (Swedish: *folkrörelse*), where wide participation was mustered—Pentecostal religion, labor movements, anti-alcohol and later anti-nuclear energy. The accounts of these popular movements tend to be rather romanticized, but they did play a part in popularizing "modern" and "progressive" values.

As the country did not partake in the world wars, its relative economic position was strengthened and it could sport an impressive growth during the "golden age" of the decades after the Second World War

The only thing special about Sweden is that it has had a relatively stable development in a relatively favorable part of the world economic system of trade, growth and exploitation—while being at a relatively short geographic, cultural and linguistic distance from the center. That's it.[9]

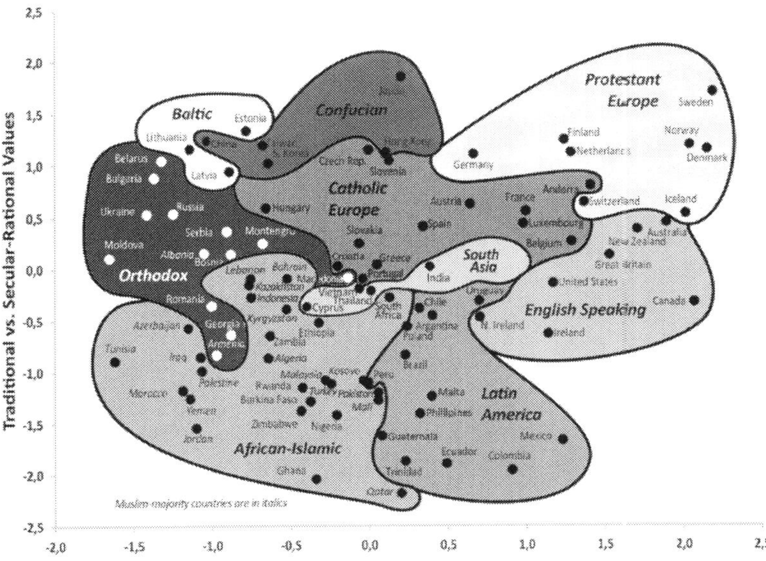

Source: A recreation of the 2015 Inglehart–Welzel cultural map of the world.

Most often, in most parts of the world, society tends to be much more tumultuous, especially during periods of rapid change and technological expansion. But for a host of different reasons, this particular part of the world, not only Sweden but also the rest of Scandinavia, managed to develop a full-blown postindustrial economy with more or less the whole of the population on board, under relatively stable circumstances. This caused the cultural values of the population to change during the last part of the 20th century, and the political landscape shifted accordingly, subtly but radically.

You are perhaps familiar with the Inglehart-Welzel Cultural Map of the World (see figure). It is based on the world's by far most encompassing sociological investigation, asking people in most countries of the world a host of survey questions, a total of over a thousand variables (although far from all participants are asked all of the questions). Over the decades it has accumulated millions of entries, studying cultural differences and trends over time. In the scientific literature there is almost a whole genre of papers directed towards criticizing different aspects of its methodology.[10] But even if criticism can be raised against different aspects of the World Values Survey, one of its main results seems rather solid: the overall picture of The Cultural Map of the World. As you can see in the figure, Protestant Europe (and especially the Nordic countries) holds the upper right corner of the two-dimensional cultural map of the world. This means that people here, on average, lean much more towards rational-secular values (vs. traditional values) and self-expression values (vs. survival values) than anywhere in the world. This is where people believe in abortion and gay rights rather than God's reign, and where they are more likely to go to India to "find themselves" on a spiritual journey rather than finish their degree on time.

It can be no coincidence that the most stable parts of the world, the parts that have had a wealthy and equitable economy for a long time, also have the "most modern" worldview among their populations. In fact, the Nordic countries have sped up in this direction during the last two decades, in the same period as they have become countries of immigration, accepting large numbers of people from more traditional societies. In a way, the figures thereby conceal a yet stronger and clearer trend: The values of late modernity are winning over the traditional values at an astounding pace. Even immigrants in Sweden tend to be "more modern"[11] than e.g. the average resident of Poland. If you zoom out to a couple of hundred years ago, and look globally, the trend becomes clear. The Swedes and Danes would have been conservative peasants back then, comparable perhaps with today's Afghans. Even if the values of countries do jerk back and forth over time, the overall progression is clear: We are headed towards a world with more cosmopolitan values; values which according to Inglehardt and Welzel's own analysis work better in modern society.

Think about it. The most secular people in say Pakistan are the richest and most educated ones—and these are the ranks that most other Pakistanis aspire to join. The wealthy Pakistanis, in turn, like to go to the US and adopt large parts of the American lifestyle and values. In the US, the liberal press has a constant upper hand on the conservative press, with TV-hosts ridiculing the rural, conservative population—and the people with the highest status are liberal New Yorkers rather than "hillbillies" and Christian fundamentalists. And among the liberal US population, Sweden and other Nordic countries have a very strong lure, being viewed as "pure" and "fresh"—or just progressive. If you are a liberal lawyer in Boston, you tend to love watching the Danish TV-series *Borgen*, (where a divorced woman and mother of two is prime minister of Denmark, dealing with a fictional Green Party to outmaneuver the crude, conservative populists). And you are likely to listen to Nordic pop artists such as Robyn, Elliphant, MØ, Röyksopp or Björk, because these subtly embody more progressive values in their artwork. And the countries keep winning the Eurovision Song Contest.

So the rapidly globalizing economic world-system has produced some pockets where the values and worldviews of a more global, digitalized civilization seem to have taken stronger hold, and they just happen to be in the Nordic countries. And these pockets have high symbolic value in the status chain of world cultures, which is evident in the growing cultural exports of these countries and the strong "Nordic brand" in proportion to the small size of the region.

None of this should be controversial. Some parts of the world seem to "develop" values ahead of others and thereby acquire "progressive" values, which in turn grant different advantages on the global market. After all, why should we expect all seven billion of us to alter our values in perfect unison with one another? And why should we expect all value systems to be of equal status on the global scene of cultural prestige?

I am *not* saying that the rest of the world is "destined" to become like the Nordic countries—technology and culture are evolving much too quickly for such silly recaps to occur. There will never be another 1960 or another 1990. Each historical moment is unique. Neither am I saying, of course, that the world is becoming irrevocably "westernized" and "secularized"—there is certainly more going on under the sun than that. But significant sociological developments have undeniably taken place here during the last century; changes that can help us understand future developments in other countries.

We are likely to see new and unexpected forms of societies emerge, for better or worse. It is in this regard that the Nordic countries offer an interesting case. If we truly want to understand the development of the global economy and the emergence of its political, cultural and socio-psychological landscapes, we should not confine our analytical gaze to the aftermaths of the Arab Spring or the struggling Kurdish state. In this coherent world-system, we should look for the locations where people have the preconditions to write new values on new tablets.

Societal progression is when lasting conditions of stability and abundance allow for changes in the games of everyday life to occur: in the workplace, in dating, in friends' groups, at home (you stop beating the kids, for one thing), in neighborhoods, at school, in the political arena, in the market—and the labor market. **The games of everyday life become milder, more sensitive, fair and forgiving as a result.**

In this perspective it becomes apparent that the Nordic countries are by far the most progressive societies that the world has ever seen. It is here that we are most likely to find the values and worldviews that best correspond, in functional terms, to a complex, digitalized, global, transnational, post-industrial society. (Now don't get cocky and patriotic on me, you stupid Swedes, it's not about you being better than anyone else.)

Post-Materialist Values

It should be noted that the development of people's fulfillment and happiness becomes less tied to material wealth once a certain level of wealth has been achieved, and that this has an important role to play in the new political landscape. There are different ways of seeing this: through happiness research, as the utility of natural resources expended and as the growth of post-materialist values in the population.

Happiness research: Let us first consider the controversial field of "happiness research" in economics, psychology, sociology and related fields. According to such research, the Nordic countries generally do very well.

You may be familiar with the famous (and now infamous) Easterlin Paradox, named after the economist Richard Easterlin who wrote a book chapter about "economics and happiness" in 1974. The paradox is that wealthy countries seem to stop increasing their level of happiness. Happiness follows economic growth but flattens out in rich countries even if they keep becoming richer. But there is plenty room for nuance and criticism in that statement.[12]

First of all, the general methodology of Easterlin's study has been attacked—he relied on different kinds of measurement crammed into one model (although other researchers have found similar results). Secondly, happiness research is itself a fishy field, using vague measures such as asking people how they are doing on a scale from one to ten. Once you start reaching higher numbers on this scale, we have good reason to assume that few people will give a ten. The ten somehow always slips farther away, because very few of us have a perfect life.

And third, the "paradox" has more or less been solved by economists who have pointed out that happiness follows economic growth, but only *logarithmically* (you have to double income to get one more point of happiness, so if you make the scale logarithmic you can actually plot it as a linear increase).[13] That explains why you get a flattening curve: First you add two dollars to someone who only make one dollar a day, and happiness goes up a lot. But when you already have a thousand bucks a day, adding two more makes no difference. Tripling the income might still make a difference, as you can now start your dream business, a foundation, etc. Once you view happiness over income logarithmically, you get a solid correlation between the two—although it should be noted that not all of "happiness" seems to be "explained" by income; living in a stable democracy with civil liberties, lower inequality and higher levels of trust (between citizens and for authorities) also helps your smile. And of course, at the level of single individuals, things like being good-looking, healthy and having fewer domestic quarrels make a lot of difference, more so than income. On another note, increasing happiness may be "more worth" when you go from 1 to 2 (on a self-reported scale of 1-10) than when you go from 7 to 8—which also says something about how the first dollar matters the most. (A better scale of subjective happiness is presented in chapters 12 and 13.)

All this—with some ifs and buts—is just to say that human happiness, in these countries, is being decoupled from money and other material wealth. Stop a moment to consider the implications of that.

Use of natural resources and technology: Another way of looking at it is that material resources are very efficient for creating happiness when the population is poor, but then becomes less efficient once you reach the level of a wealthy, liberal democracy. So increasing economic output gets lower payoff in terms of human happiness, once modern industrial society is established to a certain degree. In terms of natural resources, which we are already greatly overusing, this means that we would need a few extra planets to make the people of Sweden happier by use of material wealth (or Norway, at almost double Sweden's GDP per capita largely due to oil revenues). That is quite inefficient. The use of natural resources also connects to the overall technological and cultural development of the world-system (what the market can offer at its best). Norway-Sweden is again a good example: People are about as happy in the two countries despite large GDP differences. Both countries can afford to buy more or less the best that the world market has to offer today, so Norway's huge amount of extra money makes little difference.

Norway recently made the Guinness World Record for largest firework displays ever. They just topped a recent record in Dubai (United Arab Emirates), launching 540 382 fireworks in a spectacular 20-minute show. Dubai's display was 94 km (58 miles) long, along a coastline, just to get the proportions. And the Norwegians on the ground, gaping and ooh-ing for 20 minutes, are left with the same smartphones and medical care as in Sweden. Efficient use of resources for creating lasting human happiness?

Post-materialist values: This brings us to the third way of looking at it. Nordic people have lower "survival values" and higher "self-expression values", as we have seen. In the same countries you also have increasingly vocal attacks on the idea of the dominant role of work and professionalism in society, support of basic income projects and emphasis on "quality of life" and social entrepreneurship. In a word, people are becoming *post-materialist.*[14] Extra wealth is simply a less efficient strategy for people to achieve fulfillment and happiness in these societies.

This offers a plausible explanation for why cultural matters such as gender, identity, leisure and long-term issues such as sustainability, gain a stronger foothold in these countries. On the Left, we see the rise of what is called "identity politics", i.e. issues pertaining to the exclusion and discrimination of genders, sexualities, ethnicities, class backgrounds and disabilities. On the libertarian Right, we see more principled defenses of individual integrity and privacy, freedom from surveillance, etc. Even the neo-fascists (and the associated bloggers that make up the so-called "Dark Enlightenment" and the Alt-Right) in these societies follow a similar pattern, championing "identitarian" nationalism, the cultivation of masculinity and struggling against "cultural Marxism", which is taken to mean just about anything that the neo-fascists don't like about contemporary society.[15]

Although scholars tend to have a lot of bad things to say about the old "hierarchy of needs" proposed by Abraham Maslow, it may go some way towards explaining and understanding post-materialism.[16] When people have security, good food, a nice place to live, education and okay personal relations, they begin to want more vague and immaterial things for themselves and their families, such as self-development, happiness and meaning.

My argument is that, for society to achieve these goals, it must be qualitatively different from how society is constructed today. Our current society is designed to achieve growth of industrial output and redistributing its spoils. Future society must expand upon today's society's way of functioning; **its institutions must be geared towards achieving more psychological goals**. More goals of the soul.

One Meta-Ideology Has Already Won

So if the Nordic countries, with their growing post-materialist values, offer an interesting case for the world-system as a whole, what political patterns can we see emerging here?

The dominant meta-ideology in the Nordic countries is social-liberalism, with at least a modicum of green, environmentalist hue. We can call it "Green Social Liberalism". You only have to look at the political "game of thrones" in these countries to see that this is the case. The game of party politics has certain features that are increasingly becoming all but ridiculously evident.

When it fully blooms, liberal democracy (with a parliament, parties, market economy and publicly funded welfare) merges with Green Social Liberalism. This is why Green Social Liberalism is no longer just an alternative among others, but a meta-ideology. Believing in some version of Green Social Liberalism becomes almost as self-evident and mandatory as believing in democracy, multi-party systems and civil liberties. To be a respectable, democratic, liberal citizen is increasingly synonymous with being a green social-liberal. Let's take a few examples.

There are *no* represented parties in *any* of the Nordic countries that want to abolish or, in practice, even seriously challenge the market economy. There are, furthermore, no parties that want to abolish the welfare state—not even the young hardliner libertarians of Denmark, called Liberal Alliance. (Being the most radical of them all, their long-term goal is to lower income taxes to a not so mindboggling 40 percent.) And there are no parties that don't at least give lip service to ecological sustainability.

All parties in all Nordic countries are in effect green social-liberals. The nationalist party in Sweden, called the Sweden Democrats, founded through a merger of neo-Nazis and a "populist" tax-cut and anti-immigration party, are nominally pro-abortion, pro women's rights and claim to have a responsible environmental agenda. Their conservative program must be dressed up in social-liberal robes in order to survive at all: they are against immigration, of course, but the way they legitimize such resistance is by claiming that immigration threatens the welfare state and the liberal values of native Swedes, often revolving around women's rights, and sometimes even gay rights. They also claim to defend small-scale Swedish entrepreneurs and industries by not requiring as high tax rates to fund the often costly immigration, claiming that funds should be used for foreign aid instead of prolonged integration processes of the newly arrived. In other words: This is nationalism and social conservatism under the banner of Green Social Liberalism. The only way you can make a nationalist or conservative argument in Sweden these days is by claiming that you are conserving the national qualities of Green Social Liberalism. In order to gain respectability, the Sweden Democrats have gradually lowered their tolerance for anti-liberalism and racism, leading to the expulsions of more and more members after *faux pas* in mass- or social media. The party recently broke off with its entire youth corps, after these had elected a too nationalistically inclined young woman as leader. On their pamphlets the Sweden Democrats display their male leader on the back seat of a bike—two female politicians in front, steering the tandem bike. The message is clear: "You can trust us; we play safely within the field of the Green Social Liberal meta-ideology." And the leader of Christian Democrats joins the fray, marching in the Pride parade.

If you look at the center-left and center-right parties that have hitherto been the largest and dominant ones—indeed, having defined the major divide in politics, like in other countries—they are quite close to one another, both rhetorically and in practice. Sweden had a period of eight years of center-right government from 2006-2014, breaking its long tradition of social democracy. The center-right won, in large part, by promising not to change key features of social democracy, claiming to be the new workers' party. Indeed, they were influenced by the "third way" New Labour politics of Tony Blair and Anthony Giddens in the UK. When the Danish Social Democrats came to power in 2011, together with a socialist party that once housed many Trotskyists, and a small social-liberal party, they proceeded by more or less copying the Swedish center-right policy implementation. When the Swedish Social Democrats finally took the power back in 2015, by a very thin margin, they promised not to roll back the market-liberal reforms made by the center-right and seem to have copied the slogans of the Danish center-right, defining themselves, rather neutrally, as “the future party”.

I could go on, discussing how the Left (left of center-left) has become social-liberal, how social-liberalism has become an explicit part of the Green parties, how the actual, historical social-liberal parties have all but vanished, as their niche was taken up by all the others, and so forth. Today, some newspapers, public intellectuals and ex-politicians are even calling out for an alliance between the two major parties—the center-left and center-right—in order to leave out the nationalists and the progressive parties deemed too irresponsible. This would, of course, ruin the whole dramaturgy of the current system of party politics, causing a major drop in support both for the center-right and the center-left, as they would both lose their identities without their main adversary. But it is a telling sign that serious commentators are making such suggestions.

All the political parties are delivering the same goods, more or less. A little percentage lower taxes here, a percentage higher immigration there, but it is all within the same over-arching political framework; all parties in all the Nordic countries adhere to the same dominant Green Social Liberalism, even if wet revolutionary dreams and fascism sometimes resurface in individual politicians (who are then instantly hounded off the stage).

And when push comes to shove, all the parties will defend the state bureaucracy and institutions, despite their liberal rhetoric. During the dramatic increase of arrivals of refugees from Syria and other countries in 2015, even Sweden’s coalition between Social Democrats and Greens slammed the door shut the moment that the administrative systems became overburdened. This move was not rhetorically justified in nationalist or state bureaucracy terms but, of course, as a defense of a long-term, sustainable, liberal and social immigration policy.

There Is No “Center” of Politics

In popular parlance this phenomenon (of one winning meta-ideology) goes by different names: that all the parties have “gathered around the center”, that the “political scale has been compressed” and the like. The Left, both academic and populist, is thrilled to be shocked by how “ultra-liberal” society has become, and its adherents somehow always manage to mention Ronald Reagan and Margaret Thatcher as a kind of transcendental prime mover, explaining how the world took a wrong turn based on corporate lies and blinding neoliberal ideology. The Right, and by that I mean the socially conservative elements of society, is equally thrilled to be appalled by what appears to be an endless onslaught of political correctness, relativism, multiculturalism, and the excessive softness of the nanny welfare state. As I mentioned, the neo-fascists like to call it the victory of "cultural Marxism". What we are hearing are scattered remnants of the voices of the alternatives to Green Social Liberalism that existed under industrial modernity.

But that age has quickly passed. We are approaching a new landscape. I am not talking about what Zygmunt Bauman calls "postmodernity"[17] or "liquid modernity"[18] or what Anthony Giddens calls "late modernity"[19]. What I mean is that we have passed into a postindustrial and digitalized age where new political rules apply—and where metamodern politics becomes increasingly viable.

There is no "center" in any strict, analytical sense. What we have is one victorious meta-ideology, one recipe for society that has beaten its competitors when it comes to functionality and rhetorical edge. It is this meta-ideology that is *disguised* as a "center", as being the sensible, moderate form of politics. The "middle" is a position that under other circumstances would have appeared as extreme. Indeed, Sweden is an extremely modern, liberal country, stabilizing approximately around this equilibrium:

- An uncompromising acceptance of the market economy.
- An equally uncompromising acceptance of the welfare state.
- A gradual adaptation to the pressures of economic globalization, with a focus on economic growth, liberal markets and international competitiveness.
- An approximate 50-50% mixture of public bureaucracy and private enterprise, usually with a slight tilt towards private (Sweden, for instance, collected 50.4% of GDP in taxes at its peak in 1999, which had gone down to 43.0% by 2015).
- An uncompromising acceptance of basic liberal values.
- A rhetorical minimum of ecological awareness.

Anybody who strays from this path commits political heresy. All values, from radical feminism and veganism to anti-surveillance and anti-immigration nationalism, are justified with at least some reference to this same meta-ideology. This meta-ideology is dominant simply because it is superior to its alternatives under the current economic, technological, socio-psychological and historical circumstances. That doesn't give Green Social Liberalism any transcendental value or divine justification. It just happens to have a competitive edge under the current circumstances.

Readers will no doubt note that one can see similar tendencies in many Western countries. The point here is that these tendencies are more pronounced and have progressed farther in the Nordic countries, which is why we are studying them specifically—they may, to some extent, portend the political development in a more international, even global, context.

In the Nordic countries of today there is no real public discourse about where society is headed, no real tug-of-war pulling in different directions. There are just superficially different varieties of Green Social Liberalism. If we zoom in a little on what may be causing this ideological (but not economic or cultural) stand-still, the list looks something like this:

- The industrial society we knew has been suspended in favor of a post-industrial, digitalized service economy. Thereby the parties no longer represent real economic classes (peasants, workers and bourgeoisie) that people feel they belong to in their everyday lives.
- Individual people have increasingly complex identities, interests and ideologies (mixing, for instance, feminism with Christianity and online privacy concerns or whatnot), making them harder to represent in coherent political parties.
- Politics deals with more and more complex financial, legal, social, political, technological and ecological realities—thereby landing more power in the hands of non-elected bureaucrats and experts and making public discourse more difficult and filled with distorting simplifications.
- The increasingly mixed class and social interests make it difficult to form monolithic structures to organize and represent voter interests. For the individual person, this also makes it harder to "join" any one movement without contradicting some of one's own central values.
- If a country goes farther left it loses in the face of international competition for capital; if it goes farther towards liberalization, it suffers social paralysis and protests; if it retracts civil liberties (gay marriage, etc.) it loses valuable economic agents; if one ignores the environment or the plight of foreigners one loses the rhetorical battles for moral high-ground.

The party system we know, with a Left and a Right, is a product of the classes of an industrial society, where a majority of everyday activity was based around partaking in the production and distribution of industrial goods. The same can be said about the electoral system itself; it is constructed to house class-based parties.

In the postindustrial, digitalized and globalized economy, where the most revenue is cycled through rather abstract services, we no longer have the same class division; we no longer have the same social strata that the parties were designed to represent. Social mobility is relatively high in the Nordic countries, which also means that within one family, you can have one unemployed blue-collar person, one with depression and on sick-leave, one with a fancy international job with high salary—and a school teacher. The divisions become much more multilayered and complex. Later in this book, when we study how moral values and worldviews develop, you will understand more clearly which new divisions are emerging as the most significant ones.

In the parts of the world where this postindustrial economy has manifested most clearly, postindustrial politics follows like a shadow: liberal values together with a balance struck between free enterprise and social welfare—and sustainability. In the Nordic countries, the clout and seriousness of every political movement is measured by its dedication to the dominant meta-ideology of Green Social Liberalism. The question is no longer which society we want—one vision has won by walk-over, and it allows no alternatives—but rather, who will be most proficient at getting us there. Who is the best janitor?

What should we make of this? Is all ideological struggle over? Are we, in effect, replacing one janitor-of-a-prime-minister with another? Let's take stock of some implications.

First of all, don't be fooled by the fireworks, the displays of rhetorical and practical disputes of the politicians, who have every interest in maintaining the image of deep divisions and conflicts, an interest shared by the media who work hard to create drama concerning relatively small differences.

And secondly, admit defeat. Socialism (or anarchism) is not going to happen. And there is no national resurgence of organic community coming our way. There will be no night-watchman state and libertarian utopia where the public sector is all but removed. There will be no ecological-spiritual awakening spontaneously growing from the goodness of your heart. And no, Mr. Conservative, there will be no rolling back of gay rights, bike paths, vegan diets, animal rights and queer perspectives—they are all here to stay and expand.

You can give up on all of that nonsense. Those were whispers of another time. Let them die hard. Clear your head of these hallucinatory fantasies. They are about as meaningful today as belief in ghosts or Jesus walking across King Herod's swimming pool.

And third, you can take the bull by its horns and tame it.[20] If the ideologies and utopias of modern times are increasingly revealing themselves as bankrupted, how about taking a sober look at the new political landscape, and from there develop a new ideology based on the already dominant Green Social Liberalism? Can you take the full consequences of it—and raise it to a new and higher level? Oh, that's why we're doing this book.

See the "center" for what it is—the total victory of one ideology over all alternatives. And then use it. Break its limits.

The Voter's Raw New Deal

Another way to look at the issue is from the perspective of the individual voter and her interaction with the political system. She is faced with a situation in which party politics gradually loses much of its meaning and lure. Because the political spectrum is really a showcase for more or less of the same content, party politics becomes predictable and irrelevant.

Three perceptions of the political realm become deeply ingrained. First, that politics is boring. Secondly, that it is difficult, requiring expert knowledge of e.g. sustainability, energy or finance. And third, that our efforts won't make any difference either way. Membership of political parties drops, and has kept decreasing for decades in a very stubborn trend. Everybody claims to be "above" such petty things as party politics.

None of this should be surprising, given that one and the same political meta-ideology overshadows the bickering of day-to-day politics. The Nordic countries have proportional parliamentary systems, which favors the formation of six to ten parties, rather than two major ones. If the voter takes an online test before the elections (for party sympathies), she often finds only a small difference between her degree of agreement with the number one party and the number two on her list. Let's say the gap is five percent. Can you expect her to tie her personal identity to that party, to make it her own project, to stand up for and support it, to hand out stickers and wave flags in its name—only for those meager five percent? Truth be told, it's a raw deal. Party politics is just not the place to be anymore. The voter will likely be able to better defend her interests and find a positive, coherent civic identity elsewhere.

Whereas the politicians and the media try to inflate the political debate, focusing on differences and distinctions—as well as increasingly focusing on matters of competence, respectability and scandals (where smaller and more trivial matters begin to count as shockingly scandalous)—the electorate and media consumers grow tired of charades and petty squabbling.

There is an increasing popular demand for things such as "straight talk", not to score cheap points, not to raise your voice, not to be impolite, sticking to the argument, and bringing up relevant information. Because the electorate senses that there is no real debate and no real class struggle going on, they begin to demand a more *deliberative* form of politics (deliberative democracy is when people talk to one another and reason their way to a common ground based on mutual respect and understanding). The voter expects her representative politicians to listen more carefully, to **co-develop** political solutions by taking on multiple perspectives. Nothing is more common in Denmark or Sweden than the complaint that politicians bicker too much and too artificially about too superficial things.

The politicians and the media have not been late to catch the trend. Politicians are hurrying to recast themselves as the responsible, holistic ones, becoming increasingly reluctant to cast the first stone, portraying themselves as less ideologically blinded than their competitors. The media, for their part, increasingly try to present their TV-shows, webpages and newspapers as the ones that "take a higher perspective", to be the platform where "real deliberation" occurs.

Whereas Nordic politics has largely been based around consensus during the 20th century (primarily between organized labor and capital and their respective political representations), it is now taking another step in this direction. The individual cannot know his or her interest in advance. **Political interests are becoming vaguer and more complex—and thereby more closely related to one another in unexpected ways.** The ambiguity of life and our positions in society makes it all but impossible to form stable interest-based parties. Am I a consumer, a student, a worker, a woman or perhaps an entrepreneur, or will I soon be on sick-leave, or will someone in my family be? Am I threatened by economic crisis, immigration or ecological collapse?

Nordic politics is crystallizing around what we may call "the Nordic ideology"—a concept we will explore and deepen in the following book. In this ideology people increasingly value **co-development**: the ability to, together with others, responsibly explore the new landscapes of risks and possibilities that are opening up. Everybody knows the politicians cannot deliver full-blown libertarianism or socialism. So at least let's hear them speak honestly, and let them *listen* to one another, and listen to me, the voter.

Nordic politics has moved from consensus (and compromise between the Left and the Right), to a politics of co-development. It's a major shifting of gears that breaks the trend of the representative class system based on debate and "winning the argument". This trend is accelerating and gaining strength as we speak.

What we begin to see is a strange paradox. **Liberal representative democracy, because it is approaching its own ideals, has slowly begun to render itself obsolete.** It is precisely *because* liberal democracy has progressed (creating one relatively unified public with no clear distinction between an educated middle class and an industrial working class, in an affluent postindustrial, meritocratic service economy) that it is parting ways with its own fundamental principles. No longer is there any real choice between the different parties, between the Left and the Right. Representation is becoming weaker and the need for deliberation (rational, careful debate aiming for consensus) is becoming stronger. The different parties and their ideologies are all shifting positions, trying to find themselves, trying to find visions and goals to latch on to, copying them from one another. In the process, they come closer and closer to each other, which in turn makes mean accusations and arguments seem sillier than ever in the eyes of the voter.

Crammed up in the same political corner of Green Social Liberalism, politicians of all parties start trying to distinguish themselves by being good co-developers—all serving the emergence of the Nordic ideology.

Chapter 2

CRISIS-REVOLUTION

But all is not harmonious in the political realm of the Nordic countries. New trenches are being dug, new borders of bitter conflict. They cut through the parties, through classes and families, even through individuals and their bedrooms.

Newly Dug Trenches

The most important line is drawn between the old society and the new. **A majority of the population still do not realize that they no longer live in a national, industrial society.** They don't see that the identities and narratives of the modern industrial age simply don't apply anymore. These people are of course especially concentrated to the conservative and populist movements. The very agenda of such movements is to resist immigration, resist other aspects of globalization, fight transnationalism (a concept we discuss in chapter 5) and fight certain social aspects of information society. This resistance is what is fundamentally fuelling the electoral successes that have recently been enjoyed by the nationalist-populist parties and the rise of Trumpism in the US.

But it is not just the Nordic nationalists who are stuck in the old paradigm and who use outdated narratives. In fact, the old Left is helplessly blind to the fundamental shifts that are taking place in society. They perceive, quite incorrectly, that a nostalgically held solidarity is being attacked by neoliberal corporate greed—when in reality post-materialist values of happiness, quality of life and self-development are booming at the expense of materialist values. And government welfare spending has gone up over the decades.

And the market-libertarians, for their part, try to cling to a hopelessly outdated image of "the free market" that they imagine can be pitched against "the state", failing to recognize that those categories are long gone (and were very doubtful to begin with). Market, state and civil life are becoming intermeshed in a myriad of ways.

Center-left and center-right compete with one another about who is the best at "creating more jobs" and "keeping industries" so that they can "fund welfare" and "invest in education". They don't recognize that they are playing the wrong game altogether. The game has shifted.

A smaller axis of progressives do have intuitive and sometimes explicit understandings that the times are-a-changin'. These strata are concentrated around progressive parties such as the Pirate Party (started in Sweden, but had the most success in Germany and lately in Iceland), the Greens, the Feminist Initiative (also Sweden) and **The Alternative** (a Danish party, by far the most insightful and progressive one, discussed in chapter 5). Such parties are indicative of new progressive strata of the population, representing the groups we can call **the triple-H: hipsters, hackers and hippies**.

The triple-H people are not just annoying; they are also the main agents within crucial sectors such as IT, design and organizational development. The sociologist Richard Florida called them the creative class.[21] His theory has merits, but he failed to see the wider political implications of such shifts of values in the population. He also lacked a framework for understanding developmental psychology and he missed vital aspects of how it all links up with technological development.

It should be noted that such progressives do exist here and there within all parties, Left and Right, and to a small extent within academia. On the Right, especially the green libertarian Right, you are more likely to find the growing **yoga bourgeoisie**. The yoga bourgeoisie are rich and successful urban dwellers, usually working in the private sector. They have found that money is not the answer to a happy life and therefore begin to cultivate self-awareness, authenticity and intimacy—often in and around yoga parlors, tantra group settings, contact improvisation dance, improvisation theatre, self-help courses and coaches, and to some extent the Burning Man festival and its wider cultural sphere. These people, funnily enough, often work in tandem with the more anti-establishment triple-H people.

Progressive movements host people working *against* the values of the national industrial society, taking on a **transnational** perspective. They work to transform their countries (or cities or regions) into nodes within a larger community of states (or cities, or regions), where information is free, production of cultural goods is central, and creativity is paramount.

A major task in these groups is to achieve a transition to an ecologically sustainable society. They don't resist Green Social Liberalism, but try to expand it and build it on a transnational level. They are also much more likely to be good co-developers, valuing personal traits such as listening and humility in the face of others' perspectives. Most of all, they live in pockets of transnational networks where they partake in creative IT-companies, public-private partnerships and different forms of social entrepreneurship and research programs, often working professionally with things such as open information, climate change and organizational democratization.

The non-progressive group, the increasingly bewildered guardians of the old society, generally consists of the less favored people in the newly emerging social, cultural and technological hierarchies. If you look at voter behavior, you have an overrepresentation of men, older people, lower education and rural residents.

The progressives have the opposite profile: city-dwelling young women with higher education (and more gay people). And this struggle between the old society and the new runs deep—even into the bedrooms, where you find many lonely, frustrated rural men and an increasing number of discouraged successful, independent city women who never seem to find a satisfying match. And then there is a smaller number of men of more progressive alignment—having all the right feminist values and socio-economic merits—who are web-dating all those women, but seldom deciding to stay with them. Single households abound.

If these new borders, conflicts and tensions are more subtle and have more dimensions than the class struggles of old, they are no less embittered. The trenches—and the cruel, grinding wars—are present even within each single person, even within our own bodies and minds.

In this new society of digital culture and software, being in touch with the symbols and tempo of society—having what is sometimes called "cultural capital"—puts you at a much greater advantage than before. Whereas money, in the Nordic countries, is scattered relatively evenly across the representatives of the old society and the new, cultural capital is certainly not. **The more artsy, creative, well connected, socially intelligent, emotionally developed, idealistic, digitalized, diversified and educated you are—the more likely you are to be a rising star of the new society.** And the more likely you are to be powerful and successful in the new global economy, even without much money. A sign of this is the growing number of humanities majors who make it big within IT startups.

In the long run, the trend is clear—even if the people of the old society still vastly outnumber the people of the new, the Nordic countries will become much more progressive than they already are. The progressives are at a significant competitive advantage. This is because of the changed technological and social environment of the information age. The fight is fixed.

A yet stronger indication can be found in the statistics for the young people voting in Sweden during the 2014 elections for the European Parliament. In these elections, people often vote more in line with their true ideological convictions. If you look at the youngest voters, the Pirates, the Feminists and the Greens almost had a majority of the votes if you put them together. When the young vote from their hearts, this is the pattern that emerges. It says something about where the long term trends are pointing. Do not be fooled by recent surges of nationalist sentiment. Even the nationalists of Sweden have become a softer, more liberal and greener version of their continental European sisters.

But even if class struggle is not what it used to be, and even if the population is increasingly valuing co-development, there is still a political game. Development of societies has always produced losers and winners. It has always been a grim business. A new political reality is emerging at the heart of the most progressive countries in the world, a silent revolution pertaining to the information age. What we are seeing is not really a wave of nationalism rising across Europe or a socialist utopia lost to neoliberalism. **We are witnessing the rise of the digitalized, globalized, transnational, postindustrial society—and its discontents.** The nationalist resurgence is only that: the outdated, the outgunned, the outmaneuvered. That does not make the confusion and suffering of the losing side any less real.

Where do you fit in all this, dear reader? Are you marginalized and embittered by the onslaught of rapid change, by the new waves of immigration and sudden shifts in gender identities? If you are, your perspective also deserves a voice. It doesn't make you a bad person.

But of course, it is easier, more fun and more beneficial for the world if you side with the new society that is being born. Politics has changed. And frankly, so should you.

Hackers, Hipsters and Hippies

A little more should be said about the "triple-H population", their cultural and economic DNA and their role in bringing about a metamodern society—and why the can comfortably be grouped together. They have worldviews, interests and skills that are notably different from any of the classes of industrial society. Let's go through each of the subgroups, see what they produce, and why they are in fact becoming a new basis of power in society.

A hacker is not just a person who illegally gains access to computer systems; the hackers I refer to, self-identified (like that of Facebook's founder Mark Zuckerberg) or not (like many of those who nonetheless participate in programming events known as "hackathons"), produce digital solutions and software that reduce the complexity of society and make it manageable. Of course, not all IT-workers, computer engineers and programmers can be considered to be hackers in this sense. Only the ones who *combine* their IT and programming skills with an intimate, embodied knowledge of digital culture (and other sensitivities towards our day and age) can be considered as such. They combine software development with cultural capital and social capital, i.e. with a sensitive knowledge of the culture and age we live in, with a rich understanding of its symbols. You'll find many of these people in creative industries, ranging from smaller app startups and the independent, "indie-", game development scene, to social innovation projects, to some of the more visionary departments at Google and other major actors. They invent solutions that bypass many of the old, capitalist ways of distributing services and information: digitalizing and gamifying education (and making it more module based), finding novel applications of technologies to solve social problems (like making software for social movements to organize, or to improve the democratic deliberation in larger organizations) and democratizing medical equipment by creating mobile applications that measure everything from brain waves and heart rates to the environmental impact of our purchases, or working to create more transparent and shared data bases available to governments and publics, or working to create mobile solutions that help payments and pricing in developing economies or help sharing videos of abuses or facilitating other forms of whistleblowing. Datamining and AI play increasingly important parts in this development. The increasing saturation of computer games of everyday life offer many platforms for such endeavors. So this group is growing in importance because it offers us the software solutions that can only come from great creativity combined with cultural capital and digital know-how.

Hipsters are not just people with a particular style of fashion, or the pretentious college kids who show off their supposedly good taste in music and art. The hipsters I refer to produce the many symbols that help us to orientate ourselves in, make sense of, and find meaning in the global, digital age. Here you find a wide array of artists, designers, thinkers, social entrepreneurs, writers and bloggers. They develop the ideas of posthumanism, transhumanism, complexity and network researchers, participatory forms of politics and social movements, critique of wage labor (and the often irrational nature of work in the economy), ecological and social resilience, personal development, organizational development, the new gender and sexual relations, our forms of family and community life, the interactions of different cultures—and much more. They also, notably, *embody* these new thoughts by creating music, fashion, movies, books and games that embody these new values and ideas—and by their own taste in fashion, art and lifestyle. Whereas the hackers rely upon a combination of digital skills and cultural capital, the hipsters rely upon a greater amount of cultural capital only—combined with their personal networks, i.e. on social capital. People who adopt and successfully wield and display these symbols gain different kinds of competitive advantages: Companies turn greater revenues, individual persons appear more sensitive and sophisticated, and cities or municipalities can brand themselves as attractive, dynamic and creative hubs. The hipsters are becoming more powerful because it is becoming increasingly difficult for most of us to grasp and navigate the society of the present age—and they offer us the tools for doing so.

The **hippies**, then. I concede that this is a silly use of terms, as the word "hippie" was originally derived from the word "hipster". But since the 1950s and 60s, the two words have taken on quite different connotations, so I think we can safely separate them. The hippies are the people who produce new lifestyles, habits and practices that make life in postindustrial society happier, healthier and, perhaps, more enchanted. The hippies here are not quite the same as the hippies of old: the starry-eyed New Agers who looked to astrology, crystals, transpersonal psychologies and gurus, but rather people with highly developed skills in meditation, contemplation, bodily practices, psychedelics, diets and physical training, profound forms of intimate communication and sexuality and simple life wisdoms that apply to our day and age. You will find more rational and research based approaches to psychedelics, communities for self-development and eco-village living, science-driven meditation and stress release practices, coaches of all kinds, and elaborate forms of practices for achieving higher mental states and spiritual experiences. An important hub for all this is the Burning Man festival community of "burners" that are springing up around the world—originally held in the Nevada desert, but now with numerous offshoots. At this festival you will find a large host of MDMA-induced (a.k.a. ecstasy) art projects; large, impressive and "meaningless" structures that are built as temporary art projects for no other reason than that it is fun and interesting. So the hippies are becoming a force to recon with because they provide social and personal technologies for maintaining health, happiness, community and a sense of enchantment to an increasingly strange and alienating world. Sometimes, this takes the form of vegan diets, sustainable lifestyles, organic farming for self-sufficiency, and relative withdrawals from modern life. But the activism always reinserts itself into the mainstream; it always comes back with a will to engage with others—not least via social media. The sorts of hippies we are talking about here are generally highly educated and rely upon knowledge of medicine, physiology and psychology. This, too, can be seen as a form of cultural capital. Hippies without such cultural sensitivity fall behind and remain the old kind of hippies.

Somewhat strange bed-fellows, these three, hackers, hipsters and hippies. What, then, unites the triple-H population? One thing is that all three groups share an alternative relationship to work and the market: They are all driven by what psychologists of work call *intrinsic* motivation and self-realization, rather than extrinsic motivation, such as monetary rewards, consumption and security. This means that they work by another social and economic logic than any of the old groups in industrial society. Of course, this is an outflow of postmaterialist and highly individualized societies, in which significant parts of the population have the luxury to think much less about how to pay the bills and more about how they can change the world. Bangladesh is not full of triple-H; California is. Because of the idiosyncratic nature of their many endeavors, the triple-H folks find it hard to "fit in" within the classical, hierarchical and meritocratic organizations. Many of them will have rebelled against such structures and try to find ways to work outside and beyond them—outside academia, outside major corporations and even medium-sized companies and beside public bureaucracies. No doubt, organizations that find ways to attract and keep these agents and harness their talents will gain great competitive advantages in the future.

The second—and most significant—thing that unites them is the fact that they all rely more upon **cultural capital** (and to some extent social capital) and less upon economic capital. As such, they form a complex but united front against the capitalist society in which they take part, a subtle **revolution of cultural capital**. What you see is that, near the centers of the world economy, you find more and more people whose lives are no longer governed by the logic of economic capital. And some of these people can still be rich. Rich hipsters? How does that work? Because cultural capital is becoming more powerful than economic (as a means of organizing and coordinating people's actions and behaviors), **the cultural capital can be traded for money or other valuable resources at a favorable rate**. Hence, bit by bit, cultural capital is beginning to *dominate* economic capital in the new digital, postindustrial age. More on this in future books.

Which brings us to the third thing that unites the triple-H: their common vested interest as **a postindustrial class**. In this sense, these people are the real "creative class". When the American sociologist Richard Florida tried to describe the creative class he relied upon classical occupational statistics, but that is, needless to say, a very clumsy tool. If you want to spot this new class and their interests, you must *first* understand them qualitatively, and then analyze their socio-economic DNA, like we are doing now.

For these people, **the wage labor treadmill (and conventional work life) *hinder* the lives that they want to live, rather than being a source of security and empowerment**. Each aspiring triple-H person of course has relatively low chances of achieving financial success. She must win the trust and attention of other people in order to be able to perform her "real" work, her labor of love, fulltime. So she must make many attempts, which often leaves her back at square one, where she must again tweak her ideas and modes of work.

Hence, there is a revolving door between "the creative class", which the triple-H population largely constitutes, and the **precariat**—people in economically and socially precarious situations, at the fringes or outside of the conventional labor market. Oftentimes, it is up to the family or the state to support this growing reserve army of "failed" triple-H folks. And once these people must give up their intrinsic motivation to stand in line for menial work, reporting in to the rigid control structures for the unemployed, or adapt to the demands of not-so-postmaterialist supporting family members, they become miserable and often dysfunctional. For them, there is no clear line between fun and work. Even reading a novel or watching a TV series or playing a computer game is part and parcel of their work to change the world. If their higher aspirations fail, life seems to offer them very little and they are prone to falling into escapism and depression.

For this reason, the triple-H population generally support ideas of basic income: This would insulate them against falling into precarious situations and emancipate them in the face of demeaning bureaucratic control. This is why the triple-H population and the precariat are both classes produced by postindustrial, digital society and as such, they form an entirely different form of class interest, a line drawn between them and the classes of old: worker, middle class and the rich. What the triple-H people often *don't* understand, however, is that most people do not function like them and do indeed still find meaning and security in the conventional work life—even the ones who don't like their jobs find structure and context to their lives and earn a much valued paycheck. The demands for basic income are hence often premature and naive, not least because they overlook the developmental psychology of the population (which I present in part two). The triple-H people are children of a new society, and their needs and their solutions are, in the last instance, at odds with the modern, capitalist system. But the group is growing and so is their relative power within the global capitalist economy.

The triple-H populations suffer from a number of things that aren't an issue to most people. These are:

- uncertainty of levels of expectations,
- bullshit,
- empty networking.

I will discuss all of these in greater detail elsewhere—here we are just mentioning them. "Uncertainty of expectations" has to do with the extreme differences of responses that can be produced by their work. If you work hard and put your stuff out there most anything can happen: You can become a star, get a solid international upper middle class career, or you can be completely ignored for whatever reason. There can be fame and glory and a major breakthrough around any next corner, or there can be a lifetime of frustrations and precarious and embarrassing situations. Will your app help save a million lives or will you have wasted ten years of your life? Will people scorn you or adore you, or both? Should you continue, follow your dreams, change plans and pivot, or maybe go back to the security and humility of a conventional life and career? This is the revolving door between the creative class and the precariat; there can be great distance between expectations, strivings, hopes and realities in these non-conventional lifestyles. At least since the classical sociologist Émile Durkheim's work at the turn of the last century, it has been known that expectations minus realities is how you calculate a major factor of ill mental health and human misery (what Durkheim famously called *anomie*).

"Bullshit" means that there needs to be a lot of big talk when you deal with bigger and more abstract issues and matters. A new organizational paradigm? A revolution in how we apply datamining to new problems? A major innovation or a technical detail? A profound global movement or a club for self-admiration? Because there is so much understanding and context needed in all these projects, they may be difficult to explain, and sometimes you may need to find ways to package and sell them. In plain English, you need to wrestle the doubts and accusations that it's all just bullshit. And, needless to say, the majority of the work of the triple-H population is undeniably so. The reason that it's so valuable to society is just that some of it *isn't* bullshit and even a small percentage of genuine innovations of software, culture or lifestyle can have a huge impact. Still, you never quite know if you are the bullshitter or the hero, or if you are being sold utter bullshit.

"Empty networking" is a wasteful activity that most triple-H people know all too well: those many coffees and lunches had, Skype conferences held and evenings attended that never really led anywhere. Because the triple-H people all rely upon large networks of people to collaborate with in different projects, they must always be open to new contacts. This means curiously inviting new people, surveying the skills and assets and building personal rapport, exploring new ways to work with new people. The people they meet are friendly, like-minded and always interesting. But the productive relationships that are mutually reinforcing and become stronger over time are rare: Because it's so complex; so many expectations and assumptions and so much shared knowledge that must be in place.

So these are some of the sufferings of the triple-H population, some of their weaknesses. The parts of the world economy that are most sensitive towards these weaknesses will also become the most competitive ones as they can successfully harness the creative powers of the triple-H. Advanced science is also a key ingredient to postindustrial growth, but it doesn't necessarily create local growth without a vibrant community of creatives and people who can invent applications of ground research—the research results can be picked up by any agents around the world, at least in theory.

But favoring the creative class is never an easy issue, since there is considerable resistance from other, more conventional segments of society. Malmö, a town in southern Sweden, recently reinvented itself, going from an industrial economy where the jobs had been lost, to being a "progressive" and "hip" city, attracting the creatives. Not only were there bitter struggles around this on a political level; there has even arisen an "anti-hipster movement", placing bitter stickers downtown public spaces, attacking the hipsters. People feel a vague sense of confusion, inferiority and disgust at these new segments of the population, who displace large parts of the existing people: their favorite joints, the look of people on the streets. Ah, there it is again: the struggle between the old society and the new.

Polarization and Trumpism Explained

So that's the story about the triple-H population, but where exactly does all of this leave us when it comes to the rest of society—after all, most people are neither hackers nor hipsters nor hippies. That's where political polarization comes in.

In the US there is a clear polarization of politics, i.e. that people are increasingly gathering around strongly opposing political poles. In the past, people of "authoritarian" bent (who like strong leaders, dislike foreigners, favor harsh punishments and value order over freedom) were divided equally between the parties. Today, they are all concentrated to the Republican Party and Trumpism has risen as a result going against the party's old elites. A high "A-factor" (A for authoritarianism) is more predictive of being a Trump-supporter than education, income or gender.[22] This means that the opposite profile is of course concentrated to the Democratic Party (and fragments to the left of it). In a country like the US, the discontents of globalization are strong enough to put up a real fight. This is why you see a polarization here, rather than the victory of Green Social Liberalism. Two opposite poles are becoming increasingly distanced from and hostile towards one another. The playing field has not cleared so that a Green Social Liberalism 2.0 can emerge—no single meta-ideology has won.

If you compare this to the Swedish electorate, one poll indicated that 69% would have voted for Clinton and only 9% for Trump. Another poll, where Swedish MPs were asked the same question, reported that over 80% hoped for Clinton; only five out of 234 respondents would admit to supporting Trump. These were all male and members of nationalist Sweden Democrats, and not one of them described his candidacy as anything other than the lesser of two evils. In Denmark, the corresponding figures were, according to a YouGov poll of the general population, 4% for Trump vs. 81% for Clinton. This was before the 2016 election; but still, you can see how dominant the green social liberal meta-ideology is. Of course, large parts of the world preferred Clinton to Trump, but the Nordic countries certainly shout with the best of them.[23]

You see a corresponding pattern of polarization if you look across countries. Some are dominated by the discontents of globalization, like Russia. Hence, polarization is not only a fact within countries, but also *between* countries. The US is caught in the middle, split in half, as it were—and it can develop in either direction.

It is unavoidable that the discontents of globalization will run the show here and there for periods, but their political programs really have very little to offer in terms of improving people's lives and transitioning to a new stage of societal development. They try to defend a sinking ship, and their poor policies will only make the economies subjected to them more marginalized and outcompeted. Sure, they can stop the EU and decrease immigration—but then what? Will that stop the globalization of markets or the digitalization and robotization of work? Will it solve the manifold transnational "wicked issues", (complex problems like sustainability, etc.)? Of course not. When they are done screwing up in a decade or so, there will be more leeway for political metamodernism to offer its bid.

Polarization (and Trumpism) is in itself a kind of political crisis. But all of this would be fine in the long run, if the stakes weren't so high and the time frames so narrow. As a world-system, we really don't have the time for Trumpism and the like. Global warming and the rapid changes pertaining to the internet age won't wait. We are entering a time of unprecedented transformation and we are in dire need of politics that are progressive—in the sense that they anticipate and productively respond to the upcoming multidimensional crisis-revolution.

The Multidimensional Crisis-Revolution

You are an educated and up-to-date reader, of course, but just to make certain that you haven't missed it, I would like to underscore that we are today living in a time of unparalleled social, technological and cultural change and development. The scientific revolution of the 17th century, the Enlightenment of the 18th, the industrial and chemical revolutions of the 19th century and even the combustion engine and the communications of the 20th century were all peanuts in comparison to the scope of what is going on today. It is as if all of these revolutions were happening at once.

Today we are experiencing an era in which several extremely far-reaching revolutions of technology, thinking and behavior are occurring simultaneously. For better and/or worse, profound changes are very likely to take place in the coming decades.

The first such change is simply the maturing of information and communication technology itself. We live in an information age and this affects all parts of our lives. We think differently, we act differently, we socialize differently. Our worldviews begin to evolve much faster, as we begin sifting through more and more information. New challenges appear —from Facebook time wasted and gaming addictions to grooming pedophiles entering the bedrooms of children via computer screens, to new ways of distinguishing ourselves that tempt us to create emotionally inauthentic virtual identities, to the selectivity in our reading of news articles—the list goes on. As I write this, the so-called "dark net" is booming: anonymity at last, married of course to a stupefying quantity of criminality and all manner of online depravities.

Computers saturate every aspect of everyone's life, changing governance, production, distribution, transportation, travelling and science. Education is being made available through MOOCs (massive open online courses), Khan Academy and Coursera, and soon it will be transformed in a massive surge of gamification.

Given the dramatic changes of the last twenty years, and that these have been accelerating and becoming all the more radical, we are looking at an entirely new form of society. The amount of information is growing at what appears to be an exponential rate—and yes, here "exponential" is the correct term. The same goes for the total of computational power available, with the possibility of quantum computing becoming increasingly tangible. From the bankers of Wall Street to the Mumbai rickshaw taxi driver's daughter, the basic conditions of life are shifting. And we haven't even entered step two of this revolution: virtual reality, now appearing as gadgets, but soon as a strong opium for the people in the form of games, pornography, travel, work interfaces or online meetings in realistic 3D environments.

And peace be with us, this is only one out of several technological revolutions that seem to be at our doorstep. Another, related one, is Artificial Intelligence (AI) and robotics—and self-learning machines, "deep learning" through "stacked neural networks". We will increasingly be able to exchange complex human work with machine labor. This may or may not "cause unemployment" (a question that is likely to look sillier by the year), but it can and will cause profound shifts in the way that we live our lives, as the robots become better at learning new tasks that go far beyond running a production plant and beyond self-driving cars. The employments of doctors, teachers, programmers, musicians and research assistants can all, in principle, be challenged by the AI. The more dramatic forecasts of futurists, like those of Ray Kurzweil, suggest that we are approaching "the singularity", when computers begin to take control of their own development. Even without accepting such fanciful speculations, we can safely assume that AI will be a major force of change.

Another budding revolution is the nanotechnological one. Nanotech is likely to solve fundamental problems of scarcity and has the potential to create abundance of a whole new magnitude. The growing ability to manipulate structures at the atomic level—and the tremendous drive in scientists to successfully do so—can create all manner of useful substances with incredible properties from virtually no raw material. Nanotech also faces us with perhaps the greatest environmental risks to date; much, much worse than plastics. Not to mention the implications of its medical uses and the closing gap between organic and non-organic applied chemistry.

And then there is the even stronger and more well-funded drive to manipulate life itself. We have an ongoing genetics revolution, nearing the possibility to manipulate and shape the human genetic code—which just took a giant leap with the CRISPR technology (Clustered Interspaced Short Palindromic Repeats)—allowing anybody with a lab to alter genetic code. To this category we should add not only epigenetics, the study of gene activation and deactivation in living organisms, but also the broader field of "human enhancement", i.e. the use of various technologies to change or improve upon the human body itself—not least by merging our bodies with machine parts. The so-called transhumanist movement is gaining traction with its radical ideas about the how technology can and should be applied to change humanity itself. And transhumanist philosophers draw a following consisting largely of tech-savvy scientists, doctors and engineers who show an almost frightening zeal in their quest to remake humanity. Bio-hacking is growing in peer-to-peer communities, a form of applied do-it-yourself biology. Even within the humanities, starting with Donna Haraway (a biologist gone humanities professor), people are talking about "the cyborg", the merging of humanity and the machine, and how it relates to gender issues and whatnot.

Beyond that, we have a host of ongoing developments that by themselves are revolutionary. Look at energy prices—how solar panel energy is becoming cheaper and how many innovations are beginning to show up in this area, including new forms of nuclear power. Take a look at housing, where we are beginning to construct homes that are largely self-supporting—and cheaper, and designed by the customer with modules. Look at the 3D-printers and drones, democratizing customized production and distribution (as well as the distribution of bombs, in the case of drones). Look at the Internet of Things—connecting all of our everyday objects to the same cooperating network. Look at the peer-to-peer production movements, in which people have begun to be able to produce cars at only a small percentage of the previous costs. Look at cradle-to-cradle production and the sharing economy and what in Germany is called *Industrie 4.0* (when the customer orders a full tailor-made industrial production from scratch). Look at the mobile revolution, today driving the ongoing migration (the waves of immigrants are harder to stop because they share information with one another). Look at Big Data and data mining—the explosively useful and dangerous analysis of vast quantities of real-life information gathered by registering user behavior. Look at the Quantified Self movement and the increasing ability to measure yourself in a myriad of ways and create your own data, including information on your own genetics. Look at the Effective Altruists and their increasingly evidence-based forms of charity showing up in so many areas. Look at the rapid changes of organizational structures, where the forms of creative work have formally exploded—some examples being LEAN, AGILE, SCRUM, sociocracy, holacracy, the whole Art of Hosting movement and Frederic Laloux's *Reinventing Organizations*.[24]

Phew. Now look at the demographics, especially the ongoing population booms in countries like the unstable Nigeria, the quickly aging demographics of Japan and Europe (and increasingly other parts of the world, with birthrates below replacement rates from China to southern India to the Caribbean and Latin America). This brings us to the colossal growth of the world economy at large, with an even more radical growth in trade, and a yet sharper growth in FDI (Foreign Direct Investment). Look at all the new financial instruments, growing in size, speed and influence as the quants (mathematicians and theoretical physicists working for investment banks) use some of the sharpest minds on the planet to continuously make automated stock trading more competitive. Look at the unprecedented volume of knowledge in the hands of the equally unprecedented masses of highly educated people that are more intimately and effectively connected than ever before. Look at the sheer volume of PhDs—within more areas than I could dream of naming or even imagine.

Look at the staggering number and diversity of hi-tech companies being born, bought and sold. Not to mention the growing number of world-altering innovations brought about by talented children. Look at the block chain technologies, Bitcoin and other crypto-currencies, and the increasingly vocal and serious critique of the monetary system, banking and rents.

Look at the global political power structure of the world shifting with China, India and Brazil blazing into world prominence, their vast populations rising above poverty (whereas the middle classes of Western societies are shrinking and new poverty growing), and the order of international security changing (with Russia still dangerously stagnating, economically, politically and culturally). Look at the budding global institutions of trade, development and security, from the IMF and WTO to OECD to NATO and IPCC and the many heads of the UN hydra, not to mention the floundering EU—taking us closer, step by step to a proto-form of global polity (a World State), whether we like it or not. In a similar vein, the number of international non-governmental organizations (NGOs) has kept exploding during the last few decades.

Then look at the growth of a myriad of small institutes, organizations and even festivals such as New Economics Foundation, Alter Ego, Edgeryders, the RSA (Royal Society for the encouragement of Arts, Manufacturers and Commerce), the Ekskäret Foundation, Tellberg Foundation, World Academy, and so forth. Such platforms gather progressive global elites (in a wider sense of the term), tech savvies, researchers and activists, to overview and discuss the dramatic ongoing changes. Their long-term influence and impact are arguably outpacing those of our prime ministers and presidents.

And then turn your gaze to the seismic shifts of perspective that are taking place across our conceptual maps of the world. The physicists are giving us an entirely new view of reality, called string theory, where potentiality is real and multiple universes may be possible. Fundamental notions such as causality are being attacked as illusions of the senses and our living, participatory perspectives are proving to be ingrained into—entangled with—the very fabric of space, time and matter. The cosmologists are bending reality farther and farther beyond what we can recognize or may even comprehend. The philosophers and mystics are tearing down the idea of a separate self, an ego at the center of existence, from all sides—leaving only a longing, empty space that needs to be filled with relations and participation. Neuroscience is exploding, with its philosophical cousin cognitive science following suit and the strange next cousin computational neuroscience still being born. So-called posthumanist thinkers are radically challenging humanity's biased view of herself in relation to the other animals and the rest of reality, taking us beyond the anthropocentric (human-biased) perspectives we have hitherto lived by. The mathematicians are teaching us that most things in reality emerge through chaos and complexity and that so many of our modes of thought are outdated and dangerous, since we are oblivious of the non-linear patterns and relationships that matter the most. Systems science and systems perspectives are breaking through, from their home bases in computer science, information science, chemistry and ecology—to all aspects of life, including the interactions between physiology and psychology. The social scientists are tearing down the foundations of the state, of the market, of money and of science itself as we have known them. Economists are telling us that the economy we took so seriously was really a myth all along, just a story. Radically new spiritual movements are cropping up, notably the "atheist" practice of Syntheism. And musicians are creating stranger and stranger electrical sounds and rhythms, mixing them with strained voices, as if to underscore just how mysterious, yet peculiarly familiar, it all seems. And fashionable, tattooed young female DJs play that music on the dance floor, and we dance under flashing lights into the darkness and get high and drunk and make out, as the reality we thought we knew is being torn down and we plunge into the sublime and the unknown. And far out into the desert, under the clear skies of that luminous, open blackness lit by perfect stars, we find each other in an intimate, loving embrace. Without the slightest effort we converse for hours and all of reality melts away as we let go of our inner shields and become one. In that timeless moment of forgiving embrace we lose ourselves and find ourselves, both at once.

The next morning we wake up in new outlandish company. Or are we still dreaming? Are we alone, or are we together? Can we ever be alone or together? We'll have to discuss these questions later. This is also a time of deep, multifarious crisis. However mysteriously terrifying and sublime our age may be, we must remain sober, clear sighted, responsible.

We face no less than nine simultaneous major global ecological crises, according to the Stockholm Resilience Centre (or at least three very acute ones). We are living in an age of mass extinction of species, comparable to the one that ended the age of dinosaurs some 60 million years ago. Almost all animal biomass on land (discounting insects and the like) consists of humans and our enslaved, tortured animals under global industrial farming. Even if wildlife fauna isn't necessarily happier than domesticated animal life, the exploitative behavior towards non-human animals must be seen not only as unsustainable but also, and primarily, as ethically inexcusable.

Most of the oceans have collapsing ecosystems and most fish are dead or dying (a truly explosive development since 1950: Over a trillion aquatic animals are killed per year). The soil is eroding and climate change is striking at the heart of the frail meteorological equilibrium that constitutes our rather young current meteorological epoch. The scientists tell us that we have entered a new geological epoch, the anthropocene, in which humanity shapes the environment more than volcano eruptions and erosion.

To the definite risks we must add the uncertain but even more dramatic ones. There is the threat of nuclear war—and a host of other doomsday scenarios are surfacing as we begin to comprehend the sheer power unleashed by our own gazing into the secrets of the universe—and the universe winks right back at us with a vengeance. Haywire AI, erratic nanotech and global epidemics are the major ones. Senior scientists like Oxford philosopher Nick Bostrom and physicist Max Tegmark (both of whom founded the Future of Life Institute) warn our leaders at special UN conferences.

And the global capitalist system is based upon perpetual growth. But we have yet to see economic growth without increased exploitation of natural resources—resources that are already overused by a wide margin. Something will have to change for this system to compute and be sustainable. The financial system seems to generate both growth and crisis—and it increasingly concentrates wealth at the top, which in turn seems to hijack our politics by way of lobbying and other artful machinations. Each financial crisis reveals that our political systems are inept to deal with the dramatic changes at hand. And the political system itself is—as outlined above—in a more subtle kind of crisis, losing its grip of a runaway, globalized world.

At the micro-sociological level, most humans are doing better than ever. Yet there is so much confusion, suffering and bitter resentment. How many beautiful, privileged people have I not heard whisper to me, late at night, that if it were up to them, they would never have been born; that they are angry with the world; that they were let down; that they live with guilt and self-doubt; that their friends and families are hypocrites? These are signs of the alienation suffered by modern human beings.

The Boom Equation

If you don't already know about the things I have mentioned, you should go back up the list and look them up.[25] You may have serious holes in your education and worldview. To be a worthy reader of this text, you should at least know the basic outline of our day and age.

This is all just to point out a simple fact: the times are changing. And how could they not be? After all—just compare today to a hundred years ago, or two hundred years ago. How can we expect immobility from a universe that literally evolved from dust to Shakespeare, as one author wrote? Whatever will come, it is not likely to be business as usual. We need to bet on a good future. And the stakes are very high.

Just consider that right now, this moment, there are a million people out there, working eagerly on something that the rest of us don't yet quite understand—knowing, *knowing* that "this will change everything". If even one percent of them are not mistaken, we will literally have thousands of discoveries, inventions and insights that, each one by itself, changes society in profound and unexpected ways.

Even if some of the things I have mentioned turn out to be exaggerated or based on misconceptions, the totality will certainly be something dramatically new and different as the world-system evolves over the coming decades. What I have not ventured to discuss is that every one of these mentioned phenomena interact with the others at an accelerating pace. We live in a time of "peer-to-peer digitalized nano-bio-tech employed by means of virtual 3D to solve energy problems to address climate change"—and so forth. All of this is happening simultaneously, day by day, in one great web of interacting, evolving nodes.

Do the math—an increasing number of accelerating revolutions and crises, all cross-pollinating at an accelerating pace (the solution to the equation is "boom!"—we just don't know if it's fireworks or atom bombs).

When a multiplicity of things explode all at once, in a **multidimensional crisis-revolution**, our linear models of the world rarely work out—they cannot take on so many different variables (and variables with qualitatively different properties) and their mutual interactions. But that does not mean we should refrain from attempting to understand the times we live in; *au contraire*, we have even greater reason to analyze society and to try to see the deeper patterns that connect in the chaos.

We need directions, but these directions must necessarily be of an abstract, open-ended nature. We don't need cookbooks; we need general ideas on how to create good cookbooks, so to speak. We need stories about stories. **Meta-narratives.**

In circumstances such as these, it is only seemly to anticipate corresponding changes of the political system and how society functions in daily life. Indeed, to ignore the necessary adaptations of political, cultural and psychological development in the face of a multidimensional crisis-revolution would be highly irresponsible. In order to take responsibility we must use an intricate understanding of psychology—the science of the human soul and the behavior of the human organism—to develop **social technologies** that address the deeper issues at hand.

Politics has changed for all time. This change is part of a wide and profound shift of the world at large. We've just got our trembling hands on the boom-stick. Where do we go from here?

Chapter 3

IN A NUTSHELL

Political metamodernism arrives at the stage at a time when the old liberal, representative system of party politics begins to lose its meaning for a host of reasons, at least in the world's most advanced and progressive countries. The political debates seem increasingly hollow, all residing within the frame of the same overarching Green Social Liberalism.

Political metamodernism sees through the current spectacle of Left and Right and begins to formulate a **Green Social Liberalism 2.0**. But it does take sides: It chooses the new society of digitalized, transnational post-industrialism, its structures and values, over the old industrial capitalist nation state.

Political metamodernism takes the consequences of the current political situation and follows them to their respective logical conclusions. The aim here is to create a synthetic solution between Left and Right—to strike a new balance or to find a new equilibrium. But Green Social Liberalism 2.0 is not a matter of compromise. It is a matter of taking the three elements of Green, Social and Liberal to their utmost extremes. [26] What we are looking for is a logically and practically coherent vision of a society that is, by our measures, without poverty and social insecurity, that has fully free enterprise and that is ecologically sustainable—in other words: **an extremely social, extremely libertarian *and* extremely green society**.

Such an endeavor would simply not have been possible to undertake during the industrial age of mass media and bureaucracy. But the game has changed. New opportunities have surfaced as a result of the informational revolution, as a result of the cultural development of society and—as we shall see—because of the increasingly powerful sociological and psychological technologies at hand, reaped primarily from behavioral science.

The Basic Idea

The following presentation does not convey a thorough understanding of the listening society or of political metamodernism. What is offered here is a superficial sketch so that you know roughly what we are talking about. The basic idea is this:

- Deliberately and carefully **cultivate a deeper kind of welfare system that includes the psychological, social and emotional aspects of human beings**, so that the average person, over the length of her lifespan, becomes much more secure, authentic and happy (in a deep, meaningful sense of the word).

Once the average person is much more secure, authentic and happy, she also tends (again, on average) to develop into a braver, more mature, more idealistic and reasonable person who cooperates more easily with others and makes better priorities, both individually and politically. Such people can then recreate society in a myriad of ways, solving many of the complex, wicked problems that we are facing today.

We are talking about **generativity**—i.e. the propensity of society as a cultural, economic and social-psychological system to, on average and over time, *generate* the *conditions* for psychological thriving and growth to occur. We are *not* talking about shoving some formula for the good life down everybody's throat. We're talking about creating likelihoods for good conditions.

But what are we trying to "fix", really? What's "wrong" with society in the first place? While we cannot "repair" society once and for all, we can certainly understand some things that are deeply messed up—and address them in an efficient and productive manner.

Here's a rough diagnosis to start from. What we think of as "normal life" is simply too harsh and cruel on our psyches, too demanding and full of insoluble dilemmas. We thereby, from childhood and onwards, become mutilated versions of our fuller potentials. Because of these many wounds, scars and arrested developments, we fail to become truly kind, intelligent an open-minded. On a subtle level we fear the world; we expend energy protecting ourselves, and this means that we fail to awaken in ourselves the playful curiosity and love that are needed for us to comprehend and respond to the challenges of the world. We make poor decisions for how to live our lives, what to prioritize, what to care about, and what to produce and consume. And we hold ourselves and each other back.

Solution? So the basic idea is to institute six new forms of politics that continuously and very deliberately work with the psychological and cognitive development of human beings, our relationships to one another, and our relations to society at large (these are presented in Book Two, *Nordic*

Ideology). These are not "solutions"—although I will suggest more than a few practical policies as well—but rather **open-ended processes**.

Processes? All modern states have finances, security and schools. The fact that these phenomena exist does not in itself answer any questions about what financial policies to adopt, how to improve security or what the education of our young should entail. They just name the categories and give us general ideas about what the institutions of our society are for. Lately we have added new forms of politics to the list—environmental politics being the prime example—whereas e.g. pyramid building has taken a backseat as of late. We can add or remove different forms of politics, if we have good arguments for doing so. We can add new processes to our society's self-organization.

As a society, we haven't fully admitted to ourselves and one another just how sensitive, how utterly emotionally vulnerable, we really are. The aim here is to make this embarrassing truth publicly obvious, so that we can together reshape society thereafter—until even the most sensitive among us can blossom; indeed, until the truly sensitive become our kings and queens.

Should We Really Make People Happy?

Should we really make people happy? Is it a viable goal for society? People sometimes make the distinction between *hedonic* happiness (pleasure, enjoyment, fun) and *eudemonic* happiness (meaning, purpose in life, and peace of mind). Both of these can be supported for the long-term development of each person as well as society as a whole.

Supporting happiness means relieving suffering, which also means improving the quality of human relationships. Negative emotions such as sadness and frustration are, in manageable quantities, an integral part of a happy, productive life—but they must be effectively learned from and surmounted.[27] And that requires happiness, or mental health, or at least some goddamn peace of mind. Happiness not, then, as the opposite of sadness—but as the opposite of suffocating misery and degradation.

To seek to develop and improve the psycho-social environment in which we live our lives does *not* (I repeat: *not*, read that word again, because I find a lot of people misread this sentence) mean that people should be protected from all challenges, difficulties or pains in the name of a superficial, immediate "happiness". We're not going to induce people to burst into loud, empty, hysterical laughter at their mother's funeral or to abandon their family responsibilities to "find happiness".

It simply means that much better support can and *should* be offered to citizens, so that we are better able to productively tackle and overcome life's challenges—and to make the best of what life offers. It is a matter of increasing people's autonomy and sense of independence, not the contrary. High levels of challenge *and* high support give the best learning outcomes, and the best learning outcomes give the most sustainable positive results—this is educational psychology 101.

A libertarian reflex is to be wary of all attempts to create happiness by political measures ("it is not the role of the state to…"). While understandable, this reflex misses the point entirely. It is not that *either* states *or* markets (*or* families *or* civil society *or* individual persons) create happiness—and "if the state does it", the individual cannot. That's silly; a rather crude and, frankly, unintelligent way to look at it. All of these categories work together in a great meshwork. You can gear these different parts of society to work together well and create happy human lives—or not. Given that we already *do* have a public sphere and a market, we can either tweak them so that they tend to generate sustainable happiness, or we can develop them in ways so that they become oppressive and create misery. But we cannot avoid the choice.

But, again, do we really want a happy society in the first place? Aren't challenges and difficulties what give life its meaning and direction? And do we deserve to be happy at all?

Let's start with the last question. If I grew up neglected by my father, with a school class where one girl cut her arm, one kid never talked to anyone, most people were insecure and never really figured out love and relationships, and some took hard drugs or drank alcohol and never got jobs, and some of the people who went to college got depressions and severe stress anxieties—am I not justified to want to inflict a corresponding pain to others, so that they learn just how tough life really is?[28]

No. The current level of suffering in modern societies is not ethically justifiable. It is morally wrong to uncritically reproduce a society that displays the amount of misery and long-lasting traumas prevalent in modern countries—even the comparatively happy ones like Canada and Denmark. It's not that pre-modern societies are any better, but today we have more options available, which lends us greater moral responsibility.

Another version of the "not deserving" argument has to do with the global bottom billion—people in abject poverty. Somehow it might seem arrogant or even coldhearted to want to dramatically improve the lives of people in rich, relatively happy economies when there is quite obviously so much material inequality in the world. Isn't it unethical, or at least distasteful, to want to build a more kind, listening and inclusive society in the developed economies, when we should in fact be focusing on redistribution of wealth and more acute suffering? There are three answers to this.

The first answer is that we can and should do both, so that the poor do become richer, but once they have become so, life can actually be happy—which was the point all along. The second answer is that rich societies are going on with their development and institutions either way, so we might as well make sure they do so in an efficient and intelligent, rather than inefficient and unintelligent, manner. The third and by far strongest argument is that the world-system is evolving a whole; each part affects every other part. So one of the best things that we can do for the good of the world is to make sure that the richest and most privileged people have enough psychological security not to worry about how fancy their cars are or if they look a little fat, so that they can instead expend time, attention, energy and resources as genuinely concerned world citizens—which would benefit everyone immensely.

Happier people create more functional societies, and more functional societies are more efficient at combating inequality—locally as well as globally. We are trying to shift the whole global system into a fairer and more sustainable equilibrium, and that requires some parts of the world to culturally develop ahead of others. It's simply hard to see how we could neglect this part of the equation.

Life is just much too full of suffering and lost potential, and this is keeping our populations from developing psychologically and becoming mature, genuine world citizens. People are hurt and afraid at a subtle psychological level—and are therefore self-absorbed, incapable of taking on larger perspectives and incapable of acting upon the very real long-term risks that are threatening our global civilization. We must, at all cost, make the world population much, much happier in the deepest sense of the word.

Obviously, we don't want to obsess about consumerism and commercialized "self-development" (as happiness researchers and yogis will agree), but we can and should wish our fellow human beings genuinely happy, productive lives. If you think about it, it becomes obvious that the opposite position is untenable from an ethical standpoint. Try saying this out loud:

> "I will inflict upon you deep suffering and degradation, or refrain from preventing the hell-like mutilation of your psycho-physiology and emotions, '*cause it might be good for ya.*"

... or worse, because "it might be useful to society". When I talk about this vision of a deeper welfare, people will often bring up the argument: "Oh, but if you make people genuinely happy, society would stop functioning, because we need people to be anxious consumers (so they keep spendin' it!) and act out of fear of losing their jobs (so they keep workin' it!) for things to run smoothly." Sometimes people will even, in all seriousness, say that we need suffering to produce good books and screenplays.

Of course, this line of reasoning is in opposition to the ethics that Immanuel Kant set up for us, to treat every human being as an end in and of herself—never as a means for somebody or something else. It also breaks the older Golden Rule, to treat others as we ourselves would wish to be treated.

Besides, it's completely wrong, if you look at the facts. The Nordic countries have happy populations relative to others—and this appears to work *in tandem with* a highly functional and ordered society (producing plenty of poetry and crime novels too, for what it's worth). It is, as we shall later discuss in detail, often misery and psychological hurt that prevent productive and meaningful social, political and economic development.

The happiness of human beings—again, in a deep, psychological sense of the word—serves the common good. Deep suffering *can* have positive effects (there is an increasingly promising clinical literature on "posttraumatic growth"), but most of the time it causes lasting traumas and costs the hell out of society in terms of social work, criminality, unrest, poor health—the list goes on. Our society generates huge amounts of trauma, every day, every minute. And psychological mutilation causes suffocated souls that never get to blossom and share their unique gifts and longings with the world.

Either way, making life hurt more is the last thing in the world you have to worry about. Even in the most functional, educated, equal and healthy regions on Earth, a lot of people are traumatized, miserable wrecks. Ask any therapist, social worker or doctor who knows what goes on beneath the surface. And with all the rapid changes and crises coming up at every corner, *somebody's gonna get-a-hurt.*

That life is too easy and hurts too little is just very rarely the problem. Don't worry. Life is going to hurt, alright, even if we dramatically improve upon its quality.

Of course, overprotection from discomfort can be harmful, because it may foster unsustainable laziness and inability to deal with problems. In psychology and psychiatry there is the concept of "learned helplessness", which can be caused either by seemingly hopeless situations, by exhaustion, and by overprotection. However, being severely harmed and degraded many times over throughout your lifetime, often beginning at very early age—which happens to many if not most people—is simply not productive.

What we are looking for is not an army of spoiled fools, incapable of taking responsibility or enduring pain. We are not looking for a non-acceptance of the suffering of life (which only brings more misery), but for a profound acceptance of life as it is. Psychologically speaking, we want a radical acceptance of pain, so that we can deal with it much more productively and create happier (and less miserable) lives for people and animals. But to truly accept the pain of life and deal with it, we require a lot of comfort, support, security, meaning and happiness. This is also what the "posttraumatic growth" researchers claim, i.e. the folks who look into how people gain positive, life-changing insights in the wake of personal crises.[29]

The point is that "normal life" causes immense harm to so many people; it just happens on a subtle and non-obvious level. This grinding down of living, breathing children is currently going on at a massive, global industrial scale through many cruel social-psychological mechanisms prevalent in what we call everyday life. Maybe we cannot stop this suffering, but at least we should do our best to substantially reduce and mitigate it.

What we are looking for is to stop the mass-mutilation and torture of human beings—who are in turn fed with the agonized bodies of enslaved non-human animals.

But then again, the happiness of our children and fellow citizens does not—*should* not—require further justification. We can and should create a happy society, simply because we care. Unfortunately, I have found, this is not obvious to many professors of psychology, theologians, philosophers, economists and the like. Pond scum.

Don't Scorn Happiness

It is as fashionable to scorn happiness as it is dumb. It is popular to try to seem "wise" because one "understands" that happiness is not that important after all. And *voilà*: You can mirror yourself in Kierkegaard, Heidegger or Viktor Frankl, saying that meaning is more important. And sure, for the individual person faced with aging, sickness or concentration camps (that was Frankl), this can make sense, which is probably why most people begin to say such things after about age fifty. But at a societal level of analysis, the scorn for happiness is profoundly misplaced.

You don't think happiness is important? Now look the chronically depressed person in her eyes—we are not talking about the cute kind of depressed of cultural creatives here (like the Norwegian author Karl-Ove Knausgard) but people who really can't get up in the morning and get abandoned by their own families as a result—and say that again. Look at the unhappy, insecure kid, who desperately looked for comfort in a stranger on the web and just got raped by someone (who is also miserable), and say it again. Or how about the screaming piglet who just literally got his testicles ripped off without anesthetics. Look him in the eye and tell him his happiness is unimportant, that he should try to find meaning in it. Not so tough, huh? Kind of craps that solemn, wise style you had going there for a moment.

Happiness and misery, bliss and suffering—these are, to a large extent, continuous with one another. If you are committed to preventing and relieving the suffering of others, you are also committed to supporting their happiness.

To say something in the defense of the deriders of happiness, it's not usually that they don't care about others or that they suffer from philosophical defeatism due to a kind of Stockholm's syndrome (that you begin to excuse unhappiness because you yourself are unhappy, that your mind is "taken hostage", as it were). Their mistake lies primarily in the failure to make the *analytical* distinction between unsustainable, hysterical "happiness" on the one hand, and authentic, sustainable happiness on the other. Authentic happiness includes hedonism (pleasure, fun) and eudemonia (meaning, contentment) *as well as* the productive and responsive acceptance of pain and sorrow.

These critics also fail to see the social implications of how happy people are more productive in profound and complex ways. The critics conflate all talk of human happiness with cheap commercial self-help books and unbridled individualism: one big, hot summer party on Ibiza. They think that striving for happiness implies what I later in this book call "the denial of tragedy". Sometimes they also mistake sincere commitment to the happiness of others for the worship of the happy/successful person and a corresponding disdain for the unhappy/unsuccessful person—which is of course not what we are talking about here. Striving for the happiness of our fellow citizen is perfectly compatible with ascribing equal ethical value to the fortunate and grief-stricken alike.

On another note, some of the better informed critics point out that happiness is a rather vague societal goal, because people don't seem to agree about what makes them happy. But the argument doesn't hold up. First of all, it is perfectly possible to describe with some consistency what happiness feels like, some of its psycho-physiological correlates and so on. Even if recent research—with affective psychologist Lisa Feldman Barrett at its forefront—has revealed that there appears to be no single neurological or physiological "fingerprint" of different emotions, it is at least possible to broadly discern positive inner states from negative ones.[30] Even if the issue is an enormously difficult one, happiness constitutes a set of describable, discernible phenomena, regardless of how it is caused. And yes, we can know a lot about what causes happiness—just not by naively asking people (what a stupid method is that!), but through experimental psychology, ethology (studies of animal behavior), psycho-physiology, and so on. Secondly, and more importantly, people are rather consistent in their ideas about what makes them unhappy (social degradation, harm to the body, etc.), which again underscores that we can prevent misery in order to create happiness and vice versa.

People find many reasons to be against happiness. Such criticism of happiness is understandable, but ultimately mistaken and inexcusable. It lands you in untenable positions.

The fact that happiness isn't *everything*, that it isn't the *only* worthy personal and societal goal, doesn't mean that it's *nothing* and *no* worthy goal. Of course, if you always try to make everything about happiness only, you get in philosophical trouble, and people can start asking you those dull questions they like to ask beginner-level utilitarians, i.e. people who want to maximize the happiness in the world ("what if you had a poisonous happy-pill..."). But—and here's the reply—if you try to act in society without any concern at all about the happiness and suffering of others, you get in much worse trouble. That's the point here.

I'll say it again: **The fact that happiness isn't everything, doesn't make it into nothing**. Happiness still matters very much if you want to understand the problems of society. A growing host of research from the field of "positive psychology" and other fields, including strands of medicine and epigenetics, shows that **happiness is good for you**. A banal research finding, in a way; I'm not going to reference it here. So yes, we should make people happy, and it is simply perverse to suggest otherwise.

Don't worry, spirituality and existential development really *do* tower far beyond emotions of happiness, and yes, they *are* awesome and significant, and no, happiness alone does not exhaust the meaning of life and the universe, as we shall discuss later. We just need to get some people off their high spiritual and existential horses, so that we can get on with the argument without being stuck at point zero due to tiresomely pretentious attempts at profundity.

And then we need to set the horses free, while we're at it. Their backs aren't made for carrying other animals, you know. Horses are made for roaming on vast plains under open skies.

The Fabric of Hurt and Bliss

Let's return to the main argument. People are hurting as hell. It matters. We should do something to make them happier, if we can.

So, where were we? Let us clarify the diagnosis of late modern society, the central feature of our predicament: There is a shared, complex fabric of psychological hurt and bliss that determines our common lives and futures. Our wounds and insufficient developments do not stay with ourselves—they transmit to other people, often in unexpected and indirect ways. **The suffering and stunted development of our citizens are not individual concerns, but matters of utmost importance to society as a whole.** They are deeply political, ecological and economic matters. The stunted development caused by emotional suffering affects the individual's quality of life as well as basic societal concerns such as security, public health and the stability of our institutions.

It has been shown in large, influential studies that happiness tends to transmit through networks; a happy friend within a mile tends to make you happier—a neighbor even more; siblings or spouses work too, but to a lesser degree.[31]

But happiness and pain are "social" in an even more tangible and intimate way. Hurt, shame and fear make us become mean, controlling bosses, envious friends, lousy parents, bad teachers, thoughtless voters, uncritical consumers and ungrateful neighbors. We shift the blame, as immature people do, and believe that the ills of the world are due to people who are not like ourselves—we become poor citizens, incapable of meaningful dialogue, incapable of universal love and forgiveness. We are judgmental, short-sighted and self-righteous, raging at the "moral degenerates" and "hypocrites", and we fail to show common courtesy and respect to those we disagree with, not least in politics. We fail to take responsibility, to act productively in the interest of ourselves and others. And in our attempts at a better life, we are often severely limited or thwarted by the immature and socially inept behavior of ourselves and others.

There is a great fabric of relations, behaviors and emotions, reverberating with human and animal bliss and suffering, a web of intimate and formal relations, both direct and indirect. Nasty whirlwinds of feedback cycles blow through this great multidimensional web, pulsating with hurt and degradation. *My* lacking human development blocks *your* possible human development. My lack of understanding of you, your needs and perspectives, hurts you in a million subtle ways. I become a bad lover, a bad colleague, a bad fellow citizen and human being. We are interconnected: *You* cannot get away from *my* hurt and wounds. They will follow you all of your life—I will be your daughter's abusive boyfriend, your belligerent neighbor from hell. And you will never grow wings, because there will always be mean bosses, misunderstanding families and envious friends. And you will tell yourself that is how life must be.

But it is not how life has to be. Once you begin to be able to see the social-psychological fabric of everyday life, it becomes increasingly apparent that the fabric is relatively easy to change, to develop. **Metamodern politics aims to make everyone secure at the deepest psychological level, so that we can live authentically**; a byproduct of which is a sense of meaning in life and lasting happiness; a byproduct of which is kindness and an increased ability to cooperate with others; a byproduct of which is deeper freedom and better concrete results in the lives of everyone; a byproduct of which is a society less likely to collapse into a heap of atrocities.

Of course, it should be noted that the fabric works in complex and often contradictory ways: One form of happiness can give birth to another form of misery (and vice versa); the happiness of one person can be the downfall of another. But there *are* regularities to these patterns, and we *can* make the patterns work for collective, sustainable happiness—yes, for love.

We desperately need a deeper kind of welfare, beyond the confines of material welfare and medical security—*a listening society*, where every person is seen and heard (rather than made invisible and then put under surveillance). How can this be achieved?

Taking Up the Struggle

The answer is to be found in that we today know so much about the human mind, the brain, and the human being in her totality: her psychophysiology, her behavioral responses and patterns (including economic behaviors), her emotions, her relationships, how to make her happy, how to decrease the likelihood of psychiatric disorders, how to prevent family tragedies, how to support her in the developmental stages of childhood, adolescence and adulthood, how to support (and to some extent increase) her intelligence and creativity, how to help her to heal after hurt and loss, how to support her tendencies for universalistic values, how to support her towards developing more complex thinking—even how to support the acquisition of existential and spiritual insights that make death, pain and life's disappointments more tolerable and manageable.

And this knowledge is growing by volumes every day. There is increasing evidence that many different factors work together to help a human being flourish or to let her fall apart. In medicine this insight is called the "biopsycho-ecological paradigm".[32] In psychology it is similarly called the "bio-psycho-social model". In politics and welfare policy we can call it **the listening society**, which is the deeper form of welfare that metamodern activists strive to achieve.

Political metamodernism is the rebellious act of taking this vast knowledge into our hands—and to boldly shape it into usable politics; into wonderful but dangerous "social technologies" that can be used to fundamentally improve the lives of a majority of the citizens.

This is to be achieved within the time frame of a few generations. We are *not* talking about a dramatic revolution from one day to another, or an attempt to "set things straight once and for all", or the sudden "waking up" of everyone. Nor are we talking about a utopia in any naive sense. **We are talking about painstaking, slow reforms that nevertheless can be expected to have substantial effects on the quality of life of our fellow citizens—over longer periods, and on average.**

We take the most useful of the scientific knowledge into our hands, and begin the long path of using a multiplicity of slow, open, transparent democratic processes, with the goal of reshaping all parts of society: schools, the workplace, higher education, the market, healthcare—even the personal relationships, sex lives, gender relations, worldviews and inner selves of the citizen. **We are speaking about conscious and deliberate social-psychological and cultural development.**

As our power over nature grows, and as the social technologies allow us deeper access into the human soul, the political metamodernist takes open, deliberate and unapologetic responsibility for the psychological development of all citizens.

It is *my* responsibility that they left home for the madness of the Syrian war. It is my responsibility that most people do not see the wrongs in how we let the farm animals suffer slavery, torture and mutilation. It is my responsibility that the integration of immigrants is working poorly, that so many young women suffer from anorexia, that so many people live their lives with a pervasive lack of meaning and never truly work to improve the world.

I could have changed social reality, thereby changing the lives of these fellow beautiful creatures under God. It was me all along. It always will be. This is the commitment of the metamodern activist.

The political philosopher Elizabeth Cripps has argued that the citizen cannot hide behind her individuality in the face of collective ethical dilemmas caused by the actions of the many. One must act according to one's abilities to change the collective, given that one understands the mechanism that causes harm, and that one knows what actions can reasonably be taken. This moral obligation includes political activism.[33]

Whereas Cripps writes primarily about climate change, her ideas certainly apply to a wider context. The more you understand how society's ills are caused by the psycho-social environment (i.e. the interplay of people's inner lives and the arenas of everyday life) the more obliged you are to change and develop these realities.

Accepting the Risks

Reaching deeper into the human soul (and organism), supporting its inherent capacities for development, is dangerous business. It can easily lead to breaches of the private and personal sphere, to subtle but pervasive forms of oppression. But it is, as we shall see in the next book, a path that we have already travelled along at least since the 17th century; and it is becoming increasingly necessary, given how our technology is evolving.

Such a **cultural development** requires millions of scientific articles and careful democratic debates, trial and error, effective measurement, continuous feedback and full transparency of information and decision making. Building—or *cultivating*—the next and deeper layer of social welfare requires the ongoing posing of two questions:

- How can good conditions and prerequisites for human flourishing and "thrivability" be brought about?
- How can this be done in a manner that is open, democratic, non-manipulative—without a "creepy" undercurrent of control?

The metamodern political activist lives by both of these questions, day and night, body and soul. It is a fulltime commitment because negligence in either one of the two questions can and will have terrible consequences.

If we fail to answer and act upon the first question it means that we are not using the best knowledge available to let people lead happy and productive lives. We are thus letting people walk lonely through life, letting children be bullied, exploited and harmed in so many other ways, letting the public debate continue to be dysfunctional, letting the destruction of our environment continue, letting the torture of billions of defenseless animals continue, letting people rot away during old age and die full of angst, confusion and regrets.

Failing to answer the first question does not only mean that we are reproducing the inexcusable suffering prevalent in current society; it also means that we are making large global catastrophes much more likely, as insecure and afraid people, with poorly working social institutions, gain power over nanotech, AI and the redesign of life itself. **We are failing to evolve humanity to a maturity matching her newly won powers over nature that the information age (or rather: the multidimensional crisis-revolution) brings.**

If we fail to answer and act upon the *second* question, we are undermining freedom, democracy and human dignity—we are treating people like pawns, and contributing to a system of increasing manipulation and surveillance, where power over deep, psychological and personal issues fall into the hands of elites and bureaucracies. At the dawn of the modern age Adam Smith, the father of economics, warned us about the "man of system" who tries to arrange everything in accordance to his plans and ideas about the good society, but ends up creating unexpected consequences and misuses of political power:

> "...so enamoured with the supposed beauty of his own ideal plan of government, that he cannot suffer the smallest deviation from any part of it."[34]

You may have heard of the term "nudging", Sunstein and Thaler's behavioral-economic idea that people can be subtly "nudged" to make "better" choices by means of "libertarian paternalism". A "choice architect" can arrange how food is presented in the school's lunch line, thereby improving public health by facilitating the making of "better" choices.[35]

There is nothing wrong with this line of reasoning in principle—but it begs the question about *who* such a "choice architect" should reasonably be. In Sunstein and Thaler's discussion, the "choice architect" comes eerily close to "the man of system". At the very least, people should get to vote in a "direct democracy" manner, about how or when we want to nudged or not.

Every day we must look deep into our own eyes in the mirror—are we becoming this technocratic man of system? This is not only a contemplative question, but a political and analytical one. As you will see in the next book, the six new forms of politics suggested create checks and balances that work against the misuse of power, against manipulation and insensitive social engineering. The development of society and our increasing knowledge force us to face, and to balance out, the man of the system at new and deeper levels. We have only begun to become acquainted with this "man of system"—and this grey eminence will show his face in more subtle ways, even deep within ourselves.

The two questions go together. You cannot have the first without the second. And neither question has "one answer"—they are both open-ended, in that they will continue to produce new conundrums, dilemmas and riddles as society evolves and new challenges arise. They both require ongoing questioning and answering. They are, to use that hackneyed term again, *processes*.

Many people take pride in not even attempting to answer the first question, because they thereby avoid having to answer the second one; a position I will later call **the liberal innocent**. From that position their hands are free to attack anyone who tries to make suggestions about how society might be different and better, by labeling them control freaks, arrogant or naive. These are the people who fail to accept the risks, and thereby make themselves complicit in the suffering of all who are mutilated under the unacceptable cruelty of our prevailing society.

Higher freedom begets greater responsibility; and we are freed together, or not at all. For the reader who does not accept the risks, who asks for freedom but does not take the responsibility, I have nothing but the most severe moral condemnation.

Chapter 4

POSSIBLE AND NECESSARY

Such a deeper expansion of social welfare—seeing to that all citizens (or as many as practically possible) grow up genuinely healthy and emotionally well-developed—is both *possible* and *necessary*.

Yes, It Is Possible

It is *possible* due to the new circumstances of the internet age, the robotics revolution and the sheer growth of production and knowledge of the global economy. As the economy continues to grow, and with the expansion of technology, society simply has much greater opportunities to employ people to work with subtler, more psychological and more long-term oriented—yet deeply meaningful—tasks.

We know that the costs of one kid gone rebel in the rich world are immense, seen over a life span: not entering the labor market, taking up social costs, police work, courts and prison, causing harm to other citizens, reducing general security and causing surveillance and security costs to rise, making the public afraid and thereby more prone to dumb fear-driven politics, and so on. Lately economists and social work researchers have increasingly argued that such "bad kids" should be singled out early on and get the extra support they need; a few years of support teacher salary is a bargain in comparison.[36]

That is not what we are talking about here. We are talking about something of a much greater magnitude (and ethically on less murky waters) than singling out 4-year old ruffians. We are talking about universal measures, guaranteeing everyone more care, support and attention by redesigning all of our major institutions to improve the quality of human relations, personal development and mental health. I beg to move:

- Everybody should have the benefit of talking to a kind, listening professional therapist while growing up (just think of how the number of molestations would drop, how kids would treat each other better, how family life would improve).

- Everybody should get to learn to meditate, both with mindfulness and other techniques so that one can handle stress and get in touch with one's own emotions.
- Everybody should get a good gym coaching from early age so that they grow up to have fit bodies, good bodily awareness, positive body image, relaxed body language and healthy habits.
- Everybody should be trained in dialogue and get the chance to participate in public debates or deliberations.
- Everybody should get a year off once in a lifetime to go look for new purpose in life and make tough life decisions under professional care and support—in a kind of secular monastery.
- Everybody should be "nudged" and supported to consume both healthy and sustainable food that prevents depression and supports long-term societal goals.
- Everybody should be trained in social and emotional intelligence so that conflicts arise less often and, when they do arise, are handled more productively.
- Everybody should have a proper sexual education from early on, knowing things such as how to tackle early ejaculation, tensions in the vagina, sexual rejections, making approaches in a charming but respectful manner, how to handle competition and how to handle pornography or sexual desires that diverge from the norm.
- Everybody should get some aid in managing the fear of death and facing the hard facts of life—to help us intuitively know that our time here is precious.

This is just a very rough outline, so far. The point is that we need to shift the whole fabric of social reality, making the mental and emotional background noise of anxieties and fears less prevalent and making everyday life in general saner and kindlier. This is not a superfluous or self-evident claim. In no existing society does a corresponding level of welfare exist; not in the Swedish system, not in nice boarding schools, not in the "Gross National Happiness country" of Bhutan.

If everybody did have a support structure resembling the one briefly outlined above—all according to best practices—do you think that you would be more or less afraid of walking down the street a dark night? Do you think that you would be more or less likely to hurry past by a person in need? Would you feel more or less secure in sending your kids off to school? Do you think the integration of immigrants would be more or less hindered by prejudice and cultural tensions? Would more or fewer people become terrorists? Would the average person feel more or less compelled to buy cool clothes and cars to prove their social status? Would people build stronger or weaker local communities? Would mental and physical health be better or worse? Would society be more or less prone to violent overreactions during times of change and crisis? Would class distinctions be aggravated or leveled out, and would the hidden injuries of class be deeper or would they heal more easily? Would the average family be more or less harmonious and healthy?

The most reasonable answer is that, on average, society as a whole would be safer, saner and kinder—and that these effects would accumulate over decades and generations until a new and higher equilibrium of happiness and lower suffering is reached. People would experience a much higher degree of freedom and contentment. Life would be a lot more fun and exciting too, since much fewer people would get stuck in their lives, limited in their development by stress, anxieties or broken relationships. There would be more human bonds, trust and opportunities. This in turn would save humongous costs and let much more people spend their lifetimes in productive service of themselves and others. So the whole idea of a listening society is possible because, after its initial investments, it saves a lot more than it spends. It *saves* the increasingly pressured welfare system.

I will say it again, in case you missed it, because people really seem to have difficulties with getting this point.

- The listening society *saves* the welfare system, by being much more efficient and socially sustainable than our current system, thereby being more affordable in the long run.

What we are talking about is the deliberate, long-term management of deep, complex, social-psychological issues. These deeply seated issues affect all aspects of society in a great variety of ways that are difficult to predict precisely. But the effects are pretty easy to spot on a general level. Think about it—if the average person would just be more socially well-developed, healthier and kinder, would not society as a whole benefit immensely? How about the economy, the labor market, or the efficiency of democratic governance?

A deeper welfare, a listening society, is possible because we live in a postindustrial age and because we are now beginning to have the knowledge to execute it successfully; new social technologies are being made available. And the knowledge about how to continuously improve upon the implementation of such social technologies is growing.

The listening society is possible, moreover, because of the foundation created by the prevailing meta-ideology of Green Social Liberalism. In a country like the US, where universal health care, abortion and gay rights are still real issues, you don't yet have a stable ground to build upon. A country (or other society) must first have reached a point in the development of its political discourse in which a solid majority supports liberal, social and green values, allowing these to be used as a common ground to start from. This is to a much greater extent the case in the Nordic countries.

Once it has become a no-brainer that we want a free, fair and sustainable society, and once the first steps towards this end have been achieved, it becomes apparent that all the current parties (all of which are *de facto* green social-liberal) have become stuck as movements. They no longer have any long-term visions for society, no utopias or future goals worth mentioning.

This is an ironic turn of events; we have in fact never had greater potential to develop new forms of everyday life than we do today. The resources and knowledge at hand are simply staggering compared to only twenty years ago. The problem for the established political movements is that they all build upon ideologies that were founded during the industrial era. These ideologies are largely being abandoned in practice (the Social Democrats no longer truly want socialism, and so forth). The industrial age ideologies are all bankrupted—they have all become pale, polite butlers of Green Social Liberalism.

This leaves plenty of political and institutional leeway for new powers to emerge, offering an update upon the new political equilibrium of Green Social Liberalism.

Look. Even if the socialists got everything they wanted, life would still be full of inequalities and misery. Even if the libertarians got their way, most people would not be free. Even if the Greens got their way, society would not be sustainable in any deeper sense.

By offering a bid for a "Green Social Liberalism 2.0", one begins to build a new layer of society, *on top of* the modern society and its project of progress and enlightenment. It brings up deeper, more personal and authentic issues that constitute the very core of how society functions. Such social-psychological and existential issues are often what lie under the surface of superficial "societal problems" that we habitually think about and debate.

More and more people have begun to take interest in asking deeper questions about life and society. People long for more depth and authenticity—and the inspiration that can come from answers in these domains. There is a demand for a deeper kind of politics, and thus there is political power for the taking. This new layer of welfare breaks the limits of modern society. It begins to transform the very quality of human relations. Nobody else is doing it, so whoever starts first gains a sharp competitive edge. That's what makes it possible.

And, Yes, It Is Necessary

But Green Social Liberalism 2.0, and the listening society that it seeks to put into effect, are not just long-shot possibilities. They are, as I have argued, a moral imperative. And they constitute an institutional necessity. We are quickly moving from one kind of society to another, and failure to adopt a more efficient welfare system is likely to have very negative consequences. Our current form of liberal democracy and welfare deserve all the respect in the world—but they are insufficient, and we must help them evolve. If we do not, our society can be expected to face increasing problems, even to the point of collapse, as our old answers and institutions persistently fail to tackle the challenges brought by the new era.

The cultivation of a deeper layer of welfare is *necessary* because the current system and its political visions are increasingly bankrupted under the globalized internet age. The problem is no longer to get food on the table or to manage the successful extraction of natural resources or the production of cars and medications (although these problems may come back as results of ecological collapse). What is lacking in our day and age is the ability for people to manage complex problems that require patience, knowledge, oversight, creativity, mutual trust and friendly co-operation across sectors, scientific disciplines, cultures and subcultures. In a phrase: the management of complexity. Or, with a term we shall get back to, we require greater **collective intelligence**.

Similar social-psychological demands are also increasing for everyday choices such as consumption and how we spend our time amidst all the distractions. It even holds for personal relations, where new forms of love, family, friendships, acquaintances, co-habitation and mixed work-personal relations are mushrooming all over the world. We need people who are much more socially and psychologically functional for this new society to run smoothly in all of its crazed beauty. As a population, we are not ready to face up to and live in the society that we ourselves have created.

We are out of our depth. Or, as Robert Kegan—the Harvard adult development psychologist—has suggested, we are **in over our heads.**[37]

So basically, for people to function well as participants in the new economic landscape, the demands for psychological wellbeing and good social networks have become greater. A deeper welfare is necessary, one that increases our average psychological health and wellbeing and thereby our functionality in this bizarre new global society. We need to be stable, flexible, mature versions of ourselves, because we spend our lives playing on an increasingly complex and multi-dimensional arena, where social skills and the quality of our relations make all the difference.

Collective and personal meaning-making is another big part of this. People need to be able to create their own life stories, their own narratives about the world, to find their own meaning. Life conditions no longer force you to go out and plow the field to feed your family and society no longer offers (and/or forces upon you) a coherent worldview written down by the gods—although we still of course inherit the norms of society, its language, etc.

It is a major challenge for people to stay sane in this world full of contradictions, temptations, distractions and stressful yet devilishly vague demands. No meaningful story is given beforehand (unless you are part of some religious sect, but even these positions are increasingly precarious). Not only must we stay sane; we must find and keep direction in all of this; we must stay active, even as our activities are rarely "necessary" in any direct, concrete sense. If we fail to do this, we can easily land in socially and economically precarious situations. Many of these challenges require us to develop higher stages of personal development, as described in the second part of this book.

Consider the changing nature of professional work. The freelance part of the labor market grows and the relatively stable structures of the industrial age companies melt away (along with their employments), which means that the average person must think and act much more independently in order to thrive and be productive. And no, this does not happen because of a neoliberal conspiracy pulled on us, starting with Thatcher and Reagan, but because of the internet revolution, robotics and post-industrialism—and the mechanisms of globalization (which, of course, do deserve their fair share of criticism from the Left).

We are leaving behind the economy in which you were defined by your profession. Increasingly, people are defined and acquire their social value through a wider array of identities, including civic, personal, aesthetic and existential ones. This has two major implications.

Firstly, people will need much more emotional support in order to grow into maturity and to be able to play with the many possible and confusing identities—instead of taking them too seriously, or clinging to one job description and be crushed if one is suddenly out of work. As mentioned in the parallel discussion above, this necessitates a deeper form of welfare that supports self-knowledge and a rich life beyond the labor market.

Secondly, many new professional roles need to be invented to match the transformations of labor, as robotization and digitalization progress. "New jobs must be created", to speak that horrid language of our current leadership. Many of these jobs can and should be concerned with the meaningful activities involved in creating a listening society (a huge amount of work is needed helping kids, designing public spaces, supporting life stage transitions, improving upon diet, organizing citizen deliberation, evaluating and developing all of the above, and so forth). **So the listening society is necessary *both* as support to the citizen *and* as a new source of meaningful, productive work opportunities.**

Moreover, the listening society is necessary as a competitive edge in the global economy. The regions that will be able to create the most fertile soil for the blooming of human relations and wellbeing, are also likely to have much higher productivity in the postindustrial economy. It is well established that things such as *flow state* and *intrinsic motivation* are conductive to creativity and performance of complex tasks. Confident, happy people, who can manage more abstract and long-term goals, and who are more self-secure and thus better at taking in negative feedback (and adjusting to new information), will simply outcompete other people in the scramble for capital and central positions in the new world economy.

This is a cynical part of the argument, admittedly, but an important one. It is not just that the listening society is kinder and more ethical. **The listening society is, plainly, much more powerful in a digitalized global economy, than is the capitalist liberal democracy.** It saves so much tax money, it boosts enterprise, entrepreneurship and innovation, it attracts talent, and it attracts capital in different forms—and it grows human and social capital. We have seen similar macroeconomic effects with HDI-rankings (Human Development Index): **human development drives economic growth.** In the internet age, a deeper and more complex form of human development is highly likely to drive a deeper and more complex form of economic growth.[38]

The deeper welfare system is necessary because, without it, you will be outcompeted by other, *more* listening societies, where citizens truly do thrive. Luckily for the future of humanity, this dynamic sets the world-system on a positive feedback cycle towards greater sensitivity and care, rather than a race to the bottom.

How It Connects to Everyday Life

What people don't realize is that everyday life could be much lighter and happier if we built a saner society. Just looking at my own life, there is so much suffering around me that has to do with the psychological development of people and the quality of their relationships to one another—I am sure you can think of corresponding stories yourself.

When my parents were still alive I would visit at my mother's every now and then. After their divorce, my father's life had stagnated, professionally and personally: As an alcoholic, he survived surprisingly long on coffee, beer and cigarettes. My mother's new husband built a house by the seaside and they were doing well. They would always be kind and polite, and we would discuss matters of life and society over dinner. Even if neither of them went to college, they would follow my work at some distance. My mother's husband would ask why I was so eager to change and develop society when things were, after all, good and well these days.

I had three brothers on my father's side. Two of them died, at 39 and 45, respectively. As children they had both been abandoned by their mother, who suddenly left them—and my father—for another man. Both of them drank a lot and smoked, did so-so in school (even if one of them was quite intelligent and learned Portuguese during a month spent doing charity work in Angola, and the other was good at getting work done as a carpenter with his own company). They both left behind children and chaotic family relations. Would their stories have turned out differently had they not spent their lives with a vague sense that their mother didn't love them? Or if there would have been steady support offered early on? If they knew how to talk about and deal with emotions? I can't help but wonder.

What about my third brother? I haven't heard from him for long. His new wife made him abandon his daughter (i.e. my niece) at age fourteen and move abroad. He won't say hello, but these days he sometimes writes short Facebook messages to her for Christmas, as if nothing had happened. What makes a person so afraid and dependent that he would abandon a lovely teenage daughter if his partner asks him to, and so socially inept that he would then send mixed signals about the abandonment? And what would make a wife so protective and jealous that she would ask something like that of her husband? Could these things be different? What are the long-term societal costs of such behaviors? The human costs?

My mother's new husband had two children himself from a previous marriage: a daughter and a son, both in their forties. Last I heard of them, they were both rather unhappy in their lives. The daughter had a stroke at young age and recovered physically but was often depressed and anxious. However, she took care of her kid—and he would play video games and had no friends, living on a rather unhealthy diet. I don't know what happened to them later. I hope things went well.

My stepfather's son had the strangest wife—she would have multiple partners, lie to him, steal his things and show abusive behavior. But he didn't leave her. It went on and on for years. The family would never speak about their feelings. They simply didn't know how to. Nobody's to blame, really.

But even as I advanced in social class, and got to know highly educated and otherwise successful people, I would see suffering. I once realized that all of the smartest humanities students (the ones who wrote about advanced postmodern theory and loved French intellectuals) were struggling with severe anxieties. Had it been today, they would no doubt all have been on pills.

And when I finally, rather late in life, figured out love and relationships, I would notice how very confused and broken all of my partners were. Each one would seem happy and functional, but soon enough they would tell me their secret: a deep self-doubt, anxieties, periods of depression. How much it hurts to be a woman and never be pretty enough. How much it hurts to be nerd who isn't respected in the arenas of everyday life. How much it hurts to be the less interesting and successful one—or to be emotionally stunted, being unable to feel love and care deeply for others.

Of course, at the top of society—and here and there all over the place—you find some people who don't know as much suffering, who simply seem to have lived relatively protected and well-functioning lives. But even at the top, there is confusion and existential emptiness: drugs, sexual addictions, materialism, vanity—you know the drill. Could more of these people be much more psychologically healthy? Could we create and reproduce a society in which the average human life experience is more emotionally satisfying and spiritually productive?

I could go on, but the point I want to make is simply that you can hardly find one single cause or person to blame for what seems to be holding us back in our lives. What we *can* do is to look at the totality of these interconnected life experiences: at the fabric of hurt and bliss. Most people don't see it. They don't recognize how brutish and cruel life is even in the most developed of countries. "Things are fine nowadays". Right.

Now imagine if the average person in all of these interconnected stories had been actively supported to deal with the challenges of life. It may not have "saved" everyone from suffering, hurt and degradation. But yes, everyone would have had a better chance to live a dignified life and to treat others better. We would live in a less broken world.

Think about it—given that so many people live in such broken worlds, should it surprise us that we cannot handle transnational challenges such as climate change, globalization, poverty and the disruptive effects of technological innovation?

Am I wrong to ask why are we letting all of these things happen without any serious effort to change the situation, to the detriment of people's lives and to society?

We are doing nothing—or much too little—because we haven't yet developed society to a degree where there are safety nets, common knowledge and institutions that deal with these subtler, more sociological, sides of life.

An Empirical Example: Meditation in Schools

All this is fine, and intuitively it makes sense to believe that a more listening society would change the life courses of many or most people, letting them develop into healthier and more whole citizens. But these examples are anecdotal, just single stories. What are the *empirics* of the matter? Is there any research that can hint us towards what a listening society might look like, and give us an idea of how it improves people's lives? There is. Lots. But let's keep it short.

My favorite example **is meditation in schools.** Basically, you can teach kids to meditate in schools and you see not only lower rate of bullying and sick-leaves (among teachers especially), but also better school results, and most of all, better psychological health and the development of more pro-social behaviors. This subject has lots of studies but nothing that would assess the difference if you compare kids who have gone to twelve years of daily meditation with those who haven't. The research also lacks differentiation between different teaching styles and progressions (maybe you should start with three minutes for six-year-olds)—although once recent groundbreaking study from the Max Planck Institute suggested that different forms of meditation may show different kinds of benefits.[39]

Meditation is almost always thought about as a binary question: yes or no. In fact of course, there is a world of difference depending on if it is taught well, if the general progression is right, and which methods are used (mindfulness, Vipassana, Zen, listening to sounds, etc.).

The point of meditation in schools is of course not to inspire woo-woo beliefs or anything of the sort, but to improve people's lives and society at large. It's not a matter of turning kids and citizens into quiet, complacent little Buddha statues, but a matter of psychological and cultural development.

It works through two major mechanisms. The first mechanism is that people learn the skill of self-awareness, calming their own minds and not overreacting. That is of course useful in all walks of life. The second mechanism—and perhaps the more important one—is that it changes your mental and emotional state *then and there*. So if the average kid spends an average of fifteen minutes being guided in calming her own mind every day, she will be a little less anxious and aggressive that same day. Hence, on average, she can be expected to treat her friends and rival twelve-year-olds a little better during lunch break. Now imagine that it is not only her, but her full class of 35 people (which is, by the way, probably about optimal, as reducing class size has proven to be one of the least cost-effective way of improving the quality of education)[40] who all get this subtle nudge. Would not the whole social climate be somewhat softer and kinder, a little less tense and stressed? And now imagine that this goes on for 12 years. Do you imagine there might be an accumulation? During that time, her school experience teaches her a lot about what to expect from life. Will the social processes by which she makes friends, handles conflicts, learns who to trust have been affected? Will it affect how much she feels she can trust people, how much disdain she should have for the boys, how much time she will have spent intriguing instead of studying? Will she know herself a little better? It's not an implausible hypothesis, not at all. Here's a relevant quote by Amanda Machado, a young teacher in San Francisco who wrote in *The Atlantic*:

> "Schools have also begun experimenting with the practice and discovering that its techniques can help its students. When a school in New Haven, Connecticut, required yoga and meditation classes three times a week for its incoming freshman, studies found that after each class, students had significantly reduced levels of cortisol, a stress hormone, in their bodies. In San Francisco, schools that participated in Quiet Time, a Transcendental Meditation program, had twice as many students score proficient in English on the California Achievement Test than in similar schools where the program didn't exist. Visitacion Valley Middle School specifically reduced suspen-

> sions by 45 percent during the program's first year. Attendance rates climbed to 98 percent, grade point averages improved, and the school recorded the highest happiness levels in San Francisco on the annual California Healthy Kids Survey. Other studies have shown that mindfulness education programs improved students' self-control, attentiveness and respect for other classmates, enhanced the school climate, and improved teachers' moods."[41]

That pretty much sums it up. What these studies do not take into account are the possible and accumulative long-term effects as more people get a longer and more refined, more individualized and scientifically supported practice. Unfortunately, our governments haven't begun to take these things seriously. Just like medieval governments didn't take reading and writing skills of the population seriously—until some Protestant countries began to outrun the other European powers as literacy rose. Or like a lot of people in Africa don't see the importance of washing hands, making efficient sewer systems, brushing teeth and using condoms. (At least this is what foreign aid scholars often find in their ethnographies.)

We simply haven't advanced to that stage of thinking—a stage where you see that the inner development of each person is intrinsically connected to the development of society as a whole.

For fun, let's splash some more studies that have shown social, psychological and medical effectiveness of meditation (I have abbreviated the references, but you can find all of them if you like):

- **Improved quality of life for congestive heart failure patients**
  - Ethnicity and Disease, March 2007.
- **Enhanced longevity**
  - American Journal of Cardiology, May 2005.
- **Reduced blood pressure and use of hypertensive medication**
  - American Journal of Hypertension, January 2005.
- **Reduced blood pressure in at-risk teens**
  - American Journal of Hypertension, April 2004.
  - At-risk adolescents reduce stress, anxiety, and hyperactivity
  - Presentation at annual meeting of the *Society for Behavioral Medicine*, March 2008.
- **Increased flexibility of brain functioning**
  - Biological Psychology 55 (2000).
  - Psychophysiology 14 (1977).
- **Increased efficiency of information transfer in the brain**
  - Progress in Brain Research 54 (1980) 447–53.
  - International Journal of Neuroscience 10 (1980) 165–70.

  - Psychophysiology 26 (1989) 529.
- **Increased intelligence in secondary and college students**
  - Intelligence (2001) 419-440.
  - Journal of Personality and Individual Differences (1991): 1105–16.
  - Perceptual and Motor Skills 62 (1986) 731–38.
  - College Student Journal 15 (1981) 140–46.
  - Journal of Clinical Psychology 42 (1986): 161–64.
  - *Gedrag: Tijdschrift voor Psychologie* [Behavior: Journal of Psychology] 3 (1975) 167–82.
  - Dissertation Abstracts International 38(7) (1978) 3372B–73B.
  - Higher Education Research and Development 15 (1995) 73–82.
- **Increased creativity**
  - Journal of Personality and Social Psychology 57 (1989) 950–64.
  - The Journal of Creative Behavior 19 (1985) 270-75.
  - Dissertation Abstracts International 38(7) (1978) 3372B–73B,
- **Improved memory**
  - Memory and Cognition 10 (1982) 207–15.
- **Improved academic performance**
  - Education 107 (1986) 49–54.
  - Education 109 (1989) 302–04.
  - British Journal of Educational Psychology 55 (1985) 164–66.
- **Benefits in special education**
  - Journal of Clinical Psychiatry 42 (1981) 35–36.
  - Journal of Biomedicine 1 (1980) 73–88.
- **Increased self-confidence and self-actualization**
  - Journal of Social Behavior and Personality 6 (1991) 189–47.
  - Higher Stages of Human Development: Perspectives on Adult Growth (Oxford University Press, 1990) 286–341.
  - British Journal of Psychology 73 (1982) 57–68.
  - College Student Journal 15 (1981) 140–46.
  - Journal of Counseling Psychology 20 (1973) 565–66.
  - Journal of Counseling Psychology 19 (1972) 184–87.
- **Decreased hostility**
  - Criminal Justice and Behavior 5 (1978) 3–20.
  - Criminal Justice and Behavior 6 (1979) 13–21.
- **Decreased depression**
  - Journal of Counseling and Development 64 (1986) 212–15.
  - Journal of Humanistic Psychology 16(3) (1976) 51–60.

- *Gedrag: Tijdschrift voor Psychologie* [Behavior: Journal of Psychology] 4 (1976) 206–18.
- **Reduced anxiety**
  - Journal of Clinical Psychology 45 (1989) 957–74.
  - Anxiety, Stress, and Coping: International Journal 6 (1993) 245–62.
  - Journal of Clinical Psychology 33 (1977) 1076–78.
  - Dissertation Abstracts International 38(7) (1978) 3372B–73B.
  - Hospital & Community Psychiatry 26 (1975) 156–59.
- **School behavior: reduction of anger, absenteeism, disciplinary infractions, and suspensions**
  - Annals of Behavioral Medicine 23 (2001) 100.
  - Health and Quality of Life Outcomes 1 (2003) 10.
- **Increased tolerance**
  - The Journal of Psychology 99 (1978) 121–27.
  - International Journal of the Addictions 26 (1991) 293–325.
  - Dissertation Abstracts International 38(7) (1978) 3372B–73B.
- **Reduced substance abuse**
  - Alcoholism Treatment Quarterly 11 (1994) 1–524.
  - Bulletin of the Society of Psychologists in Addictive Behaviors 2 (1983) 28–33.
  - The International Journal of the Addictions 12 (1977) 729–54.
  - Journal of Offender Rehabilitation 36 (2003) 127–60.
  - American Journal of Psychiatry 132 (1975) 942–45.
  - American Journal of Psychiatry 131 (1974) 60–63.
- **Decreased insomnia**
  - The New Zealand Family Physician 9 (1982) 62–65.
  - Journal of Counseling and Development 64 (1986) 212–15.
  - Japanese Journal of Public Health 37 (1990) 729.
- **Healthier family life**
  - Psychological Reports 51 (1982) 887–90.
  - Journal of Counseling and Development 64 (1986) 212–15.
  - Lower health insurance utilization rates
  - Psychosomatic Medicine 49 (1987) 493–507.
  - American Journal of Health Promotion 10 (1996) 208–16.
- **Increased efficiency in government offices**
  - Impact of Vipassana in Government (2004).
- **Reduced criminal propensity among jail inmates**
  - Vipassana: Its relevance to the present world (Delhi, 1994) 38–55.

- Research report from Vipassana Research Institute (1995) *Psychological effects of Vipassana on Tihar Jail Inmates.*
- Research report from Vipassana Research Institute (2002) Effect of Vipassana Meditation on Quality of Life, Subjective Well-Being, and Criminal Propensity among Inmates of Tihar Jail.

Even if some of the cited studies are a bit old, there has been an exponential increase in the number of mindfulness studies in scientific journals—which is one, but far from the only, form of meditation. The last few years it has really taken off. As we speak, we're getting several new peer reviewed studies *per day*. This means we'll probably have a much clearer picture pretty soon. Here's a graph I borrowed.[42]

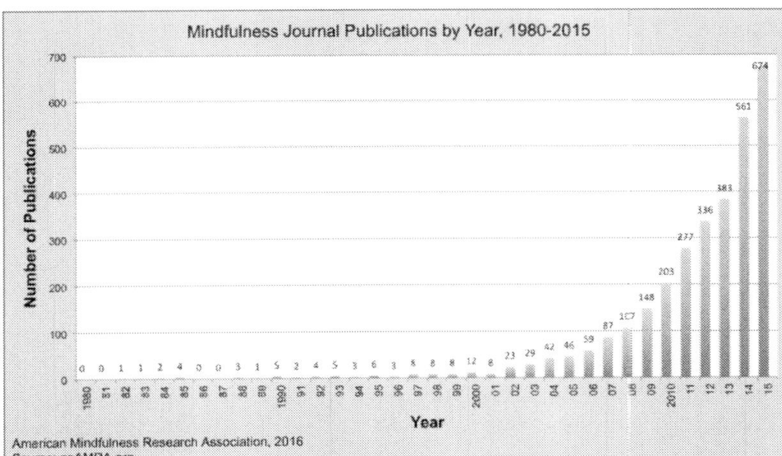

Source: American Mindfulness Research Association, 2016.

Now, even if we don't yet have the major studies about cumulative effects on groups that stack up over time, it should be obvious that there is an interesting field here. How much disease, suffering, depression, criminality and social misery could we prevent? Probably a lot.

The costs are extremely low and the effects quite wide-reaching. What would happen if we had serious, scientifically driven meditation teachers designing the best possible programs for schools? Probably a lot. Now ask yourself what would be the effect if millions of people had twelve years of this kind of training and then interact in society. Would there be changes to the overall patterns of such a society? Would the effects stack up over generations—what if your grandmother, your dad and you all get to grow up in a somewhat more emotionally nourishing environment? Would that affect your life? Probably a lot.

I have friends who study meditation in schools and other institutions from a more *critical* perspective. Meditation is certainly no magic bullet. You have to consider the social-psychological aspects: What happens if somebody feels pressured to meditate in a situation where they are not comfortable? Or when someone gets frustrated because the others seem to experience it as more pleasant than oneself? And sometimes, it has been shown, meditation seems to *cause* anxieties rather than reduce them.

All of this is not different from, say, gym class: In Sweden alone 30 000 kids are treated in hospitals each year from physical injuries in school (and another 60 000 from spare time sports injuries). That doesn't mean sports are bad. And mathematics causes a lot of anxieties and frustrations—but it doesn't mean that it should be excluded from education or society at large. It just means that there are problems we should be aware of and deal with as we go along.

Meditation in schools is one of my own favorite examples. But it is far from the only one. For instance, giving all kids access to simpler forms of talk-therapy can dramatically reduce depression and suicide rates (this was tried in a provincial town in northern Sweden recently; the depression rate dropped from 9.5 to 1.5 percent in two years).[43] Or you can make people run at maximum heart rate for a few minutes, and their wellness and immune system will be boosted for the entire day. Or you can give people more nuts, berries and green vegetables, which reduces long-term risks of depression and facilitates healthy aging. Or you can make people participate in games in which they share and cooperate, which increases their propensity for pro-social behavior. Or you can develop sexual education dramatically, which makes people less prone to sexual violence and more likely to form productive relationships. Or you can use carefully and professionally guided forms of massage and other non-sexual touch to increase oxytocin levels in the brain and make people treat one another better and thus uphold social orders in a more egalitarian manner. Or you can change the surroundings in the inner cities to that they promote meetings between strangers and generally feel less stressful (more lush green often does the trick).

You could make lists of studies around all of these topics as well. The point is, we as a society have not yet developed to a stage where these deeper issues—issues that affect all aspects of life and society—are part of our general social, economic and political awareness. In terms of money, such long-term investment, if properly supported by science, can be extremely cost effective. And yes, it can boost the economy, as the average person gains more trust, better social relations and becomes happier.

The great economist Amartya Sen coined the term "development as freedom". He meant that human development and civil liberties could be drivers to lift populations out of poverty. Psychological and social development can—and will—lift us out of spiritual and emotional poverty.

EMOTIONAL, SOCIAL AND COLLECTIVE INTELLIGENCE

What would happen if we substantially increased the average emotional, social and collective intelligence of the population? What would happen if our public institutions, educational systems and civil society worked intently towards this end—employing the best methods according to evidence? Let's discuss these three forms of intelligence briefly.

You have probably heard of **emotional intelligence**, a term popularized in Daniel Goleman's 1995 book with the same title. Of course, Goleman's theory was far from perfect, and even many of the later developments of it have been lacking in scientific rigor. But that being said; wouldn't it make sense for society to very actively and deliberately work to increase the emotional intelligence of the population?

Emotional intelligence, Goleman-style, includes:

1. **Self-awareness:** the ability to know one's emotions, strengths, weaknesses, drives, values and goals and recognize their impact on others while using gut feelings to guide decisions.
2. **Self-regulation:** involves controlling or redirecting one's disruptive emotions and impulses and adapting to changing circumstances.
3. **Social skill:** managing relationships to move people in the desired direction.
4. **Empathy:** considering other people's feelings especially when making decisions.
5. **Motivation:** being driven to achieve for the sake of achievement.

The point is that these aren't inherent moral qualities that people either have or don't. They are, to a certain extent, *skills* that can be learned, honed, maintained and developed. Emotional intelligence can be associated with better psychological and physical health, less bullying, and better leadership performance. Just training people in emotional intelligence for four hours seems to significantly improve their performance (in emotional intelligence) even six months later.[44] Maybe these ideas will soon be outdated. But there *does* appear to be something very interesting going on here. Worth exploring? Yes.

Social intelligence is also a term associated with Goleman (but a bit less so). Social intelligence has more to do with managing *other* people. Obviously, emotional and social intelligence overlap.

Looking at social intelligence, you can show that people are at dramatically different levels of skill when it comes to correctly recognizing the feelings of others, that their brains light up more or less when they see happiness or suffering (this part seems to depend a lot on genetics). There are also differences in how well they can have mastered skills such as using their voices and body languages or otherwise managing the impressions that they make vis-à-vis other people.

When it comes to the romantic and sexual games of everyday life, there is a huge difference between the people who are skilled and sensitive to norms, and those who are not.

All of these things are relatively easily learnable. The scientific literature on improving our general social skills is rather thin, however. This is because the scientific community of psychologists and medical researchers generally think of training social skills only when it comes to kids with autism, extreme shyness or the like. Fewer have considered the fact that most normal people are terribly socially inept.

Might we have a goldmine here in terms of long-term effects on welfare? I think we might. Too bad we as a society aren't looking in the right direction.

Collective intelligence is the general problem-solving ability of a group, organization or society. The best source of knowledge about it in the world today is the MIT (Massachusetts Institute of Technology) Center for Collective Intelligence.

Sometimes, when I talk about this issue, some dimwit thinks I mean "collective consciousness", i.e. the idea that there would be some kind of ghost floating around among a group of people with a mind of its own. Just to be very clear: That is not what I mean. The study of collective intelligence is a serious scientific endeavor.

One of the central findings of this research program is that a group's collective ability to solve problems and perform tasks is *not* strongly correlated to the average and maximum IQ of the members (although there is a small correlation). So even if you stick ten people together who are all in the top one percent in terms of IQ, and make them cooperate, they generally won't do much better than ten people of average intelligence. Nevertheless, groups of people do show dramatically varying levels of performance, different levels of collective intelligence. What, then, determines the performance of a group?

Researchers have let groups perform a wide array of different tasks (creative brainstorming problems, puzzles involving verbal or mathematical reasoning, negotiation tasks, and moral-reasoning problems, etc.). And yes, there does appear to be smart groups and dumb ones. They vary about as much as individuals—a finding that has been replicated in a number of recent studies. Two major factors seem to determine the smarts of the group as a whole:

1) The average *social* intelligence of the members (again, rather than IQ). This means that groups containing higher percentage of women generally do better, even up to 100% women, as women commonly have a slight advantage over men in this area. This holds true even if people interact online only by text chats.
2) The structure of the group. More evenly distributed talking time, more total communication, less of a clear leader, more democratic decision making, moderate level of diversity among group members when it comes to personality, etc.

And there's more. Collectively intelligent student groups do better on group assignments even if the students don't do better on individual assignments. More intelligent groups learn faster.[45]

This research is only in its early stages. Can the intelligence of organizations be measured? Of markets? Or how about countries? If collective intelligence varies across different small groups, can it vary across larger units of analysis as well?

Would it be so strange if the parts of the world economy—cities, corporations, hub regions, countries—that become most proficient at increasing emotional, social and collective intelligence, will also become the most competitive ones in terms of innovation, capital investment and quality of life? I wouldn't be so surprised. In other words, where there are more listening societies, these are likely to outcompete other parts of the world market, until regions around the world begin competing to create the most listening society. I discuss this subject in greater detail in my other book, *Outcompeting Capitalism*.

If I'm right, this would set the world on a positive feedback cycle, towards a more emotionally mature, sensitive civilization.

Feeling Provoked Yet?

Many people feel quite provoked by any talk of positive global feedback cycles in politics and economics, paths that may lead to happy, sustainable outcomes. Somehow it might seem frivolous, or even insolent, to speak of a "listening society", of deeper care for the citizen and the higher human needs such as fulfillment and existential insight, in the midst of a world in crisis, with such great risks and so much poverty, conflict and suffering. Aren't these first world problems, far removed from the plights of most of our fellow world citizens?

Others feel provoked by the opposite—the ingratitude of thinkers who criticize a society that is obviously happier and more functional than it was before. After all, many things have been getting better. I sit here in a nice house in the Swiss Alps, with a long education, hooked up to the internet and a Jacuzzi bubbling in the background. It just seems a bit out of touch to complain, wanting to radically change a society that has given me all that I have. If I think it's so bad, would I rather have lived in the 19th century, or in today's Sudan or North Korea?

Both sides are partly right. The world really is a tragic and grim place, and yes, society really has made great progress in important respects. But you need to see both these sides simultaneously to get out of the grid-lock.

If you don't allow yourself to explore what positive feedback cycles are possible, you are also stopping yourself from looking at realistic paths ahead. Because, after all, the world really has changed many times before—so why not again? If we deem all visions of a better future disrespectful, we are precluding all real possibilities of substantial, positive change that can come through intentional efforts. Since the fate of the world's poor is intimately connected with the inner selves and conceptual horizons of the world's more progressive populations—like in Scandinavia—it makes perfect sense to want to cultivate a deeper layer of welfare in these societies.

And if you insist on being grateful for all the wealth and progress, you are stopping yourself from reacting against things that are obviously still unjust and terribly wrong with the world—such as climate change, global poverty and animal slavery. If things have been getting better, it makes sense to also admit that this is at least partly due to people's efforts to make them so, and that in retrospect, all earlier societies have been pretty messed up. So why not think of today's society as profoundly messed up as well? We're just adding one to the list.

I bring this up because, for every one person who enthusiastically and playfully (but realistically) embraces the idea of criticizing and reforming society, I meet ten people who just get angry and resentful. If you learn and understand the ideas of this book, you are likely to have the same experience when communicating with others. Either people get angry because you are suggesting that the future might be good, or they get mad because you suggest that society today is bad.

What, then, is the way out of this grid-lock? Fundamentally, it is a matter of understanding that society is *both* very, very good *and* simultaneously very, very bad. Reality is rich. It has room for plenty of extremes. It has multitudes of contradictions. We must increasingly learn to live and deal with such paradoxes.

You don't have to choose one side. Both are true. This means that there is nothing inherently naive or frivolous about suggesting positive paths forward, since one is still acknowledging the suffering of the world and the great risks ahead of us. Likewise, there is nothing arrogant or disrespectful about wanting to change society, because one is still admitting that there is much good in people and that great progress has been made. Again, it is *because* the world is both a wonderful and terrible place, because humanity is both divine and depraved, that the only sane and respectful attitude towards society is to be both critical and optimistic. I would even claim that it is slightly insane *not* to take the great potentials of the world seriously, given the great changes that have already occurred and the ones that are undeniably underway.

A second part of the answer, one that I have mentioned before, is that life is always an experiment. After the Second World War, Germany was famously united under Konrad Adenauer's Christian-Democratic slogan: *Keine Experimente* (no experiments). And that was a good thing. I don't advocate frivolousness and carelessness; very great suffering can and will befall us, which is why the development of society is no joke. But we need to take that profound seriousness together with a dose of experimental playfulness. Beyond the slogans, the rebuilding of Germany and Europe—with the Marshall Plan and the policies that lead to the German growth wonder—was in fact an experiment of gigantic proportions.

If there is one thing you learn from the study of history, it is this: people don't have a clue about what they are doing. The first lesson of sociology and critical social science is this: People don't know what they're doing. Psychology 101 is this: not a clue, boy.

Economics, humanities, arts—it's the same story. The society we live in today is just an experiment. Nobody has the answers. Nobody knows where it's going, or why. We don't even know where we would like it to go. There's no grown-up out there, looking out for us.

Nobody's home. It's just one big, glorious chaos engine; busy, busy spawning all manner of unimaginable creatures, existences, relations, exquisite beauties and excruciating tragedies. When you truly see this, an experimental attitude towards society suddenly seems much less reckless or disrespectful. It is the only appropriate stance.

Don't let provoked feelings stop you from thinking. You have every right to try to see where society can and should be going, and you have the same right as any other member of the world population to speak your mind and act accordingly.

No issue is too grand for you. Why would it be? This world is your experiment as much as everybody else's. You are the creator.

Chapter 5

THE ALTERNATIVE

Who makes metamodern politics happen; at what political level; is it Left or Right; what's the plan; how do you win political power with metamodern thoughts; in which country; and who are the elites that can lead this development?

In this chapter, we look at some new and important agents on the political playing field. One such agent is the process oriented party, exemplified here with the Danish party The Alternative. Another such agent is the loose group of people I call the metamodern aristocracy.

Let's go!

Party about Nothing

So we have this long-term vision for cultivating a deeper kind of welfare, which revolves around looking after the psychological development of the citizen in an open and democratic way: the listening society. And we are doing this within the framework of a new meta-ideology: Green Social Liberalism 2.0, by means of co-development, i.e. developing "the Nordic ideology". But *whose* political project is this? Who makes it happen?

The process oriented political party does—a party that is less about content, and more about the political processes that lead up to the best policies. A party about nothing.

The closest thing to a truly process oriented political party to date is the Danish party **The Alternative**, founded by the former minister of culture Uffe Elbæk in late 2013. The party was ridiculed in the press and by members of the other parties upon its founding, partly for not having a fixed program to begin with, but entered parliament less than two years later with about 5% of the votes (2% is needed to enter parliament) and has since gained in the polls. Apparently the Danish public was ready for a "party about nothing".

Instead of being based on a readymade political program, the party was formed around a set of principles and values for how to conduct good political discourse and dialogue. The party also has political content, of course, a program with things they want to change, but this was subsequently crowd sourced by its members after the party got founded. Most central to the party's founding and organization is still the *how*, rather than the *what*.

Starting with the *what*, the party has three main issues in focus.

- Transition to a sustainable society (drawing partly on the Transition Town movement, originally from the UK);
- supporting entrepreneurship and social entrepreneurship; and
- changing the culture of political dialogue (as well as supporting art and culture in general).

As you can see, at the time of writing, the party has yet to discover the idea of the listening society; but still, it is a quite promising movement. Let's hope some of the members read this book.

The Alternative has its electoral and organizational base mainly in the urban creative class—the triple-H (hipsters, hackers and hippies) as well as some yoga bourgeoisie; these social groups we discussed in chapter 2. Thereby, the party can employ a lot of its cultural muscle to compete in the world of mass and social media—not least with the help of gifted designers working for free, people who are sensitive to cultural trends and currents.

The old Left intellectuals of Denmark tend to stay with the socialist movements, whereas The Alternative steals away the triple-H and yoga bourgeoisie people, creating a platform for their interests and expressions. The party represents a merger of the artistic, digital and sustainability-concerned elements of society. It is, in a way, the party of artists and their often eccentric, playful, post-materialist lifestyles.

The party is successful because it represents the new interests being born in a postindustrial society: not only **the creative class** but also what British economist Guy Standing elaborated and popularized as **the precariat** (people in precarious economic and social positions, who fall outside the classic class categories).[46] The precariat is supported by an ambitious program for simplifying life for the often surveyed and controlled unemployed, who get stuck in nasty bureaucratic state practices that in reality seldom lead to employment.

A second reason for the party's early success is that you have so much **cultural capital** gathered in once place, so much know-how about making the best meetings, dialogues, media events, parties, campaigns, posters and so on.[47] In a media landscape where everyone competes for attention, the people who are more fun and imaginative get an upper hand—not the richest and "most proper" people.

In a way, you could say that The Alternative represents the revolution of cultural capital against economic capital. The Conservative party of Denmark had much greater campaign expenditure and all the contacts with Danish industry, but still a much less successful election campaign. The Alternative beat them in many different ways. For instance, they had smaller, shrieking green election posters and made a point of not rushing the publicly designated starting time for when putting up posters was allowed. When all the other parties had cheated their way to all the most prominent spots, they calmly squeezed their smaller green posters into whatever cracks remained with the message "There is also The Alternative". A happy, kind-looking 20-year-old reported to the rolling TV-cameras that there is no need to cheat, because "there is room for everyone". When the party was widely accused of being "clowns" in the press, members scrambled to create a YouTube video featuring the leading candidates performing all manner of clown acts while reciting that they are happy to be jesters if that's what it takes to get their serious policy issues, such as transition to a sustainable society, on the agenda.

You have here a party formation born out of the progressive values of the urban creatives, people who are generally rather privileged, happy and functional. Naivety is also part of such progressiveness. At its best, this kind of movement combines the childlike openness of the idealist with a shrewd political pragmatism that comes with high concentrations of cultural capital. Cultural capital, as you may know, is a measure of the extent to which people possess a sensitive, intimate understanding of the time they live in.

As in the 2011 *Metamodernist Manifesto* (which I discuss in the appendix) we can see "informed naivety", or "pragmatic idealism"—terms explicitly used by the Alternativists, although coined independently from metamodernist scholars.

At its worst, this amounts to good old uninformed naivety and unworkable idealism (for instance, too much yoga woo-woo and too little intellectual rigor, or stifling moralism and what I in Book Two call **game denial**). On the worrying side, the party also attracts its fair share of over-spiritual, pot smoking conspiracy theorists (from the "astrology precariat", a social group we will also come back to). We'll see which way it goes. Probably both.

A unique thing about this party is its central focus; as mentioned, not its content, but rather its form or process—its *how*. It is based explicitly upon the idea of harnessing the **collective intelligence** of citizens and using their inspiration and creative ideas to achieve a transition to a sustainable society—ecologically, socially and economically. The party members use so-called "political laboratories", and an "alternative citizen parliament" (in the real parliament building) to invite ordinary citizens into dialogue and deliberation, gathering ideas and popular impulses, with relatively simple entry paths to participation and responsibility.

The most central tenets of the party are a set of six core values: courage, generosity, transparency, humility, humor, and empathy. These do not promise the voter a certain political program. Rather, they promise a kind of social environment within which the program is brought into being. The members of the party commit first and foremost to these values. This avoids some of the complications for the voter in an increasingly complex and contradictory political reality of postindustrial society, in which, as we have discussed, it is very difficult to even know what one's own interests are and the effects of policies are difficult to overview. When a party promises a better democratic process, you at least know what you get—albeit in a somewhat more non-linear fashion (see the discussion on non-linear politics in the next chapter). If politicians act better, you will get smarter politics by means of increased collective intelligence. Let's take a further look.

In addition to the core values, the party representatives are committed to six "dogma of debate". Notice this wording, "dogma" (a word with a more positive meaning in Danish as it has been used by progressive film makers to refer to a certain artistic method); it suggests something immutable and strictly upheld. This is where you can see metamodern logic in action. The party has rather loose policies, but does *not* shy away from holding its members to strict "dogma" when it comes to behavior and demeanor. Indeed, you will find this structure nowhere within the Left or the environmental movement, where beliefs in specific policies dominate but everyone would nevertheless be deeply allergic to words such as dogma, or prescriptions for people's behavior. Neither could you find anything like it in the many NGOs informed by more postmodern thinking.

Metamodernism, as a cultural logic, creates new forms of politics. The Alternative is putting *culture* first. They are committed to the deliberate shaping and development of political culture, by means of participating in the public debate in a transparent and kindly fashion. Thereby, they lift their gaze from the concrete issues of ecological sustainability, and target the cultural context within which such long-term politics become possible and meaningful.

For instance, at the party's inaugural address upon entering parliament, one of the newly elected MPs gave a speech in which he commended the different qualities and perspectives of all the other parties—including their ideological Nationalist adversaries. This is a sign of **transpartisanism**—the principle of seeing the interchange of all parties as vital to democracy, and to seek to implement one's policies by means of affecting the other parties (rather than antagonizing them). The Alternative can be described as a **transpartisan** movement.

Another example of transpartisanism. During the increasing pressures of migration, party leader Uffe Elbæk wrote an open letter in the paper, kindly asking the center-right prime minister (who is rather restrictive on immigration) for a dialogue on how to avoid bitter polarization of the Danish public on this hot topic. So what are the dogmas of debate? There are six of them, renamed "debate principles" on their English homepage:

- We will openly discuss both the advantages and the disadvantages of a certain argument or line of action.
- We will listen more than we speak, and we will meet our political opponents on their own ground.
- We will emphasize the core set of values that guide our arguments.
- We will acknowledge when we have no answer to a question or when we make mistakes.
- We will be curious about each and every person with whom we are debating.
- We will argue openly and factually as to how The Alternative's political vision can be realized.

As voters, many of us often recognize that we cannot know the answers to all the complicated societal questions. And frankly, neither can the politicians reasonably be expected to. But what we *can* know with some reliability is that if politicians are more humble in their opinions—and more open to new information and thereby more intelligent in their dialogue and debate with others—we are likely to get more balanced and sound politics.

And we can know that the process oriented party vouches for a better dialogue, thereby improving the climate for discussion and deliberation throughout the political realm, not just within that particular party, but within and between *all* parties. Hence, this approach speaks to the tendency of the electorate to be increasingly disenchanted with the ongoing debates in postindustrial party politics. It targets a deep nerve within the population of a liberal democracy, where the Left and Right no longer represent clearly defined class interests, and people long for a more honest and nuanced discussion.

A party like The Alternative can only pop up once there is a significant population with a certain set of values, norms and social skills. If you scratch the surface of this party, it is both highly egalitarian (spreading power, including people in dialogue, etc.) *and* built on the implicit creation of new hierarchies. Of course, almost all the members of The Alternative would object violently to that last part, as they tend to be deeply egalitarian and against hierarchies and elitism (their current leader Uffe Elbæk half-jokingly calls himself a Buddhist anarchist). But look at their dogma of debate. When they state that they will meet their adversaries where these are coming from, they are implicitly saying that they must be able to understand and see the perspectives of others, but don't expect the same treatment in return. A subtle hierarchy is being introduced. When they say that they will accentuate values, they are in fact saying that they will hold a more abstract and general level than others in their thinking. Another subtle hierarchy.

We are here approaching one of the strange paradoxes of our time, one of the many cases where a both-and thinking is required. The paradox is this: We need to simultaneously deal with increasingly clear and well-defined hierarchies, *and* we need society to become more democratic and inclusive.

The people who end up on top in this strange new hierarchy are the *most democratic ones*—the people who have the personalities, skills and cultural codes necessary to create social settings that are more inclusive and nuanced. Such social settings can handle contradicting views, allow for more autonomy and experimentation, and can handle a greater number of relationships with fewer conflicts. Conflicts are resolved with greater openness and less carnage. In other words, this is the golden age of caring, creative, socially intelligent, psychologically healthy beta boys and girls.

This tendency spills over into other areas—the new main agents of the symbol-based informational economy have the same profile. The artistic, sensitive, complex and multitalented **social entrepreneur** is increasingly becoming the ideal type of the new economy. Social entrepreneurship, peer-to-peer production, sharing economy, democratic dialogue techniques such as Art of Hosting—this is part and parcel of The Alternative's ideology and movement.

The Alternative is also looking for ways to form a commercial company and an NGO. In tune with the metamodern cultural logic, you see how the process oriented party works to reintegrate the personal, civic and professional aspects of (late) modern life.

GOT THAT EDGE

In the internet age pockets with concentrations of cultural capital (knowledge of arts, culture, philosophy and so forth) can contribute to the birth of metamodern political movements. And political metamodernism is fundamentally a sensitive balancing of sincerity and irony. **This balancing of sincerity and irony gives progressive movements (like The Alternative) a great competitive advantage in the media and on the political stage—a sharp edge.**

The metamodern activist can cut through the irony of everyday life and media and aspire towards higher ideals, without looking like an embarrassment or a joke. Instead, the joke is on anyone who lacks that same sincerity, who never dared to be vulnerable.

The marriage of irony and sincerity helps us to take the perspectives of others: the racist, the exaggerated feminist, the conservative. Each ironic position you play with is simultaneously saturated with sincerity, which means that you can *honestly* be with their feelings and values while still being in opposition to them. This saves a lot energy that would otherwise be expended on anger and resentment and it helps creating mutual understanding or even unexpected alliances and synergies. It helps you play the game of politics. Strangely, it is much easier to defeat someone if you honestly care about them and see the world with their eyes, stand in their shoes.

Even if there is currently a widespread mental resistance and difficulty to both communicating and understanding metamodernism, it has all the deeper structures of society working in its favor. The long-term game is rigged. In this way, metamodernism spreads like a virus, by hacking and hijacking the thoughts, words, practices and institutions of modern society, bit by bit sneaking its way into the programs of all parties, Left and Right. And it does not work by means of silent conspiracies—it works psycho-actively, in broad daylight, just as I am planting metamodern modes of thought in you right now, without any shame or apology.

Metamodern principles are already inherent to the contradictions of modern society; late modern society is pregnant with metamodernism. **People need irony in order to build interpersonal trust based on self-**

knowledge, humor and critical thinking. Only when such trust is in place can we successfully gather around a meaningful struggle for something greater than ourselves, like the climate crisis.

There, another ironic quirk of our age: Irony brings trust. And trust crowns a winner.

Violins, please.

Transnationalism, Truly

Please take note of the following, dear reader. People really can't seem to get their head around this next point. I hope you can.

When I speak about this metamodern political program with a listening society, a deeper kind of welfare, new kinds of political movements and the like, I deliberately refrain from bolting down exactly at what administrative or political level it can or should occur.

When I say that "society" should change in this or that direction, I *don't* mean Denmark or Sweden, but *society in general*, in a more abstract sense. We can still work with the nation state as a starting point, because it is how we are most comfortable thinking and speaking about politics, but we're not really taking a hard stance on at which level metamodern politics can and should manifest. This is largely because the world is slowly becoming transnational.

An important feature of The Alternative is that it was founded as a transnational movement from its very beginning. In practice, this means that the day-to-day politics are not led by the party leader, Uffe Elbæk, who instead travels the world, building a wide and diverse network. He recently met with the US presidential candidate Bernie Sanders—who found the time to see him during an ongoing election campaign. The Alternative hook up with all manner of think-tanks, activists, movements, parties and businesses around the world—and find "ambassadors" in each country who are local representatives of the party.

But at its core, **transnationalism** is about much more than building a network across and beyond national borders for process oriented, progressive parties and movements (you will find connections to e.g. the Spanish neo-leftwing party Podemos or the Italian accountant-gone-comedian Beppe Grillo's direct democracy party, the Five Star Movement). Transnationalism whispers something under its breath: the long-term, approximate aim of dismantling the modern nation state, at least as we normally think of it.

I don't think that is what the Alternativists are explicitly about these days, but it certainly lies in the extension of their cosmopolitan, world-centric, ecological political program (with slogans such as "a Denmark that is good for the world").

Issues such as universal freedom of migration, international security, terrorism, internet policing, climate crisis, ecological sustainability, stabilizing international finance and banking, global poverty, basic material security, basic income, labor rights, human and animal rights all share one fundamental trait: they are *transnational* by nature. They all function *through* borders and *beyond* nations. You are probably familiar with these issues as being different versions of "prisoners' dilemma games", where nation states are pitched against one another and all end up losing unless they manage the risk that mutual cooperation necessarily entails.

In the long run, we know that the nation state cannot remain the primary, or at least not the hegemonic, building block of our governance and self-organization. There are two simple reasons for this. The first is that we are increasingly facing problems that are not solvable at the national level. The second is that there are a growing number of "societies" that don't correspond to nation state constructs, such as dynamic economic regions built around major transnational cities—with growing, influential and successful populations who lead lives beyond nation state identities and national legislative or symbolic frameworks. **Basically, there are a growing lot of issues and people and cities that just don't fit into the nation state.**

The state can remain, of course, as a kind of administrative and democratic "train station" in a larger meshwork of governance: local, regional, city-based, corporate, continental, digital and global. In other words, the long-term *attractor* (the point we are likely to approach) is some kind of more intricate meshwork of governance structures and institutions. There are other forms of governance that are beginning to work beyond states—supranational institutions, administrations of strong city regions (often more in tune with the day and age than national parliaments), corporate structures and NGOs. It is true that nation states still control the armies, but warfare is becoming less central to political reality—even if militaristic relapses of geopolitics and wars are unavoidable.

To be clear, the transnational way of thinking first of all means that "metamodernists know no borders", that the ethics and values are world-centric, or perhaps cosmo-centric. It also means that you have a general way of thinking where the nation state or region are not the primary categories of society, but rather just tools or train stations in a longer journey of the historical development of governance, of human self-organization.

This also means that you refrain from over-essentializing nationalities and ethnicities. Frenchness, Chineseness, Arabicness, the Nordic ideology, the German ideology—it's all nonsense; just temporary, contingent patterns, cutting through water. The cultures evolve; the forms of governance, languages and economies continuously transmute. National cultures are what Irish-American anthropologist Benedict Anderson called "imagined communities", continuously being reimagined. They are based on what Norwegian anthropologist Fredrik Barth called "ethnic boundary making": I am German because I am *not* Danish, and so forth.

So you can use the features of any one culture or nation state or form of governance, but the goals remain world-centric. The metamodernist does not hate or despise nations or nationalism. It's just that they are treated instrumentally; a nation is only worth anything to the extent that it serves all humans; indeed, all animals. We seek to hijack these structures, to remote-control them for purposes that lie beyond them.[48]

There is no American spirit, just different moods of different geographies, living conditions and epochs. Indeed, metamodernism knows no nation and, in a sense, no family. Our nation is the blue sky, our family the millions of tortured piglets of factory farms, the asphyxiated fish of the Baltic Sea, and the nomadic tribes of evolving, intertwined selves in an increasingly virtual, transnational reality where the distances of old crumble and vanish.

Violins, please, this time played *molto fortissimo* in A major.[49]

The Metamodern Aristocracy

The metamodern aristocracy are people who have a combination of factors in their psychological, existential and cognitive constitutions that allow them to play a certain role on the new historical world stage (see the developmental models in the second part of this book). But they are also people of social, economic and cultural privilege, who have the time, energy and emotional fuel to expend for abstract endeavors such as developing the future of the world-system.

What we are looking for is a nicer, softer, more nuanced and flexible form of Leninism, an *avant-garde*, or vanguard, of people who recognize and align with some of the deep structures and long-term attractors of our age, and who cooperate transnationally to bring about profound changes in global society. These people have little else in common than a metamodern perspective. They find each other in a variety of settings, often through the internet.[50]

The Leninist idea of a global, progressive movement with its own power playing, radical vanguard is not all bad. The vanguard just need a much clearer understanding of the development of society, and of developmental psychology, than what Lenin and his contemporaries had. And we need a code of ethics that they lacked—starting with non-violence and a commitment to understand, empathize with and listen to others.

The members of this group have to love power. But not the power of self over others; rather, the power of selves *and* others, the power to self-organize in complex fashions—**transpersonal power** ("transpersonal" is explained in the following chapter). Not your power or mine, but yes, the brutal capability to coordinate living systems, to make events come into being. What we think of as oppressive power is really an expression of imbalances of power, between rich and poor, privileged and deprived, humans and non-human animals.[51] The world does not have too much power, but too much powerlessness. If we have pathological, sickly wants for power, it is because we are really powerless. **Lovers of transpersonal power seek the empowerment of selves *and* others—realizing that power and freedom are sisters.** Superficial readings of social philosophers such as the Frankfurt School (or their fellow traveler Erich Fromm) can make us believe that power in itself is pathological. But in reality, even the softest souls and most tender bleeding hearts must long for power.

The metamodern aristocracy doesn't work according to a linear plan about what will come (like those damned communists). They just share some common conceptual maps, personal traits, perspectives and political sentiments. This makes them difficult to spot with the naked eye. They are a loose network of people who recognize each other and who share some common overarching perspectives. They work together in a myriad of different ways—lending resources and support for the development of ideas, arranging key events, starting businesses and other organizations or projects, and affecting policy making.

Who are the members of the metamodern aristocracy, these soft-hearted lovers of transpersonal power? And how are they different from the general members of the world population? The Swedish philosophers Alexander Bard and Jan Söderqvist suggest that the information age is creating a new class of "netocrats", people who govern and control value creation on the internet and related media, where attention, rather than money, is the primary value. They further suggest that there are three forms of netocrats that ally with one another: the new kind of social entrepreneurs, the web-savvy philosophers who understand the deeply dynamic and transient nature of things (called "eternalists"), and the networkers who actively and deliberately make themselves into central, connecting nodes within this new multidimensional web of people, perspectives and opportunities.

Because these netocrats are not after money anymore, or have enough of it, they "imploit" (rather than exploit) people and resources.[52] Like me; I sit here in a beautiful house, without much concern about who owns the place. All I care about is peace and quiet and a powerful mountain view that makes me feel like Nietzsche. I am an aristocrat in the sense that I can be as eccentric as I like, in a morning robe on a late afternoon. The primary driver in my life is not food on the table, or even a struggle for interests, but an ethically fueled playfulness and sense of adventure, concerned to a large extent with directing people's time, emotions and attention towards novel ideas. To imploit means to use things for their subjective, existential and non-exhaustible value—in a way, to play with them.

Not bad. That might account for what the metamodern aristocrat is like, at least to some extent. But I would be wary of applying a class analysis and equating the metamodern aristocracy with "netocrats". The metamodern aristocracy are people who have a combination of two things: great privilege and high personal development.

The privilege I speak of is high "total capital" (a concept we get back to in Book Two, *Nordic Ideology*), meaning that we are not necessarily rich in the conventional sense, but that we have enough opportunities and support around us to do pretty much whatever we want with our lives (so, total capital is a combination of social capital, cultural capital, economic capital, emotional capital, sexual capital and good health). High total capital means that you can live your life relatively unafraid.

The second part, about personal development, is that we have "high" **effective value meme**, the meaning of which we will discuss in the second part of the book. In a word, it just means that these people are genuinely progressive and have the values of a global, sustainable internet age civilization. But who are they as persons?

We are playful eccentrics of various sorts. We are screwed-up and brilliant million dollar babies; people who have somehow fallen outside of the normal meaning making processes of everyday life—without breaking apart—and for whom there is no going back to a bourgeois lifestyle. You will find metamodern swashbucklers, mavericks, hackers, intellectual revolver men; subtle enemies of the bourgeois lifestyle (in which you are supposed to take life very seriously, especially your job, but never seriously aspire to truly change the world).

The metamodern aristocracy is the playful vanguard of a new form of society in which people are free in a deeper sense than what everyday life in modern society normally allows. Something picks up speed, gains momentum; the aristocracy acts with the kind of elegant conviction that can flow only from an embrace of the paradoxical and complex nature of reality.

So, besides the transnational, process oriented party—which works from an informed naivety, beyond Left and Right, with non-linear politics, in order to bring about a deeper welfare called the listening society—you have another historical agent in our story: a small vanguard, a metamodern aristocracy, consisting of people who are much more consciously and deliberately concerned with bringing about a transnational metamodern development.

These people are armed with more advanced and updated conceptual maps of the world than the average member of the process oriented party. The metamodern aristocracy is teaming up worldwide and conspiring to change the functioning of the global world-system. **They are "hacking the world-soul", as it were, injecting doses of metamodern DNA into key areas of society, hijacking the political, economic and cultural systems of modern life in order to bring about a more fair, transparent, sustainable and caring future.**

To these aristocrats it is simply obvious that today's world is undemocratic, unscientific and primitive. But they don't rage and revolt against it. They surf it, ride its waves, and implant bits of metamodern cultural code deep into the structures and dynamics of society. They work together with, in tandem with, the existing political movements, businesses, NGOs and governments. In a way, you could say that they manipulate and conspire, but it is a very democratic and transparent form of manipulation, and a very non-linear and open-ended form of conspiracy, taking place within a very loose network.

To *con-spire* means to breathe together. The conspiracy is to educate and seduce humanity into taking the path towards a more existential and sustainable civilization. To educate and to seduce—these two words come from the same Latin root. To this playful aristocracy, the world stage is a great, multidimensional puzzle, where the aim is to find unexpected synergies that work in the direction of human development—by way of playing, educating, seducing. They don't press their agenda on others, but they tickle the dialectic processes to see what emerges, having strong intuitions about in which directions it might go. Often, this is done through art and cultural expression, hinting at new perspectives and potentials. Just by breathing the same air, the fresh air of a potential—but not predetermined—future society.

Metamodern thinking involves an increased acceptance of the paradoxical nature of things. All this talk of aristocrats rests upon a central paradox of political metamodernism (which I have mentioned before): the deep, unyielding struggle for greater egalitarianism, inclusion and democracy—together with a renewed tolerance towards and understanding of hierarchy and elitism.

On the one hand, the new global vanguard is emerging; that is just a fact of life. And it must recognize itself as such in order to be fully efficient. On the other hand, the metamodern aristocracy fails its own moral standards if it does not work for a much more democratic, transparent and open world—it loses all legitimacy without a deep commitment to egalitarian values and the dignity of all humans and non-human animals.

So the metamodern aristocracy is not anywhere "high up", at great distance from others, hoarding privileges from within certain organizations. Rather, its constituting principle is nothing else than the spontaneous self-organization of a new layer within the world-system—a cultural development pertaining to the globalized information age. They are simply the people who live metamodern lives, with metamodern values, within the still predominantly modern world-system. But as such, they do have an important role to play.

As all other social groups, the metamodern aristocracy is both good and bad. Don't blame me for telling you about their existence. No shooting of messengers, please. We do exist, and we do have a role to play, and that role can and should be recognized with all its risks and uncertainties. I don't mean to glorify or exaggerate it, but there it is.

The metamodern aristocracy isn't *actually* going to rule the world. We're going to tweak it, somewhat, in a favorable direction. And it's going to be fun. It already is.

Are you part of this aristocracy? Your reading of this book is a way of testing just that. If your reading goes smoothly and what I say is intuitive to you, and you recognize the things I am speaking of, you're a candidate. If you are also part of a vast, diverse transnational network and you have more ideas for changing the world than you can possibly act upon, and your everyday life revolves around making some of these things happen—you're it.

For most readers, you're not it, and that's okay. It's still advantageous for you to know about the existence of the metamodern aristocracy, just like you can benefit from knowing about other groups in society, such as the precariat, the cultural creatives, the hackers or the ultra-rich.

I suppose this book is a bit of an invitation to participating in the metamodern aristocracy, to be a co-creator of the new society. So I lay down the analytical bricks, but you get to build the castle (and of course, challenge the ideas and develop them). If I'm Marx, you get to be Lenin. If I'm Jesus, you get to be Mohammed, who *really* meant business with this thing about God's kingdom. If I'm Rousseau, you get to be Robespierre.

Just promise me three things. You won't send peasants to death camps, you won't conquer North Africa—and please don't behead the king.

No, I'm serious. It's up to you to make these things happen in the world, by means of starting cool companies, becoming prime minister or some such. But if it ever comes to killing anyone or doing anything else nasty and harmful in the name of these ideas, just forget about it. Put away the book, forget I told you about this and disown the whole thing. We're exploring ideas. We're being open-minded and curios about the potentials. But we are not laying down "the one path", and if it ever leads us in the direction of killing, lying, cheating, torturing—we need to drop it and think again. It's not worth it. And if my ideas press you towards such conclusions, we can be certain I was mistaken all along.

The more serious questions and matters you play with, the greater the moral demands. Almost all political ideas have led to atrocities. As I write this down, I can almost feel the mutilation of innocents going on in closed prisons, somehow non-linearly emanating from my fingertips.

No violins.

Chapter 6

POLITICAL PHILOSOPHY

> "You see" said the professor, "it is not that black and white, not at all. There are many shades of grey, many nuances we must get to know, each by its own appropriate method."
>
> "You couldn't be more right and mistaken, both at once" the little green devil replied, a sly smirk nudging his thin lips again. "It is not so black and white, that the truth it is *either* black and white, *or* many shades of grey. Sometimes, it really *is* black and white. And sometimes, even, it is only a deeper shade of black. And sometimes blackness itself is luminous. In fact, it always is."

A lot of people don't care much about philosophy. Philosophy means the love of truth (or knowledge, more precisely). It is not a specific activity, but the foundation of your reality. You can either be a co-creator of it, or you can be a dog, letting your philosophical reality be created for you by your masters. No offence meant to dogs.

In the appendix, you can get a more detailed look "under the hood" of the metamodern philosophical engine. In this chapter I spell out some of the conclusions; how we should think about society. And why you can throw what they taught you at school out the window.

In this chapter we question the human rights of the individual, explain what it really means to go beyond Left and Right, and why we cannot remain believers in liberal democracy.

But enough talk. Have at thee!

Transpersonal Perspective: Beyond Individuals

In modern society there is a widespread idea about "the individual". The idea of the individual is actually an ingenious solution to a difficult social-philosophical problem: Should we focus on society as a whole, or on its different parts and singular processes?

If a society focuses on its totality and wholeness, it can easily repress or deny processes that follow their own, partly independent, logics and social orders: legal systems, business, personal love relations, party politics and so forth (think Soviet communism). On the other hand, if a society (not necessarily a nation state) fails to integrate the many parts into a whole, it can easily suffer serious consequences: that people work against one another, environmental degradation, failure to address wider issues such as social exclusion.

The idea of *the individual* provides a kind of solution to this problem. It basically says that each human being, over the stretch of her lifespan, is an indivisible whole unto herself. This idea thereby creates a series of smaller "whole" systems, "individuals", each being a "life project" that ties together many different societal processes into one seamless fabric: childhood, personal life, education, work, family, political opinions, and so on. By use of this idea, modern society finds a golden mean that addresses the dilemma between the whole and the parts: Within each single individual, the many processes of society come together into a whole. By means of the individual, all of society can be integrated into a microcosm.

Individual means "that which cannot be broken down into smaller parts", if we look at its Latin root. The Greek translation of the same word is "atom". In actual reality, of course, there are no "individuals" in any deeper sense that corresponds to the theory of atoms in physics: We are just animal bodies that move through a series of socially defined realities. Our bodies are always in a flux, always being changed by the environment. After five years, all mass in our body has been exchanged (at least more than 99%).

The life story about our "individual self" is always just that: a story. There really is nothing to our individuality that makes us very unique: All of our wants, dreams, words and ideas come from the social environment. Even our name and our idea of a self come from interactions with other people, who in turn have been defined by *their* social surroundings. And the individual has no real "free will". Even if we are organisms with intentionality of our own, we are always deeply shaped by the social environment; this includes our thoughts and intentions. The same conclusion is apparent to all people trained in meditation or otherwise versed in Eastern philosophy: When we quiet down our "talking head" minds and observe our thoughts, it becomes evident that the voice speaking in our head runs automatically and largely beyond our own "will". Where in all this is the individual located?

After all, even atoms turned out to be divisible; their very existence non-local and always based upon interactions. But the reason that political metamodernism must go beyond the idea of the individual, and "see through" the individual person, is not just philosophical, not just a matter of being correct in an analytical sense. It has profound practical and political implications.

The idea of the individual was a smart solution under the circumstances that modern, industrial society produced. In today's globalized information society, however, when the problems of society are of a much deeper and more complex nature, the idea of the individual tends to blind us to the problems as well as to their solutions. **The idea of the "individual" no longer fulfills its function as an effective unit of society's self-organization. As a solution to the problems of society, it no longer does its job.** This is because the problems of society increasingly stem from deep layers of the psyche—and their interactions with the world—that are hard to access for us as individual persons. How do you make the average person trust her fellow citizens more? How do you make those same fellow citizens more trustworthy in the first place? How do you make people have genuine solidarity with all people and animals (which, truth be told, most of us simply don't have)? How do you make the average person more far-sighted, creative and complex? How do you make the average family have more stable and loving relationships? How do you break the evil cycle of insecurity, commercialism and over-consumption?

In turn, such deeper layers of the psyche are fundamentally intertwined with the collective structures of society. For instance: how everyday life in school is, how the labor market is, how love and sex function (or don't), what words we are taught to discuss the universe and our place in it. All of these things depend on our surroundings so much more than on individual choices.

But society cannot be viewed solely as "collective structures" or "networks", either, because that would make us blind to the deeply lived and felt perspectives and experiences of singular human beings—and to the fact that the collective structures are largely defined and determined by such deep, psychological processes within each one of us.

The French philosopher Deleuze proposes that we should see society as made up by **dividuals**, i.e. that we all are in fact part of one another and affect one another. We consist of many different influences, roles and perspectives, within a multitude of contexts.

I am offering a related bid for anti-individualism: **the transpersonal perspective**. The transpersonal perspective holds two seemingly opposed, but in reality complementary, positions.

The first position is to see society as determined by the deep, inner lives—the most personal relations and tender emotions—of human beings. This takes the unique lived experience of each human being very seriously. Such lived experience is taken to be the very foundation of society: if there is anger or love in our hearts, if there is peace in our minds, and if all manner of psychological issues have been properly dealt with. Such things determine if we turn out engaged world citizens, mindless consumers or bitter reactionaries.

The second position is that this deeply human and personal experience is in turn *created* by societal processes that are largely invisible to each single person, and accessible only through a profound and systematic sociological and psychological analysis of society.

So this lands us in an apparent paradox: To *really* see the singular human being, to really respect her rights and uniqueness, we must go *beyond* the idea of the individual; we must see through it and strive to see how society is present within each single person as well as in the relationships through which she is born as a "self". We go from the idea of the individual (vs. "the collective"), to simply seeing society as an evolving, interlinked set of **transindividuals**. This is the transpersonal perspective. It's not just that we are each a billiard ball that "interacts" with other people. We co-emerge. Or, as the physicist-philosopher Karen Barad has put it: we **intra-act**.

Initially, it may seem counter-intuitive to think of humans as something other than individuals: After all, don't we all have one body each, one voice and one inner monologue? But even neuroscience challenges this assumption. Ever heard of what is popularly called "split-brain"? It occurs in rare cases when the bridge between the left and right hemispheres of the brain is surgically removed to treat severe epilepsy. People with "split-brain" show a number of deeply puzzling features; they appear to have two different selves, each controlling one side of the body. Sometimes these two sides work past one another, the conscious mind (or rather: the linguistically endowed "talking" mind of the dominant hemisphere) even making excuses and rationalizations for the behaviors of the ghostly left hand which seems to gain a will of its own.

Or, you can show a picture to one eye and not the other—and the split-brain person will act as if he has seen the picture. But if you ask him, *he is still unaware* of having seen the picture and gives rationalizations for why he acted as if he had seen the picture. What you can see here is that the brain becomes split in half, and each part seems to have a mind of its own—although sometimes the two communicate indirectly. This truly is bizarre, at least from a perspective where humans are thought to have an individual self and will of their own.

Or you may have heard of the cranially conjoined child twins (meaning that their heads are partly physically merged into one) from Vancouver, Krista and Tatiana Hogan, who seem to be able to pass visual impressions to one another directly through their brains: You can ask one girl what the other sees and she will know. Such cases make the reality of the dividual clearly apparent: The single human mind is not indivisible, not a "single atom". It's just not; not even biologically speaking. But these uncommon cases serve only to underscore something more fundamental that involves all of us: Nowhere can you find a single, individual "self"; it's always connected to everything around us.

To the metamodern activist, the rights and interests of the transindividual are seen as much deeper, more real and more important than the rights of the individual. Just like modern society scrapped the rights of the clan or the family in favor of the individual, we are now scrapping the individual in favor of the much more morally entitled and more analytically valid transindividual.

The idea of the listening society serves the transindividual: The human being is seen as more than a unique, separate life story. The idea of the transindividual sees the human being as inseparable from her language, her deep unconscious, her relations, roles, societal positions, values, emotions, developmental psychology, biological organism and so forth. Each human being is viewed as an open and social process, a whirlwind of participation and co-creation of society. Society as a whole is viewed as a self-organizing system which creates such transindividuals who are in turn able to recreate society.

To sum up, the idea of the individual and her rights and freedom has served us well, but now we need to move on—lest society come crashing down on us like London Bridge.

Metamodern politics, working from sincere irony, applies a transpersonal perspective to society, serving the transindividual, her rights and interests. You can use the words transpersonalism and transindividualism more or less interchangeably. Just remember this: **It is by looking at deep psychological issues, the inner development of each of us, and how such properties are generated within society, that we address the core of society's problems.** In the appendix, you will find some more condensed definitions of what the transpersonal perspective means.

Let's take an example. How about a terrorist like Anders Behring Breivik, the Norwegian guy who killed 77 people (mostly social-democratic youth) and injured more than 300 people on that fateful day in July 2011. There are two major explanations people use to account for his acts of terror: that it is a political issue (the spread of neo-Nazi ideas in the wake of rising populist nationalism) or that it is a mental health issue (the guy is crazy). A third, less common, explanation is the suggestion that Breivik is the result of neoliberal developments of society, which have purportedly made people unhappy and narcissistic (obviously championed by mainstream Left sociologists). Some social-psychological observers have suggested that the long process with years of isolation and self-disciplining while preparing for such a grave transgression of norms is the main issue: How did someone like Breivik at all manage to get himself to follow through?

What all sides agree upon is that online forums played a big part; that Breivik is at least in part an internet phenomenon.

These discussions choose between an individual and a societal (collective) perspective. From a more transpersonal viewpoint, the issue appears quite differently. The matter at hand is instead the social psychology of a long sequence of everyday events: Somehow and somewhere in everyday life, this young man became very embittered, and was clearly unable to handle life in a productive manner. Breivik, the mass murderer, was born in the school yard, in the dysfunctional family, in the peer group, on the internet, in the labor market, in failed love aspirations, in sexual frustrations, in failed masculinity (a recurring theme in his crazed "manifesto", released the same day as the killings occurred—he even spent his last night with two expensive prostitutes and champagne), in hurt pride, in failed interethnic relations and stalling integration processes. In short, he was born as a result of the entire fabric of society.

So Breivik planned for nine years and then went out and killed people. In doing so he of course violated the rights of each unique person, and the rights of their loved ones.

Think about it; the only way to have prevented this from occurring would be if people like Breivik were simply much less likely to emerge in the first place. We can't really protect each single person from the ill will of all conceivable wrongdoers, not even with super-efficient policing. No matter how much we "stand up for the rights of the individual", the individual will still be limited and harmed in a million ways, even to the point of being murdered, if we don't see her deeper insides and the social-psychological contexts of which she is part—if we fail to see the trans-individual and stand up for *her* rights.

We cannot do much about the sporadic occurrence of pathological psychopaths, as psychopathy clearly has strong hereditary or genetic factors. Nor can we make crazy Nazi ideologies disappear from the internet (or do-it-yourself guides for terrorists, for that matter). In any case, neither psychopathy nor internet extremism is sufficient to explain Breivik the terrorist.

What we *can* do, however, is to make sure that the average person is happier and healthier, has better relationships, better self-knowledge and more support. Because the terrible truth is that Breivik is you and me. He is a direct result of the society we create and uphold every day. He is not an alien force. He is that kid from school who came back and killed our kids. It's all interconnected. We are all interconnected. Obviously Breivik is an extreme example of social deviance, but he emerges in continuity with the rest of us. Somehow, we are made of the same stuff. The answer to the horror show that Breivik unleashed is to be found deep within ourselves.

Would Breivik have become who he became if the whole fabric of bliss and suffering had been more intelligently weaved? It is a matter of likelihood: Some societies generate more terrorists than others, Norway usually being relatively peaceful, but evidently not without its fair share of social tensions. It is a transpersonal issue; it goes *beyond and through* the individual person. But as such, it still is, and will remain, deeply personal, in the sense that it involves matters that are exquisitely intimate and emotional.

Let us go beyond the terrorism example. Extend this transpersonal perspective to all kinds of other issues: unemployment, where the issue is not only how many are employed, but how it feels to be unemployed, what it means to people and why; or bullying, where the whole environment and social setting of schooling and the educational system set the limits for interpersonal trust and solidarity throughout society; or public health, where the lifestyles of our friends and relatives affect our habits and therefore our lifespan—which in turn depends on how well they are doing psychologically in terms of happiness, which in turn depends a lot on the quality of their relationships, which in turn depends on how much people are forced to compete for social status, and so on. So the great fabric of hurt and bliss that explains acts of terror is the same one that explains so many other miseries in our lives.

There is of course not "one explanation" for the gruesome mystery of Breivik, but some perspectives are much better at dealing with the complex nature of these issues than others. The inner life of the singular citizen is married to the collective structures of society, and vice versa. Our failure as a society to see this interconnectedness is the real explanation that people flip out and become murderous Nazis. None of the other perspectives can stop the next Breivik; only a transpersonal perspective can.

To serve the individual—or the collective—is thus increasingly becoming regressive and harmful. "The individual" and "the collective" are analytically faulty positions. We are not simply balancing individual and collective interests; we are attacking both in the name of the transindividual.

To see human beings as "individuals" in an obviously interconnected and co-evolving universe is not only poor social philosophy. It is an unforgivable insult to the greatness of the human soul. We are *more* than individuals; we are much larger beings. This is why, in a transpersonal perspective, I can say in all sincerity: Death to the individual.

Long live the dividual—or the transindividual.

The View from Complexity

In our days, there is a lot of talk about chaos and complexity. And it's not just buzz and academic fashion—as some commentators have claimed—but a real development that has bearings on pretty much all the sciences.

When it comes to understanding society, you have the mushrooming field of complexity economics and some very promising developments in mathematical sociology. Major sociologists like the recently deceased John Urry have attempted to draw conclusions for a view of society, what you might call "a view from complexity".[53] You even have a gathering of prominent scientists called the "Gulbekian Commission" in which Immanuel Wallerstein (the originator of the world-systems theory, which is a big deal in leftwing economics) works together with the systems theorist and chemist Ilya Prigogine (he won a Nobel Prize but his reputation has since been tarnished due to his spiritual leanings) to help introduce the understanding of chaos, complexity and emergence into our way of thinking about society.

I suppose you could say that you have preludes to this development already in the so-called cybernetics back in the 1950s—and notably in the work of the polymath biologist Gregory Bateson.

Today, the by far best source for understanding chaos and complexity is the Santa Fe Institute, a research center that gathers some of the top people in computational science and actually from most other sciences (in Santa Fe, New Mexico).[54] And you have a growing community of people from around the world—from all sciences—who are inspired by the work of Albert-László Barabási, a Hungarian physicist known for his work on network theory.

But when it comes to understanding society and politics, what is the "view from complexity"? Can we bring it down to some general understanding? Yes, we can.

One of the first examples of complexity taught in textbooks is what they call a Schelling simulation. And it shows us something about how racism and segregation works. Basically it's a chessboard with rings and crosses that move across the board. Every time you press enter on the computer, the rings and crosses move one step or stay put. So you keep pressing enter and the markers keep moving around the chessboard.

Now if you program the rings and crosses to only have a *slight* preference for moving closer to their own kind, patterns will soon emerge and stabilize: patterns of *dramatic* segregation. And not only that—in some cases a somewhat *lower* level of preference your own kind can cause a *more* segregated chessboard.

If you look at the pattern that emerges, you would think that these rings and crosses must be really racist. But that's not necessarily the case. They're just a little racist. The dramatic segregation is an *emergent property* of the system as a whole. Where a leftwing, critical sociologist would rage against power structures and the historical supremacy of rings over crosses, and the psychoanalyst would speculate about a deeply ingrained racism in their unconscious, with the view from complexity one sees that these explanations can only ever be very partial. Relatively small, simple changes in the behaviors of each single ring or cross can produce an entirely different chessboard.

And you would think that racism is a nasty variable that "causes" segregation. But sometimes, even tolerance can actually "cause" segregation. There is no "evil essence" that you can get rid of; only variables you can tweak, with different—often unexpected and counter-intuitive—results.

With the view from complexity, it becomes apparent that you can't really blame the individual behaviors of the many people who interact, and you can't really identify an evil "power structure" out there, which you can just get rid of and things will be fine. You have to look at the rules of the game, at the patterns of interactions, and how we create one another through those interactions—and how that in turn produces society as a whole.

If you want to change society, you need to change these games. You have to change minute things in people's behaviors and you have to develop the quality of their relationships.

Let's take another example, one from criminology and police research. In 1992, a British criminologist named Robert Reiner noted that there appears to be five interacting mechanisms that make the police direct more attention towards certain ethnic minorities:

- Categorical discrimination, i.e. that the police themselves choose to stop and frisk more black people (or other minorities).
- Transferred discrimination, i.e. that people in the general public call the police more often when they see black people around.
- Interactional discretion, i.e. that the police have more cultural difficulties when it comes to interacting with certain groups and hence more often end up in situation that escalate to violence and arrest.
- Institutionalized discrimination, i.e. that some areas with higher criminality are patrolled more and thus more people in these areas are put under surveillance.
- Statistical discrimination, i.e. that the crime statistics of certain groups start bad cycles as the police direct their attention to these groups and hence reinforce the statistical overrepresentation of criminality within this group.

Reiner contended that categorical discrimination—the one we generally think of when it comes to police racism—is the *least* powerful mechanism. In other words, Reiner was telling us that the **rules of the game** generated racism and discrimination (rather than the racism of the police officers themselves).[55] In my own work on police ethnography, I have found plenty of reasons to believe that Reiner was right. With the view from complexity you see, again, that racism is an emergent pattern; a phenomenon that emerges not through the actions of individual people, but as a result of the interactions of many different people.

Another example: sexist commercials. A lot of women feel objectified. They also feel that they have to compare themselves to constantly tooted impossible ideals whenever they move around downtown. It's everywhere: fashion models wearing the latest underwear, being all thin when they eat ice-cream with perfect skin and perfect teeth. It's just too much; it makes a lot of women and young girls uncomfortable (and it has psychologically adverse effects on men as well). Surely it must be the social power of males and patriarchy, allied to capitalism, that subjects us to this treatment?

Well, think about it. If only *some* people are only a *little* more likely to buy things when the person on the commercial is more good-looking, this means that the companies that have more good-looking people in their ads will sell a little more. And in the long run, they will outcompete those that don't. This means that most companies are likely to have good-looking models on pictures with their products. And not only that, the companies who then have *more* good-looking people, *and* are better at displaying them, will have an advantage over the others. This creates a competition *ad absurdum*—a bizarre race for sexiness, which in turn creates a whole market for marketing companies, models, photographers and photoshoppers.

Now ask yourself—and be honest—do you yourself have a slight tendency to spontaneously like good-looking people better? If your honest answer is yes—and it is—this means that you have just explained a large part of our super-sexist woman-objectifying urban landscapes. This small, relatively innocent urge within yourself is what grows through complex interactions and creates a terribly sexist society that nobody wants and many of us are suffering from.

Adam Smith, the father of economics, described "the invisible hand" of the free market, i.e. the emergent property of economic growth and increasing wealth within industrializing open markets. But there is really no reason to assume that the invisible hand only does benevolent things. The moment we look away, it can also subject us to racism, sexism and environmental degradation.

The view from complexity may seem less exiting than images of a villainous patriarchy or the grim towers of capitalism. Somehow, it seems silly to gather in the hundreds and march down the street shouting: "Let's develop our behaviors and slightly tweak the games of everyday life so that we, together, in the long run, produce dramatically better emergent properties!" There's just not that oomph, not that "zing". If you know what I mean.

But here's the deal. The more primitive and stupid your ideas about society, the cruder your "bad-guy theory" will be. To the Nazis, the bad-guys are the Jews, plain and simple. To the nationalist conservatives, the bad-guys are not necessarily Arabs, but certain problematic aspects of their culture and religion. To the modern libertarian, the bad-guys are laziness and lacking sense of responsibility—and all those pesky leftwing control freaks. To the Left it is capitalism. To the critical sociologist it is power structures. To the ecologist it is industrialism and a consumer society disconnected from the ecological systems.

To the metamodernist, there are almost no bad-guys left, nobody and nothing to blame: not even an impersonal structure. With the view from complexity, there is only the painstaking tweaking of many small things that can help us fix the failures of our society and mitigate the tragedies of existence. Fighting the power structures and killing the Jews might be more exciting. But it won't solve our problems, I'm afraid.

Beyond Left and Right, at Long Last

It has become increasingly commonplace in our days to speak of the classical Left-Right scale as outdated, but somehow few people seem to be able to clearly articulate what that means. Sometimes you will hear about an economic scale (high or low redistribution) and a social one (traditional vs. liberal values), a space with four quadrants. Sometimes people will pitch progressiveness against conservativeness—but then in reality the nationalist conservatives often team up with welfare defending left-wingers. Jonathan Haidt shows us how liberal and conservative values seem to match each other and create a sum greater than its parts.[56] Anthony Giddens tried to synthesize Left and Right in order to create a dynamic economy that was able to support progressive welfare and solidarity (Tony Blair's New Labour showed us the results of that—hardly a satisfying radicalization of politics, from a Left perspective).[57] There's also the "fourth political theory" of Alexandr Dugin, which must be described as Russian neo-fascism, but let's not go down that path.

Although there are some merits to each of these developments—perhaps Haidt especially, who looks at how conservative and liberal sentiments create a whole greater than the sum of its parts—I think that none of them fully capture the structure of metamodern politics. None of them sufficiently explicate the philosophical underpinnings and political consequences of an ideology that genuinely lies beyond Left and Right.

On the surface, metamodern politics and the Nordic ideology, with its Green Social Liberalism 2.0 and the vision of the listening society and a vast expansion of welfare into the social-psychological realms of life, might look like a far-left project. And, in many ways, it is. We are, after all, looking to dramatically increase the quality of welfare that each citizen enjoys.

But note that we have not said anything about *how*, through which mechanisms, such a development takes place: by democratically controlled state bureaucracy, by market solutions or the civil sphere (or, more likely, by synergistic development of all three). This is up for discussion and debate—we are not *a priori* defining how such goals must be achieved. We are just noting that there is an undeniably political side to them.

Going "beyond Left and Right" means that we make questions of the relations between public sector, private sector and civil sphere into open discussions where the best empirical arguments for each mechanism, in each case, must be taken into consideration. For instance, do "free markets" work more or less efficiently than state bureaucracies? The answer depends on what area of society we are studying, what values need to be taken into account in our common goals within this area, and what kind of state bureaucracy and how functional a market we have available.

People on the Left tend to believe, irrationally and *a priori*, that democratic control through the public sector is better in and of itself. The Right tends to believe that "the market" (whatever that is taken to mean) is *in and of itself* a more intelligent mechanism than bureaucracy, that it serves a naturally given order, sometimes compared to Darwinian evolution. People of Green (and often anarchist) persuasion often believe that civic, informal and personal relationships are *in and of themselves* kinder, fairer and less oppressive than both markets and bureaucracies.[58]

But once we say these assumptions out loud, they somehow fall flat on the ground. They are revealed for what they really are: prejudices. To *a priori* assume that democratic control through public bureaucracy is more efficient, fair and morally superior to a "free market" solution is simply nonsensical. It is a religious belief in the negative sense of the word. In the future, people will look at these beliefs, being Left or Right, much as we today look at medieval beliefs such as being Christian or Muslim.

These are case sensitive questions. The answers vary. There is no one answer. It all depends on what institutions, levels of psychological development, technologies and information processes we have available—and which area of social life we are discussing. There is nothing irrational or inefficient in the public sphere itself, just as there is nothing inherently rational and right in a "market equilibrium". And there is nothing inherently humane, kind and cozy about the civil sphere.

A large part of this issue is to transcend one's own **political allergies**. Let's try out a few words, allergies of the Left: market, power, capitalism, authority, profit—and of the Right: radical, social, feminism, revolution, public.

If you get a sense of spontaneous disgust or aggression upon reading any of these words, if the word itself comes out on the paper sheet as repulsive, you have a political allergy, hijacking your political mind. One needs to recognize that these are not inherent essences or givens. They can all be good or bad, depending on the context—and more pertinently, they are all good *and* bad. It just makes relatively little sense to "hate" or "be against" such vague and open categories as "the market". It limits your thinking. It makes you dumb.

All of these three systems—democratic bureaucracy, the market and civil sphere—are simply forms of governance that process information about the behavior of humans, coordinating our actions in order to create desirable common and individual results. Each of them has its pathologies, its own sicknesses, its own limitations as well as its own magnificent qualities. There are intelligent and unintelligent markets, intelligent and unintelligent bureaucracies and democratic institutions, and the civil sphere can be equally inclusive as it can be oppressive.

The three systems depend upon one another for their functioning, for their very existence. There are no countries without markets—and no larger markets without regulating states and bureaucracies (as "the father of sociology" Max Weber pointed out). And the civil sphere, in the sense that the great master of German social theory Jürgen Habermas first described it, grows and gains its force as the modern state comes alive. When the modern state is introduced, people have this penetrating, overarching entity that determines much of their lives, which gives us something in common to talk about—in the national news, papers or cafés. And the modern nation state makes it possible for us to have a "personal sphere", where we are expected to keep our own "individual" dreams, close relations and sexualities at some distance from the public and professional realms.[59]

In some important ways, the systems have become more independent from one another under modernity, during the last 200 years or so. As Weber's classical sociology established, the genius of modernity, the spirit of modern society, is its ability to tease out different dimensions of social reality from one another: 1. the rational/scientific objective truth, 2. the subjective/personal aesthetic, and 3. the interpersonal/moral realm.

You can't burn someone at the stake for making a scientific claim anymore. You can have sexual relations without it necessarily having economic implications. You can elect officials based on merits rather than who they are related to or how rich they are (in theory, sigh). You can start a business without it threatening your family relations—and so forth.

The spheres gain a certain form of independence or autonomy. And this is a wondrous thing, really: Fair markets are ideally free from cozy friendships that make for crony capitalism, bureaucracy sees all citizens as equals and should ideally work independently of market interests, and love should ideally be free from power relations and gold-digging.

However, such a teasing out (with a fancier word: *differentiation*) of the different dimensions of social life is never complete. The systems interpenetrate. They continue to affect one another. **When a modern society fails to differentiate these three spheres, this brings all kinds of social diseases**: corruption, favoritism, inequality before the law, misuses of public office, formations of cartels and unfair monopolies, breaches of the personal privacy of people—the list of horrors is endless. Consider what happens if your boss is sleeping with your wife, or the bureaucracy works to help certain ethnicities or clans over others. In modern society we want to be rid of such things. Good riddance.

But the glory of modernity has a dark side: In the meantime we become split up; the same person is a family member, a citizen and a professional. These spheres of life are kept at a certain distance from one another. This is one of the major sources of alienation in modern society. In sociology, this nasty baby goes by many names (all of which catch slightly different meanings): fragmentation, the postmodern condition, the corrosion of character, and so forth.

But society is now shifting past this stage. In our days, democracy, markets and the civil sphere are finding *new* ways of saturating one another. They are being integrated again—not like in traditional society, but in a distinctly postindustrial manner that pertains to the internet age. These new forms of re-integration are not the same as failed differentiations (which causes corruption and the like). The new re-integration is, to some extent, a good thing. If carried out intelligently, it can make us much less split-up, much less alienated. And it can make politics, markets and personal relationships work much more intelligently.

So you need to keep three stages in mind. *One*: markets, politics and personal relations are not clearly differentiated; *two*: in modern society these three spheres gain a great measure of independence from one another; *three*: in metamodern society, these three spheres are being re-integrated, ideally without any one of them dominating or contaminating the other two.

Examples of this re-integration abound. Let's mention just a few: Market mechanisms applied to public sector organization; planning of "triple helix models" for regional economic development (triple helix means collaborations between public, private and university agents in a region); an increasing pressure from civil sphere influence to break the alienating management and bureaucracy of both private corporations and the public sector; and personal relations within professional firms being increasingly honed and invested in. Again, this is a major process of our time. These examples are just a few superficial such changes visible in today's society.

The growing re-integration of these three different spheres of social life—the **civic** (politics, democracy, bureaucracy, public), the **professional** (market exchange) and the **personal** (the civil sphere, family life, communities)—requires of us a kind of political thought that does not take one of the dimensions as fundamental or inherently superior to the other two. We must see the totality of social and political life.

This is what it means to go beyond Left and Right, and this is the philosophy which allows us to update the Nordic ideology into effective metamodern politics. An example of such re-integration is the growing importance of "the fourth sector", consisting of hybrid organizations, public-private initiatives and, above all, of social entrepreneurs—as mentioned, the social entrepreneur being the ideal type person of the new global economy.

At a very trivial level it is of course easy to see how no one political movement or direction can be the eternally "correct" one. Almost nobody would in all seriousness believe that all the Left has done, wanted and thought of during the last century has been good and that all the Right has ever done has been inherently wrong and mistaken. It is simply an untenable position, revealing itself as nonsense the moment it is recognized.

Of course, there has to be some kind of dialogue, competition, development, evolution—or *dialectic*—going on, where different ideas, practices and policies are tested against one another and co-developed in a larger process that no single thinker or movement can fully predict. Even the gravest of mistakes can in retrospect prove valuable. As I have argued, this dialectic development does seem to point in certain directions, as is becoming visible in the Nordic countries. Co-development.

But there really is an underpinning to all of this, a central insight. The philosophical principle of metamodern politics is as simple as it is elegant. This principle holds that social life is of *fractal* nature, and that society consists of three interdependent dimensions that always repeat themselves but ultimately depend on one another: solidarity, trade and competition.

- **Solidarity**—in all societies that have ever existed, there has been cooperation and what the anarchist classic Peter Kropotkin termed "mutual aid". And in all of our lives, there are always at least some aspects of such things as caring, brotherhood, friendship, cooperation, help, charity, alliances, affiliation, liking, love and so forth. The principle is: *you, rather than me.*

- **Trade**—in all societies that have ever existed, and in everyone's life, in every relationship, there is an element of *exchange*: tit for tat, something for something. The principle is: *me and you, but only conditionally.* "Only conditionally" serves to underscore that we only make trade transactions if there is something for us to gain.
- **Competition**—in all societies that have ever existed, and in everyone's life, in every goddamn relationship, there is an element of competition: conflicting interests, power relations, struggle, manipulations, violence, animosity, enmity and so on. The principle is: *me, not you.*

The unstated, irrational belief that people have, is that one of these three dimensions somehow makes up a higher truth than the other two. The Left somehow believes, in a subtle but pervasive manner, that solidarity is the highest truth. The libertarian Right believes that trade is the first principle. The conservative and the fascist believe in their hearts that fierce competition lies beyond the other two, that it ultimately defines social reality.

The metamodern political activist makes no such mistake, has no such prejudices, and recognizes that each of these three beliefs is equally dishonest and violent against the nature of reality. Each of these prejudices comes at a terrible cost in terms of human and animal suffering—we shall return to the topic in the next book, *Nordic Ideology*, when we discuss "game change".

A fractal, as you probably know, means that if you zoom in on one part of its (mathematical) structure, you see that the same function repeats itself, creating self-similar patterns on a new level, even if you zoom in or out a thousand times or more. The fractal applies the same ingredients or principles (a function applied to itself), but it produces ever new results at each level you study. The patterns of each level of zoom are still somehow self-similar, however; you can recognize what kind of fractal you are studying. Instead of having "three dimensions", you can have fractions of dimensions (one-and-a-half dimensions, and so forth); that's where the word "fractal" comes from. You can break up any dimension into smaller parts and see how it repeats itself. You can break up friendship and see how it consists of trade and conflict.

Now look at any relationship, let's stay with a friendship. Does it not contain at least an ounce of competition? Does it not contain trade, an exchange where both parties gain something valuable? In fact, if there is no gain at all for one party, it is difficult to imagine how the friendship could be sustainable. Would a one-sided friendship not amount to exploitation?

And does the definition of a friendship not subtly exclude the non-friend—which again means that it relies upon competition?

Or look at the Second World War; did this major conflict not include incredible sacrifice, love and solidarity—indeed, did it not rely upon these for its existence? Or the very fact that you were born into this world—is it not a violent act, that you have eaten your way through other organic matter, as much as the result of a mating competition and the authentic bond between your parents? Your very body is organic matter under violent control; killed, chewed, digested and brought into new cooperative relations. Recent research has revealed an evolutionary struggle even between the pregnant mother and her fetus—the growing child's evolutionary interests are somewhat different from those of the mother (who may increase the chances of spreading her genes by having more children, and hence not be too drained by this particular fetus). No matter how profoundly symbiotic and loving a relationship, there is an element of struggle.

At its heart, metamodern political thought fully accepts and acknowledges these three dimensions of social life: **solidarity, trade and competition** (and their intertwined, fractal nature). As such, it avoids the self-imposed blind spots of the Left and Right, going beyond them as analytical categories. Being Left or Right becomes merely a matter of taste or preference—just as you can choose to call your god Allah, Brahman, Jehovah, the Pastafari monster or nothing at all.

Once you accept the metamodern fractal perspective, you don't seek to colonize and destroy fundamental and necessary dimensions of social life anymore. You are not, for instance, against enmity and competition. If you try to be "against enmity", you are creating enmity between yourself and others who don't share your view, views that you then by definition seek to conquer and defeat. You see, you cannot escape any of the three dimensions.

So instead, we begin to look for how solidarity, trade and conflict can develop together, into new forms of social life—and indeed, how they *have* developed throughout history. This means that we no longer hate (or romanticize) the state, the market or personal life (with its often irrational and unfair complications). We can no longer believe that one of the categories holds the solutions to the "evil" or "problems" of the other two. We simply begin to grasp social life itself as a dialectical, developmental process, which is at least partly in our hands—and that its categories (state, market, civil sphere) are always slipping, always shifting. They don't have eternal, inherent qualities of good or evil. They don't have essences.

You can play the same game with another, related triad: **equality**, **freedom** and **order**. They sometimes work against one another, sometimes create synergies—but they cannot even *exist* without one another. If you love freedom, you must also see that, at its very core, freedom is born through order and equality, both of which in turn need freedom to exist. Higher degrees of order is often what allows for greater freedom—but only if the order is of a general and abstract form. Simply making people "organized" by having them march together, as in North Korea, hardly makes for a free society. Having functional policing, orderly statistics and revision of public finances, might.

So when you begin to create a Green Social Liberalism 2.0, you use this fractal philosophy in order to go beyond Left, Right and feeble "center" compromises between the two. You look at how the new economy and its political and psychological landscape can take us to a higher equilibrium balance, where society is farther Left, farther Right and much more sustainable than today—how such synergies can become possible.

For that we have to allow our minds to think paradoxical thoughts, make experimental leaps, and dream dangerous dreams.

Non-Linear Politics

Another foundational metamodern principle holds that you must continuously doubt your own ideological position. People are good at reconstructing their past, telling themselves that they always had this or that opinion or worldview. In reality, people are a lot more flexible, adjusting as we go along in order to fit the norms. How on Earth did everyone (at least in the Nordic countries) go from being homophobic to being pro-gay rights in just a few decades? We all neatly and discreetly changed our views when new social pressures arose.

Look very honestly at yourself—how many of your current views did you *really* hold ten years ago? Have you had any new insights, adopted new opinions or taken up any new values? Personally, I have continuously changed throughout my life. Other people, hopefully often (but certainly not always) the ones better informed than myself, have rewritten me and recoded me in a thousand ways—most of which happened outside of my conscious awareness, but not necessarily outside of theirs. And, most likely, the same goes for you.

I have already mentioned the bizarre notion of one ideology or movement or just a relative direction such as "left" or "right" being "the correct one". In retrospect, it is quite obvious that the grinding of different ideas and perspectives against one another has been necessary for today's "correct" opinions to evolve—including the ones that you currently hold to be correct. The dialectic that unfolds through the interactions of different perspectives seems to be an integral and necessary part of each political movement. There can be no Left without a Right. The Left needs the Right, would be impossible without it; it would lose all energy and meaning without this polarity.

To see that perspectives and movements co-evolve doesn't mean that you cannot choose sides. Some people still turn out to be right, and others mistaken. But one group or movement or perspective is never continuously correct in all conceivable ways. The metamodernist can choose sides only from a **transpartisan** position—you understand that there is always a larger process that goes beyond and through your current ideological, partisan position. There is always something to learn from the other parties, even from your most bitter adversary. And your purposes are often best served by using the interplay of different parties and perspectives, rather than by taking one monolithic path.

Now apply this principle of dialectic development to yourself, to your own views and opinions—even your most cherished values. Is it not obvious that, whatever you think and believe today, it cannot be fully correct or acceptable from some future vantage point, where better knowledge is on the table?

Is it not obviously the case, furthermore, that there are other people alive today, most likely in your direct vicinity, who have understandings and perspectives that simply go beyond what you can see at this particular time, perhaps what you will ever be able to grasp—but that you simply fail to recognize it, because of limits inherent to your current perspective?

We are not only speaking of fields of expertise. We can all readily admit that the heart surgeon has skills and understanding that we lack, or that a physicist has insights that would put us to shame were we to discuss how sound waves function. But other than that, we tend to take our more common everyday understanding of reality, ourselves and society as relatively correct.

Looking around us, we see so many other people who harbor obviously false or preposterous ideas and perspectives. If we zoom out for a moment, looking at ourselves from the outside, it suddenly seems highly unlikely that the particular story about reality that this particular person is telling herself—this organism of this particular species, in this particular time, in this particular position in the world, at this particular point of its lifespan—would be especially correct, scientific, ethical, universal and sane.

Indeed, the very fact that we manage to take ourselves this seriously, when we are almost certain to be utterly blind, confused and downright mistaken about so many, so fundamental issues, can only be described as a form of madness. We are all staring at the incomprehensible, absurd mess that is reality—and with the glazed eyes of mad conviction, we somehow manage to believe that we really get it. Preposterous, really.

Socrates, as you know, taught that the wisest of the Greeks is he who realizes that he knows nothing (which was himself, by the way). There are Chinese proverbs and Confucian teachings to the same effect. Socratic unknowing saturates the metamodern understanding of politics. This principle necessitates a certain approach to all matters social and political: **the non-linear process**.

The simplest definition of a non-linear system is that the output (outcome) is disproportional to the input (the effort made). More money doesn't have to mean less poverty. Longer education does not have to mean higher understanding. Less regulation does not have to mean greater freedom. Social problems don't necessarily shrink in proportion to social expenditure. Higher rates of immigration do not necessarily translate to greater cosmopolitanism and global solidarity. And so on.

A cute way of saying this, that a lot of people like, is that both the mind and society are *ecosystems*. They self-regulate, self-reproduce, keep up a certain "homeostasis" for periods of time, and then they either develop or crash through crisis. "Crisis" occurs when some variables are jacked up on self-strengthening feedback cycles and run off the charts in "far from equilibrium states". Because it's a very widely discussed concept that you can find in any source about chaos and complexity, I'll refrain from delving deeper into the discussion here. The point is that the ecosystem as a whole develops as a result of many autonomous parts that both compete and cooperate in complex (indeed, as I have said, *fractal*) ways. So if you think that foxes are bad and pigeons good, and the world just needs us to kill the fox and breed the pigeon, you are very likely mistaken. Society's political thought and our political agency are like developing ecosystems.

Given that we are dealing with a social reality under development—of which we ourselves form an integral part—we must take into account that the very nature of our understanding changes as we go along. **So our**

goals and efforts evolve; they always turn out to be something different than we initially think.

This is why we need to engage in **non-linear politics**. Even if this is a truism and sounds trivial when you say it, the point is certainly not self-evident or superfluous. People have a strong propensity towards linear thinking. Non-linear thinking often befuddles us; it just seems counter-intuitive. But our intuitions betray us. Without noticing it, we continuously and repeatedly squeeze non-linear phenomena into linear models that our minds are more comfortable with—a kind of analytical violence stemming from the crudeness and developmental simplicity of our minds.

The cardinal of all such linear models in politics the belief that "if only people were like me, had my opinions, the world would be alright". This is the point zero of political understanding. If you have this feeling, you know nothing.

The point is that everybody already *is* like you—a very limited, vulnerable, hurt, single human being with almost infinite distortions and blind spots, working from within the narrow frames of her emotions, intellect and experience. And that is exactly why the world is a complete, utter mess. And because the world is a mess, you are a mess. You cannot trust yourself and your current conceptions and ideas.

What then, *can* we trust? We can—or, at least, we have to—trust the processes that come out of our communication with one another, given that such processes are fair, open, without excessive emotional pressures and are conducted in a shared language. We must trust that if enough people break their ideas and emotional investments against one another, on average, and over time, something better (authentic, resilient, sustainable) can come out of it.[60]

In other words, we can partake in *non-linear politics*, where we simply know that whatever we think we are working for is going to turn out to be something entirely different and that we are going to need the best possible democratic processes for this dialectic to play out successfully.

So in metamodern, non-linear politics we don't work according to a certain plan going from A to B, but we see the larger, deeper structures of an evolving global society and we play the game of life in accordance with the long-term trends of that picture, in order to increase the likelihood of certain desirable events to occur. Metamodern activists relentlessly make naive efforts to do great things, things that are unlikely to occur at each attempt, but almost certain to occur in the long run, somewhere, somehow. This may feel a little bit pathetic and embarrassing at times. But it is a simple fact that the play-it-safes, in their villas, are not going to change the world. People who make repeated efforts at great things, working with good roadmaps, will.

The more correct, abstract and complex your map of reality, the greater non-linearity you can afford in your thinking and agency, since you hook up with deeper and more universal structures of how society is evolving. That is how it works: The Heracles, Prometheus or Achilles of our age is whoever can think the most abstractly and act the most non-linearly—those who can live with and skillfully handle uncertainty and not be paralyzed by it. To do so, one must manage to stay determined even when the expected paths and results are largely unknown.

The non-linear stance is needed all the more today, given how complex global society is becoming, how difficult it is to predict each specific event. That being said, we still need a sense of direction. So we go ahead to sincerely building a listening society, a deeper kind of welfare, a new kind of politics and economy. We go ahead with informed naivety, with an ironic smile at our own self-importance.

Liberal Innocence Lost

On a last note of this first part of the book, I would like to clarify something that has been mentioned and hinted towards, but not yet clearly stated.

Metamodern political thinking constitutes a breach with liberalism and liberal democracy as we know them. We can no longer take the stance of **the liberal innocent**. It is this innocent that has to die. We must hereby issue a *fatwa*; shoot on sight.

The liberal innocent holds a few deeply seated beliefs that hail from the modern, industrial view of life, existence and society—beliefs that I contend are outdated and increasingly harmful.

The first such belief is that one can hold a "pure" or "correct" ideological position within a parliamentarian party system; that one can be "on the right side" of things, the Left, the Right or something similar. But this is increasingly becoming an untenable position. As I have argued, liberal democracy *cancels itself* the same moment as its ideals are approached.

Liberal democracy cancelling itself? Let's take a little detour to again examine what I mean when I say that. This is a difficult, abstract part of the argument, so you might have to make an effort. Here goes: the death of the liberal innocent.

The ideals of liberal democracy are formed around the notion of the educated "concerned citizen" (an ideal showing up from Alexis de Tocqueville to John Dewey and George Herbert Mead through Paolo Freire's radical pedagogy of the sixties to Jürgen Habermas and other leading theorists of democracy). This informed citizen must be able to take on a general perspective of society and deliberate with others, as equals, about the common good.

In reality, liberal democracy in industrial society has been a party-political trench war between working class (worker, employee) and bourgeois (industry, professional, consumer, share owner) interests. Industrial society, its classes and categories, has spliced aspects of us into different shards, from which political identities have been formed. From these different identities we could then form parties and belief systems about what modern life is and should be.

Liberal democracy works as a power balance between these different aspects of ourselves, as a dialectical process resulting from the interaction of different ideas—ideas that by themselves are partial and largely mistaken, but that together form a dynamic process that we know as the liberal, democratic market economy with public welfare (leading up to Green Social Liberalism). It never actually worked through the "informed citizen" and certainly not the "public intellectual". The ideological positions, Left and Right, were false all along. **What we hailed as liberal democracy was never based on deliberation about the common good, but rather on the dialectic between conflicting interests, checked in a dynamic power balance.**

It is only when industrial society fully blooms into postindustrial society (and education levels rise dramatically and class distinctions and the categories of class become blurred), that liberal democracy begins to live up to its own mythos as a deliberation between equal citizens. In such societies we begin to observe a situation in which arguments and reasoning of informed citizens actually *do* matter. This is what pushes us towards "the Nordic ideology" and its more self-consciously deliberative co-development.

It is a popular sentiment that democracy has lost its vitality these days. Political scientists in country after country show appalling research results—the younger generation would sell their votes, don't care about democracy, and would even support dictators. But that democracy is losing ground is a superficial analysis, an illusion. Truth be told, democracy (as the rule of informed, deliberating citizens) is only becoming real once society develops past the trench wars of industrial class parties. Before that, we never had democracy in any deeper, qualitative sense anyway. The whole system was built around the fact that our interests were at odds. You couldn't actually unite "the people" or "let the people rule".

Exclamations such as "United and free" (Soviet anthem) or "In the name of democracy, let us all unite!" (Charlie Chaplin in *The Great Dictator*) remain oxymorons, self-contradiction. Democracy and freedom, as we have known them thus far, are born from the very fact that we are and remain largely divided into the classes of industrial society, nationally and globally.

It is because the social categories of modern, industrial society are losing their relevance, that we suddenly land in a much more interesting position—one in which it is hard to know what my own interests are, long-term or short-term, let alone tell your interests apart from mine. **The *divisions*, not the unity, that made possible the party system we know as "liberal democracy", are breaking down.** So when democracy begins to fulfill its promise of a people ruling itself through deliberation—it ironically wrecks the whole game that we know as party politics, around which our democratic system is built, because the necessary party division interests break down. By its dialectic development, by the logic of its own productive contradictions, liberal democracy cancels itself.

In this strange new state of affairs we have every reason to engage in an open-ended, democratic dialogue and deliberation with one another—to do "real" democracy, more according to the classical and Habermasian ideals. But the system of governance is still running on the engine of a modern, industrial society. This is where the frustrations and disappointments with the ongoing political debate are coming from: People are recognizing that the boxing matches between Left and Right are increasingly devoid of substance. We begin to long for a real, honest talk about society and the future. But we find ourselves unable of speaking and listening, these being a much more difficult tasks than we imagined.

When you take up that thread, when you begin to deliberate about the evolution of society as a whole, you must admit that your own position on an ideological scale must always be partial, inherently harmful and limited in some respects.

Liberal democracy begins to reveal that it never worked in the first place. The different positions we are offered within its game of party politics no longer make any deeper sense.

That is—you can no longer be innocently Left or Right, no longer believe that you're the good guy and that the other positions are false, because it is becoming apparent that the real action happens in the honest deliberation between your position and theirs.

You can no longer believe that you are the libertarian defender of freedom, up against the odds with so many nasty control freaks of the Left and conservatives. You can no longer be the defender of the poor against the high bosses of neoliberalism and capital. You can no longer be the upstanding citizen, reacting against multiculturalism and relativist degeneracy, no longer a Green environmentalist reacting against the excesses of industrial society.

All these positions still believe in those little shards that were one part of the greater whole. Once you see the larger process and identify with the dialectic of society as a whole, each of these positions is revealed as a partial, silly belief, a childish dream.

There is something endearing, almost cute, about being so blinded by the current forms of liberal democracy, that you think that you can take one position within it, and it just so happens to be the right one. It is *innocent*, in a way. It is very much like when people in pre-modern times used to believe in Jesus or Mohammed just because they happened to be born on opposite sides of the Mediterranean; the highest cosmic truth was in all seriousness believed to be determined by flukes of geography. **Modern people are "religious" in a corresponding way; they believe that the people born and raised in their position in society have the "correct" beliefs and values**; that the truth is somehow dependent on where you are situated on a sociological map.

Once you adopt the metamodern perspective on politics, you lose that innocence. You become *secular* in a more profound and systematic way. The modern worldviews, such as those of libertarians or socialists, appear as irrational as Kali, goddess of creation, with blue skin and four arms.

You realize that there is no "safe" political position. Whatever position you take, it will work its non-linear way through reality and sneak off to murder, torture, maim, destroy, exploit, defeat others, deprive others of their meaning making, and press itself upon social and political reality. The truth is that you don't have the truth; that you never will. And even if you turn out to be right about something, there will always be a time when your opinion is outdated or at least incomplete. Whatever direction you move in, it will lead to contradiction, self-destruction and decay, sooner or later. **Your perspective or opinion always has a systemic limit, a breaking point; it always breaks down under its own weight, just like any engine, organism or economic system.** You never get to be the good guy in the end. You are not innocent.

And that leads us to a second, even deeper, belief of the liberal innocent: That you can choose not to act, and just be a normal citizen, and that you are thereby innocent. The belief holds that, if you "don't want to control others" and "just live your life", you are innocent; that only the politicians, reformists and dictators bear the true responsibility.

But you are society as a whole, more than Louis XIV, the Sun King, ever was the state (the one who said *l'état, c'est moi*). Society is you—Left and Right, up and down. There is no "default position" to which you can revert, no way of "just being normal". Ours is a meat-eating, animal-exploiting, cruel, capitalist, alienating, unfair, oppressive, unscientific, undemocratic, unsustainable society. If you partake in it, you are complicit in its crimes, mistakes and vices.

And if you tolerate this, your children will be next. When I make suggestions about how to improve society, and you say no, but offer nothing in return, you are not being innocent, a liberal defender of freedom—you are killing children and burying them in invisible graves. When you call yourself an anarchist, an environmentalist, an anti-capitalist or just an honest working citizen, you are not pure, not taking the "right path" and leaving it to others to mess up the world. You are hiding behind a small shard of the totality of human existence and failing to take responsibility.

Third and last. Once you see, with a transpersonal perspective, that you *are* the whole process of evolving language games, that you *are* the polarities and dynamics of the social and political developments, you also recognize that all of your positions, all of your opinions, all of your choices, *both* do good *and* cause harm. You are causing harm, doctor. You are causing harm.

If you, like me, are against animal exploitation, you are also saying that you want to denigrate the social status and livelihood of millions of human beings, the honest folks working for generations with animal husbandry. Yes, I admit it. I would destroy their lives for the greater good of all sentient beings, if that's what it takes.

If you, like me, tend towards liberal stances on narcotics, you are also saying that you would cause many young, innocent people to suffer irreparable psychiatric harm, let them live through unimaginable hells, in order for humanity to stop the global terrorism, civil wars, criminality and prison-industrial excesses emanating from drug bans. Yes, I admit it; I will cause them harm.[61]

It is a question of choosing totality over partiality. Partiality is only possible if you believe in the liberal innocent. **Once you choose totality, once you begin to see society as a whole, liberal innocence is lost.**

The universe seems to have presented us with a mean, ironic twist: Any true freedom, revolution or open horizon is simultaneously a call to power, a crown to grasp, an adversary to conquer. Even the most heart-warming idealism, be it feminism, peace work or abolitionist animal rights, must act violently to create new hierarchies, new winners and losers. In that violent act, we can never know for certain if we are good or evil; an inconvenient truth if there ever was one. We only know that if we choose innocence, we have chosen evil.

When we identify with ideas, ideals and deeper political movements, we are also challenging other patterns of thought, other "memes". The metamodern thinker and activist challenges modern society. This is not revolution on the barricades, and no harm needs to come to human bodies. But people are deeply invested in their ideas and worldviews. To challenge their ways of thinking and sensing is also an act of cruelty and aggression; shattering people's beliefs, their sense of security, self, ethics and reality. Nothing could be less innocent.

But the gods of modernity are false idols—the individual self, liberal democracy, liberal innocence, Left and Right, humanism, rationality (and "free will"), scientism, many forms of linear causation and to some extent even equality (as the following chapters reveal) are all outdated ideas. In the information age, and the new life conditions it brings, these golden calves must be rejected—even at great cost. We must discipline ourselves to be temple thieves; to pillage and desecrate the symbols of modern society.

So while bodies are spared, and no physical violence is needed, the souls of our fellow human beings do not go unharmed. As we build a program to develop a metamodern society, we must crush the resistance that the defenders of liberal democracy muster, applying just the right balance of ruse and tenderness, guns and roses.

The modern worldview is ridden with inherent self-contradictions, with analytical dead-ends that cause intolerable suffering and are likely to eventually lead to the collapse of civilization. Against these dead-end brick walls of contradiction we must round up the ideas of modern life, the dearly held beliefs of people we love and care about, and execute them in the name of the revolution.

When analytical rifles shoot ideas, they also shoot the human souls that worship them. We are attacking your time, your society and your way of life. Let the mass killings of liberal innocents begin.[62]

PART TWO

Psychological Development

Chapter 7

ON STAGE THEORIES

Okay, so before we go on, you should know that stage-based adult development theory puts your mind on crack. Developmental theory of this kind is incredibly useful, but equally seductive, and it can lead to pretty grave delusions and downright arrogant and nasty attitudes or behaviors if you are not careful. Not the cute kind of nasty like the literary excesses of Hanzi Freinacht, but the bad kind of nasty.

Poorly constructed or misinterpreted developmental theories have been used for all manner of oppression, the formation of sects, and worse. A likely hypothesis to account for this would be that our brains are wired with powerful reward and punishment responses for knowing "who's who": Am I above you or below you? Is this or that person important? This leaves us vulnerable to bad developmental stage theories—or perverted uses of good ones.

Once you learn this stuff and it "clicks" for you, you may never see the world, or the people in it, in quite the same way. If you think the next few chapters are obvious or trivial, rest assured, it hasn't clicked. This goes for people acquainted with adult development too, since I am not only introducing the field—I am redefining it.

But just to make sure you want to do this—you may want to stop reading the book here. After all, you got some rough basics in the first part of this book, and maybe that's more than enough for you. And in that case, it's okay. Stop here, put down the book, and don't go any farther. Boundaries, respect.

It's alright, and there is nothing wrong with you if you choose to stop at this point. This isn't therapy, after all, and it's not necessarily nice or healthy. I am not just doing reverse psychology; you might *actually* want to stop here. Real philosophy is a chainsaw up your guts. And in this book, we are chainsawing the world-soul like it's Friday the 13th.

Still reading? Okay. Remember—you can just stop later for any reason; *you* are doing this reading. No hard feelings.

After this introductory chapter, the following ten chapters present a comprehensive developmental theory of human beings, focusing on adult development and its main dimensions.

- The next two chapters are on cognitive development ("smarts");
- chapters 10 and 11 are on what I call "coding" or "symbolic toolkit" ("learning");
- chapters 12 and 13 are on lived or experienced "states" ("wellbeing");
- chapters 14 and 15 are on "existential depth" ("wisdom"); and
- chapters 16 and 17 put these pieces together into the political-psychological concept of the "effective value meme" (a kind of average value of the other forms of development).

But before we dig into cognitive development, let's discuss developmental theory a little more generally. Why is it important? And is it really okay to study stages of human development in the first place?

In this chapter we talk *about* stage theories—but we won't really describe any of them, or get to know the stages. Patience, *padawan*, we'll get there.

And yes, you will get enough information to deduce your own stage, as well as the stages of people you know, your family, work environment and social groups in society—and yes, if you are reading and understanding this, you are probably at a higher stage than most, including this and that person that you find too simpleminded and annoying (often your boss). But let's not rush things. And remember, stage is not everything; it's just useful theory.

Unintelligent people don't like theory. They don't understand that the word theory just means "seeing", and that without it you miss out on seeing vital aspects of reality. Don't be like that. Theoreticians built this world; the rest of y'all just live in it.

A Missing Piece of the Puzzle

Want to know the reason why moral philosophy almost never makes a difference, why most academic moral philosophers remain rather useless? After all, we are obliged to ask: Why don't they manage talking people into being vegans, selling their cars and giving away more of their money to charity, and being more selfless generally? Or even getting us to do what makes us happy either way, according to happiness research (give away your stuff, exercise, do mindfulness, eat healthy, walk in nature, don't stress, have more sex and care about others)? A moral philosopher can still help us come to the right conclusions, given we agree on the premises, but they seldom seem to drive the ethical development of society.

It's because they don't have their behavioral science and psychology straight. They don't understand that humans are, in a manner of speaking, behavioral robots.

Of course, we're not robots in the sense that we don't have real feelings, thoughts and sensations. And the robot metaphor should not blind us to the depths and rich ecologies of our co-evolving minds and emotions. However, it does underscore the very hard facts of behavioral science. We are not free and rational individuals who you can just talk into one rational conclusion or another, thereby dramatically altering our social values and behaviors. For any moral philosophy, you must consider who, when, what and where: Are we talking about children, or cats, or mice, or educated people, or rich people, or scared people, or mentally disabled people, in Denmark or Saudi Arabia? Such questions generally fall into the background of humanist, analytical philosophy—and, unfortunately, of continental philosophy as well. There is no "default human" from which moral philosophy can start.

One of the most important aspects of understanding behavior, human or animal, instrumental or moral, and what can reasonably be expected from an organism, is the overall **developmental stage** of that organism. That's where developmental psychology comes in handy—and, in particular, the stages of adult development. As I mentioned in the introduction to this book, before a person understands this part, they tend to have great trouble grasping what metamodern politics is.

A good behavioral and developmental psychology, one that recognizes the stages of human beings, is the missing piece of the puzzle for us to make society more rational and ethical.

In Defense of Hierarchies among Humans

Developmental stage, aye? But who is to say that someone or something is of a "higher" or "more advanced" stage of development? Maybe ants are more advanced than people, just in ways we wouldn't think of? Children towering far above their parents in their intensively alive experience of the human condition? The Jarawa tribes folk of the Andaman Islands leading lives far beyond anything a modern professor in Mexico or China could ever imagine?

But development *does* matter, and it *can* be studied in coherent and reliable ways. **The terrible truth is this: Adult human beings are not**

equals. We are as different from one another as adults from children, albeit in various ways and in different regards.

This is a trivial point when it comes to single skills: I have friends who lift more than four times what I can on the bench press, some who read at more than three times my speed, some that speak twice as many languages, some that know more medicine than I could dream of, some that have much, much higher IQ, some that are much better at making money (and can easily make a dozen times or more than me in a given period), some who write books at five times my speed (I kid you not) and so on.

There is no reason to believe that we do not *also* vary greatly in terms of overall developmental stages (the four dimensions being *cognitive development*, *cultural coding*, *state* and *depth*, as we will discuss).

And this makes all the difference when it comes to understanding politics and society, even personal relationships. This scientifically uncontroversial—but politically very sensitive—insight is central to understanding behavior. Understanding the developmental stages of humans is mandatory for all who seek to change and develop society. Without the insight that humans can be described with subsequently unfolding developmental stages, you are driving in **developmental blindness**. It's worse than drunk driving. And it kills or harms considerably more people, literally speaking.

So in this second part of the book we work through ten chapters discussing what personal, psychological development can mean. The bogeyman here is of course the H-word. We've addressed it before, briefly, but now we must stop to face it full frontal.

Hierarchy. We are introducing hierarchy into the study of human beings; scientifically supported and enduring—but not immutable—hierarchy. Some people are just much more developed, more evolved, than others. Ouch.

> "Introduce hierarchy! Who would do such a thing? And why? Is it not a pretext for claiming that some people should be put above and beyond others, some unfair privileges unduly legitimized? After all, we are still working hard all over the world to get rid of the postcolonial heritage, of male privilege, white privilege, Eurocentrism, the exploitation of the global South, discrimination against animals, anthropocentrism in relation to the rest of the biosphere and the many hidden injuries of class! And you want to discuss *hierarchy*? What demonic purpose would possess you to invoke such *forbidden phantoms*™? I forbid it! Do not venture into this research of adult development! Do not go there to see with your own eyes! In the name of equality, choose ignorance! Do not ask forbidden questions!"

You are correct, dear reader. This can be bad news. And it's even worse than that. Once we open the Pandora's Box of hierarchy—who knows what might come out of it? New sources of neurotic self-blame? New ideologies of domination? Exploitation under the auspices of scientific legitimacy? Eugenics? A new class society, like the one in Aldous Huxley's *Brave New World*, where the population is divided into bio-engineered castes? Shiver me timbers.

Despite these risks, all of which I fully acknowledge, I am convinced that we are better off with a sound developmental stage perspective than without one. And to study development, we must admit that there *are* hierarchies—that some opinions, behaviors or psyches are, at least in some sense, more developed. It is possible to take this stance without being an asshole.

The risks associated with developmental blindness are simply so much greater, the consequences so much more harmful. I contend, without blinking, that an understanding of the stages of human development is key to emancipation, to freedom and equality in the globalized internet age. In this strange new wonderland, the developmentally blind become the oppressors, much like Christianity went from being a liberating force to having its own landed elites and an inquisition. **A progressive thinker and activist of today must know and accept hierarchy**; a rebel heart must love hierarchical development—and use it, against all masters, against all unjust hierarchies, and against the chaos and entropy inherent to the cosmos.

Wait a minute; I don't think you heard me. Didn't I say it slowly, didn't I make it clear? I am saying that if you *fail* to understand hierarchies and human development, you end up being primitive, conservative and oppressive. *You*, not I, are the oppressor. *You* speak the language of opp-ression.

Let me explain some important principles to clarify this. Being pro hierarchy only makes progressive sense if you meticulously apply these eight principles. So here's a user's guide.

The Hitchhiker's Guide to Hierarchy

1. Non-judgment. The first principle is that stages of development in humans and other organisms must be studied in the light of a *radical acceptance*, a pervasive *non-judgment*—much like Christianity (in its liberating forms) teaches, really. Every creature has an inalienable right to be who she is, even the least likable among us. So whenever you see farther than someone else, whenever you are more ethical or intelligent or sensitive, you are manifesting a privilege over that creature. The reason that she is not like you is that you are more privileged, at least in that particular regard. Even things you learned through suffering, and insights or capabilities that are painful to bear, in some sense put you at an advantage. When you acknowledge this hierarchy, you are no longer judging. The perspective shifts from judging people for not being like us (damning all who are racist, not socialist, uneducated, not environmentally minded, not sensitive, not good listeners, etc.), to trying to give a universal account for why our own position is better than theirs (why it would trump their position on their own terms) and explaining why the same insight or capability is not available to them at this time. Such explanations can be: it's just a kid, he didn't have the chance to learn this, she wasn't allowed the peace of mind to think this through, he's in a too precarious position to allow himself to think along these lines—etc. In this way, the acceptance of hierarchy serves non-judgment and forgiveness.

2. Not a moral order. The second principle is that the developmental stages do *not constitute a moral order*, in which a higher or later stage would be morally "more worth" than a lower or earlier one. For instance, as we will see in the next chapter, kids generally are of lower cognitive stage than adults—but they of course have the same priceless value. And they can often be kinder and "better people" than adults, more honest, empathetic, etc. The jury is still out on who should count as morally valuable or not, but a good starting point might still be Jeremy Bentham's old "...the question is not, Can they reason? nor, Can they talk? but, Can they suffer?".[63]

3. Natural and dominator hierarchies. The third principle is that there is a difference between *natural hierarchies* and *dominator hierarchies*. Dominator hierarchies are the ones that you cannot find any universal arguments for and that are used to legitimize exploitation: men over women, whites over non-whites, H&M (the clothing store) customers and stock owners over Bangladeshi sweatshop workers, humans over non-human animals, nobility over commoners, masters over slaves. Natural hierarchies are different—no exploitation is inherent to the hierarchy; it builds on a universal argument that benefits all parties, and it is limited to the specific area in which that benefit can be argued for. Examples: student driver and driving instructor (probably the clearest and best example), child and parent, patient and doctor, pupil and teacher. Of course, each of these natural hierarchies can be misused, the power imbalance exploited for other purposes (if the doctor wants sex for medicine, etc.)—but that is not in itself inherent to the definition of the hierarchy. Developmental hierarchies can, if used correctly, support such natural hierarchies. Remember, however: All dominator hierarchies disguise themselves as natural ones, to make them appear as "the triple-N" of all hidden oppression: Natural, Normal, Necessary.[64]

4. Does not transmit. The fourth principle is that the hierarchy *does not transmit* to other, irrelevant areas or power relations. They should not give "halo effects". For instance, that you are at a higher cognitive stage than me, doesn't mean you should get lower taxes or sleep with my wife. Also, I can still be a much better figure skater, listener or mathematician than you are, even if you are able to think more complex thoughts—in which case I still deserve recognition for my talents. Developmental stage is not the same as skill.

5. Humility. The fifth principle is *humility*. Hierarchical models with several stages are more humble, not less, than non-hierarchical visions of reality. Let's say for instance that you, giving yourself medals for being noble defender of plurality and equality, are "against" hierarchical stage models in science and humanities. You are thereby in effect creating a hierarchy yourself: The people who have your opinion are placed "above" the people who don't—it's better to be against hierarchy than to be for it, right? The very preference creates a two-step hierarchy, in a sense. By doing that you just made several moves that are anything but humble. To start with, you are reducing the richness of possible answers to just your own position "and all others". This means that you are squeezing together many, perhaps very qualitatively different, answers and labeling them under one category (the non-correct one). There is just your way or the highway, and no internal ranking is possible between all the other possible answers. You are also precluding all possibilities of there being stages *above* your own—because there only are two stages, and you're already at the higher one. So you don't need to learn from others, right? But hierarchical stage models that have more stages don't allow for these mistakes: You are obliged to describe all the relevant stages, how they relate to one another, and you must always admit that there can be higher stages than your own, stages that you don't yet understand. Rather counter--intuitively, hierarchy, understood correctly, serves openness and humility towards the perspectives of others.[65]

6. Different dimensions. The sixth principle is simply to know that hierarchical stage theories of human development have *different dimensions* and that development in one dimension does not necessarily translate into development within another. The dimensions do interact, however—as we shall see in the coming chapters. In fact, you will find, the development of one dimension can possibly even hamper development in another dimension.

7. Sensitivity. The seventh principle is *sensitivity*. One must recognize that all hierarchies can and do hurt people's feelings. After all, nobody likes continuously being picked last for the football team. And when you reveal enduring, deep-seated developmental structures that describe vast, qualitative differences between real people, it tends to make some feel elated and others degraded—most of us are, after all, not at the highest stages of human development. That somebody is at a "higher stage" than me, somehow tends to hurt more than the fact that someone has higher grades, has higher IQ, or lifts heavier weights. Developmental hierarchies are just an extremely sensitive topic. What does it feel like to recognize that someone I know genuinely understands deeper aspects of reality than I do? Or that I am less morally developed than another person, a person who adheres to values and ideals that are lost on me? That my mind is more or less permanently incapable of doing what you do routinely? It hurts, quite simply. Maybe not if I think of Einstein at great distance, but if I realize that this younger, junior colleague is hierarchically above me, and that the distance is qualitative and permanent, it tends to really hurt in soft places deep within. So—to deal with these issues, we have to be very emotionally sensitive to everyone involved. The sensitivity of this topic is probably, by the way, the main reason that this field of research hasn't gone farther: Nobody wants to be an insensitive prick.

8. Not all there is. The eighth and last principle is that stages of development are important, but they are obviously *not all there is* to life, knowledge, talent and meaning, and so they should only be treated as useful psychological tools, never be revered as anything more than that. Just as you can be blind by not understanding the stages of human development, so you can be blinded by staring too much at them. Like the sun, really: Without it, you walk in darkness—but if you keep staring at it all day, you also go blind. It's when the sun shines on other things that you see them more clearly.

So you need to remember these eight principles for hierarchy to make sense in a progressive, egalitarian manner. But all in all—*not* understanding the hierarchical stages of human development leaves you more judgmental, more prejudiced, more arrogantly narrow-minded, less competent to understand and empathize with others, and less likely to successfully interpret and predict behaviors (and the events in society). And in order to understand the stages of human development you must admit that they are, at least in some ways, hierarchically ordered. Thus, dealing with hierarchy is not a "necessary evil"; no, it is simply an evil to refuse. Hierarchy, correctly understood, serves the greater good. Again, this only holds true, of course, if we follow the eight principles outlined above. Otherwise we can end up legitimizing dominator hierarchies, contributing to oppression of all sorts.

The point is not to obsess about hierarchy. The point is that if you see hierarchies clearly and don't imbue them with emotional value, you can relate to them in a more rational and detached manner. There is no need to pretend that we are the driving instructor when we are the student driver—and both parties benefit. The aim here is of course to create a more equal and egalitarian society, where hierarchy matters less, and only in ways that make sense.

If you still don't like where this is going, I think your heart will soften once you—after the next ten chapters—see the direction in which the hierarchical development goes: towards greater inclusivity, understanding and acceptance of others and towards challenging one's own certainty.

Introducing Adult Development

Studying the field of adult development can mean a few different things; the field is often tied up with healthy aging and the like. What we mean here is **the study of hierarchically organized stages of psychological development in adult human beings**.

We are looking for clear patterns in the thoughts and behaviors of people—even in our ways of sensing and experiencing the world—and how these patterns tend to evolve under favorable circumstances. What countless researchers have found is that people can shift from one recognizable stage to another, and that this occurs in recognizable sequences.

Proponents of adult development will sometimes introduce the field by asking what happens after someone turns eighteen or twenty: Does all development stop once one is "grown up", or does one continue to "mature", to grow and evolve throughout one's lifetime?

This way of framing it usually wins people's sympathies. Surely I, at fifty-five, must have developed and "matured" since I was eighteen? But unfortunately, there is little reason to be very optimistic about such age-related development. Most people, the vast majority, stall in their (hierarchical stage) development relatively early during adult life. Most of us never experience any profound shifts of worldview or perspective after adolescence, let alone increases in the overall complexity of our thinking and behavior. We go through the *phases* of life in more or less harmonious or tumultuous sequences: love, companionship, work, career, family life, old age—these are best described by the classic psychologist Erik Erikson who identified eight phases from infancy to old age. And in that sense, we all "mature". But such phases should not, under any circumstances, be confused with the developmental stages we are speaking of here.

Stages are different: They represent a logical sequence, where later stages build upon earlier ones; the later stage **transcending and including** the earlier stage. It builds upon the earlier stage, adding something to it. Whereas an Eriksonian phase, like old age, can in theory occur even in a young person who gets terminally ill, or just in a population where the average life span is much shorter—a developmental stage is simply not possible to achieve unless you have passed through the earlier stages (a statement that may warrant some further discussion, stay tuned). You have to learn to count before you can add or subtract—it's just a fact of life. There is a clear *stage* difference between the two.[66]

After infancy, childhood and adolescence (where hierarchical development follows a roughly predictable age pattern), developmental stages should *not* be confused with aging or the number of years you have lived. In that case Jonathan, the Seychelles giant tortoise, hatched in 1832 (the oldest known living animal), would put us all to developmental shame. (Or actually there turned out to be artic sharks that grow much older due to their slow metabolism, but never mind.)

And stage should not be confused with "skills"; the most masterful and silent navigator in the jungle is probably a humming bird, not a human—it is more "skillful", due to its biological properties, its swiftness and humble size, but it is certainly at a lower stage of cognitive and psychological development than any human jungle dwellers.

And, here's another one, psychological stages of development should not be confused with psychologies of "personality". Psychologies of personality are much more well-known, more academically kosher, and more widely taught than the developmental stage theories. Studies of personality were famously used by the early critical social psychologists in attempts to explain authoritarianism and how people would change under consumer capitalism, etc. There are personality tests such as "the big five" (which looks at traits such as extroversion and conscientiousness), the Holland scale for what people find interesting (if you like fixing cars, helping kids or learning science), studies of cultural patterns of personality (such as Hofstede's famous research on different countries' work culture), sibling studies (which more or less lack evidence, apart from small IQ differences) or the tests for different psychopathologies (the psychiatric scales used clinically). But, except perhaps for the psychiatric tests, none of these personality tests have anywhere near the explanatory power and importance as differences in developmental stage—with stage, we're talking ten times stronger correlations or more. Developmental stage explains a lot of why a person acts like she does: her reasoning, morality, aesthetics, leadership style, close relationships, values, income (even more than class background), and much else. Whereas the psychiatric diagnoses are only good at understanding behaviors in a smaller part of the population (those who have the diagnoses), the stage theories help us understand "normal" behavior in society at large. Please remember, stage is something other than personality.

And—perhaps the easiest trap to fall into—stage development should not be confused with "healthy" psychological development, which is usually what is studied under the headline of "developmental psychology" (if someone has healthy emotional attachment patterns, positive self-image, has dealt with her traumas and whatnot). It is perfectly possible to have a healthy low-stage two-year-old (or a psychologically healthy 184 year old turtle, for that matter) and a psychologically messed up high-stage adult human being. But note that lower stage doesn't guarantee psychological health, either; we've all met a crazy cat at some point. There is all the reason to believe, however, that the development of a human's psychological health may interact in complex ways with her development into higher stages. Usually this means that a healthy, not too painful, psychological development supports higher stages of development, but not always. Psychopathologies (mental imbalances or sicknesses) of different kinds can also *spur* psychological development, either by causing discomfort and thereby making us work harder to challenge our current equilibrium—or simply by removing some psychological property that would otherwise have been an obstacle to our growth. For instance, if you have almost no sense of shame, you may not be psychologically "normal", which causes you to seem "weird", but this may in turn allow you to make unique experiences and to act with little inhibition—thereby spiking your learning curve and helping you achieve higher stages of development.

And, again, developmental stage is *not* the Eriksonian life phase, in which case the most highly developed people would be found in retirement homes. A romantic and appealing idea, but it's simply not the case.

So what is "a stage" anyway? **It is *an equilibrium* at a certain degree of complexity, a form of self-supporting balance within your mind, brain,**

organism—located within an open system of continuously ongoing interactions with the environment. It is the pattern of a self-perpetuating feedback cycle in the organism, a pattern supported by the environment. The living organism is always in a kind of flow, a whirlwind working its way through new matter (metabolism), new impressions, new actions and interactions. And this flow always follows a pattern according to the developmental stage of the organism. Examples, please.

Look at a three-year-old and a (normally developed) eighteen-year-old. There is a *qualitative* difference between the two organisms. The three-year-old will consistently produce behaviors that are different from those of the young adult—we're not just talking physiological differences, like size, teeth and sexual maturity. The teenager has better chances of replicating the behaviors of the small child than vice versa and she can produce a range of behaviors and thoughts that may be replicable by her classmates but not by the three-year-old (such as playing the guitar or solving equations at math class). Every day, from the moment they wake up in the morning, the three-year-old and the eighteen-year-old will continuously reproduce equilibria that set them apart. This goes on until some dramatic shift occurs in the three-year-old, who then quickly shifts from one stage to another—and some of the gap closes.

Twenty years later, one is 23 and the other 38. Let's now assume that the younger one has had a much better upbringing, education, health and also has a better genetic makeup for being intelligent ("high cognitive stage"). They both live in the same modern society—but the younger one may now have achieved much more advanced ways of reasoning, partaking in more complex behaviors—and perhaps even be more emotionally mature and existentially profound—than her older fellow citizen. It's not that the older one has had an awful time or anything, everything has been going on "as usual" for the last two decades, and so she hasn't really gone through any fundamental changes. She is at the same equilibrium as she was two decades ago, whereas the 23-year-old has gone through profound changes time and again. The system of thoughts and behaviors has been shocked, both by biological changes and new environments, and major developmental leaps have been made. **Changes of stage usually happen in relatively short leaps that bridge more stable and longer periods of equilibrium.** But such stage changes are relatively rare in the lives of adult human beings.

Our little kiddo has now advanced to a *higher stage* than her fifteen years older fellow citizen, for instance having acquired philosophical insight, being able to systematically question her own society. But note that the 38-year-old may still be a "better person", being friendlier, more loving, etc. And she may have skills that the 23-year-old lacks, for instance, being a good professional pianist or a skilled doctor. Again, higher or lower stage does not determine such things—even if it does interact with them.

Domain-Specific Developmental Theories

What, then, *does* higher or lower stage determine? It depends a bit. Roughly speaking, there are two main groups of adult development theories: domain-specific theories (one area of life) and "global" theories (the organism as a whole). And in the scientific community, there are currently some unresolved conflicts between and around the two—much of which I try to resolve in the following chapters.

The domain-specific theories study the stage advancement within a certain area of life. The classic example is Lawrence "Larry" Kohlberg's six stages of moral development and reasoning, where, as you may know, people gave different answers to the same moral dilemmas and accounted for their answers in different ways—the answers were interpreted and coded as "preconventional", "conventional" and "postconventional".

Preconventional answers did not yet fully take the norms of society into account (being more of a "selfish" kind), *conventional* answers did—and *postconventional* ones reflected critically upon what people in their surroundings thought of as right and wrong. Kohlberg was a colorful and emotionally complicated genius at Harvard who left behind a rich tradition; his work was foundational but has since been challenged in many ways, notably by Carol Gilligan who claimed that women and men advance through parallel but somewhat different sequences.[67]

Since then, moral reasoning has been considered a "domain" of adult development. But the domain-specific theories have multiplied and taken many forms. There are stages for:

- Leadership styles (Bill Torbert's "action logic", Bill Joiner & Stephen Joseph's "leadership agility", Jonathan Reims);
- Religious faith (James H. Fowler, James Meredith Day);
- Teaching styles and academic learning (Erik Jan van Rossum & Rebecca Hamers);
- Critical thinking (Patricia King & Karen Kitchener);
- Psychotherapy (Michael Basseches & Michael F. Mascolo);
- Ecological awareness (Sean-Esbjörn Hargens & Michael Zimmerman);

- Governing patterns of organizations (an attempt at corresponding collective theory by Frederic Laloux)...

...and much else. All of these are stage theories in the sense I have described—they don't just describe phases, but a kind of maturity that builds upon itself in a fractal manner that creates a consistent *hierarchical* order. You'll be able to find stage theories about painting, aesthetics, sports, nursing styles, sexuality, masculinity, love relationships, political thinking, mountaineering, conflict resolution, far-sightedness, and more.

Of course, not all of these theories are very good, and not all of them are based on sound empirical analysis. Then again, some of the most empirically researched theories are the most miserable ones. The quality of the theory generally depends on how clever and well-informed the theorist is. But there is a lot of ingenious work here, no doubt about it.

There is a general pattern to all of these stage sequences. They are, to some extent, possible to line up alongside one another and certain comparisons become all but obvious.

The pattern that emerges is that you go from earlier stages with simpler, more black-and-white and mechanical or linear ways of functioning, towards being more self-critical, more nuanced, diverse, and—a recurring theme—towards more *dialectical* forms of thinking and acting. Some developmentalists make it their trademark to talk about how fabulous dialectical thinking is, the kind of thinking pioneered by Hegel and extended by Theodor Adorno, where you become less rigid in your thought structure (much as I have argued in chapter 6).

Another recurring pattern to all of these theories is that you go from focusing on more narrow frameworks (like yourself) towards wider ones (like universal principles, the network of relations you partake in, etc.). This plays out so that the middle stages let you make more and better *differentiations*, where you notice more and more nuances or differences, and the later stages are when you put these new pieces together in new ways, creating more *integrated*, overarching wholes. **You go from simple black-and-white thinking, to complex and nuanced thinking, and from there to finding *new* simplicities in the form of underlying, universal, guiding principles: towards what you might call a "second simplicity".**

And perhaps the most obvious pattern is that these stages follow normal distributions in the populations. There are fewer people at the early stages, more people at the middle stages—and fewer people again at the later stages. This goes for all the areas where you study these stages.

However, although some overall patterns do exist, the boat starts leaking as soon as you try to put the theories together. There is a general problem with comparisons between these different stage theories: to delineate the difference between the "developmental lines". What would be a logical, coherent way of saying which areas of development should constitute a developmental line or "domain" in itself? As it is today, what counts as a line is determined simply by the researchers' choice of subject, which is just silly and *ad hoc*. The consequence of this quickly becomes absurd: Should there be a line for ballet and one for bird-spotting? We end up with theories about learning skills in general. This takes us into the field of more general learning theory (which is also important, but we must leave aside here).[68]

Kurt Fischer's "dynamic skill theory" holds that there are indeed many developmental lines, even thousands of them, and that they develop by interacting with one another as well as competing for attention and time.[69] They unfold as a rich ecology within the mind and body of the person—in a multiplicity of micro-developments. But this proposition doesn't really solve the problem. We still need a developmental line for bird-spotting (silly), and somehow we fail to grasp what might be a good map for the overall stage of an adult human being—a map that we can use for understanding metamodern politics and the overall development of a population.

That's where the global developmental stage theories come in—even Fischer and his colleagues end up presenting an overarching theory of development (developmental "levels"). But let's take a look at some other ones.[70]

"Global" Developmental Stage Theories

But are there really different lines of development in the first place; are there different "domains", that each require their own stages—or is there something more fundamental at play, like the overall, qualitative difference between a three-year-old and an eighteen-year-old; something underlying that would explain the other differences?

The *global* developmental stage theories try to describe the overall development of the person, which is more in line with the purpose of this book. The first philosopher to very explicitly write about such stages of development is Rousseau in *Émile ou De l'education*, published in 1762. In an American context, we might mention the work of James Baldwin—who influenced both of the chief names in educational psychology: Jean Piaget and Lev Vygotsky.

The great classic theorist of "global development" is the Swiss psychologist (and "epistemologist", i.e. theorist of knowledge-making) Jean Piaget, who studied the major stages of how the cognition of children advances until adulthood, identifying four of them.[71] For instance, you begin to recognize yourself in a mirror, or understand that things farther away are not smaller. At each stage, your whole world changes, and you begin to display a host of new behaviors associated with that stage, as you manage to understand that the world around you is not yourself; that things don't revolve around you.

The Piagetian model is generally taught in educational science and psychology, but is often considered to be outdated in mainstream academia—where the early Soviet theorist Lev Vygotsky's ideas of learning as context-bound are more popular (together with other similar ideas, often from the sociology of education). Most scientists are somewhat familiar with Piaget but they generally don't quite recognize his profound importance.

But in the quiet background, Piaget's tradition is alive and kicking—and researchers have been expanding his thinking (or founding other traditions in similar veins).[72] The "global" adult development theorists are the ones that have attempted to see overarching patterns in adult human beings, some of whom are seen as "more developed" than others in a general sense.

Not all "global" theorists can be called "neo-Piagetian", but all have in some way been influenced by his tradition. I would like to mention six such research programs:

- **Robert "Bob" Kegan's** development of self-perception, wherein the sense of "self" is studied in people. People advance towards more abstract ideas of who they "really are" in the higher stages—he uses five stages and has good data for it. Each stage gains the ability to reflect critically upon the earlier stage, how they used to see themselves. Only older people, in their fifties and older, are thought to reach the highest stages.
- **Jane Loevinger's** theory (and Susanne Cook-Greuter's elaborate extension of it: "Nine Levels of Increasing Embrace"), which describes overall patterns of how people's personalities tend to change as they develop and mature. This tradition is built on a "sentence completion test", where researchers score people's answers. Also here, mostly old people are thought to reach the highest stages, where the later stages are generally thought of as more spiritual and existential than earlier ones.

- **Clare Graves'** model, developed and popularized by Don Beck and Chris Cowan as *Spiral Dynamics*, in which people are thought to belong to "vMemes" (value memes) that are named with color codes, RED (warrior society), BLUE (traditional), ORANGE (modern), GREEN (postmodern), YELLOW (metamodern) and so on. This model has taken a lot of fire for being too colorful, simplified and popularized, but it certainly has some merits: It elegantly describes how there is a certain unifying logic to each stage pattern of people's thoughts and moral reasoning, and it describes how each stage tends to come with a corresponding cultural logic.[73] We discuss this theory more closely in chapter 16.
- **Ken Wilber's** theory, in which a person's spiritual and cognitive development are taken to be two aspects that don't always match—a theme that I will elaborate upon. Others researching and working in this vein are Zachary "Zak" Stein and Terri O'Fallon (O'Fallon should perhaps primarily be seen as a follow-up to Cook-Greuter), both of whom have gone somewhat beyond Wilber. Even if Wilber never conducted research on his own, he is perhaps the foremost general theorist of adult development, having identified several fundamental patterns of development.[74]
- **Gerald "Gary" Young's** explicitly neo-Piagetian theory, in which an attempt is made to integrate cognitive development with emotional development (such as in emotional attachment theory and the Eriksonian life phases), into a model with 25 stages (five major stages, each with five recurring "steps")—an intuitively interesting but unfortunately largely mistaken move, at least in its current form. Young's theory holds that emotions and cognition must develop together and that only old people reach the highest stages—which is obviously confused, as cognitive genius generally shows up around ages 25, most often around 30, latest at 40—and in most people, simply never.[75]
- **Michael Lamport Commons'** neo-Piagetian **MHC: *the Model of Hierarchical Complexity***. This model is by far the most scientifically viable and consistent one, and the one that indisputably has the strongest empirical evidence, the strongest explanatory power, and the widest applicability. Based on pure behaviorist psychology, it does not look at anything other than how organisms solve tasks of different "orders of complexity". These tasks are rated by a mathematical system for understanding at which order of complexity a task is. The model can be used, and often is, for other animals as well. We'll spend the next two chapters on this theory.

So the fundamental tension here, among the global theories of adult development, is between more *holistic* ones and the more reductionist Model of Hierarchical Complexity (MHC) of Michael Commons. In this sense, Commons' theory stands alone against all of the others.

Whereas Kegan's psychoanalytically influenced theory (drawing on the humanities rather than behavioral science) relates to intimate things such as the evolving sense of self, the MHC does nothing of the sort. It just looks at how complex a task someone can handle, and goes on from there to see how that correlates with other variables, such as income[76] or attitudes (and usually it correlates a lot, a whole lot more than any of the other theories).

But the MHC does not tackle the other issues at hand—what about overall growth of a person's personality? What about the development of his or her set of values and their worldview, like in Spiral Dynamics? What happens with someone's emotional development, or existential development, for that matter? Is cognitive complexity really enough to explain all that? I don't think it is.

All of the mentioned theories, other than the MHC, attempt to be holistic, to really grasp the overall picture of a multifaceted human being developing in many ways, and yet they all fall out less generally applicable than the MHC—a theory that can be used to rank the difficulty of tasks, predict behaviors, describe animals, describe political opinions and many other things. Yet, there really does appear to be more to growing as a human being, than the purely cognitive development of the MHC.

I hold that all of the holistic adult development theories are on to something, but that they all fail to grasp quite what it is. They all make the same mistake: **They *smash* together different forms of development into one and the same model, and *force* these (interrelated but still distinct and often independently developed) dimensions into the same stages**. This is because they fail to distinguish between the dimensions of development with sufficient clarity.

Some of the theories mix things up even worse. Robert Kegan's theory mixes up stage with Eriksonian life phases, which turns him into a hopeless "gerontophile": Age is glorified to an almost religious extent. The same goes for Gary Young, perhaps the worst gerontophile[77] of the lot, whose theory in all seriousness implicates that people would become cognitive geniuses only in their fifties and sixties or even later, and only if they manage to work through the emotional family issues pertinent to that age. A similar mistake is apparent in Loevinger's and Cook-Greuter's tradition, both of whom even manage to blend in issues of personality into the different stages *and* spice it up with a bit of psychiatric diagnostics (where the lower stages are described as psychopaths, more or less).[78] Spiral Dynamics is perhaps the most simplistic model, and thereby mixes things a lot, too. It is fashionable among the developmental researchers to disdain it—but it still manages to be the most widely used, perhaps not only because of its simplicity. The model has real merits in that it is at good describing the overall *cultural* logic inherent to each stage, as I discuss further in chapter 16.

Wilber's model comes closest to understanding these issues. He speaks of two kinds of development: one of spiritual states and one of cognitive stages. But his model (called the Wilber-Combs lattice) is still spaghetti, mixing up very crucial aspects, which leaves the theory full of weak spots. Perhaps his worst sin is to overemphasize spirituality so that he, for instance, in his detailed maps over human development, places the Indian mystic Sri Aurobindo's later stages of spiritual development right *on top of* Michael Commons' stages of cognitive development—a deeply confused move. Terri O'Fallon elaborates upon Wilber's model a bit, but she doesn't quite solve its problems—also dramatically exaggerating the role of spirituality. None of the "Wilberians" seem to have figured out that Wilber *smashes together* four dimensions into two and that his description of spiritual "states" is lacking in essential aspects, as they fail to account for the varieties of everyday experience (even if Wilber's writings on spirituality are undeniably insightful).

What all of the holistic models are on to is that purely cognitive development (which is what Commons' theory describes) leaves out something crucial. But when they attempt to put that "other stuff" in, their models become blurred and much weaker—and certainly much less clear, logical and elegant—than Commons' theory.

The other theorists have all failed to make some important analytical distinctions: to differentiate between the relevant dimensions of psychological development. And because they haven't teased out the correct dimensions, they all fail in their attempts to integrate the dimensions into one whole, "holistic" developmental model.

Here is what I believe: Commons is the only one that has discovered one of the *four* fundamental dimensions of development—that of cognitive development. That's why his model shows up with so much greater clarity and consistency—and better research results.

What we are going to do in these following chapters is to go through these four dimensions—and discuss some of their interrelations—starting with Commons' MHC for cognitive development, then continuing with *code*, *state* and *depth*, each of which will get simplified but workable definitions. Note however, that the MHC is the only aspect that so far has got a satisfying research program. If you're a smart scientist, maybe you can help out by operationalizing research on one of the other three dimensions and have a fascinating, pioneering career. Cheers.

We will also explore how these four dimensions tend to work together to generate overall patterns that we call **effective value memes**—which is a more stringent version of the Spiral Dynamics model, solving its main problems and clearing some of the confusions around it, but still keeping its bird's eye view.

It is especially this *effective value meme* that has a vital role to play in pretty much all societal, economic and political matters. It is when you get this part that you begin to be able to "do" metamodern politics yourself—and you begin to see why metamodern politics is simply a necessity for us to have a flying chance of dealing with the challenges of our age.

Chapter 8

COGNITIVE DEVELOPMENT

So, we have zoomed in on cognitive development, and on the Model of Hierarchical Complexity (MHC) especially, as one out of four fundamental facets of a person's overall stage (their *effective value meme*). The basic idea of the MHC is that people are distributed across different stages of hierarchical development, so that some people can think thoughts and perform tasks that are *more complex* than others. The model leads to some rather counter-intuitive conclusions that can be hard to swallow—but are shockingly obvious once you see them.

In this chapter we pretty much just go through the MHC theory. You will learn the logic by which it works.

Meister L. Commons

First of all, I should probably say a few words about Michael Lamport Commons, the main originator of MHC. He's born in the late 1930s and was a collaborator of Larry Kohlberg (the one who did the stages of moral reasoning) back in the days. Michael is an old school, tough-headed scientist through-and-through: materialist, reductionist, behaviorist, empiricist, positivist, atheist and (a probabilistic) determinist. It is somewhat ironic, but not surprising, that a man like that should have come up with the by far best model of adult development—a field that generally draws holistically inclined people. As a young man Michael studied at UC Berkeley with Lois Alvarez (a particle physicist who was awarded the Nobel Prize and came up with the hypothesis that a comet killed the dinosaurs)[79] and later as a Harvard mathematician and psychologist. He loves hard research, rigid theories and solid results—and he despises speculative philosophy and spirituality, and even the "softer" sciences, not to mention psychoanalysis. He likes precise, measurable variables and reliable methods—vague things like "level of education" simply won't do in his book. In a world seemingly obsessed with education, he'd simply mutter: "It's a crap variable".

At thirteen, he was inspired by Isaac Asimov's *Foundation* trilogy, the novels in which the prophetic scholar Hari Seldon worked out a fictional "psychohistory", a mathematical way of describing and predicting human behavior. Later in life, his greatest inspirations were Ernst Mach, the Austrian physicist-philosopher (after whom we've named the speed of sound) and Gustav Fechner, who first described the principles of psychophysics—the discipline in which you study how intensively organisms perceive different stimuli and how they react. You may know, for instance, that the same water will be perceived as warm to a cold left hand and cold to a warm right hand—even if you stick them both in the water at the same time. So it's a no-bullshit, rather mechanical, way to study human behavior. Such science has blind spots, for sure, but it can also be very illuminating and useful.

As a person Michael is loud, confrontational and bossy. An old man, he is bald, with a white beard; his body short and chubby, his gaze steely and direct. He speaks with a commanding, grumpy voice, always with the kind of self-certainty you'd only find in movie characters. I know, because I stayed at his home for quite some time, a classic New England house where he lives with his family in Cambridge, Massachusetts. Even if I listened and learned, and mostly did what he told me to, we would occasionally have fierce arguments and disagreements, him being an American (cultural) Jew from Hollywood who loved cars and business, me a romantically and philosophically inclined European full of Buddhist sentiments and without a driver's license—fights that somehow never seemed to compromise our relationship of scholarly mentorship and camaraderie.

Listening to Michael was an art in itself. He would scatter his thoughts into morsels distributed irregularly over days or even weeks, suddenly bursting into long tirades on something we had discussed much earlier, without giving any forewarning or context. I would hurry to note things down, and over time I learned to collect his thoughts into longer chains, struggling to see how they connected to one another. And they always did. His ideas were to be found in the broader pattern of these talks, in the pattern that connects.

And then he would suddenly stop speaking to indulge in one of his many odd quirks: to walk up to some other guests in a restaurant and—hovering over their dinner table conversation—start guessing details about their lives (like Sherlock Holmes, he was always right), take a turn off the main road while in the car to inspect the industries of any neighborhood he passed, talk about his results in orienteering (the sport where you find your way through the woods with a map), make a huge cup of chocolate coffee with ridiculous amounts of artificial sweetener ("it has to saturate" he would say with a kind of gravity, as a ghastly sugary white hill amassed at the surface) or just quiz people, acquainted and stranger alike, in a domineering manner that only he would get away with. Other Harvard professors, lawyers and psychiatrists, often people with fancier formal positions, would let him push them around in a surprising manner. I was far from his only admirer and follower—but, to be frank, a lot of people disliked and shunned him, something of which Doctor Commons seemed charmingly oblivious.

As a scholar, Michael is extremely productive. His lifetime output is several times greater than what you might expect from a normal academic professor. A lot of the work consists of collaborations with other researchers who find different applications of his theory (over a very wide range of topics and sciences). Another body of work consists of substantial advances to the theoretical framework of the MHC itself.

Although hardly a philosophical kin spirit to myself, and despite our quite fundamental differences, I must concede that Michael is by far the most brilliant person I've had the pleasure of knowing.

Here's a toast to the maestro.

The Model of Hierarchical Complexity (MHC)

The theory that is today the Model of Hierarchical Complexity was first presented by Commons and Richards in the early 1980s. It builds directly upon the Piagetian model and the work of Kohlberg and can be considered as **neo-Piagetian** (although some call it "post-Piagetian"), because it largely supposes that the Piagetian model (with cognitive stages) is correct, but that **there are several stages *above* what a normal human adult achieves, higher stages that only a minority of the adult population reach**. According to the neo-Piagetians the study of these stages can explain a lot about humanity and society.[80]

Commons first formulated the theory after having taken a year off from work to study mathematics, where the language of abstract algebra helped him to describe the formal relationships between the different stages.

Once this formal relationship was in place, the different stages could be described with generalizable **orders of complexity**. The order of complexity is the complexity of a certain task (such as getting three green balls, a task in which you must coordinate the shape, number and color with the verb "get"—this is stage 5, Sentential, in the model below). The MHC research program is based on **task analysis** and is thereby dependent on the inventions of tasks and dilemmas to test people—it is a branch of experimental psychology. But once you know the stages well enough, you begin to be able to understand at which stage people operate when they do things in everyday life as well (and, yes, you also begin to be able to see which stages your fellow researchers operate at and what order of complexity their work is).

All the other theorists had built their theories by observing the development of children or adults. Commons and Richards mapped the stages mathematically—and then found that the data mapped their theory much more elegantly and precisely than any of the other theories. Besides, you could use the same models for animals. Clearly, they were on to something important.

Initially, Commons and Richards themselves failed to see the wider implications of their theory. They had primarily devised it as a response to criticism of Kohlberg, as some scholars did not believe in there being higher stages than what a normal adult human being reaches at ages 11-14 (the formal-operational stage). But Commons and Richards' model, in all its reductionist crudeness, took on a life of its own, and impressive results started appearing: people—and their behaviors—mapped onto the different stages with an almost frightening precision and consistency.[81]

I am not going to discuss the evolution of the model, but just skip to the latest version of it, now in 2017. The model covers everything from germs and amoeba right up to Einstein. But it does not, as we will see, describe existential depth, i.e. it doesn't account for the Buddha or Kierkegaard.

So—sixteen stages, let's go baby (we'll revisit the four most relevant ones, stages 10-13, in the next chapter; in this list I have underlined them):

0. **Calculatory Stage (molecules)**
   - Can distinguish between 0 and 1 (something versus nothing), much like a digital computer.
   - Can only react to stimuli without any distinguishing for strength of reaction; "organisms at the edge of life", like DNA itself.
   - Humans pass this stage long before we are born; indeed, before we are even conceived.
1. **Automatic Stage[82] (cells)**
   - Can react to stimuli depending on different quantities, but only by automatic response and never through learning.
   - No coordination of different stimuli, there is just a single stimulus-response.

- Single cell organisms; humans pass the stage before we are born.

2. Sensory or Motor Stage (amoeba)

- Can react in different ways to different stimuli, and can coordinate two stimuli responses (but not invent new responses). Move body parts.
- For instance a leech, if you both shine on it with a lamp and shock it with electricity several times, you can get it to respond to just the lamp as if there was an electric shock.
- Amoeba, slugs, mollusks, early human fetus.

3. Circular Sensory-Motor Stage (insect, fish, newborn human)

- Can reach, touch, grab, shake objects, babble, make single sounds (phonemes).
- Can move body parts after having perceived objects and can recognize things.
- Most predatory fish, insects, newborn humans.[83] (Note that cognitive stage can be the same even if brain size, cognitive speed and perhaps the degree of "sentience" vary greatly. Counter-intuitive but true!)

4. Sensory-Motor Stage (rat, small baby)

- Can do a series of movements that are calibrated after one another and build upon one another to achieve something.
- This includes putting several sounds together so that you can form a morpheme, at least in the language-prone species of humans (you can use combinations of sounds to "express something" but not yet use a full word consistently).
- Rats, young baby humans.

5. Nominal Stage (pigeon, one-year-old toddlers)

- Can find relations among concept and make them into words: single words, exclamations, knowing the meaning of a word. "Nominal" because you can name stuff.
- Can begin to understand what other organisms "mean".
- Laboratory pigeons, one-year-old toddlers.

6. Sentential Stage (two/three years old)

- Can put words together into *sentences*, and see a series of simple tasks that need to be coordinated, imitate a sequence.
- This allows for the use of pronouns like I, mine you, yours it, etc.—these being more abstract than names of things.
- Parrots (as famously described by Irene Pepperberg; trained parrots can go up to this stage), cats, toddlers around two to three.[84]

7. Pre-Operational Stage (three to five year olds)

- Can make simple deductions (but not spot contradictions), follow lists of sequential acts, and tell short stories (by coordinating several sentences).
- Can use connectives (in humans): if, then, as, when, etc. Puts together several sentences into a "paragraph".
- Dogs and small children, three to five years old.

8. Primary Stage (five to seven years old)

- Can do logical deduction and use empirical rules; adds, subtracts, divides, multiplies, proves, does series of tasks on its own.
- Can relate to times, places, can count acts and relate to separate actors. Can construct relatively coherent narratives ("groups of paragraphs"); these create accounts and ideas about what's going on.
- Chimpanzees and rhesus monkeys; in humans, five to seven year olds.

9. Concrete Stage (seven to eleven)

- Can do long division, follow complex social rules, takes on roles and coordinates self with others.
- Can create meaningful, concrete stories and keep the same story intact and consequential over time. Puts together groups of paragraphs into a story. Can thus keep track of interrelations (which is the best tool, and how would you test it, etc.), social events, what happened among others, reasonable deals, history, geography.
- Normal in humans at ages seven to eleven, but also a significant portion of the adult population. In the famous bonobo chimpanzee studies of Frans de Waal, there are examples of concrete stage behaviors, such as testing several tools to determine which is the best one.[85]

10. <u>Abstract Stage</u> (ages eleven to fourteen)

- Can form abstract ideas and thoughts: single, generalized variables that fall beyond the concrete sequences of events in a story—can make and quantify abstract propositions.
- Relates to categories and uses "cases of events" to incrementally improve the understanding of these categories.
- Humans eleven and older, a significant part of the adult population, about 30%. No known non-human animals.

11. **<u>Formal Stage</u> (ages fourteen to eighteen, if at all)**
    - Can identify relations between abstract variables and reflect upon these relations, devise ways to test them, etc. Solves problems using algebra with one unknown, uses logic and empiricism.
    - Can speak a full, rich language with self-reflection, uses logical sequences of connectives: *if* this, *then* that, in all cases.
    - Fourteen years and onwards. The most common stage in adult human beings, about 40% of the adult population—only a minority go beyond this stage.
12. **<u>Systematic Stage</u> (eighteen and above, if at all)**
    - Can identify patterns among linear relationships, thus forming systems of relations among abstract variables and how these interact. Can thereby also solve equations with several unknowns. The first "postformal" stage, i.e. it was not described by Piaget, but implicated in Kohlberg's work.
    - Begins to discuss legal systems, social structures, ecosystems, economic systems and the like.
    - Can be found in about 20% of adult humans, usually after age eighteen.
13. **<u>Metasystematic Stage</u> (early twenties and above, if at all)**
    - Can compare and synthesize several systems with differing logics, put together "metasystems" or conclusions that hold true across different system, reflect upon and name general properties of systems.
    - Understands that things can be "homomorphic", "isomorphic", etc. This means that you can see how one system can be changed in corresponding or differing ways to another system.
    - Can be found in about 1.5% of the adult population, usually only after early twenties.
14. **Paradigmatic Stage (mid-twenties and above, if at all)**
    - Can deal with several very abstract metasystems to create new ways of thinking of the world, new paradigms, new sciences or branches within sciences.
    - Has a fractal way of thinking, so that the universal principles found are applicable to many different levels of analysis and phenomena.
    - Prevalence unknown, but if the pattern holds and every stage seems to increase with about a standard deviation[86], it should be a little more than one adult in a thousand in a normal population, mostly at ages 25+. This makes it rare, but still some three million

people in the world (one thousandth of the functional adults above 25). Although the stage is theoretically formulated, there is no reliable test for it.[87]

15. Crossparadigmatic Stage (late twenties and above, if at all)

- Can deal with several paradigms to create new fields.
- Examples are: Newton's reformulation of physics, Darwin's theory of evolution, Einstein's theory of relativity, the invention of quantum physics, the invention of chaos mathematics and complexity, the invention of computing, the invention of postmodern philosophy, the invention of the holistic "integral theory" of Ken Wilber, the invention of string theory, the invention of the MHC theory.
- Prevalence unknown, found only in adults older than twenty and who have privileged circumstances. It most often shows up around 30. No reliable test for this stage.[88]

What you get here is a model of cognitive complexity that places humans and other animals on the same scale. This kind of thinking leads us towards questioning some of the "speciesist" assumptions of our day and age: that there would be anything "special" about humans.

Admittedly, there are some things unique to humans, such as our propensity for language use—which appears to be a certain genetic property; in 2009, researchers transplanted such genes to mice and heard them make more interesting squeaks.[89] This is also in line with what Noam Chomsky's linguistic theory would suggest; that we should view language as a biological property of humans.

Commons' theory naturally focuses on language (words, sentences, increasingly complex grammar, narratives, concepts…) because it is mostly used to study humans. But the MHC stages or "orders of complexity" are perfectly possible to describe in non-linguistic terms, such as abstract algebra, which is what Commons initially did. So even animals that don't speak (like the pigeon at stage 5 Nominal) can display behaviors at equal or higher orders of complexity than e.g. young human children, even if kids talk and pigeons don't. Speech is a useful tool when it comes to accomplishing complex tasks, but it is not *in itself* necessary for cognitive complexity (or sentience, for that matter: having subjective experience, feelings, etc.). This should insulate us against linguistically based speciesism, where humanity's "specialness" is legitimized by the fact that we have language use.

Before we go on, let's just note again that cognitive stage according to MHC is not a moral order—we have noticed for instance that human newborns can be described at the same stage as an insect (stage 3 Circular Sensory-Motor), but we'd hardly ascribe the same moral value to the two. Moreover, you can see variations of MHC stage in animals of the same species. This goes for newly born cubs versus fully developed adult dogs, as well as individual differences where some dogs out-stage their fellow canines. Irene Pepperberg's parrot was trained, after years of hard work, to go up one stage from 5 Nominal—where it could get a ball (out of several options, with cubes, rings, etc.) in order to claim a reward—to 6 Sentential, where it could get "two yellow balls", etc. The parrot just had to think for a very long time to figure it out, its brain being much smaller than a human one. This means that a human at the same stage, but having a far "higher IQ", would reach the same conclusion as the parrot, just at a much faster pace.

So we are not taking anything away from the fact that members of two different species, who are at the same stage, can still be very different from one another. Just consider the fact that some species have mate selection by means of bloody tournaments, like baboons (and a relatively short-lived rock n' roll lifestyle alpha male gets all the *punani* and offspring, before he is violently dethroned), and others through pair-bonding, like bonobo chimps (most of the population procreates and guys help out with the kids)—with humans being somewhere in between, judging from our physiological traits such as moderately larger males than females and medium sperm competition (as implied by testicle size, and, uhm, I guess by our sexual behavior). These species (baboons, bonobo chimps and humans) are behaviorally and psychologically quite different from one another even if their cognitive stages partly overlap.[90]

Of course, such species-specific traits shape behavior, and of course there is plenty of evolutionary psychology to account for much of what goes on in humans and other animals. But still, the *complexity* of those behaviors can be described with the help of our new friend—the MHC—and that puts all animals on the same scale, a scale on which adult human beings, surprisingly perhaps, differ vastly from one another.

This last part is both counter-intuitive and controversial. So let's examine it closer. We will now discuss what intelligence really is and then, in the following chapter, turn to the four most prevalent MHC stages in adult humans.

What Is Intelligence? The Parrot Speaks

A question we can hardly avoid is the definition of intelligence. In older Western sources, from the early 20th century or the 19th century, the word "intelligence" is sometimes used synonymously with "consciousness", which is an unfortunate mistake, one that sometimes haunts everyday parlance to this day.

So first of all, intelligence is not the same as consciousness. This, among other things, has implications for the whole "intelligent machines" debate. Intelligence here simply means "smarts", as in the capacity to perform tasks.

Secondly, we have already mentioned Alex, a great figure in science who tragically passed away from a virus infection in 2011—that is, Irene Pepperberg's famous grey African parrot. Alex reached stage 6 Sentential, and since parrots are linguistically endowed, he also learned about a hundred words (differentiating between objects, colors, materials, and shapes) and knew how to combine them; i.e. he was not just "parroting"—he was talking. A clear indication of this is that he could correct other parrots when they made mistakes.

But Alex's brain was, as mentioned, much smaller than that of a new-born human, who nevertheless can do nothing of the sort when it comes to the intellectual stunts that this grey African parrot was pulling off.[91] The human brain is just huge and superfast, and during early childhood it is full of so-called "glial cells" that support further growth and the creation of new patterns. Its growth rate and plasticity (the brain's capacity to form new patterns) are just staggering—although a newly born infant cannot even coordinate different reflexes, which means that it is stage 3 "Circular Sensory-Motor", like an insect.

By the time the human will have reached stage 6 Sentential, she will be able to do a lot more actions per timeframe, much more smoothly, with fewer mistakes, and she will learn much more quickly, have much greater memory capacity (easily knowing more words than a hundred).

What we are comparing now is **horizontal complexity** and **vertical complexity**. Horizontal complexity is simply a measure of how many calculations you have to make (how many yes-no questions you manage to answer). So this is basically how quick and efficient your brain is. A human newborn has much greater *horizontal* complexity than an adult parrot, even while being at a lower stage. But then again, a computer can have greater horizontal complexity than a human (while still being at stage 0 Computational).

IQ-tests will primarily measure horizontal complexity, given that the test taker is at a certain minimum stage so that they can actually take the test. The more difficult of these tests can include questions at stage 12 Systematic, but not really above that. Most of all, they measure how easily you recognize relatively simple patterns. Obviously, IQ (or "g factor") is not unimportant, and "intelligence" should perhaps be seen as a combination of horizontal and vertical complexity.

On the other hand, you have organizations like Mensa (top two percent of IQ scores, 132+) and Triple Nine Society (for folks way above Mensa level, at the 99.9^{th} percentile, 146+ IQ)—and somehow these places are hardly full of inventive geniuses, busy changing the world in all manner of ways. So what's going on here?

It's that high IQ, in humans, seems to only be loosely correlated with MHC stage. Mensa folks are seldom at the lower adult stages, but they tend to be at stage 11 Formal or stage 12 Systematic. So you have people whose brains are very quick and efficient—but without necessarily climbing to the more abstract forms of thought and behavior of higher *vertical* complexity. About 67% of your IQ score seems to depend on your MHC stage (or at least, that's how much the two seem to go hand in hand).[92]

So, what is vertical complexity? The MHC stages measure orders of vertical complexity. This means that **each stage coordinates the actions at the preceding stage.** You go from constructing stories to finding abstract variables in those stories, to finding relationships between abstract variables, to finding systems of relationships, to finding common properties in systems, and so on. There are actually five rules that determine the relationships between the stages, but here we just need to mention the three most basic ones—it's a bit technical, but bear with me:

- Higher-order actions are defined in terms of lower-order actions. This makes the higher-order tasks include the lower ones and requires that lower-order actions are hierarchically contained within the relative definitions of the higher-order tasks.
- Higher order of complexity actions organize lower-order actions. This makes them more powerful. Lower-order actions are organized by the actions undertaken with higher order of complexity, i.e., more complex tasks.
- Higher order of complexity actions organize those lower-order actions in a *non-arbitrary* way.[93]

A simple example. Alex the parrot increased in stage when he learned to combine words into sentences—in ways that made sense. There is a *hier-*

archy between sentences and single words—and the sentences are more powerful.

Basically, you can imagine a pyramid, where different people create original thoughts and behaviors at different heights. The organisms at higher cognitive stages can then master taller pyramids—and high IQ people can master broader ones. If you don't like the image of pyramids (because it feels imperialist, or whatever) you can switch it for something cuter or more organic, like a "network of networks", drawing on biological metaphors.

The super-intelligent folks of world history are the ones who happen to have *both* exceptionally high IQ *and* MHC stage—the clearest example being John von Neumann, a Hungarian 20th century Jew who moved to the US, and arguably the smartest person who ever lived. A super child prodigy, his displayed behavior clearly reached stage 15 Crossparadigmatic already in his early twenties, when he was able to apply very abstract principles to a wide host of problems. He "invented the computer" (almost), developed game theory (which may have contributed to saving us from nuclear holocaust—or perhaps brought us to the brink of one), predicted the Second World War, contributed to cybernetics, information science and quantum physics—and worked on more strands of mathematics and physics than perhaps any other scientist. All before he died at age 53.

Why then aren't all the high IQ folks over at Triple Nine Society doing the same as von Neumann? Because they don't *also* have exceptionally high cognitive MHC stage, that's why. Their "cognitive pyramids" are wide but not necessarily tall.

But then again, whereas von Neumann may be a role model for testosterone jacked boys who want to be the best and smartest and "conquer the world", he is perhaps not the highest ideal for a mature humanity. He did work on the Manhattan Project to develop nuclear arms, after all. He was not ahead of his time in terms of progressive values (being a militaristic anti-communist), he had a failed first marriage, was a notoriously bad driver who would read books while driving—and on his deathbed he betrayed his agnostic principles, suddenly converting to Catholicism (perhaps in fear of death). In other words, there may be other dimensions to human development than intellectual brilliance. It's safe to say, that when it comes to spiritual or existential development, von Neumann was about average, like the most of us. He was exceptionally intelligent, but probably not exceptionally "wise".

Either way, we can't all be like von Neumann in terms of smarts: It appears to necessitate a fluke of nature. Both IQ and MHC appear to have rather large genetic components. In a human population, both seem to be about 70% heredity, meaning that the IQ and stage of your parents explain a lot, but far from all of your own intelligence (but of course, the discussion is more complicated than that). There is currently (almost) no genetic *or* neurological research on MHC stages in humans.[94] This leaves the question open as to how possible it is to affect the development of MHC stages by means of changing the environment.[95] According to Michael Commons himself, MHC stage is relatively fixed for most adult people, given a relatively "normal" development (obviously, if you lock someone in a dark basement on their first birthday, and keep them there until their 25th, stage development is stunted).

Note, however, that the existence of MHC stages can hardly be used to excuse income inequalities in the name of a "genetically determined meritocracy". As succinctly argued by the British political scientist Brian Barry (in a parallel discussion about income, heritability and IQ) we cannot conclude that there is a pre-specified "innate potential" in each person, because it might very well be the case that different family environments, educational systems, diets etc. might spur different levels of development in people of different genetic constitutions.[96] Some may increase in MHC stage in a more musical environment, some in an environment with more challenges and adversities, and so on. Hence it is a simplistic—and politically inappropriate—idea that high MHC people should be targeted and granted privileges.

But maybe, once we know more about learning and the brain—and perhaps epigenetics (i.e. how genes change with the environment)—we will be able to affect the development of MHC stage and IQ, likely by design of living conditions from childhood and onwards. After all, we know about the so-called "Flynn effect", i.e. the observation that, in modern societies, IQ seems to increase with every generation—this goes both for what they call *crystallized* intelligence (based on prior knowledge and habit) and *fluid* intelligence (working memory, speed, etc.). Would it be possible to find a similar pattern for MHC?

One thing that would suggest that MHC stage is more volatile than Commons suggests, is the fact that the same MHC stages can show up in brains of very different sizes and shapes: The parrot's brain displays the same stage as a human three-year-old. Maybe, then, the "stage" is some kind of pattern in the overall communication of the brain, a pattern than can shift by being stimulated by the environment? The future holds the answers.

What we indisputably *can* do, however, is to affect the development of the other three dimensions: code, state and depth. These three are more volatile and subject to change. And that makes all the difference when it comes to politics and a deeper welfare system. Stay tuned.[97]

Chapter 9

THE IMPORTANT STAGES

People like the super-genius John von Neumann are exceedingly rare. Most of us are at lower MHC stages and have normal IQ scores. It is true that individuals like him or Einstein, or even Marx, can have great historical significance, but that doesn't really help us when it comes to understanding the wider demography (and ourselves) in cognitive-developmental terms. Whereas the qualitative difference between ourselves and such intellectual giants may be obvious and uncontroversial, the MHC theory also holds that there are great differences even between people within a "normal" population, differences that span over several MHC stages.

If we look at the four stages 10 Abstract, 11 Formal, 12 Systematic and 13 Metasystematic, we cover about 90% of a normal adult human population. A small percentage fall below this range (being stage 9 Concrete, which is still within the normal range, or below that, which is less common) and only a negligible fraction fall above it (being at stages 14 Paradigmatic and 15 Crossparadigmatic). If you learn to recognize these four stages, you will be able to see at which stage almost everyone in your vicinity operates.

In each of the following subchapters, we zoom in on one of these stages: what people can do at this stage, what they cannot do, and how to spot a person at this stage.

Now, before we go on, remember that this stuff really tends to hurt your ego in soft places, because we all obviously think it's more flattering to resemble Einstein than a grey African parrot. So: shields down. Relax your shoulders. Take a breath.

Stage 10 Abstract

Who? Emerges at ages 11-14. Observed only in humans.
How many? About 30% of a normal adult population in modern countries reach and stay at this stage throughout their lifetime.

INTRODUCTION TO STAGE 10 ABSTRACT

To "be at this stage" means to display only behaviors and cognitive operations of this order of complexity or below—i.e. that you produce *original* thoughts, reasoning and behaviors which are maximally this complex. However, of course, your development doesn't stop at age 14 just because your MHC stage does. You still learn, develop and change in other ways throughout your lifetime.

INTUITIVE EXAMPLE FROM THE HISTORY OF SCIENCE

Remember: In terms of language use, stage 9 Concrete means that you can put together many different paragraphs into one overarching narrative and name that narrative: the Iliad, etc. But whereas Homer's Iliad contains a lot of succinct and interesting human understanding, you don't find it abstracting variables and defining them.

The pre-Socratic natural philosophers, however, did exactly that: the essence of the world is water, suggested Thales; Heraclitus held that only change is constant, and so on. The ancient Greeks obviously could perform many actions that were of stage 10 Abstract or beyond: ship building, planning trade and conquests, administration, navigation and so forth. But philosophy that corresponds to stage 10 Abstract was not yet present in early literature and drama, and only showed up with the pre-Socratics (about 6th century BCE).

I chose the example with Greek literature and drama and the birth of Western philosophy simply because you here have a clear shift from explicitly expressed thoughts at stage 9 Concrete to stage 10 Abstract ideas or variables. Of course, this shift is possible in many other non-explicit and non-linguistic forms.

YES CAN DO

At stage 10 Abstract, we can invent our own **abstractions**: not just chairs and tables, but furniture; not just furniture and domestic appliances, but "all movable objects you put in a home"; not just home and office but all indoors environment—and so forth.

This is not just mimicking words like "furniture" used by others, but actually *creating* novel abstract concepts or **variables** themselves.

The stage 10 Abstract thinker can then use quantification of these variables: some of the furniture, some of the time. This can refine the variables, make new distinctions and let the abstract concepts acquire new meanings.

The abstractions are taken from stories about concrete things, people and events. These abstractions—furniture, love, justice, animosity, weight, volume—take on meanings that go beyond the particular story they are a part of.

INVENTED EXAMPLE

Let's invent a variable to try this out: the ruggedness of mountain cliffs. We can have more or less of it, relate it to time, say that this variable causes mountains to be difficult to climb, etc. We can name the variable a new word: blefuscity (it's a made up word).

Unlike the word "ruggedness", blefuscity only denotes ruggedness in the way that *mountains* are rugged—not the way that a person can have a rugged look. "High blefuscity" means that the cliff range has many sharp edges and "low blefuscity" means it has fewer such edges and that it is smoother.

Now blefuscity takes on a life of its own, beyond the singular, concrete story. But in the next story we tell (let's say it's a story about mountaineering), we notice that the cliffs are hard to climb but undeniably have "low blefuscity". The mountain slope was steep and smooth. So we make a distinction between "blefuscity" and "steepness". We have thus refined the meaning of "blefuscity", but it can always be further refined or challenged.

And so—the world we live in soon becomes a world of abstractions, a world of abstract concepts that have definitions and quantifiable properties. When we conceptualize reality at this stage, narratives still matter (this and that happened, I am from that place, etc.), but they are hinged on abstractions: "a story about love", etc.

Whoa. So that's pretty good. And the only creature that has ever been observed to do this is *Homo sapiens* (but we can probably count in the Neanderthals and other hominids). We can name, relate to and quantify a world of abstract things.

Shakespeare would have said: "Oh, wonder! How many goodly creatures are there here! How beauteous mankind is! O brave new world. That has such people in 't! MIRANDA. How amazing!"

NO CAN DO

What the stage 10 Abstract *cannot* do, however, is to describe regular relations *between* different such abstract ideas.

We can still, however, by means of a shared language, take part of the ideas that other people produce at higher orders of complexity. (We can also, if guided through the sequences of actions, perform tasks that are up to two stages above; we'll get back to that).

By definition, if we never ourselves have displayed original behaviors higher than this stage, we are said to "be at" stage 10 Abstract.

Let's return to our example with steepness and the invented abstract variable "blefuscity". For instance, very high steepness tends to create an even slope, which then means low blefuscity (few sharp edges)—which still makes for a very difficult climb (whereas our stage 10 Abstract thinking would have us believe that low blefuscity should make the climb easy).

This means that we easily land in false conclusions because we alternate between using steepness and blefuscity in our thinking, but fail to clearly and distinctively formulate the even more abstract *rule* which guides how we should use the two variables. We fail to see the *formal* relationship between the different abstract variables.

Why is this a problem? Because, as it turns out, the world around us—and inside us—behaves in ways that are so often not sufficiently and productively described by a single abstract variable. This means that, as stage 10 Abstract thinkers, we will very often respond to the world around us in simplified manners: in black-and-white, either-or ways. In everyday life that may be more than sufficient. But unfortunately modern people, at least as a collective, have to deal with much more complex issues than creating, choosing and quantifying single variables.

SOME STAGE 10 ABSTRACT TASKS

As mentioned earlier, the MHC research is based on "task analysis", i.e. the idea that every task has an "order of complexity" that can be analyzed: Getting through a maze is more complex than walking down a road and so forth. The order of complexity is not the same as "difficulty", which is much more context bound. Now let's look at some tasks in everyday life that would require stage 10 Abstract thinking. We will get back to a corresponding list of tasks when we discuss the higher stages.

- Writing a conclusion in an essay that ties the whole thing together.
- Pointing out the common denominator in a few different stories (love story, story about deceit and revenge, the same moral of the story).
- Inventing new words for things that are not concretely present.
- Driving a bus (following traffic rules and keeping in mind the length of the bus and other factors that are out of your sight).

- Simple nursing (categorizations of patient behavior and reporting back to doctor, quantifying several medical variables, relating to these rather abstract variables, etc.)
- Non-investigative journalism: reporting events and abstracting what "the story" is.
- Accurately drawing 2D objects (without conceptualizing new styles or art forms).
- Artisanship or building that requires a planned idea (but no engineering or physics calculation).
- Creating a map, or reading one without assistance.
- Teaching kids to read and write.

SOME STAGE 10 ABSTRACT REASONING ABOUT POLITICS

Our stage of hierarchical complexity also affects how we think about politics and society. Regardless of political persuasion, we can think more or less complexly about political issues. Let's look at some stage 10 Abstract arguments of different political hues.

- **Anti-racist argument:** Racism is bad: It is a self-contained and self-explanatory essence that spreads by itself unless you stop it, causing discrimination and possibly tyranny and war.
- **Conservative argument:** The Arabicness inherent to Arabs gives them traits that are irreconcilable with Western civilization.
- **Feminist argument:** Feminism means to stand up for women and crush patriarchy.
- **Libertarian argument:** The less state control, the better.
- **Green argument:** Human greed causes crises and destroys the environment.
- **Day-to-day politics:** I am frustrated both by high taxes and low spending; by both high unemployment and low starting wages.

HOW TO SPOT A STAGE 10

As stage 10 Abstract thinkers, we cannot see the general rules that govern *when* our abstractions should apply, when they can be expected to have certain properties and so forth. This means that we will tend to focus on one single variable and want to either increase or decrease its quantitative value: less immigration, lower taxes, more love, more dialogue, less greed etc.

If confronted with a counter-argument (e.g. that more dialogue also means more time-consuming squabble, which in turn may not serve the purpose) the stage 10 Abstract thinker will simply insist upon having both: more dialogue *and* less time-consuming squabble. This is the less complex form of both-and thinking: not accounting for a productive tension between both sides, but simply denying that one's argument has trade-offs or downsides.

As stage 10 Abstract thinkers we can sometimes insist upon doing things that to others is apparently counter-productive. For instance, the management department at a (modern, computerized) hospital can decide to cut the budget and make a decision to close down many of the printers. In effect, this may cause the nurses to walk much longer stretches to the printers farther away, in effect costing much higher wages if seen per hour and reducing efficiency—just to save some ink. In this case (which is taken from real life) the management uses the singular variable ("saving costs") but fails to coordinate it with other variables ("cost per effective hour of work") and in effect make budget cuts that are directly wasteful.

Have you ever been in an argument where you patiently and politely address the inconsistencies of your counterpart's argument, but they seem to repeat the same phrase or concept as if it were an answer in itself? This is probably a stage 10 Abstract thinker. At this stage we can spot obvious factual inconsistencies, but we cannot spot inconsistencies in how we apply abstract variables: for instance, lower taxes and higher welfare, please! And if you point out that there may be a trade-off, the stage 10 Abstract thinker will think that you are being vague and just playing with words.

Thinkers of each stage have this kind of **complexity bias**. Complexity bias means that we intuitively prefer forms of reasoning that correspond to our own stage of complexity. Explanations of lower complexity seem crude and simplistic to us, whereas higher stage explanations seem vague or counter-intuitive.

Stage 11 Formal

Who? Adolescent and adult humans. Emerges, if at all, at ages 14 and older.
How many? About 40% of adult humans in a normal, modern population.

INTRODUCTION TO STAGE 11 FORMAL

This is the most common adult human stage and where Inhelder and Piaget's original model ended (this is somewhat of a simplification, but never mind). That someone is at this stage means that they perform tasks of this order of complexity—*original* behaviors not guided by others. Again, we don't know what this means in terms of the organism internally, but we can certainly *observe behaviors* at this stage.

Even if this stage emerges in adolescence and relatively few people grow beyond it, people of course continue to change and develop in other ways throughout their lifespan.

INTUITIVE EXAMPLE FROM THE HISTORY OF SCIENCE:

In the history of science, understanding Newton's three laws of motion is an example of stage 11 Formal thinking. To successfully coordinate the three laws, however, requires the next stage (stage 12 Systematic)—not to mention inventing these laws in a time before natural science was clearly established (which requires a much higher stage).

This is just to give a clear example of stage 11 Formal when formalized in scientific theory. Of course, outside of science, a lot of people were performing stage 11 Formal tasks: coordinating prices with demand, investments with risks and rewards, setting up rules and legal systems, building advanced structures, handling relationships between people with different interests by means of fair rules, creating ways to compare different measure units and currencies, and so forth.

YES CAN DO

We can now invent our own rules or principles that describe or guide the relationship between several abstract variables. The relationships can be linear or not, but they make us see some kind of plotted line.

This means that our thinking and our actions become guided by such rules or principles: *if* this, under these circumstances, *then* that.

It also means that, because we know the rules guiding the relationships between different abstract variables, we can guess the value of an abstract variable simply by knowing the values of the other related variables. We can "see around corners" and think ahead in ways that children cannot.

INVENTED EXAMPLE

Let us return to the invented variables blefuscity (the ruggedness of cliffs) and steepness. We concluded that blefuscity and steepness both cause the climb to be more difficult.

But let's assume that, on a very steep cliff, you can only climb it if it also has high blefuscity: Otherwise there is simply nothing to hold on to.

If you only study blefuscity, you don't notice this: All steep cliffs with high blefuscity are difficult to climb, as are all not-so-steep cliffs with high blefuscity. It is only when you compare different steep cliffs, that you notice that high blefuscity makes for an easier climb.

So what we assumed was a property, an essence, inherent to the variable, was in fact only true under some circumstances. We have gone from a thinking with "blefuscity *and* steepness" to one where we relate to "blefuscity *and/or/if* steepness". And our whole view of the situation changes.

We have invented a rule that describes the relationship between three variables: Blefuscity causes greater difficulty under low steepness and lower difficulty under high steepness. We call it "the general rule of blefuscity". An elegant rule of the universe. And the stars glisten.

NO CAN DO

What we *cannot* do as stage 11 Formal thinkers, and what most adult people actually never quite do during our lifetimes, is to relate several such formalized rules to one another and form one coherent system of thought.

This is partly where the MHC theory becomes so counter-intuitive that it loses many adherents: It just seems implausible. The simplest systems are such things as a "catch-22" or a feedback cycle, or a balance of two simultaneous processes. Could it really be that almost 80% of all adult humans never think such thoughts or perform the corresponding actions? I will discuss this in a section after the four major stages have been presented. Suffice to note, at this point, that we are speaking of the ability to create *original* thoughts and behaviors of that stage. This means that, in a civilization that is global and has many, many millions of people inventing behaviors and concepts above stage 11 Formal, there will simply be so many higher stage actions and concepts around, which can be taught and performed with help, or simply misunderstood. So we tend to not notice that a minority of people are actually doing most of the more complex inventing.

If recognizing the "catch-22" as a concept is so easy, how come there wasn't even a word for it before John Heller's 1953 novel with that title? You may have read or heard of Malcolm Gladwell's 2008 book *Outliers*, which points out the great significance that unusual, exceptionally talented people called "outliers" have in society's development—although he quickly and famously points out that such people always have good circumstances, that they put in 10 000 hours of practice, and always rely upon some help of their friends.

Or you may know of Clay Shirky's 2008 book on the participatory potentials of the internet *Here Comes Everybody*, where he points out that, after all, only a small minority of the users of e.g. Wikipedia actually create the content. This may also be because relatively few people have complex enough understandings of many of the topics.

I agree with Michael Commons: It appears as though most people never construct complex systems of thought or behavior. But then again, most tasks in everyday life can be successfully managed with stage 10 Abstract and stage 11 Formal behaviors or below.

The challenge to stage 11 Formal thinking comes primarily when we deal with systematic issues of society, ecology, economy, organizations, social psychology and the like. For instance, we may have problems with seeing how the messiness in the college kitchen dorm is a result of systemic properties of sharing a kitchen, rather than as someone's breach of the rules. We tend to think that a single rule, or breach thereof, explains issues that indeed require us to consider the system as a whole.

Paul Haggis' 2004 movie *Crash* focuses on issues of race and class in Los Angeles. It's the darling film of sociologists, even with direct references to sociological research (the lines from the opening scene are directly taken from the American sociologist Jack Katz's ethnography on road rage).[98] The movie shows how the many characters are by themselves relatively innocent, each being a victim of their respective circumstances—but the collective result of all the characters' perceptions and actions create a tense, racist and violent society.

Let's just say that if the script writers were at stage 11 Formal, this movie would have looked quite differently, with a much more linear plotline and single-cause explanation of racism.

SOME STAGE 11 FORMAL TASKS

- Writing a conclusion in an essay that ties the whole thing together and fruitfully compares it to other texts.
- Pointing out the patterns of how plotlines evolve in stories of different genres and explaining the logic to why this is so.
- Inventing new words or expressions for processes, rules or general principles.
- Driving a large truck with multiple trailers (meaning, you have to consider how the trailers affect one another when you drive backwards out of a garage, etc.).
- Medical work with independent decision making (qualifying diagnosis, weighing, choosing and applying one or several treatments, etc.).
- Economic journalism: how businesses are affected by changes in the economy, etc.

- Accurately drawing 3D objects (without designing novel styles or art forms).
- Artisanship or building that requires a planned idea and engineering or physics calculations.
- Creating a map, and providing correct instructions on how to read it.
- Teaching kids to read and write, using different methods for depending on the characteristics of the children.

SOME STAGE 11 FORMAL REASONING ABOUT POLITICS

- **Anti-racist argument:** Racism results from economic and social inequalities in society and causes further inequality and discrimination.
- **Conservative argument:** Some cultural norms followed by Arabs may be irreconcilable with Western civilization.
- **Feminist argument:** Feminism is to apply the principles of gender equality and to make these principles prevalent throughout society.
- **Libertarian argument:** The less state control, the better, except that maintaining law and order is necessary. To establish law and order may temporarily require increased state control in "failed state" areas.
- **Green argument:** The lacking proportionality between our emphasis on human interests, especially those of rich people, and the interests of animals and ecosystems, is what causes crises and destroys the environment.
- **Day-to-day politics:** I see a trade-off between high taxes and high spending, between low unemployment and high starting wages.

HOW TO SPOT A STAGE 11

Generally, because of cognitive bias, stage 11 Formal thinkers will tend to like to stick with certain principles. Of course, sometimes finding the simple principle or rule that guides the apparent messiness of reality can be a mark of much higher cognitive stages (think Newton). But if people like to stick with rules and principles not invented by themselves and they tend to make linear plans about the future and tend to focus on single if-this-then-that principles, you are probably dealing with stage 11 Formal thinking.

In politics, stage 11 Formal thinkers generally have a penchant for clear ideologies or doctrines: socialism, libertarianism and the like. They are likely to repeat one common wisdom, e.g. the conservative idea that things often go wrong when you try to be utopian or the radical idea that most social change has come through struggle.

Remember, this is the most common stage. Adult middle class people in a modern society will very often be of this stage of cognitive complexity. At this stage we don't really produce our own theories or solutions, simply following the rules and habits set out by others. We can of course still be intelligent (high IQ), artistic, imaginative, skilled and so forth.

Stage 12 Systematic

Who? Adult humans, or late adolescents.
How many? About 20% of a normal adult population in modern countries.
Intuitive example from science? Darwin's theory of evolution (Darwin himself was higher stage, of course).[99]

YES CAN DO

As stage 12 Systematic thinkers we can coordinate several formal rules or simple equations (not necessarily in formalized, mathematical language, of course) to see how they form a larger system.

We can hence solve equations with several unknowns. You may remember equation systems from high school math. This is a simple form of system, where we relate two linear equations to one another and thereby solve them (or determine that they cannot be solved or have different possible solutions).

But most people can pass these tests? Yes, of course: under the circumstances where someone is walking us through the steps. But does our brain spontaneously and repeatedly create thoughts that relate to such systems? In about 20% of us, it does. In most of us, it doesn't.

If you look around at how our politicians and the electorate reason on various issues, or indeed even how much, if not most, of academic research is conducted, you notice that it does not really reason beyond stage 11 Formal models.

INVENTED EXAMPLE

So we had the thing with blefuscity (ruggedness of cliffs), steepness and the difficulty of the climb: "the general rule of blefuscity". Now let's add another rule: the climber's characteristics. The climber can be tall or short (with corresponding length of arms) and she can be a good or bad climber.

Are we just adding more factors to our equation? Is this not just more of the same? No. We are looking now at something completely different:

how the entirety of the system (the climbing of the mountain) is affected by the interactions of two quite different sets of variables.

Let's say that the climber generally is better at climbing if she's taller. But then it turns out that *this* only holds true under some circumstances: Sometimes shorter arms and legs are better. Shorter legs are better when there is very small distance between each crack and protrusion in the cliff.

So now we have to break up the variable "blefuscity" into three constituent parts: the frequency, sharpness and size of the cracks/protrusions of the rock. At very high frequency (low distance between the cracks), shorter arms make for a better climber, and at medium or low frequency (greater distance between each of the cracks), longer arms are advantageous.

Also, the better the climber, the more she can use blefuscity to her advantage. In fact, the best climbers actually are demotivated by long, easy climbs, thus in practice climbing the more difficult mountains with greater vigor and skill.

This makes us re-evaluate the "general rule of blefuscity" that our friend at stage 11 Formal formulated (that blefuscity makes for a more difficult climb *unless* it's a very steep climb, in which the reverse is true). It turns out to be not-so-general after all: Even steepness can make for an easier climb, because, together with the *right kind* of blefuscity, it motivates the climber and breaks up the climb into manageable and interesting parts.

Here, at a view from stage 12 Systematic, we see that neither blefuscity, steepness nor indeed "difficulty", were what they seemed. They are all so much more contextual than we would have thought.

Of course, in a discussion, the stage 10 Abstract thinker may appear more certain and common sense: Blefuscity makes for a difficult climb! The systematic stage 12 thinker may seem less sure of herself, having to think longer, to explain herself more technically and wordily, but she has nevertheless a much deeper understanding. And she can make for the best mountaineering. And she alone can formulate "the theory of mountaineering". Glory days.

NO CAN DO

But even as stage 12 Systematic thinkers, we are limited to thinking of one system at a time. We don't see that systems follow fundamentally different logics.

So at the stage 12 Systematic we tend to want to squeeze everything one and the same coherent system, not being able to compare different systems with quite different properties. If we are engineers, we tend to believe that the world consists of systems resembling engineering, if we are sociologists we believe it is made up of social constructions and tend to misinterpret and undervalue e.g. biology and psychiatry—and so on.

The main problem of many of the adult development theorists, from Jane Loevinger and Susanne Cook-Greuter to Robert Kegan, stems from the fact that their authors are at this cognitive stage. This is why their minds smash development into one unified model of one-dimensional development. They fail to see that there are different forms of developmental systems and that the logic of one such dimension cannot unproblematically be applied to the others. These thinkers tend to have great existential depth (as discussed in the following chapters), but that does *not* cancel out their cognitive shortcomings.

So stage 12 Systematic cannot solve deep, wicked issues that span across sectors of society and the sciences. The high esteem that "interdisciplinarity" holds within academia these days is really a vaguely formulated grasp for stage 13 Metasystematic solutions. Simply mixing panels with different scientists is only lip-service to the complexity of our day and age.

SOME STAGE 12 SYSTEMATIC TASKS

- Writing a conclusion in an essay which criticizes and goes beyond the thinking presented in other comparable essays (teaching at university level, I can say that only a few students manage to do this, even among the ones who study very hard).
- Inventing a new form of plotline or genre within literature.
- Inventing new words for theories, systems or "principles about principles".
- Overseeing the traffic system in a city, reducing risk, bottlenecks and pollution.
- Medical work with applied critical thinking within science, comparing different research results and perhaps putting forward novel theories and methods.
- Critical investigative journalism: being able to see cracks and loopholes in the system and putting these in focus.
- Accurately drawing or otherwise representing multidimensional objects (including by successful use of the multiperspectivalism of (post-) modern art).
- Artisanship or building that requires the creation of novel methods, applying physics or engineering in unconventional ways

- Providing instructions for creating good maps and how to provide instruction for reading them.
- Comparing and inventing different methods for teaching kids to read and write.

SOME STAGE 12 SYSTEMATIC REASONING (POLITICS):

- **Anti-racist argument:** Racism is an emergent property of all societies and interacts with things like inequality. Blaming and pointing fingers is generally unproductive and one should instead try to address the long-term issues that may be causing ethnic tensions under these particular circumstances.
- **Conservative argument:** There are challenges in reconciling Western and Islamic culture which depend on how these categories interact, rather than flaws inherent to either category.
- **Feminist argument:** Feminism means to work towards a long-term equilibrium where self-reproducing inequalities have petered out and people of all sexes and genders have less reason to feel insecure and frustrated.
- **Libertarian argument:** State control and policy implementation tend to have unexpected and unwanted consequences as society is always more complex than we recognize. It is therefore good to be restrictive with regulation and policy.
- **Green argument:** There are serious systemic flaws in our economic system that cause crises and may lead to ecological collapse.
- **Day-to-day politics:** Public spending should carefully follow and counter international trends—this optimizes the labor market. But the labor market can unfortunately not be expected to function perfectly; it always lets some people down.

HOW TO SPOT A STAGE 12

Stage 12 Systematic thinkers will tend to have less rigid opinions but more rigid argumentations. So one way to spot them is simply to ask them questions about their opinions: If there are few rules of thumb and clear conclusions, but much weighing of different factors, it may be stage 12 Systematic.

The stage 12 Systematic thinkers are often more inventive than others, so if the person has made unconventional innovations, this may indicate this stage.

But perhaps the easiest way may be by means of their cognitive biases: Stage 12 Systematic thinkers tend to believe that the world consists of systems and their properties. So you find a strong bias towards explanations of this kind: structures, patterns, regularities, the economy, the biological body, Darwinian evolution, the gender norms and so forth.

Stage 13 Metasystematic

Who? Adult humans from early 20s and onwards.
How many? Only about 1.5-2% of a normal adult human population.

In the history of science and philosophy you might find ideas that embody this stage of complexity in relative recent branches such as general information theory, cybernetics, complexity science, chaos theory, the systems sciences, metatheory (theory about theory), Wilberian integral theory and perhaps epigenetics. Of course, just studying these sciences doesn't mean that the student is automatically a stage 13 Metasystematic thinker. And most of the innovators within these fields are of still higher cognitive stages (14 Paradigmatic or 15 Crossparadigmatic).

I will present this stage more briefly. The point is that the stage 13 Metasystematic thinker is capable of comparing the general properties of systems, naming these properties and reasoning about when they generalize or not. Let's jump right to the invented example.

Invented Example

We can observe then, that it is not blefuscity (and its sub-factors), even combined with steepness, that determines how good a climb (how much *value*, recreational or practical) we get. Nor is it the characteristics of the climber that determines the climb. Rather, it is a property of the system as a whole: how well-aligned the different variables, across both systems (cliff and climber), are to one another, with regard to value created by the cliff/climber system as a whole. So the overall alignment of the system determines the climb: not any single variable like blefuscity. Our previous ideas about blefuscity reveal themselves as "true, but partial".

So we have added a term, alignment, to describe the system as a whole. Let's expand that term: How much can you adjust the different variables so as to increase their alignment? We are now introducing an invented meta-systematic term: alignability.

The cliff/climber system has low *alignability* (a property of the system): It is difficult—or it has high cost—to change any one variable (to, for instance, make the cliff less rugged), and the different variables effect almost no change upon one another. The low alignability of the cliff/ climber system will only produce value in relatively few cases.

Compare this to another system: the market economy. Each of its parts is much more dependent on the other parts. Things like supply, demand, distribution systems, and legal frameworks change all the time. Because of the market system's high alignability, it aligns into value-creating (and thereby behaviorally self-sustaining) equilibria all the time. It is not logically necessary to have a market to produce food or to create other value—so there is no *logical necessity* for why markets should be so much more central to most humans than is mountaineering.

The reason that markets are much more prevalent and important is that there is a certain property of this system that e.g. mountaineering does not have: high "alignability". If it were mountaineering that had such high alignability, it would be more central: We could just align its different parts in ways that created more value. The market can steer the right people to the right mountains, with the right equipment and most other people to other activities, such as skiing.

There is a long stretch between the stage 10 Abstract concept of "blefuscity" and the Stage 13 Metasystematic concept of "alignability". We have made a major climb, into more abstract heights, viewing the world from a much more elevated conceptual vantage point. We have traveled away from concrete reality: Whereas "blefuscity" is an abstract concept, you can still *see* it with your eyes, feel it with your hands. And we have arrived at a much less tangible world: the "alignability" of systems and how it creates value.

We have also made conceptual leaps: from discussing relatively concrete and small matters, to grasping a wider world.

And we have abandoned the topic (mountaineering). That's what a cognitive advance often looks like: That which seemed so important at an earlier stage seems less so—and more contingent—when viewed from a higher cognitive vantage point.

From here, let's go straight to the political reasoning examples.

SOME STAGE 13 METASYSTEMATIC REASONING ABOUT POLITICS

- **Anti-racist argument:** Racism emerges as different cultures and status hierarchies interact, where ethnic markers are used in order to increase one's position in the status hierarchy. It should be prevented by the creation of both greater psychological security and by the facilitation of productive dialogue about cultural differences.

- **Conservative argument:** Liberal values prevalent in Western countries may be more functional in late modern society than the more traditionalist values of many Arab Muslims, but for the successful integration of these different cultures one must take the perspectives of all parties seriously.
- **Feminist argument:** Feminism is an interest group movement as well as a social justice movement. As an interest group movement it must be weighed against other interests and perspectives. As a social justice movement it must be coordinated with other social justice issues such as class, ethnicity, global inequality, other gender issues (including men's issues), and the exploitation of animals and nature.
- **Libertarian argument:** State control and policy implementation always interact with other societal systems and are dependent upon these for their successful functioning. It is thus important to carefully weigh state regulation and policy against other possibilities: markets, culture, and civil sphere. State regulation is often not the best path ahead.
- **Green argument:** The logic inherent to the economic system is fundamentally alien to the logic of the ecosystems of the many biotopes. This means that there is no self-regulating feedback cycle directly present between our economic and technological expansion and the ecosystems upon which we depend. This lack of feedback means that we have to drive the ecosystem to collapse before the market self-adjusts. We must thereby create some other feedback, e.g. by means of policy, public awareness or cultural development.
- **Day-to-day politics:** Public spending can be high or low, where higher spending is generally made possible by strong institutions such as rule of law, policing, democracy and free press. This keeps corruption down and allows for public support of spending and makes spending less wasteful. There is no one answer about high or low taxes; you have to coordinate it with the other societal systems.

Note that the different political stances at stage 13 Metasystematic generally have more in common with one another than with the corresponding ideological positions at the earlier stages. This has important implications for metamodern politics.[100]

And that concludes our brief guide to the four most important stages of cognitive adult development. There is more to it, but that's all you need to know for the purposes of this book.[101]

No, I Still Can't Believe It. I Won't!

No doubt, you have some resistance against the MHC model. When I first learned about MHC it seemed quite counter-intuitive to me. That most adult people can't construct systems of thought containing several linear equations? That they cannot recognize even a simple system with a feedback loop or a "catch-22" (the simplest form of stage 12 Systematic reasoning)? It seemed not only condescending and disrespectful, but simply incorrect. I thought to myself: "No, it doesn't make sense. In reality, the same person can sometimes be smart, sometimes dumb, depending a lot on if they are doing something they are good at or not, the context she is in, etc. They don't have one fixed stage!"

But then two things happened. One thing is that I had learned the stages and could start seeing the people around me (and myself) with their help. And an almost terrifying pattern emerged: People, including colleagues and loved ones, seemed to never—never-ever—produce ideas or thoughts above a certain stage, even if they were "smart" and skilled in many ways. Their line of reasoning was always, always within the limits of for instance stage 10 Abstract: Producing abstractions but never drawing conclusions from their interrelations.

These were alive, intelligent, conscious people in my direct presence—people I still know and love—who suddenly seemed to "act like robots" in the sense that they followed the patterns of the MHC stages with such frightening precision. Everybody appeared to be a much less "free thinker" than what I had previously felt. Within academia, in my case in sociology, a similar insight dawned on me: Almost nobody ever comes up with a new idea (a real new theory). The ideas are always reused versions of things others have said, or simply applications of these ideas, or at most a small, often rather questionable, tweak to someone else's theory. The very top people of each field seemed to be the ones who had come up with *one* new theory—and out of these only very few theories seemed to make much sense. Then turn to people like Jürgen Habermas (the world top dog sociologist-philosopher) and *voilà*: from age 30 and onwards, a long string of novel ideas, of theoretical pearls that link up the ideas of others and create a shift of paradigm within sociology. High stage, man. High stage. So this explains, I would argue, why so few people ever really come up with anything quite new.

The other thing that happened was that I learned more about cognitive development (more generally, not just the MHC) and came across ideas that nuance the picture. I'd like to bring two of them to the table here: **downward assimilation** and **scaffolding**.

Downward assimilation means that, because of our ability to share a common language, you can take a word, symbol, sentence or even an attitude, that originated at a higher order of complexity, and still use it. Your *use* of that symbol will then inevitably follow the logic of your own stage, but it might still bring some meaning with it, and you can perhaps partake in conversations that would otherwise lie beyond your own stage of complexity. The complex symbol is *assimilated* "downwards".

For instance, we can imagine teaching Alex the grey African parrot a word like "structure" or "negative feedback loop". Whereas Alex really *could* "talk" about crackers and yellow rings, he would only be able to "parrot" a discussion about structural gender inequality. That's of course an extreme form of downward assimilation. Let's take a more sociologically relevant example.

In societies like Sweden, it is popular, especially among the younger citizens, to speak about things like "norms", "structures" and "identity". However, only a minority tend to be able to actually understand these concepts at stage 12 Systematic or above. This certainly includes students of sociology, the often idealistic young people I've had the pleasure of teaching. Instead, people will recast these concepts at stages Abstract 10 and Formal 11. Norms are taken to mean "social rules that create inequalities" and are always seen as bad. "Structures" become a kind of evil spirits that can be exorcized by the sufficiently faithful followers of the Left, often with linear interpretations of "feminism" as a good essence that you can apply to anything in order to purify it from evil—the more of it, the better. And "identity" comes to mean self-confidence, rather than the interactive construction of a "self" as discussed by the classical social psychologists.[102]

The second concept, scaffolding, brings some hope to this misery. It is possible, namely, through the means of language and communicative actions, to *support* someone's cognitive stage upwards—not just one, but *two* stages. Language has to be nature's most awesome creation! Through language and interaction you create a "scaffold" that helps the other person to partake in behaviors that would otherwise be beyond his or her cognitive stage. African grey parrots generally don't say even single words to one another—but Alex was different. Through the use of shared language (Alex was Anglophonic) he was supported, when interacting with very, very patient humans, to think and communicate two orders of complexity above his fellow parrots (going from stage 4 to stage 6).

The same goes for the rest of us: Language structures seem to be able to help us more than a bit. That's largely how education works. But it usually takes long hours of interaction with people who are of higher stage than ourselves and who really walk us through the correct sequences again and again.

So this social-psychological aspect of development creates plenty of room for flexibility (if you like, a compromise between Piaget's rigid stages and Vygotsky's faith in social context and human malleability).

The common language also "stores" structures and patterns for us to use, so that a certain thought or behavior becomes more easily attainable. For instance, it is easier to understand what a "gravity field" is once people have discovered, named and explained it. So scaffolding is the other side of the coin of "downward assimilation"; when we grasp for notions that are out of our cognitive depth, we also stretch our minds, and we come under the influence of thoughts and ideas that would otherwise be beyond us.

These two concepts, downward assimilation and scaffolding, explain a lot about why the MHC stages are so difficult to spot in the fussy world around us: We simply misinterpret the MHC stages because of their dependence on contexts and interactions. Add to this that we have three more dimensions of adult development (code, state and depth), and also IQ, specific skills, different levels of education, psychological health, and different ways to evaluate each other's smarts. To further complicate things, the transition between two stages seems to happen in eight steps, where you gradually learn to coordinate things at the preceding order of complexity (the discussion of which I have omitted from this text).[103] Phew! It should come as no surprise that the MHC stages are hidden in plain sight.

When the underlying order in the chaos is so difficult to see, it can be very tempting to conclude that the world is simply fussy, disordered—and even to wear that skeptical conclusion as a badge of anti-reductionist honor, as a mark of our own open-mindedness, humility and spirituality. **But there is nothing open-minded, humble or spiritual in *failing* to see—and properly respond to—the undeniable regularities in human behavior that are revealed by the elegant but merciless simplicity of experimental, empirical science.**

People try to resist these perspectives and theories in many ways, the most common perhaps being to attempt to *typify* the stages, making them into different "types" that cannot really be compared, thus relativizing the differences. It is a tempting move, because types are a so much less sensitive topic.

Such relativization is in fact an inversion of what 19th century colonial thinkers did when they "stageified" different types (human races) into dominator hierarchies (white above black, etc.). Just as the Europeans invented false and arbitrary stage theories to justify their colonial political stances, so do people today invent false and arbitrary type theories to defend *their* political stances (ignoring the relevant research results of stage theories)—to defend ideals of equality.

But you can't wish the stage differences away. It's just dishonest and counter-productive. There really *is* a logic to the order, and being at stage 10 Abstract is *not* simply "same, same but different" as being at stage 13 Metasystematic. There is a *huge* qualitative difference.

Developmental *stages* should not be confused with "types" (black/white, male/female, East/West, quiet/talkative, etc.). Types are those things that really are beyond hierarchical comparison, indeed "same, same but different". Stages constitute a logical, hierarchical and empirically verifiable order.

If you are to prove that stage theories are wrong, you are obliged to puncture the so far solid research program of the adult development, which is getting stronger results than any other part of psychology. *Or* you have to explain their strong results with some other theory that better fits the data. Good luck with that.

We can resist these ideas for reasons of protecting our own self-image (that we personally are most likely, after all, not very high stage) or for more heartwarming reasons, such as a dislike of the inequality that is implied in the model, and for concern about how such ideas could be misused.

But remember what David Hume taught us: an "ought" cannot be derived from an "is". The fact that something happens to be true doesn't make it *right* in a moral sense. Likewise, the opposite is true: an "is" cannot be derived from and "ought". That something factual doesn't rhyme with a *moral* intuition we have, doesn't make it fictional. No matter how provocative—it's still true, whether we like it or not, and then we have to make the best of it. The fact that splitting the atom leads to an explosive release of energy and atom bombs (as well as a sad goodbye to Democritus) doesn't make it any less true that atoms can be split. It's the truth, like it or not.

Listen, the fact is that people are of different cognitive stages, plain and simple. Deal with it, and use it for something good. Because, again, the facts of the matter are just *one* part of reality. The *real* reality comes into being when we use the facts to tell new stories, to create new realities.

Implications for Society

Then again—so what? Is the point that we should find ourselves a benevolent dictator at stage 15 Crossparadigmatic and everything will be fine? If only Chairman Mao and Comrade Stalin had been at stage 15 Crossparadigmatic, happy days would be here to stay?

That's obviously *not* it. That would be a simplistic, "low stage" application of the theory. We haven't yet discussed the notion of "democratization politics" (featured in Book Two).

Higher cognitive stage folks aren't necessarily "right" about things. If you have kids, you may have noticed how surprisingly often these keen little creatures can correct us, in spite of their "lower" cognitive stage. And again, stage doesn't mean skill—you still have to learn things from others even if you have higher cognitive stage.

In the future of democracy cognitive stages may have an important role to play. But the point is *not* to exclude the voices of all the stage 10 Abstract and stage 11 Formal thinkers—that would be unethical and sure to backfire dramatically. The point is to create processes in which people's perspectives make up a part of a larger whole, a whole which resides at a higher order of complexity.

The main political implications have to do with the cultivation and design of a *deeper* democracy, not the contrary. In our current political system we are not nearly democratic enough, and that's exactly what holds the more complex ideas and solutions in check. **In a good democracy the more complex answers to life's problems can emerge, answers that are more inclusive to a multiplicity of interests and perspectives. In a poor democracy, the lowest common denominator sets the limit.**

Remember, then, that MHC stage is just a piece in the bigger puzzle here—it can help us explain how we can create progressive, cosmopolitan and sustainable values, behaviors and societies, but we still need the other pieces of the puzzle. Stay tuned.

Chapter 10

SYMBOLIC DEVELOPMENT

If cognitive development seems to be relatively inherent to the single person, what about the language structures that the same person has available? Surely there must be a difference if you are only ever taught the two words "yes" and "no" or if you are taught fifty thousand words and get a 20 year long education? Yes, there's a difference.

Or another way to approach the problem. Pablo Picasso was, at least according to Michael Commons and his friend Albert Erdynast, cognitively at stage 15 Crossparadigmatic—so he produced art at this stage.[104] What then happens to the "field" of art? Does *it* become stage 15 Crossparadigmatic in itself, so that all who continue working from Picasso's insights as a starting point produce art at this stage?

Or how about the Newtonian universe? Do we all, after Newton's stage 15 Crossparadigmatic genius, do physics at the highest known cognitive stage, because his physics "were at Crossparadigmatic"?

On the other hand, consider a medieval philosopher like Thomas of Aquinas. Newtonian physics require stage 11 Formal logic to follow and understand authentically. But Aquinas, writing centuries before Newton, did not have access to the Newtonian worldview—only theology, Aristotle and his Islamic commentaries, his philosophy being largely contained within the dictates of the Catholic faith dominant at the time. Does that mean that the greatest philosopher of the 13th century was only at stage 10 Abstract?

In each of these three cases the answer is a resounding: of course not! The cognitive stage of the individual is *not* the same as the stage of the symbolic universe that she has available, the words and ideas that she has learned and "internalized" and been "socialized" into. We are speaking here of two relatively different processes: one in the single person (MHC stages), and one of **symbolic development**; that is, the evolution of the world of language and shared symbolic universes. Picasso and Newton updated the cultural "code", the symbols, so that people after them had new symbolic tools available. It was this "code" that a medieval thinker like Aquinas simply lacked, but that any modern fourteen-year-old has access to through public schools.

Let's use a computer analogy; they're so popular these days. If the last two chapters discussed the cognitive *hardware* (processing power, etc.), this chapter discusses the *software*, hence the choice of word "code". How smart a cultural piece of software are you "programmed" with?

The relation between hardware (brains) and software (symbols) is obviously one of many complex interactions—for instance, you can't run too advanced software on too simple a computer (we can teach the parrot about "two yellow rings", but not about structural gender inequality), and the right software can help speed up your computer, clearing out viruses or the like (going to school can help you see more complex patterns in reality). But stage and code are still two very distinct dimensions of development. We should not split development into one "intra-cranial" and one "cultural" part, since they interact. But we *should* acknowledge the difference between a medieval genius and an average modern fifteen-year-old.

My claim in this chapter is that there is a *stage difference* between the various forms of cultural code available to people today, and that this stage difference follows a logic inherent to the meanings of the symbols and their interrelations, rather than being inherent to the cognitive stage of the specific organism. Each such code contains within itself a *toolkit* consisting of interrelated symbols, which can be used to interpret the world. These symbolic toolkits determine a large part of how a person sees the world and how she acts within it.

We are looking here at a development quite different from simply how cognitively advanced our brains are. This development depends upon there being communities of people who speak a language—it is the development *of* that language: **symbolic development**.

Realdialektik

A central claim here is that this stage difference follows a distinct, dialectical logic, a logic that I call, with a German word, ***Realdialektik***. In English you might say "real dialectics", but please note that the German meaning of the word "real" is more closely related to "factual necessity" than the English connotation "opposite of unreal" or "not fake".

Each of the stages creates language code that is inherently more advanced than the previous stage. There is something *real* in the logic of how each symbolic universe is constructed, and this realness *forces* the direction of human history. It does not force specific events upon the world, of course, but it *does* compel society to develop in some directions rather than others: Large and old social systems are the ones that develop a greater number of words, and find more abstract relations between these words, etc.

> "History developing in a certain direction? Pah! Surely Hanzi has not been paying attention in university history class the last few decades. We all know that is nonsense!"

Or is it? Think about it: What comes first—the wheel, the combustion engine or the airplane? Could we imagine a "historical contingency" in which the airplane would come first? I would be hard pressed to find a reason that airplanes should show up before the wheel. You need wheels to create wagons, and you need wagons that you want to propel in order to create the combustion engine (which also necessitates circular motion) and you need combustion engines to propel a Boeing jet. Is there a *Realdialektik* to this, a logical directionality, or is it just me?

We are speaking of the evolutionary development of *memes* (non-biological cultural patterns that spread through communication)—where some memes can only show up in more complex societies. It simply never happened in a tribe of 150 people on a remote island that someone developed modern physics and a poststructuralist critique of literature.

This chapter isn't really about how societies develop such memes—you'll find a thorough discussion of this in one of my other books (*The 6 Hidden Patterns of World History*), which discusses the historical development of ***"meta"-memes***, i.e. the overall patterns that set the logic for what memes can be expected to show up at a certain stage of societal development.[105] This chapter is simply about the idea that different such codes are downloaded into the single individual—with lasting effects on his or her developmental psychology.

Let's not dwell on the concept of *Realdialektik* and how it works. The central point here is just that there is a dialectical development inherent to the symbols of culture, and that this makes it possible to arrange the metamemes (or cultural logics that people follow) into several stages.

Whereas the later stages of cultural **metamemes** by necessity must emerge later in historical time than earlier ones, their spread is very far from even and cannot easily be contained within a specific "historical period". For instance, just consider the metameme of secular modern life, which in fact originates in Renaissance art through the Scientific Revolution of the 17th century and the Enlightenment of the 18th century. At the beginning of the 20th century, amidst the full melee of cars and electric lights, most people were still adherents of traditional religions and worldviews. Hundreds of years after the emergence of a metameme that is so strong it mercilessly shreds its way through history, most people still haven't downloaded its cultural code. Even today, the majority of the world's population, by quite a margin, still operate primarily with premodern cultural code.

But in the meantime, the modern symbols have broken down under their own weight. This has produced a new cultural code, which is here called "post"-modernism. And then—even postmodernism has broken down, and in comes "meta"-modernism. There is a pattern to this, a *Realdialektik*: You cannot go from traditional religion directly to metamodernism. Only when postmodernism has been around for decades, can metamodern symbols start breaking through and become part of society.

In different social, technological and economic environments different metamemes gain competitive traction over the others—which also follows a predictable dynamic or *Realdialektik*. In our days, the metamodern symbols are especially powerful, which means that they are likely to spread. However, we will also leave this developmental-evolutionary discussion aside here to only focus on what matters for our main argument: the symbolic development of the individual person.

So language has evolved throughout human history, crystallizing into different code systems, some more advanced than others, and a person living today can "download" and "install" any of them—depending on her own capabilities, her position in the world and so on. The seven metamemes or "symbol-stages" are (here assigned capital letter codes A-G):

A.	Archaic:	Earliest humans and their closest relatives, Neanderthals etc.
B.	Animistic: (or "Post"-Archaic)	The magical and ritualistic thinking of tribal society.
C.	Faustian:	The mythical thinking of agricultural warrior society, Neolithic and onwards.
D.	"Post"-Faustian:	The mythic-rational, transcendental thinking of traditional, religious society.
E.	Modern:	The rational, scientific thinking of the developed world today.
F.	"Post"-Modern:	The post-rational, systemic critique of modern life and society.
G.	"Meta"-Modern:	Read this book, please.

Each of these metamemes operates as a set of thousands of propositions and assumptions about the world which interlock into a self-supporting whole, a kind of ecosystem or equilibrium. Each of them is a kind of underlying structure of the symbolic universes that constitute our lived and shared realities. So each one of them roughly have an ontology (theory of reality and what is "really real"), an ideology ("theory of what is right and good") and an identity, an idea of who or what the self is. Basically, the metamemes have an idea or story about reality in what is sometimes called 3rd, 2nd and 1st person.[106] This is the pattern I use to describe the postfaustian, modern, postmodern and metamodern "effective value memes", once when we get to chapter 16.

Since the metamemes are underlying patterns in knowledge (the beams and struts of our ways of thinking) they can take any number of forms—just imagine the inexhaustible plethora of animistic stories, traditional religions and modern sciences. So what we're going after here are the general patterns of such symbols. Once you begin to recognize them, you will begin to be able to see them all around you. And you will see their profound significance for understanding society and its dynamics.

The stages of symbolic development show up as structures in language, logically organized into ever more complex, differentiated and integrated patterns. They each create a blueprint for the creation of narratives: So the language tools are not only metamemes, but also **meta-*narratives***. There is always a rough, underlying story (narrative) about reality from which humans operate, from which they create new "code", new knowledge.

Code and Cognitive Development

The ability to understand a longer story or a narrative requires MHC stage 9 Concrete, as discussed in the previous chapter. Most adult people have been at this stage or above for the last 200 000 years. So a normally developed adult can "download" or install any of the metamemes, at least as an overall story about reality. Still, human beings live in symbolic universes that are of very different levels of abstraction.

In intelligence research, there is a classic story of the Russian psychologist Alexander Luria, who went to the farther reaches of the Soviet Empire and interviewed rural Uzbeks, whose intelligence he wanted to test. So he asked a young Uzbek man: "In the far north, where there is snow, all bears are white. Novaya Zemlya is in the far north, and there is always snow. What color are the bears there?" He wouldn't get an answer; just that the young man had only ever seen a black bear. And when he persisted, the Uzbek explained: "If a man had been sixty or eighty, and said that he had seen a white bear and told about it, he would be believed. But I've never seen one and hence I can't say. That's my last word. Only those who saw can tell, and those who didn't can't say anything!"[107]

Clearly, the young Uzbek is adhering to a kind of empiricism. He won't just take some stranger's word for there being white bears, and asserts that he himself would be presumptuous to speak on the matter. He also explains who in the social order (a man sixty or eighty) might be credible, and under what circumstances (having seen a white bear for oneself), such a claim would be believable. These are, of course, perfectly intelligent replies. The difference between him and the Russian scientist has to do with how abstract a symbolic world they are participants of. The young man simply doesn't buy into Alexander Luria's could've-should've.

Each society is bound up with a world of symbols, a world of knowledge. What is the pattern of knowledge itself, including everyday understanding, seen as a unified theory that works across cultures? The sociology of knowledge—from its origins in Marx and Engels, to its fruition in Scheeler and Mannheim, to its later developments in Berger and Luckmann and in our days perhaps Latour, Gibbons and Nowotny, Rabinow or Knorr-Cetina—has grappled with trying to see the deeper, underlying patterns of knowledge. However, for all of its eye-opening perspectives, the sociology of knowledge has yet to produce a genuinely useful typology or general theory of knowledge-in-society. The discussions of epistemeology in philosophy of science tend to ignore the question altogether.

That being said, some theorists have argued, from Jean Gebser, to Jürgen Habermas (in *The Philosophical Discourse of Modernity*) and the German developmental sociologist Günter Dux, that there is a kind of connection between the overall development of cognitive stage and of the development of symbolic toolkits available in language—the development of society. Or actually, they don't really make the distinction between cognition and language, but that's the idea they're all getting at without quite catching it. They all *smash* the different dimensions of development together into one single sequence.

Michael Commons has also given it a shot, but in my view he also misses the mark here. He obviously has access to the MHC model, but he instead *reduces* development to it (in his model, you become "ultramodern" as you reach the postformal stages, so his model in effect stops at modernity). To be fair, Michael agrees with me that there is a difference between cognitive complexity and code, but he doesn't describe the postmodern and metamodern cultural codes accurately.

So yes, there is a connection, the "code" of each metameme following the logic pertaining to a specific order of hierarchical complexity. That's the fundamental *Realdialektik* at play. It looks like this (again, assigning the symbol-stages capital letters A-G):

• A. Archaic:	Stage 7 Pre-Operational
• B. Animistic:	Stage 8 Primary
• C. Faustian:	Stage 9 Concrete
• D. "Post"-Faustian:	Stage 10 Abstract
• E. Modern:	Stage 11 Formal
• F. "Post"-Modern:	Stage 12 Systematic
• G. "Meta"-Modern:	Stage 13 Metasystematic

So, please take note here. This is not just a technical detail; it is absolutely crucial. The fact that someone is at stage 13 Metasystematic (or even above), does not mean that they use a Metamodern symbolic toolkit when describing the world. The vast majority of prominent scientists in the world today, while often *cognitively* being at MHC stages 13, 14 and even 15, still primarily rely on the modern symbolic toolkit.

This *also* means that people who, for instance, did not have a modern symbolic toolkit available, could still be at the highest cognitive stages, as was the case with Plato and Aristotle. It is continuously people at the highest cognitive stages who play key roles in challenging, updating and reinventing the symbolic codes.

And it *also* means that people can have access to a postmodern code without being at MHC stage 12 Systematic, which is in fact necessary to operate it in a coherent way. We have already discussed the issue of "downward assimilation" during the last chapter. **The majority of people with access to postmodern code accordingly use a "flattened" and simplified version of it.** By necessity, the same goes for metamodern code, which only less than two percent have the cognitive hardware to operate successfully. This makes the path ahead pretty dangerous—people are very likely to use simplified interpretations of e.g. political metamodernism. And misunderstanding a political paradigm is dangerous business. People at MHC stage Abstract 10 or below also tend to misinterpret and simplify modern science.

You may have noted that I have not included cultural metamemes that, in their logical structure, correspond to the two highest orders of complexity (14 Paradigmatic and 15 Crossparadigmatic). This is simply because these symbolic universes don't yet exist—and if somebody tries to claim to have invented them, they are either a fraud or deluding themselves. To invent a whole symbolic universe takes a civilization, and the metamodern symbolic toolkit is yet being born. So even if a person happens to be at a high cognitive stage and is developed in other regards (state and depth, as you will see), this doesn't mean that they magically gain access to the symbolic worlds of future civilizations. It only means that they can help develop new code at this particular point in history—just like Plato, Aristotle, Aquinas or Newton. They were each way ahead of their times, but they did not magically have access to chaos theory, network theory or the poststructural literature critique of our days.

Remember, remember: The code is *its own* developmental dimension, not to be confused with the cognitive hardware. And it is developed *collectively* through the ongoing use of language throughout history, then "downloaded" by the single human organism, who then uses her MHC stage (and, as we shall see, the two other dimensions of development) to interpret the code, either simplifying it, or using it in accordance to its logic—or, in rare cases, developing it further.

Yes, high MHC-stage folks can develop new code, in effect reinventing or updating the symbolic construction of the world they live in. Of course, by far the most developments of new code die out in the Darwinian struggle between memes. Most symbolic mutations are simply not fit to survive, just as most genetic ones aren't. In theory, the disciplines of "analytical philosophy" and "moral philosophy" should sift out the best symbolic codes. But in practice, that's not really how it works; academic philosophers generally stay safely within the boundaries of their own symbol-stage and don't really communicate across them.

There is one more aspect we should bring up before we go along: the amount of information or code at each symbol-stage. So let's make one more distinction with the help of our computer analogy: There is a difference between *installing* an entire symbol-stage and *downloading* more content at that stage. With time the content can easily take up more space on a hard drive than the program, but the installed program still determines how well the content files can be used, if at all.

So imagine the medieval Catholic scholar Thomas of Aquinas again. Did he not have to know *a lot* in order to write the *Summa Theologica*? Of course he did. He needed pretty much all of the learning available in his scholastic (symbol-stage D Postfaustian) times. While even an average 13-year-old of our days has managed to *install* the modern code, they of course cannot by any means match the downloaded content, or sheer knowledge, of this pre-modern genius thinker.

Likewise, most natural scientists of our days fail to understand even the simplest postmodern ideas (because they haven't "installed" symbol-stage F Postmodern), but they know modern science extremely well (having both "installed" symbol-stage E Modern and "downloaded" loads of content at that symbol-stage).

The different stages produce new forms of code, and the individual can install these stages, and then download—or create—different quantities of useful information at each stage (as well as information of different quality).

And... one more aspect of the relationship between code and cognitive development should be highlighted. We have already noted that there is a non-obvious, dynamic relation between MHC stage and symbol-stage; they can support or thwart one another, etc. It should still be noted, however, that **higher MHC stage makes the "installment" and "downloading" of a higher symbol-stage of code *more likely***—given that several types of code are available within the same society.

So for instance, we can expect, in today's Western countries, a greater likelihood for:

- MHC stage 10 Abstract thinkers to be attracted to the symbol-stage D Postfaustian (that you have a soft spot for traditional religion, monolithic nationalism, etc.);
- stage 11 Formal thinkers to be overrepresented with the symbol-stage E Modern (mainstream society, liberalism);
- stage 12 Systematic thinkers to gravitate towards symbol-stage F Postmodern (critical thinking, counterculture, etc.);
- and stage 13 Metasystematic thinkers to more often having installed a symbol-stage G Metamodern toolkit (ideas such as in this book).

But, as we shall see in the coming chapters, a person's MHC stage is not the only thing that affects what code you tend to install, or how you tend to use and interpret it—so the relationship is far from a solid one.

Teleology and Determinism?

So does this whole *Realdialektik* business, with its inherent developmental directionality, imply that history and humanity's destiny are somehow "guided" by a force or will with its own set goals? And is the future of society already determined? This discussion perhaps belongs elsewhere, since it goes for all of the developmental perspectives presented in this book, but I will just quickly address it here and kill it before it grows into a brain tumor.

The answer is no. None of this implies *either* teleology (that nature or God or whatever "wants" certain things to happen) *or* determinism (that it is already determined exactly what will happen).

Let's start with teleology. According to Aristotle and the medieval physics based on his philosophy, everything in nature "wants" something, it has its own inherent *telos* or goal, which in turn is set by God. Modern consciousness and science expelled this telos from nature and showed that it was in fact a lingering imaginary spirit, a superstition that has no explanatory power in mechanics. Since then, however, teleology has had a strange, stubborn habit of showing up again and again in more subtle guises: first as an *élan vital* in biology (the "force of life" that in the 19th century was still believed to animate organisms), then as "the will of evolution" in the pathological forms of social Darwinism (where people believed that certain classes and races were "wanted" by evolution to dominate others), or more recently, when people make "evolutionary" arguments about what diets people should have (usually lots of juicy steaks)—or when sociologists theorized to understand what "society wants" (so-called functionalism), or when people explain social phenomena by simply giving a "historical" background (as if history in itself could explain matters of social science)—or just in popular science when we teach the kids that the electron "wants" to balance out its negative charge.

The list goes on. In more spiritual circles you might find more explicit ideas of an *Eros*, a force of love that guides the evolution of the cosmos—or teleological interpretations of Lovelock's famous Gaia theory (a theory that by no means needs to imply teleology). Some people will also use the concepts of complexity and emergence in corresponding, teleological, manners. For this reason—that teleology seems to sneak in pretty much everywhere—there is good reason to be wary.

So when I talk about stages that are ordered according to an inherent *Realdialektik*, am I not making the same mistake? Am I being teleological? Nay. All I am saying is that there is a *pattern* or *logic* inherent to this kind of development, and that this pattern can be described. It's the same as saying that when a child grows, they will become taller and gain weight. That's it. It's in the very definition of a child growing with age—more inches and pounds. Or when a population grows, that the number of people increases. It's not that nature or God "wants" height, weight or an increased number of people, it's simply a description of important aspects of these forms of growth. There is an inherent logic to it. It is *in the definitions.*

What about determinism? Am I saying, by discussing stages of symbolic development, that it is already determined—ordained—what is going to happen in the future? Nay. For instance, describing that kids become taller and heavier between ages of five and seven does not say that this particular kid necessarily will. His growth can be stunted due to malnourishment or disease or any number of genetic or biochemical reasons. Or he can just get hit by a car and loose his legs.

Likewise, even if societies develop symbolic metamemes according to a certain *Realdialektik*, there's no set destiny in sight: We can still get hit by a comet or ecological collapse tomorrow, and then that will be it. In this sense, *shit just happens.* So we're not determining the future here, just pointing out some relevant patterns. We live in a *could've-should've* world, hinging on an absurd number of contingencies.

Shit just happens. But it happens in recognizable patterns that can be described (or at least metaphorically approached) with symbols. And these patterns are always interruptible and the description of such patterns does not take into account every specific detail.[108]

Still, then, there are patterns of development. For instance, it was, as a matter of *Realdialektik*, somehow determined that once the combustion engine was invented and the physics of aerodynamics discovered, eventually someone would build an airplane—the rise and fall of the Red Baron (the legendary German fighter pilot of the First World War), however, remains a particularity beyond the scope of any dialectic explanations, one of the many historical twists and turns beneath the overarching patterns of development.

Another side of this should be mentioned. Even if we can describe certain patterns of how societies develop and how the metamemes follow an inherent *Realdialektik*, we have not said anything about what effects or *meanings* these patterns may have. Depending on other issues, such as technological development, ecological crises, etc., the developmental sequences can play out in any number of ways and come to have any number of meanings in history. It also depends on the perspective of the interpreter: You can interpret and use the developmental patterns I describe in any number of ways.

I guess I am just saying this: NO, the following sequence of symbol-stages isn't a monolithic railway path that society can and must follow, a mold into which people can and should be forced. And I didn't fully address *fatalism*, which is teleology and determinism put together ("destiny"), which is of course even worse.

Symbolic stage development is just a useful pattern to recognize—and the people who fail to recognize it will be considerably worse off than the people who manage to. Okay, ready?

Chapter 11

THE SYMBOL-STAGES

The first four symbol-stages are less relevant to understanding metamodern politics and how to create a metamodern society, but they are discussed in my book on history, titled *The 6 Hidden Patterns of World History*. Even if we will mention them again a bit later, I will be very brief in presenting them and then go on to the traditional, modern, postmodern and metamodern symbolic toolkits.

So what we have here is language travelling through history, picking up new symbols and meanings as larger societies and more complex interactions between greater numbers of humans over greater distances emerge. But they all keep existing for quite some time even after their subsequent stages have emerged.

The First Three Symbol-Stages: A, B and C

Before recorded history we can see plenty of evidence of an animistic culture with Stone Age art and mysticism, totemism, ancestral worship and tribal relations. But then again, even before that, Homo sapiens have been around for at least 70 000 years counting from today (that's when humans are believed to have been both anatomically and cognitively much like today's people)—long before such traces appeared. And for a long time, there were at least six species of hominids (Homo erectus, Neanderthals, and so forth). Strangely, they did not leave such traces behind. So people must have had forms of culture that preceded the animistic one, "archaic" cultures that to a lesser degree conjured imaginary worlds of art and mysticism, but still buried their dead (albeit without much ornaments) and cared for the sick and elderly. This is **symbol-stage A Archaic**.

Archaic cultures did not leave behind artwork. The traces we do have of cave paintings and the like, from 40 000 years ago and onwards, seem to more resemble the tribal hunter-gatherer cultures of today. Such cultures are well described in modern anthropology, where the staggering variety of tribes and peoples around the world still follow some recognizable patterns: magic, animism, spirit worship, nature lore, etc. Whereas such cultural expressions are relatively common in modern people (astrology, belief in magic, angels, ghosts, ancestors, spiritual medicine etc.) it does not really inform any of our political movements, sciences or major religions. That's **symbol-stage B Animism**.

With the advent and development of agriculture we have what I call a faustian age; symbol-stage C. I call it "faustian" because people can now reach for power, glory and mastery over others through organized violence and accumulation of military prowess—controlling territories, resources and populations. Like in the story about Faust, you can "sell your soul" for ascension and power. Agriculture brings a first corresponding control over nature, and the end of nomadic life makes possible accumulations of tools created through artisanship, which in turn makes possible and necessitates the differentiation of labor (people become smiths, potters and bakers). In the cultural code produced at this stage you get heroic stories, like Gilgamesh, who in his death lives forever in the walls of Uruk, and the many gods of the Indo-European pantheons, from Greeks to Vikings and Slavs, and their counterparts in e.g. the Aztec faith. In the stories produced in these mythologies, heroes can turn on the universal forces of nature and rebel against the gods. This is also when "the lamp of history" is lit, with Herodotus' accounts of times past and Homer's epics. These constitute coordinations of (groups of) paragraphs into coherent narratives, which corresponds to MHC stage 9 Concrete.

Symbolic toolkits and symbolic universes at the faustian stage are still being invented and used today—you can see it in (often criminal) gangs, neo-Nazi organizations, some of the gang and tribe related religious practices in West Africa, and to a certain extent, in some of the cultural expressions of adolescents in Western countries. But the symbol-stage emerging from this metameme is still less relevant to understanding political reality in the Nordic countries—even if it may be very relevant to other issues. Anyway, that's **symbol-stage C Faustian**.

Symbol-Stage D: Postfaustian (or Traditional)

Around 2500 years ago, across the Eurasian continent, there was a widespread critique of the "might makes right" logic of the growing faustian societies. This cultural critique is what I discuss as "the Axial age" in the Hanzi book on world history. You have a cultural critique of faustianism, which is why we call it "post-faustian" (just like "post"-modern critique of modernity).

What is relevant at this point is simply to get a brief idea or sample of this stage of symbolic development. It is here that you find all the classical religions: from Judaism on to Christianity and Islam, over Zoroastrianism to Hinduism with the birth of the Buddhist and Jain traditions—and the Confucian and Taoist traditions. The Greek Socratic philosophy shows many structural similarities in its critique of the faustian pantheon.

All of these traditions *abstract* from the stories and narratives of their time, certain *universal* understandings (you go from MHC stage 9 Concrete stories to stage 10 Abstract concepts). There is not just "the gods", but a "God above all gods"—the ultimate abstraction. But this is not only found in Abrahamic religions, you have the Brahman in Hinduism, formless emptiness as the ground of being in Buddhism, the Tao in Taoism, the Tian (heaven above all the gods) in Confucianism, Ahura Mazda (the lord of wisdom) in Zoroastrianism, not to mention how Plato and Aristotle began speaking of "God" in singular despite the fact that they were brought up with the polytheistic Greek pantheon, without any contact with Abrahamic religions.

I am of course not claiming that these traditions had no significant qualitative differences between them (or that any of them make up one monolithic system). Particularly Socratic philosophy, Taoism and Jainism stand out, I would argue, as more radically critical of their own societies. But I *am* claiming that it is no coincidence that they appear under comparable historical circumstances (viz. within highly developed agrarian regimes with literary traditions) and that there is an underlying logic that explains this fact—again, see the history book, *The 6 Hidden Patterns of World History*.

What is the logic encoded into the postfaustian symbols? The basic idea is that there is something unnamable beyond all stories we mere mortals can tell ourselves, a universal truth beyond anything we can comprehend, to which we must ultimately surrender. Exit the god-king, the pharaoh; in walks the righteous rebel. Exit Prometheus and his defiance of the gods—and the saints come marching in. Exit rebellion, violence and power; enter surrender, peace and harmony. **Beyond all human affairs, beyond all of our dramas and passions, lies something far more absolute, a reality more real than our everyday lives.**

You have a God or Universal Truth, and the human being has a soul of her own. And the postfaustians are telling us: Don't sell your soul for pleasure and power! It just ain't worth it.

This existence of a Universal Truth with a capital T means that rebellion is futile: The rebel Satan is no longer a cool prince or demigod, but the ultimate symbol of evil. Competing "power gods" like Baal become demoted to demon status; there is only one God (or other fundamental principle, as in the Eastern traditions).

But, and this is a big but, **this also means that no king, ruler or wielder of power can have any ultimate authority beyond serving the universal truth**. So the saints and prophets are righteous critics and rebels, wishing to align their societies with a deeper, universal order of the cosmos. The Chinese emperor remains, but only as long as he upholds the Mandate of Heaven; no longer is he a god in earthly robes, now merely a divinely dressed man on a contract from God. And in India, all rulers must submit to the *rajadharma*, the path of kings. Sure, render unto Caesar what belongs to him; but remember, that in the last instance the law of the heart precedes any law of the land, says Jesus. And to speak out against an unjust ruler, adds another prophet, is the highest form of jihad.

Traditional society is born from a radical postfaustian critique of injustice, war, slavery, oppression and degradation—of the arbitrary use and abuse of power. It is here that humanity realizes that the truth will set her free. Still operating within the limits of agricultural, pre-industrial societies, these traditions set out to create disciplined spiritual practices to develop the human soul towards realization of the ultimate truth, towards some form of inner ascension. And they set out to create just, harmonious societies based on the truth as revealed by the enlightened ones, the prophets or messengers of God. The kings begin to try to show that their particular rule is indeed the most faithful one, that their power is universally justifiable as the natural order of things, that their supremacy serves the truth.

But what truth? There is always *one* true path set for us by the prophets—even in the relatively open-minded faith of Jainism—and the other perspectives are ultimately false. This creates a blind spot of humongous proportions: **ethnocentricity**, i.e. that you only see the perspective and interests of one ethnic group, culture or civilization.

Sure, anybody can be Christian, but what happens if somebody is just not? As soon as the "universal truth", like the word of Jesus, is seriously challenged, this creates an open wound in our whole reality. If those other people, say the Muslims, do *not* believe in this truth, then either the truth must be false, or they must be collectively mistaken, misguided or degenerate.

If the One Truth is false, it also means that the reality itself that I live in, that the one source of good, love and hope in this harsh world, is nowhere to be found—that the justification for all my morality is false. It means that my soul, which is given to me eternally by God, does not exist. If others can find reasons to defy this faith, perhaps its truth is not universal after all? No, it cannot be so! Let the infidels die and burn in hell—or convert.

One becomes prepared to oppress and destroy others in order to resist such challenges to one's ontology (sense of reality), ideology (sense of what a good society is) and sense of self (the social construction of an ego), to protect and maintain the boundaries of one's symbolic universe. In fact, every infidel becomes a threat to one's entire symbolic universe. And the heretic becomes even more menacing—one of our own who knows the Truth, but *still* betrays it. Just notice how gruesomely the word "heretic" appears even in its written form; this is a heritage from the post-faustian symbol-stage.

In its grasp for universality, this kind of code creates a mindless defense of its own particularity, where the deviant and the stranger are harshly discriminated against and punished. Where it reaches for universal solidarity and sisterhood, it creates boundaries and holy wars. Instead of setting us on a search for universal truth, it says it already has the Truth and installs the inquisition; it suppresses all other perspectives in zeal and missionary madness. And as it reaches for mercy and kindness in the name of the poor and wretched, it creates justifications for kings and bishops to rule us and fool us.

Even today, a large proportion of all adults, globally speaking, still subscribe to one religious faith or another—or at least to monolithic and mono-perspectival traditions of one country or culture. While certainly not in majority within e.g. the Nordic countries, this type of code is still the most installed and downloaded one in human organisms. While most of our institutions are perhaps informed by modern thinking, humanity, demographically speaking, still mainly runs on the **symbol-stage D Post-faustian** code.

And our friends "the New Atheists" (Dawkins, Dennett, Harris, the late Hitchens) still have a lot of work to do.

Symbol-Stage E: Modern

But if the "truth" is to be *truly* universal, said the pioneers of the Scientific Revolution and the Enlightenment, shouldn't it be verifiable by everyone? **That is, shouldn't it be *inter-subjectively* confirmable (or "falsifiable", as Blaise Pascal and Karl Popper clarified), so that we make certain that what you see is what I see?**

Why should we trust the words of others, even of the messengers of God, if we can't check for ourselves and then let others double-check our own perceptions? If both you and I see the moons of Jupiter, then surely the moons of Jupiter are there? If only I see angels and hobgoblins, and none of you do, is it not safer to assume, that there are no angels and hobgoblins?

This line of thinking leads us down the path of materialism, reductionism, positivism, determinism and scientism: There is a real reality "out there", and by means of inter-subjectivity, by verification, by *science* and the scientific method (induction, deduction and abduction), we can go beyond the shackles of subjective illusion and see the *real* world for the first time.

Beyond our senses, our stories, feelings, thoughts and social conventions lies a grey, colorless world consisting only of meaningless stuff that blindly follows an unchangeable, mechanical logic set out by no-one and nothing at the dawn of the universe. The world of *facts*. Everything, including our consciousness, is a giant machine, consisting of particles or waves that collide and together create all of the phenomena we know: evolution, DNA, energy, entropy, atoms, symmetry, quanta, cosmology, spacetime—all bound within the same basic arithmetic. But even the particles and waves are only superficial aspects of the ever-present fields that saturate and constitute the universe. The scientific method, and the instruments that go beyond our perceptions, help us "lose our senses": because our senses betray us. They were only evolved to see and relate to a thin slice of reality, as was our reasoning mind. By disciplining and bending our minds, we are breaking the shackles of illusion.

Physics becomes chemistry becomes biochemistry becomes biology becomes psychology becomes sociology. With each step you lose some elegance and precision—but this is only because of the imperfection of our knowledge. And at each level, the same Baconian scientific method (invented by Francis Bacon) reigns supreme. There is only one reality, one truth carved in stone. In physics.

Initially René Descartes kept "the soul" as a strange ghost in the machine, but soon enough all such ghosts could be exorcized and left was only the machine. The machine—in blind, perpetual, meaningless, mechanical motion—is the ultimate reality, the final truth beyond all truths. Laplace said it: If there was a "demon" who knew and could calculate all positions and all speeds of all particles in the universe, this entity would know all things that will ever occur. What of God? asked Napoleon, and Laplace replied: "Your majesty, I have no use for that hypothesis".[109]

Exit God. Exit Jesus and Mohammed and all the saints and their arbitrary stories, always hinging on subjective opinion and historical contingencies. We have been fooled and manipulated by what is ultimately just a bunch of power hungry and self-righteous potheads who dreamed up realities that suited them. But now we are waking up, maturing, and the *individual* can take responsibility and see for herself, see if it makes sense. The individual is freed and empowered by science—the dignity of man born under its electric light. Literally speaking: deaths in childbirth and child mortality fall dramatically.

We leave behind the *private revelations*, the ones found in remote caves after forty days of solitude, and bring forth the *public revelation*—that which can be confirmed by every human being by virtue of her own senses, reason and rationality. No longer is humanity a slave to the authoritative claims of others. Man can think for himself, and for the first time, in universal knowledge, he meets his fellow as an equal: the informed citizen is born.

Enter Francis Bacon, Newton, Darwin and Einstein! Enter inventions, from James Watt's steam engine, to Thomas Edison's refinement of the light bulb to Nikola Tesla's alternating current to penicillin and the computer. The long history of darkness, ignorance and prejudice is over. Progress has begun.

Have we, the moderns, lost spirituality? No, we are *more* spiritual than the people of traditional religions ever were. We are enlightened. The traditions speak of God and divine universals, of heaven and the individual soul. But we find the true universals, the SI base units, the reality beyond our senses—and in its dazzling elegance and unfathomable vastness, our universe is far greater, more awe-inspiring, beautiful and mysterious than yours. Look at those pristine, crystal clear lines that define the order of the cosmos, resting just beneath every seemingly chaotic surface and event. It's objective. Can you taste that beautiful word? *Objective* science about *objective* reality, through which we can obtain our societal and personal *objectives*.

The individual is no longer defined by authority, but finds herself anew in relation to the laws of nature, laws that we must continuously explore, in an honestly discussing community of equals, where every person has the dignity to find her own path and think for herself.

And we find the *real* heavens, conquering the skies, crossing space itself, landing on the moon, and bringing salvation through the ingenious advances of medicine—medicine that *works*; better than any of your prayers ever did. We feed the people of the world; we create untold abundance.

Moses didn't split and cross the Red Sea; that was a filthy lie they had to tell for people to follow him. But even if he did, we wouldn't be impressed. Our god, science, the knowledge of truth itself, is still so much greater. Parting the sea? Was that the best you could think of? We cross it in a Boeing jet at one hundred times the speed, having coffee, with no blisters on our feet, and a much better view. And we also abolished slavery, *globally*. Toodeloo, Moses.

You say that your "god" brings universal order. But all the societies you have created have been full of bizarre contingencies. We create an ordered bureaucracy with rule of law which organizes a highly productive and innovative market which fuels a welfare state. Universal peace? You have been belligerent from day one, religious wars raging to this day. Has there ever been a war about science, even one small skirmish? No.

Perhaps it would be cute if there really was a heaven, if humans really did have souls who lived on after we died, if there was a pre-given meaning for us, inscribed into the very fabric of reality itself. But ultimately, these were only ever fantasies. Humans made them up, either because we lacked the *real* explanations for things, or because we wanted to believe in them. Lullabies.

But *real* maturity can face up to reality. Sure, so when I die, I bloody well die. Is that so bad? Do I have to be a cry-baby about it and think I'm going to flutter around in the skies with grandma and a gilded harp? Sure, so the universe is a dead machine that is, always was, and always will be ultimately blind and indifferent to me and all of humanity. Okay, that's alright. Just face it and it doesn't get scary. Actually it feels fresh, clear and good in a way. Either way, it's still the truth, the only one you'll ever get. So just deal with it and get on with your life.

I can understand that people in the past who really didn't know any better believed all sorts of bizarre things. I mean, I would too if I wasn't taught about science, about the *real* reality. But actually, to persist, in the face of the modern world and science, with that narcissistic, self-righteous, inbred nonsense about this whole of reality being about you and yourself—is just not cute anymore. It's hurting people, it's causing unnecessary moral guilt and prejudices and conflicts, and it's getting in the way of real progress and the real solutions to our problems.

Yours is a smaller world, for a smaller human being. And actually, in all honesty, your ideas are crap. A universe which has no pre-given meaning, which is just pristine, open meaninglessness and where we ourselves have to create meaning—be it scientific exploration, political struggle, artistic expression or just comfort, love and fun—is so much *more* exciting. And actually dying, which is just reversing the fact of having been born, is much more comforting than an eternity of self-indulgent harp playing.

Still though, I'm not going to judge you. If you really need that lullaby, go ahead; who am I to pass judgment? Because after all, it's up to the *individual*. It's up to you. And unlike you, I am so certain of my reality, that I don't feel the need to threaten others with metaphysical coercion (hell) or force anything down their throats with threats of violence. I'm not like you—my universality doesn't come from the barrel of a gun (which I invented), but from reason and fair debate. What I do insist upon, however, is that everybody gets the best available information so that they can make informed decisions. Nobody should be kept in the dark and forced to believe preposterous things out of ignorance. Everybody should get a fair chance.

But what I *cannot* forgive, dear *compadre*, is the use of false scientific authority for dubious purposes and disgusting religious cop-outs: the purple and turquoise glowing "subtle energies" and "quantum healing" of New Age charlatans, always selling us self-help books and worthless gems, always turning our attention away from the real issues of life. Louise Hay, who says cancer is caused by your personal issues and that you can think it away. Deepak Chopra who habitually and ritually rapes quantum physics with his profound-sounding, incoherent nonsense. You just crossed the line, mister. There can be no mercy towards the spread of pseudo-science and cult leaders and proponents of "indigo children" ideas. The predators and hypocrites that create all of this pseudo-science show no mercy for the poor, confused people they fool, exploit and molest—and so they can expect none from me.

Reality is a harsh mistress. But in a way, reality is fair. People tend to get what they deserve. The people who are strong enough to face the truth (and don't cop out and start navel-gazing the hell out of the universe) will win out in the end. While those losers were on their knees fantasizing about a birthday cake from their gods, or hoping to be "special" with secret magic powers, we were out in the real world and discovered evolution, relativity, quantum mechanics, genetics and computation. We had more fun *and* our knowledge produces results: real, clear, hard, effective, reliable, repeatable, delicious results. The truth, by logic, rewards those who know the truth. And those who shy away from it, by the same clear logic, are punished.

And when their gods fail them, they come crawling to our modern hospitals, begging for a cure that only painstakingly hard-earned science can grant them. And we patch them up and take responsibility for them. Because somebody has to. Sheesh.

So this was **symbol-stage E Modern**, often operating from MHC stage 11 Formal logic.

Symbol-Stage F: Postmodern

But wait a minute—say the Romantic 19th century critic, the poststructuralist, the critical social theorist, the counter-culture movement and the deep ecologist and the intellectual hipster queer feminist—**if your claim on reality is based on intersubjective verifiability, shouldn't *all* perspectives be included and get a voice?**

There is a central flaw to the whole idea of intersubjective verification: Namely that it presupposes that each individual is independent of her social context. But what if something in that context affects *all* the individuals present, so that they all verify something that, under different circumstances, would be seen as false? There are things like common language, social hierarchies, peer pressure, hidden or unconscious assumptions, prejudices and economic interests. All of these shape the *context* within which any intersubjective verification can be made: thus shaping what is taken to be "the truth". And these things don't show up in any haphazard manner: They follow clear patterns, repeatedly and systematically excluding some voices, truths and perspectives. And the most absurd, violent and oppressive beliefs are hailed as intersubjectively verified truths, because we're all in on it. Surely we can't all be wrong? Yes, mister President, we can.

If your truth is so universal, how come it only really makes sense from a modern, educated, middle class (often white and male) perspective? Not that I argue with the specific results of science—if you drop a rock, it falls, I agree, and if a medicine works, it works—but how come your modern, universal worldview has oppressed so many people and animals?

Let's start with indigenous cultures. So when modern civilization showed up at Greenland and "civilized" the Inuits (by the hand of those pesky Danes), their culture crumbled like a house of cards. Unbelievable misery ensued and many of them became alcoholics at the very bottom of Danish "modern" society. If you go a little farther back in time, the Europeans consciously and deliberately conquered and exploited others in the name of civilization and modernity, claiming that this was the scientifically supported order of things. But even if you don't go back to colonialism, today most indigenous and traditional cultures around the world are taking heavy hits as they face an endless onslaught of commercialization, instrumentalization, bureaucratization and social degradation. Are those just road kill on the path to the universal truth you say you found in a high school physics class?

Or how about the process of modernization itself. You said there are no science wars. But did you ever notice there are other wars going on, stemming directly from the vanity of the modern project? Look at how China and the Soviet Union modernized—millions and millions of people died. Oh, that wasn't *real* modernization? Only Western modernization is real? They did become modern countries, you know. And what about the US, if it's so enlightened, how come its black book of human rights abuses is so thick? Those victims don't get a say in the universal truth found in chemistry 101? Speaking of chemistry, did you know that the British Empire started using chemical dyes and then instantly collapsed the Indian indigo cloth dye market—that the Empire had created—and let millions starve to death? Oh, that wasn't real modernity either, was it? How about the Indian traditional society, they don't get a say on this? Do you know that the biggest and bloodiest war going on right now is in the Congo? A long-term result of some of the worst atrocities in recorded history, committed by enlightened, modern Westerners who used their oh-so-hailed rationality to force native Africans to produce cocoa and rubber instead of food so that you can enjoy that delicious fine Belgian chocolate. Have you thought about that? Oh, and where do the minerals in your Smartphone come from?

And if every individual is being freed by this universal order of enlightenment that you are so graciously sharing with the rest of the world, how come a Bangladeshi female semi-slave made the shirt you are wearing, not under direct threat perhaps, but lest her kids be prostituted to Western tourists? Once she does work at the sweatshop, though, she *is* physically threatened—and her physical health is certainly compromised. What a beautiful universal order that is. Good thing we can continuously check in on it intersubjectively and verify that her life still sucks.

Or how about the patients? Modern medicine is powerful, you're right. Vaccines are good, most of the time. But the history of modern medicine is a marathon of abuses by doctors who were convinced they had objective science on their side. How much power have they not misused to lobotomize and lock up and castrate people—until *political*, not scientific, currents in society changed? Oh, those patients were weak and crazy. They don't get a perspective on universal truth, of course.

And how come this universal intersubjectivity always makes the men right and leaves the women out? I mean, you really have to work hard to find the women in the history of science.

And how come, with these super-objective sciences, that the paradigms keep shifting every generation or so, depending on who wins the academic power struggles? You go from a Newtonian universe to Einstein's universe, and now Einstein turned out to be wrong about quantum physics, and the universe really does do "spooky things at a distance" after all—and God plays a whole lot of quantum dice. Everyone is so sure of themselves, that they have the *real* reality, that they are being objective, but all the time they turn out to be wrong—their understanding again and again found to be more bound by their culture, their time and their own interests, than anybody had expected. Not so universal, after all, it is?

What about verifying stuff that is beyond someone's understanding in terms of education, stage of cognitive complexity, or access to information? I mean—what if people do not verify some great discovery simply because they are too stupid, afraid or invested in some other idea? Did that ever happen? Is it still happening all over science? You betcha.

And when the scientific community *does* agree on stuff, does it make a difference that most of them are recruited from more or less the same strata in society? Wouldn't they ask other questions if they came from other groups, with other interests? And how about big pharma, the meat industry, the sugar industry and the tobacco industry? Suppose any of these little cuties ever affected science; this holy, objective, super-effective effectiveness to which all strong no-bullshit people like yourself are so committed?

And who gets to say what is "effective" anyway? What if I have the best method? And the results are many times more effective "per dollar spent" than your method—at killing Jews. Oh, you think killing Jews is bad? That's your *opinion*. I'm looking at the *facts*, yo. And it just so happens, that I am *objectively* right and you are wrong. My method is more effective. Science says. Right.

The world, my dear modernista, before it ever becomes "objective" science, is **phenomenological**. First and foremost, you only ever have your subjective experience of things-as-they-are, always in right-this-moment. And that's the only "objective" reality you ever really get.

And the phenomenological experience of reality is always bound by **social constructions**. You can't ever reach the "real" reality by anything but the use of symbols: If you look at a chair, the moment you see it, you interpret it as a chair—which is a symbol, not an "objective reality".

Even an idea in physics, such as the hydrogen atom, is only accessible to you through the use of socially constructed symbols. No matter how many university credits you get in physics, or if you win a Nobel Prize, you still only ever get to understand the world through symbols that others have taught you. And, again, those symbols are *not* a direct link to objective reality. It's just that some symbols turn out to be more useful metaphors for describing the patterns of relations between other symbols. That's it. You've been living the illusion that you're beyond illusions.

You say you've matured and killed God, that you've grown out of it. But I, the postmodern mind, find you as a helplessly god-fearing believer. This is because you think that there is an "objective" view from nowhere, a universal, grey background reality that never depends on anyone's perspective. But *where* exactly do you find this reality, other than as a subset of your own subjective experience and your symbols, which other people have taught you in school? How do you *really* get beyond your own perspective, created by you in interaction with others? Mind if I ask?

Oh, you persist? You just *know* it's there, don't you? You can't see it, touch it, or feel it, beyond your own subjectivity, or beyond the symbols, but you fiercely… What's that word? Yes, you *believe* it. You simply take the leap of faith, that there really is a grey, colorless machine-world out there, with one Truth, One Universal Existence in the Non-Eyes of the Non-God.

Yep, there you have it. **You never stopped believing in God, you punk. You only pushed Him backstage by means of a simple negation.** But that negation still posits a God. You're still doing the same move as Newton and Descartes did: Except they actually admitted that they assumed that reality was made possible by the eyes of God. You didn't kill God; you hid him away.

You've been sitting in His holy lap this entire time. But your Non-God with a "view from nowhere" is just utter nonsense. It is a religious belief and nothing else. And from that "objective" position, which is, and only ever was, a filthy lie—you have been objectifying and instrumentalizing the world, justifying a giant extraction project where you get to exploit everything as your legally owned resources. It's disgraceful, dishonest and deeply harmful.

Now, tell me again. All scientific evidence points to a simple fact: that humans are animals like any other species. That means that a pig or a cow is as valuable as a little kid. It is undeniably so, from a natural scientific perspective. There is really no controversy here. So tell me exactly, how your universal science justifies that you let sixty billion land animals—many of whom correspond to billions of human children—be enslaved, tortured and slit up with knives every year; to be condemned without trial, to die by the fork. Explain to me exactly, how that is "progress in the light of universal science". Tell me again, about your universally valid perspective, about how beautifully intersubjectively verifiable it all is. Didn't think so.

And this civilization you've built. You bragged a while ago about being better than Moses, with your Boeing jet and all. But Moses didn't sink the Maldives into the ocean by means of global warming. You're managing to do that, not least with the help of the jet plane's CO^2-emissions. And "under the sea" isn't a very interesting place to live anymore—because *you* killed all the fish and other aquatic animals, over a trillion a year. Of that, Moses is innocent and you are guilty as charged. Fish have pretty advanced sensory experiences, you know.[110] And you're letting them die really cruel deaths *en masse*. In your enlightened objectivity, you then polluted the rest of the sea so that you could have more plastic bags for the snacks you're eating while watching TV and playing video games.

You do realize that the civilization you've built is not sustainable anyway, don't you? All "objective" analysis says that we're running major risks, but still you're not really responding, busy as you are wearing a suit and all and making money, stacking stuff in a villa. Serious things. *Responsible* things.

> "SHUT UP! Shut up, you shit-cunt!! Or I'll split your skull open and watch your disgusting relativist, moralistic, snob-hipster brains smear the street!"

Whoa, whoa! Modernism, is that *you*? Where have you been? You look awfully rugged. Have you been drinking? Now, will you *please* put that crowbar down. Slowly, where I can see it. Listen, even if you do split my head open, I'll just end up looking like a Picasso, and in my death, my multi-perspectival critique of your worldview will prevail again. It ain't worth it.

> "Don't you say another word. I've been nice. I've been listening to your *rotten shit* for a long time—and I know your kind all too well. You're one of those people who just talk and talk, and you're not really out to help anyone. You're just out to relativize everything and score cheap moralistic points on ME while living off the society THAT I CREATED for you. And then YOU showed up and turned it into a decadent fuckfest of pretentious 'modern art' and irony and self-flattery and almost no rigid science or results, and

YOU keep getting all the credit. But I am an individual who can think for myself, and I won't fall for your sophistry."

That's right, you did create me. My multiplistic, postmodern perspective simply wouldn't be possible without your hard work and centuries of modern progress. And you're right, I'm often doing better, in terms of privileges and status, than you are, not least because I tend to understand the cultural and psychological aspects of the world better than you do. And I do generally get to score the moral goals and come off as more sophisticated.

But then again, what did you expect? To create free expression and institutions that support critical thinking—and that nobody would ever go beyond you, ever speak against you? That I would sit there like a good schoolgirl and be grateful for your alienating, soulless, mindless, hypocritical and oppressive society? That I would watch reality soaps and play your sports and computer games and never ask another question? Thanks for the offer, but fuck you very much. Weren't you the one who said that whoever can deal with reality the most proficiently should win? Well, here it is for you: you're on the losing side of history.

And I realize that this may be a bad time to say this, but you're not *actually* an individual with independent thoughts. You're really just acting out the structural relations inherent to society, and the true reason that you are reacting this way has little to do with your own faculties as an independent thinker. You don't have a "self" in that sense; you're not making choices, only being like people in your position in society generally are. These are just structures and properties of the cultural system. So you didn't just keep God, you kept the soul, and you built your whole life around it, just renaming it "the individual".

Some poor modernistas even believe that they have a free will tied to this "individual". Are you one of them? How cute, but silly you, weren't you supposed to be all scientific? How does that work in a mechanistic, objective universe where everything can be explained by cause and effect? (Okay, granted, some of you may have read Daniel Dennett's more sophisticated case for free will in a deterministic universe, but even then there are unresolved issues.)

You just assumed, no, you—and there's that word again—*believed*, that you had some kind of individual will making all those "rational" decisions. Why don't you just come out of the closet alright, you zealous believer of metaphysical nonsense and make-believe. Why don't you just admit that you really don't have a clue, but that you put your faith in the great

Bible of Nature—a book you, come on admit it, haven't really read but merely put your hand on.

But hey, if you need that lullaby, who am I to judge? What I'm telling you are all things that you, dear modernism, don't yet understand. But rest assured, your kids probably will when I'm done with them. And then they'll join me in all kinds of homoerotic extravaganzas, deconstruct your worldview, make awkward dinner conversations and laugh at old grumpy dad, all paid for by you at the nearest liberal arts college.

It's just that this is bigger than you and your psychological comfort. The way that you limit your perspective to "objective reality" means that all kinds of important aspects of reality get locked out. For instance, if only what is intersubjectively verifiable ever counts as universal, and therefore as real and important, what happens to all of those who cannot partake in the intersubjective discussion? Like the animals—or poorly educated people. You can't ask the animals, but does that mean they don't have subjective experience? Your perspective turns everything into one big "object" and it silences so many voices. This opens the way for abuses, as the world is turned into dead, cold resources under your mechanical, exploitative regime.

It will be a solemn pleasure, I can tell you, to watch your colossus of false objectivity and progress crumble and fall under a multiplicity of critical perspectives that will tear it down from all sides and reveal your true nature (yes, I know there's no "true nature", it's a manner of expression). And it is in the cracks and ruins of your world, in a perpetual questioning and criticism, that humanity is truly emancipated.

You see, the problem isn't that you are too modern, too scientific or too objective. The problem is that you are not nearly modern, scientific or *secular* enough. It is because your ideas of science, objectivity and reality are too limited, because they have too much lingering stuff of religions left in every nook and cranny, that you keep creating a world of narrow-mindedness and self-deceit. Your "enlightened liberation" and "progress" become vulnerable to any number of hidden, arbitrary, unfair and particularistic power structures. While you say that you are fair and impartial, you in fact end up serving power and oppressing the weak. Systematically, again and again.

Freud was right, to a large extent: There is a lot of unconscious stuff going on. If you look inside your own mind, you will find that this is correct. For instance, modernists have a strong feeling that if you work hard and bow to the Real Hard Reality (the one that your Non-God is watching over with His Holy Eyes of Objectivity), then you will be rewarded by the universe. Or that if you apply yourself enough, you should get to live in the Real World. Or that if you are Really Objective and you plan ahead well, you should get to be the winner—the leader. Or that "smart" people are more deserving.

But, you see, the universe *really* doesn't care about you. Nobody gives a shit. It's not about you. It's not about your "science" or smarts. You really *are* thoroughly meaningless, just like you said it yourself (you just failed to take the full consequences of it). And you never get to hit the "bottom line" with "real reality"—it will always be just another story you tell yourself, and you will never have come up with it yourself; it will always be forced upon you by social structures that lie beyond you. Even if you're the best kid in math class, the universe doesn't care. It doesn't budge and disclose itself to you.

Hey, modernista, sorry to break it to you, but there are a few things you need to catch up on. You *do* know that your science grew directly out of the ancient philosophy and medieval scholastics that you feel so superior to, don't you? You *do* know that philosophy didn't end with you, that you are not the end of history? You *do* know that your whole worldview and sense of reality will one day look exactly as infantile and stupid as the Old Testament does to you? Indeed, that it already does; that people better informed and more scientifically minded than you, have been laughing at you and ridiculing you for almost two generations already? And you *do* know, don't you, that you are guilty of the worst crimes against life and humanity that have ever been committed, all in the name of your superficially understood "progress"?

So that was **symbol-stage F Postmodern**, which often, but far from always, operates from MHC stage 12 Systematic. Exit Newton. Enter Foucault. Michel Foucault, the leading French philosopher of the 1960s and 70s, is perhaps the most emblematic of the innovators of the postmodern cultural code.[111] The philosophically most stringent one is probably Jacques Derrida. Actually, let's quote Derrida himself:

> "Instead of singing the advent of the ideal of liberal democracy and of the capitalist market in the euphoria of the end of history, instead of celebrating the 'end of ideologies' and the end of the great emancipatory discourses, let us never neglect this obvious macroscopic fact, made up of innumerable singular sites of suffering: no degree of progress allows one to ignore that never before, in absolute figures, have so many men, women and children been subjugated, starved or exterminated on the earth."[112]

But today, of course, a lot of people are "installing" the postmodern code without ever having heard of these philosophers. And you can pretty much install it even without any philosophical underpinnings to speak of, like the case of Noam Chomsky.[113]

As you can see, postmodernism follows a similar pattern as postfaustianism: They both criticize the former stage (faustianism and modernism, respectively) from a cultural or philosophical standpoint, pointing out their inherent inconsistencies—and the negative consequences of these. They are both a kind of "moral" projects, seeking to reform society by critical thinking and self-scrutiny.

Symbol-Stage G: Metamodern

Of course, symbol-stage G Metamodern is what this whole book is about (as well as the other Hanzi books). You also get most of it in the appendix—the ideas about reality, society, self and humanity that constitute this symbol-stage—in a very condensed form. But still, let's take a look.

Wait a minute—says the metamodernist[114]—if all perspectives are to be included for us to be able to strive towards universal values, how come that the only perspective you pomos (postmodernists)[115] seem to value is your own? Doesn't the inclusion of all perspectives require the successful *accommodation* of those perspectives, including the modernism that you so vehemently oppose? **You aren't really taking the other perspectives seriously, if you don't evaluate, compare and connect them—and give each perspective its due credit.**

You say that you go beyond modern society by means of critical thinking, but what do *you* really offer us? You are against all **grand narratives**, all stories about how the world at large is evolving, because you find them monolithic and oppressive. You are against all overarching maps of society and reality, because you think they reduce the richness of life and existence too much. And you always strive to be on the critical side of things, always against stuff. And you say you don't really believe in progress and development, only in changes of cultures, interpretations and power structures.

When you vote you often go with the Left or the Greens—and in some cases with intellectual forms of libertarianism. But whenever any of these powers come close to government, the same modern, bureaucratic structures reemerge.

While you criticize the often exaggerated "objectivity" of modern science, and you have produced some interesting research programs in social science and humanities (such as ethnomethodology, interactionism, discourse analysis, cultural studies, postcolonialism, eco-feminism, queer theory, etc.), you have not really produced a new science equaling the 17th century Scientific Revolution.

And what about the Enlightenment—its ideas inform the constitutions of most countries in the world. You had the 1968 student revolution in France and the counterculture in the US and other countries, authors like Herbert Marcuse and Aldous Huxley leading the fray; but where is your new society?

Increasingly, you have got crammed up at university departments where you write critiques of everything from IMF (International Monetary Fund) reports to pop songs and music videos—but where is the alternative you offer? For a while it was "democratic socialism", but after 1989 we haven't really seen any credible claims for it. Then it was "deep ecology", but the world is industrializing and consuming and modernizing faster than ever. Then you came up with queer feminism and updated versions of radical feminism, which is nice, but nowhere is there any evidence that "breaking the hetero norm" and "crushing patriarchy" bring forth any true revolution, or lead to an otherwise fair society. Frankly, women have been more liberated by the pill and other advances of medicine, than by postmodern theory. And then you have been going on about neoliberalism, which you take to be an evil spirit that has possessed the world, but you have yet to produce any alternative beyond bureaucratic control. Occupy Wall Street didn't offer more than a buzz. All of your projects have fallen to the ground, without any of them deeply changing society. There have been some shifts, yes, but we still live in what must be seen as a modern society: still capitalist, alienating, unequal and ecologically disastrous.

Let's look at your pomo heroes. Foucault was good at criticizing modern society, I'll give you that. But what did he believe in? He wanted to make it legal for adults to have sex with kids (no age limit) and was deeply enthused by the Iranian revolution. He never came up with one useful solution. What about Erich Fromm, this wise guru? He wanted a centralized planning taking over all production, making sure that we only heard classical music on the radio, that a bunch of exceptionally wise people should rule (clearly having himself and folks like Einstein in mind), loved Suzuki (the Japanese Zen teacher who had supported the Japanese regime during the Second World War, giving very Zen accounts of how to poke an eye out with a bayonet) *and* he despised gay people. I could go on. The point is—as soon as it's your turn to offer a vision and a new path, your neck is exposed.

The problem you have, dear pomo, is that you fail to construct or suggest anything useful or durable, because you are only truly interested in being an anti-thesis to the existing society.

You don't *truly* use a multiplicity of perspectives; your "multiplicity of perspectives" is limited to an epistemological one (views of knowledge and how it is attained)—it is never an ***ontological*** **multiplicity** (viewing reality itself as shifting according to perspectives).

From a symbol-stage G Metamodern perspective, this is just not enough. You have to make yourself more vulnerable than that: You have to try to construct a synthesis from all that you know from the earlier symbol-stages, in order to create a society that solves the three major problems of modern life: the excessive global inequalities, the alienation or neurotic anxieties of modern life, and ecological unsustainability.

This synthesis must of course be open-ended and continuously revised, a **proto-synthesis**. You have to offer a path to Utopia yourself, and it has to *really* include the traditional, modern and postmodern—even while knowing that this path will never be the only one or "the right one". We do it because we have to, even at the very great risk of being wrong.

And this requires that you take all the former metamemes much more seriously: you have to actually deal with the prospect of One Universal Truth, that you harbor and cultivate within yourself a deep, sincere faith (symbol-stage D Postfaustian); you must look for objective truth that we can all agree upon and seek to wield it to engender progress (symbol-stage E Modern); and you must seek to criticize and find all possible cracks and excluded voices in that story (symbol-stage F Postmodern).

Every symbol-stage creates an unending beauty, cavalcades of new truths, new realities, new melodies of the universe. Multiplicity is not the only melody of the cosmos: It plays within a larger orchestra, consisting of unity, universality and faith, all of which are important—and comparable to one another.

Dear pomo, you have been monolithic in your embrace of multiplicity, narrow-minded in your attempts at open-mindedness, judgmental in your non-judgment, hierarchical in your anti-hierarchy. **In a few words, your problem is not that you have been too critical, postmodern and mulitiplistic—you have not been nearly critical, postmodern and multiplistic enough.**

If you are so good at taking perspectives and including everybody, how come the modernist showed up at your doorstep, completely destroyed, drunk and with a crowbar? Have you been imperialist and oppressive without noticing it? Have you been using your cognitive and cultural superiority for the sordid pleasures of oppression and making others, in weaker positions, feel helpless and deprived of their sense of self, morality and reality? And have you been doing this while telling yourself that you were defending the weak? If you are justified in this symbolic violence, where then, is the new society you were to bring about?

Here's what I believe: **To have solidarity with someone, you must also have solidarity with their perspective**. This means that one must also understand power hierarchies—not just as "evil spirits" in the form of class structures, patriarchy, discourses, etc. to be exorcized with "critical perspectives"—but as **differences of developmental stage**. And pomos are generally at a higher developmental stage than modernists.

If you deny the differences of developmental stage, you also fail to recognize something important: that to be in position to critique someone, from their own premises, is to act from a position of superiority—from a position of power. Isn't the realization of privilege at the core of your beliefs? Did you really believe that you were an underdog barking at the powerful? You have been a highly privileged, well-informed elitist kicking downwards all along. You, my dear pomo, armed with vast amounts of cultural capital and superior perspectives, belong to the highest strata of global society, the upper class of late modernity—so you should better acknowledge your privilege and take some responsibility for including the perspectives of your fellow citizens. The pomos are in positions of power, more so than George W. Bush ever was.

The metamodern mind takes all of the earlier perspectives at face value, as *real*; it's just that some of them are *more* real than others. They are ranked, compared and balanced against one another. And for that, one must be able to truly listen to and understand—and to a certain extent agree with—even one's most bitter enemy. We must learn to listen to another person and to see with her eyes and to merge our reality with hers, to see how her perspective is a *real*, ontological, part of reality. Listening to a stranger becomes the highest form of jihad.

> "You would rank people's perspectives and put them together in unifying visions to improve society? How arrogant and power hungry you must be! You think there are many realities at once, not just many views of the same reality? How utterly confused and crazed! And you want to define 'progress' for society? How dangerous! You seemed to be an okay person for a while, but now that I see where you are going, you fill me with utter disgust!"

Oh, is that *you*, postmodernism? I thought you might show up here. Well, I don't mean to be nasty or arrogant, really. It's just that I am born through you. Everything about you ultimately leads to me. Can't you see it? I am you. And if you don't accept my insights, you are still left in the clutches of modernism.

> "I am nothing like *them*! *You* are like them! Obsessed with rankings and stages and progress and power! But I'm not like you; I will resist, I will critique!"

Listen, if you don't like what I am saying, and you think that I have regressed to modernism, you are admitting that I am right—i.e. that there *are* in fact stages of development. Otherwise no "regression" would be possible.

If you want to include all perspectives and treat them fairly, you have to be able to compare them to one another, and see how they are each an important part of reality, and how they fit together. Otherwise you are being condescending and monolithic yourself.

If you want to transcend and leave behind the obsession with hierarchies, you must be able to dispassionately describe hierarchies and relate to them productively. If you resent hierarchies and deny them, you are still in their grip, still obsessed with them. Precisely by demystifying hierarchy we can free ourselves from this obsession.

If you want to be humble and self-critical, isn't it more humble to assume that there are hierarchical stages beyond your own, that there are people with worldviews that would trump your own on its own premises, even people you may know? As indicated earlier in this book, stage theories make for greater epistemological humility.

If you want to be progressive, you have to admit that progress is at least provisionally possible—which then necessitates that you define, at least for the time being, in what direction such progress can and should unfold.

If you see that social reality is constructed, that it is a form of patterned "meta-narrative", and that there are serious gaps and limitations in that narrative—aren't you obliged to try to reconstruct it? To create a new story about humanity, society, reality and progress? To suggest a proto-synthesis?

And if you want to include the excluded voices, don't you need to show at least some solidarity with all perspectives, even the ones you don't like or that you feel superior to?

I, the metamodern mind, can no longer believe in the postmodern critique of modern society. I see it as lacking in crucial aspects. We must move on. By virtue of its own dialectical logic, by the structure of its symbols and their interrelations and by its inherent self-contradictions, postmodernism is the midwife of metamodernism.

Now let's get out there and kick some pomo ass.

Last Notes on Symbol-Stages

And that was a very brief taste of **symbol-stage G Metamodern**, which corresponds cognitively to MHC stage 13 Metasystematic.

Okay, I realize we just covered quite a stretch, and some of it may have been emotional for you. So congratulations for making it here without burning the book.

As I have indicated, the different symbol-stages don't particularly like one another. Each of them is built precisely upon challenging everything that the former one holds to be most sacred—and each of them (viewed on average over time) mercilessly trashes the former one at its own game, forcing them to swallow things that are counter-intuitive and downright painful. Each symbol-stage shreds the symbolic universe (ontology, ideology and self) of the former one—there is a *Realdialektik* that determines how they unfold, an inherent developmental logic, direction and sequentiality. Metamodern ideas cannot emerge from postfaustianism, and so on. The development has to roughly follow this sequence: A person can **out-code** another, by having installed a more advanced symbolic toolkit. A, B, C, D, E, F and G—in *that* order.

The emotions and some of the "attitudes" that I have indicated in these examples of the symbol-stages are not really part of the symbols themselves, so my description could, truth be told, be made more analytically pure: The symbol-stages are in fact a sequence of *logical* constructs. I have included the emotions because they tend to correlate with the stages quite closely, and thus it becomes simpler to convey how the stages manifest in real people: They are always tied up with hopes, dreams and festering resentments.

Note that even in the animosity between the symbol-stages you can see a certain *progression*—as the earlier stages are more insensitively hostile to one another. Symbol-stage D Postfaustian simply kills deviants and threatens with hell for eternity; symbol-stage E Modern despises the former but certainly lets them live; and symbol-stage F Postmodern mocks and condemns modernity but not more than that; whereas symbol-stage G Metamodern teases postmodernism a bit, but then seeks synthesis and reconciliation between all of the former symbol-stages. Don't know about you, but I feel a little hope for humanity when I see this pattern: unfolding tolerance, acceptance, inclusivity and universality (however bumpy the ride).

So another note. Obviously, now we have only discussed the basic "installment" of the different symbol-stages. You can then "download" more content at any of these symbol-stages (or create new content). A 20-

year-old sociology student who is a pomo would of course not have a flying chance in a political debate against Milton Friedman, a potent economist at the modern symbol-stage. Thus you have a *vertical* axis (the symbol-stage) and a *horizontal* one (the amount and quality of knowledge and information pertinent to that stage)—in a manner corresponding to cognitive development (where, as you remember, vertical is the MHC stage and horizontal the IQ).

Another aspect of this is, again, that people will operate the symbol-stages differently according to their own MHC stage of cognitive complexity. And this brings us to the last note, one we have already mentioned. **The cognitive requirements for successfully operating the symbol-stages increase with one MHC stage per symbol-stage.** This has two important implications.

First of all, the later symbol-stages are more difficult to install, which means that fewer people will manage to install them (E and G in particular). This largely explains why the majority of the adult world population, hundreds of years after the Scientific Revolution, is still running on the symbol-stage D Postfaustian. You can't just transplant these stages. They all come with entire symbolic universes, belief-systems and emotional investments. They have "prerequisites" or "requirements"—of the cognitive, psychological, physiological, cultural and economic kind. We simply cannot let all people download the metamodern symbol-stage and be done with it.

The second, perhaps even more disparaging, implication is that **fewer and fewer people can be expected to successfully operate the later symbol-stages**. This means that even if people manage to install the symbol-stage G Metamodern, most of us will undeniably use a "flattened" or "downward assimilated" version of its code. People will tend strongly towards using very skewed and perverted versions of metamodern ideas. This is because literally 98% of adults are, in terms of cognitive complexity, simply below stage 13 Metasystematic.

Ouch. There's an inconvenient truth. It constitutes a major developmental challenge for humanity. If anything, it makes it all the more important that people who are at stage 13 Metasystematic and above successfully "install" the symbol-stage G Metamodern. Indeed, the world depends upon it.

Reading this book can of course do rather little for your MHC stage, or for the dimensions of state and depth discussed in the following chapters. But it *can* help you install the metamodern symbol-stage. Perhaps, even, this book, together with the other Hanzi books, is the most efficient source of the metamodern code to date.

Chapter 12

SUBJECTIVE STATES

> "*The hour-hand of life.* Life consists of rare, isolated moments of the greatest significance, and of innumerably many intervals, during which at best the silhouettes of those moments hover above us. Love, springtime, every beautiful melody, mountains, the moon, the sea—all these speak to the heart but once, if they in fact ever do get a chance to speak completely. For many men do not have those moments at all, and are themselves intervals and intermissions in the symphony of real life."[116]

We now turn our gazes inwards.

Thus far we have explored two facets of development in the singular organism: her cognitive complexity, and the development of the cultural "code" she has "installed" through her participation in society. Both of these constitute a kind of "exterior" reality, meaning that they can both be intersubjectively recognized and in some sense "objectively" studied. There really is an empirically *observable* side to these two: You can put people or animals through cognitive tests and they will consistently behave according to a certain cognitive stage, and you can study the pattern of their symbolic understanding of the world, in which case they will consistently gravitate towards postfaustian, modern or postmodern code.

But what about the organism's own *inner* experience? I promised in the introduction to this book that we would not only deal with developmental blindness, but also with **inner dimensions blindness**—the failure to recognize and understand the primary importance that people's inner lives have in society. Here we are.

For understandable reasons, this area is much less researched and scientifically developed than the more observable sides of human behavior. I mean no disrespect to the rich traditions of phenomenology within the psychological, sociological and philosophical fields—for instance, existential therapy—but it must simply be admitted that these fields have yet to produce a systematic theory of development equaling the MHC.

There is also the field of "transpersonal psychology" (note that the word "transpersonal" in that context is used differently from how I employ it), but it is primarily concerned with spiritual experiences and other "altered" states of mind, which means that it is more difficult to apply in everyday life, much less to a political psychology like the one in this book.[117] As you will notice, there are some quite long endnotes in this chapter, simply because there are so many things to discuss and clarify. If curiosity or healthy skepticism compels you, please consult these endnotes.

We are now going to do something for which the Romantics and existentialists were too sentimental, and for which the mainstream of our days is too reductionist: namely, describe **a quantifiable scale of subjective states.**[118]

Romantic Revenge

I listened to the piano playing this morning, a song by Ludovico Einaudi, *Una Mattina*. The melody is clear, elegant and tender. I looked out at the mountains, having breakfast on the balcony, but I couldn't see very far. Even a spring day like today, there is a blanket of sterling silver snow and the mountain tops are enshrouded in mist. As the music was playing, just for a few moments, I remembered being at kindergarten, maybe aged four, a spring day like today.

I must have known much fewer words back then, had fewer thoughts, less understanding. I had less experience, for sure. I wasn't even really a "person"; fully relying on my parents and other caretakers, unable to take responsibility even for myself.

And still, unless my vague memory deceives me, I saw the spring day with greater clarity than my blasé adult eyes could hope for, even with a view of the Alps. There was something wordlessly self-evident about the grace and novelty of spring, of day-light, mist, green sprouts and melting snow. Am I mistaken, or was there even no sense of "grasping", no sense of "ah, this is what I want"? Beauty and its intrinsic mystery were so self-evidently present that I did not even reflect upon it—indeed, I think I was unable to. The *experience* of a spring day.

Or how about a fancier example than a snotty little Hanzi. Here's an anecdote about Master Zhuang, the Taoist philosopher, in the second chapter of the classic text Zhuangzi:

> "Once upon a time, Zhuang Zhou dreamed he was a butterfly, a butterfly flitting about happily, enjoying himself. He did not know that he was Zhou. Suddenly he awoke, and was palpably Zhou. He did not know whether he was Zhou, who had dreamed of being a butterfly, or a butterfly dreaming

that he was Zhou. Now, there must be a difference between Zhou and the butterfly. This is called the transformation of things."

This little story underscores how **subjective experience**, not the facts of the world, lies at the heart of reality. It doesn't really matter, in the last instance, if you are Master Zhou or a butterfly; we are always, in a way, in a dream. Subjective experience is and remains all that we have. When the world changes, it is subjective experience that transforms. And whatever reality we are currently experiencing as self-evident and true, it can always, in a sense, be awakened from. All that seems real melts as snow in the sun on an early spring morning.

I am of course not defending the idea that "our thoughts create the world" and that there "are no objective facts". If you can measure something through more than one channel (giving it e.g. both mass and volume) it has an objective existence that others can verify for themselves. What I am saying is simply that our subjective experience is an integral, fundamental aspect of reality, and, if this kind of statement at all makes any sense, I would claim that it is the most important one.

Let us not dwell upon the philosophy of the Romantics and their heirs in spiritualism, phenomenology and existentialism (from Schiller, Schelling, Herder and Goethe, to Kierkegaard, to Bergson, Camus and Sartre, to Emerson and Blake and William James or Whitehead or Heidegger and beyond), or upon Zen teachings, or upon Taoism, or the inner landscapes described in Christian and Western mystics like John of the Cross, Teresa of Ávila, Meister Eckhart or the anonymously written *Cloud of Unknowing*.

The point that I want to make here is simply that subjective states of organisms—regardless of things such as cognitive stage or "knowledge"—are what must be of ultimate significance in life and society.

I hold, then, that other things, such as the economic system, science and logic, even the development of our brains and symbolic universes, are only of *value* insofar as they translate into or otherwise affect subjective experiences. **The reason we need to be scientific and objective is that, in the last instance, it serves a sense of truth and meaning, and it can help us change life for the better—or prevent us from making it worse.** Because, as was discovered already during the Axial Age, the truth sets us free. This doesn't have to land us in crude utilitarianism (the quantitative maximization of pleasure), only in the recognition of the primacy of inner experience of all sentient beings and the interconnectedness of all perspectives.

The inner landscapes of subjective experience are as vast as physical space. We can easily get lost in their endless spaciousness, in tragic labyrinths of confusion, in pain and fear and madness.

The capacity of consciousness, of a living organism, to *experience*, seems to be unimaginably vast—if not endless. What does a small child experience when she has longed for her mother, felt abandoned, and is suddenly embraced by warmth and unconditional, caring love? What does the schizophrenic experience when reality breaks apart into the darkest confusion? What does the torture victim experience? What happens when you accept a terrible truth and surrender to reality in deep acceptance, and your heart breaks open as the skies?

These are *real* aspects of reality. There are in our world, right this moment, inner prisons within prisons, raging hells of unimaginable horror and darkness, and, yes, there are heavens upon heavens—and there is love, deep and unyielding, and there is intense pleasure and pain, and longing and lust. And there is freshness and beauty—and infinite, mysterious expanses of awe and wonder. And there is everyday life: boredom, frustration, doubt, fun, relief, satisfaction, dissatisfaction, fascination, excitement and comfort—endless variations of sensations, moods and feelings.

These are vast **inner landscapes**. The greatest capacity of this universe is not so much its ability to organize into and follow elegant "laws" of nature (or habits: the standard model in physics has four fundamental forces), but its innate ability to *experience*, to *live*. The power to *feel*; indeed, the power to *be*. To "be", then, has a deeper meaning than existing solely as an object; to "be" is to have subjective awareness.

However, not unlike when Adam and Eve tasted the fruit of knowledge, this power comes at a terrible price: the universe becomes imbued with **non-indifference**. Reality is not just a mechanical machine, dead matter, but things begin *to* matter. And as "we, the universe" self-organize into living, conscious beings—albeit organisms with transient bodies and fleeting experiences—we begin to *see* the world, feel it, taste it and know it. We begin to know ourselves. The fabric of bliss and suffering comes alive, and we can no longer stay indifferent. To have a perspective, any perspective, be it that of a four-year-old German kid or Master Zhou or a butterfly, is, in some sense, to care. **When the world is conscious, when it sees and feels, it also cares.**[119]

For our current purposes it is sufficient to note that such inner landscapes do exist, that they are fully intertwined with raw, naked subjectivity, that they can take any number of forms, and that all ethical "value" (i.e. all that we care about) stems from the immense qualitative differences that are possible within these landscapes. [120]

We should note, moreover, that the inner landscapes are **transformable**—not only by means of *Bildung* (cultural and educational refinement), but also, and primarily, by felt and embodied encounters with the beauties, mysteries and tragedies of life itself (which, by the way, was what the Romantics meant by *Bildung* in the first place). And yes, our inner horizons are also transformable by deliberate changes to the organism itself, by means of applied medical, behavioral and social science—and increasingly by use of technological enhancements and other manipulations; a potential to which we are only now waking up. And, of course, subjective experience can be transformed by means of spiritual and contemplative practices as described in the wisdom traditions of pre-modern societies.

We can always (in theory, at least) *change* how reality is experienced for an organism: we can make a dark world of unspeakable horrors clear out and be filled with a quiet ocean of comfort and relief; we can make an enchanted universe seem dull and lackluster. When walking in the desert for too long, a simple drink of fresh spring water can change your entire cosmos. Resentment can be transmuted into acceptance and productive action. The heart's longing and passion can fester and rot into self-hatred and a perverted will to harm. The vast inner landscapes can (and always do) transform—as Master Zhou into a butterfly, then back again, into a new Master Zhou, whose memories and experiences have now changed.

And, what's more, it is an uncontroversial fact that **these vast potentials of feeling, sensing and being have not nearly been exhausted through world history**. Think about it. Has the worst possible horror occurred? Have organisms yet experienced the greatest possible realization of their ability to sense the world? Has bliss been fully realized? Have all the possible moods, colors and emotions been known, shared and experienced? The possibilities of the inner realm are far greater than the combined experience of world history, of the history of all life on our planet. The unfathomable potentialities of inner experience; this is serious business.

So, after all is said and done when it comes to science and theories and knowledge and empiricism, the world is still singing, still screaming. It's alive. And, as the Romantics taught us, this fundament of reality is transformable. And, in the end, such transformations are what truly matters.

A respect for science does not necessitate that we turn the world into a dead object, the universe into a machine. And, in fact, to see the subjective realm, and to describe its landscapes, however provisionally, is an important tool for understanding politics and the development of society.

Too long have we cast out "the baby" of the subjective realm and its fundamental significance with "the bathwater" of particularistic, arbitrary opinion. We did it in the name of objectivity, in the name of science.

Well guess what. The baby's back. And she's grown bigger and badder than Chucky the evil doll. Time for romantic revenge. In postmodern irony, sincerity has a new friend: Because irony allows us a self-critical playfulness, we can again begin to speak about transforming our inner landscapes. Here comes the **pragmatic romanticism**.

High States, Low States

The first thing I posit is that, based on *my own experience*,[121] every lived moment that I have ever had, has *felt* like something and that this "something" has at least in part been good or bad. Maybe in some very profound philosophical or spiritual sense, this can be denied: "that reality simply is". But let us leave that aside for the moment.

I further posit that we all sometimes feel better and sometimes worse—*and* that each moment has some kind of sum or totality of how we feel. Even if our experiences are mixed, there is something distinctively different between a moment of light, hopeful joy and a moment of deep angst and terror. There is a sum or **totality of inner experience in every now**. I am not claiming that it should be seen as a matter of simple addition. If you don't like the word "sum", just stay with totality.

So basically, I posit that every organism, every moment of its life, is in some kind of non-indifferent subjective state. We could add a discussion about falling unconscious, being in coma, or deep-freezing bacteria—but let's also leave that aside here.

Are you with me so far? Okay, let's go on then. Here are some words that to varying degrees may have significance to you; they may (or may not) induce some sense or feeling in you. I want you to read this list slowly and taste each of the words, *really* taste them and see if you have a sense of them.

- Magnificence, majesty, vastness, greatness, splendor, love, joy, clarity, openness, compassion, certitude, flow, jubilation, playfulness, fullness, enlightenment, lightness, peace, presence, power, realness, humility, freedom, creation, freshness, birth, wonder, victory, serenity, divinity, purity, meaning, unity, union, communion, uniqueness, chosenness, awe, fulfillment, insight, grace, refinement, subtlety, simplicity, gratefulness, substance, radiant emptiness.

What does *magnificence* feel like? How do you recognize a vast, open *freedom* at long last? No doubt, some of the words leave you cold or don't speak to you. No matter. Focus on the ones that do—the ones you recognize and know from within. Have you ever had a great victory? Did you ever feel entirely present in the moment? Do you have memories of moments of simple lightness without worry, or when your heart was humbled by gratitude?

I assume there is more than one word on this list that you recognize as a felt experience, that you know from within? Alright. Now, please stop for a moment to consider *what unites* these different words. After all, they are very different from one another, but they are somehow still interconnected.

I am certain that neuroscience and behavioral medicine can help us elucidate the matter, but at this point I would simply like to suggest one way of understanding the commonality of all the words and expressions on the list above: **They are all expressions of *higher* subjective states**.

Higher states are the lived, experienced moments in which reality itself becomes crisp, clear, self-evident: when there is a deep inner silence and the experience of life itself emerges in full. It is when the mind is brought to its knees, the soul surrenders and reality wins and reveals itself.

High states. You have a sense that life is large, reality vast. Things are magical; reality becomes enchanted, even if only for a brief moment. We tend to have ideas and expectations about *when* such high states should occur: when we watch a sunset, the day we get married, when we read Plato. But life doesn't yield to such planning or expectations.[122] The highest state of one's entire life may well be that spring morning in kindergarten. In all their pristine meaninglessness, streaks of high state flicker past us at the strangest moments—perhaps only on a few occasions in a lifetime, perhaps interspersed by many years or what may feel as whole lives.

All the higher states are not exactly the same. Of course there is a world of difference between, for instance, sensing the majesty of the Tsar as described in Tolstoy's *War and Peace* and the aching but satisfied heart that can be felt when we are moved by profound compassion. But somehow these very different forms of experience are connected; they quite clearly have a common denominator.

Higher states are not bound to certain emotions, even if they may, in a profound sense, be very the essence of "meaning and happiness in life".

High states can show up through gritted work, in bitter struggle, in releases of righteous rage, in vengeance, in the deep satisfaction of surrender, in heart-opening sadness and overflowing sorrow.[123]

Such subjective states can interact in any number of ways with the content of our thoughts, feelings and sensations. It is possible to have pleasant experiences that don't touch upon higher states, and it is possible to have high states during moments of great anger and sadness.

So again, **the overall subjective state of the organism is not its emotions. It is something more fundamental.** In a stricter sense, when we wish for the happiness of ourselves and others, we wish for higher subjective states and the avoidance or passing of lower ones: We don't necessarily mean the *feelings* of happiness, even if that may also be important.

What would that mean, in terms of physiology, i.e. we can recognize with biological measures? When looking for the physiological correlates to self-reported subjective states, so-called "heart rate variability" might be a promising place to start, given that it has been shown to correlate with things such as low stress and high willpower.[124] When it comes to animals, stress levels can be measured either by behavioral cues in experiments, or chemically by looking at urine or the like; these are ways to try to understand the subjective states of creatures we cannot simply ask. But let us leave the biology aside for now.

Let us then turn to lower states. Of course, if subjective states can be high, this suggests some kind of directionality; that they can also be low. So what are low states?

I have already indicated that they are not synonymous with anger and sadness or with the lack of feelings of happiness. Rather, I suggest that the lower states are the moments of existence when reality "lacks wholeness": when there is split and brokenness and separation in our experience; when reality is lost and a formless, chaotic confusion reigns, together with untruth. Try these words:

- Anxiety, angst, rage, hatred, bitterness, imprisonment, slavery, humiliation, loss, loneliness, meaninglessness, unrealness, confusion, boredom, filth, torture, oppression, suffocation, unsettlement, darkness, dead meat, rot, painful emptiness, powerlessness, heaviness, uncertainty, grossness, hopelessness, unlife, half-life, screaming, woundedness, suffering, unbearable pain, complication, terror, exposedness.

Getting a sense of any of them? Some of the words of course indicate lower states than others. But I would argue that there is a common theme to these many words: They all indicate some kind of prisons of the soul, anathema to a free and full life in peace. A starved, harmed or sick body generally manifests lower subjective states. But, as Michel Foucault famously observed (in *Discipline and Punish*), "the soul" is also the prison of the body: The body is restrained and suffers from the ailments of the soul, the soul being molded by society's power structures.

I once lived with a woman whom I loved very dearly, who suffered from great anxieties and was later diagnosed with a severe psychiatric disorder (and, to my knowledge, still lives with the same disorder). Cross my heart, I don't think it would be an exaggeration to say that most of the above words would describe what was (and perhaps still is) experienced by her during one single day, most days of the year. The human organism's capacity for suffering is immense.

The organism bears no metaphysical "personal responsibility" for its own suffering. When we ascribe responsibility to one another, it is really only a social convention to regulate behaviors. Every organism obviously attempts to self-organize into higher subjective states: But the limits and contradictions of existence create disharmonious and formless, broken subjective states. This is the tragedy inherent to the self-aware, non-indifferent universe. Nature brings into being low states in organisms with the same self-evident automaticity with which life is created and perpetuated, and with which the physical world follows its laws.

Low states are not the same as difficult emotions. You will sometimes hear people say things like: "I have struggled this life. I have been so afraid, so sad, and I have worked so hard, suffered such pain. But it has been *intense* and, in a strange way, beautiful. It was all worth it." This is a statement about painful and difficult *feelings*.

What you never heard a person say, and you never will, is the following: "I have lived a life full of anxiety and angst; self-hatred has filled my days. I have never found meaning and reality has been utterly confusing, and still is. I regret almost everything. I feel suffocated, degraded, filthy, disgusting, worthless. I hate my mother, I would like to murder her in the cruelest manner; and I hate myself for having these thoughts and feelings… But it is beautiful! It has all been worth it. Could I live this life again, I would, even a thousand times!"

Can you notice the difference between the two statements? Why is the first one realistic and the second one not? Because the first one looks at emotions—and challenges that have been surmounted—and the second one tells us about ongoing low states.

It's not beautiful. But, of course, the low states are part of life, inherent to reality, and as such their existence must be accepted. The lower states may be avoided for periods, for a single person, even for lifetimes. But they still exist as an inescapable part of our shared reality.

In the religions and wisdom traditions of East and West you have concepts like hell, the purgatory, the hungry ghost realm in Buddhism, and other variations. As is often observed, these concepts have become "beliefs" in everyday life, stories that are used to maintain social orders and symbolic universes, to frighten people into compliance with norms. However, there is a deeper, esoteric meaning to such teachings. They simply indicate the very serious predicament of living in a non-indifferent universe: Worlds upon worlds of seeming eternities of decay and suffering are ever-present, both as *potentials* (in the sense that such fates can befall each and every living creature), and as *actualities* (that such low states are perpetually happening in the world at any given moment). We live in a screaming world. Because there is suffering untold, existence has us eternally by the balls. This inescapable, unyielding **by-the-ballness**[125] is our predicament—to which there can ultimately be only one response: to care. The question, then, is only *how* we care.

Stop for a moment to consider that: The world is screaming, right-this-moment, and that's a fact no matter how well your own life turns out. And it seems highly unlikely that our (we, the universe) greatest suffering lies in the past; it is very, very likely to lie in the future.

By-the-ballness is what the religious traditions have tried to warn us about: We should better get on our knees before God, and yes, we should fear God's wrath, and yes, hell is real, and yes, suffering is a necessary and unavoidable part of life in *samsara* (the worldly realm of illusion in Eastern traditions).

I don't know if you like the classic 20th century German philosopher Martin Heidegger or not, and his most renowned work from 1927, *Sein und Zeit* (*Being and Time*). But I would like to bring up an important distinction made in that book: the one between *Sein* (being) and *Da-sein* (being-in-the-world). When we are talking about subjectivity as a scale from higher to lower states, we are not actually speaking of pure being, what is sometimes called pure "suchness". This is because the quality of awareness itself seems to be constant: We are always-already effortlessly aware of all that arises in our inner world. That is *Sein*—just pure being.

In this chapter, we are instead speaking of *Da-sein*: the being-there or being-in-the-world, which is *how* we show up in existence (including *who* we show up as). This is a more relative or relational category: The organism can feel what it is like to be this organism at this very moment. It is, then, *Da-sein* which is the transformable side of consciousness: the side of consciousness that can be higher or lower.[126]

Okay. Are you still tagging along? Our self-organizing universe has subjective experience, which is non-indifferent, which means that organisms have subjective states that are higher or lower. The existence of higher and lower subjective states can be taken to be a general property inherent to the universe. In a word: by-the-ballness.

The Scale of Subjective States

We have yet to discuss the "medium" states that generally make up everyday life for most of us. So medium states are the stretch that constitutes our normal experience: unease, comfort, fun, pleasantness, boredom, frustration, irritation, drudgery, tiredness, the mood at the office, the feel of the kitchen sink, the too chilly morning breeze.

But what is "the experienced self" *really*?[127] At any given moment we have a whole subjective universe, an inner horizon in which all of our experienced phenomena arise: the coldness of our toes, our thoughts, subtle emotions and more things than we could name.

Obviously, the totality of subjective experience is impossible to catch in a number from one to ten. But if we posit that subjective states can be higher or lower, it is possible to assign numbers to descriptions of them. This creates a hierarchical scale which is considerably less arbitrary than simply "one to ten".[128]

Even so, the scale I propose must of course still be very crude, leaving out the content of experience (such as the emotions) and smashing together different forms of subjective states into the same one-dimensional scale. For instance, we know that some people are in deep "flow states" and have high levels of dopamine, being super-active and immersed in activities, which is quite different from the ones being showered with oxytocin and are overcome with compassion and closeness to their fellow beings, or just ride a wave of serotonin and endorphin wellness; and some are struck with an enormous clarity and serenity of religious surrender. Surely, these are very different phenomena in our brains, not least biochemically speaking. Correspondingly, there are many nuances of hell.

Here's the scale, from the lowest states to the highest ones.

Lower states:
1. Hell
2. Horrific (phenomenological reality breaks down)
3. Tortured
4. Tormented

Medium states:
5. Very uneasy
6. Uneasy, uncomfortable
7. Somewhat uneasy, "okay", full of small faults
8. Satisfied, well
9. Good, lively
10. Joyous, full of light, invigorated

High states:
11. Vast, grand, open
12. Blissful, saintly
13. Enlightened, spiritual unity

The different altitudes of subjective state may require closer definitions—but that discussion would be a too lengthy. The important takeaway here is simply to begin to see the subjective states, and that they can be higher or lower, and to get a rough, intuitive sense of what such states might entail. In its current form, this is what they call an "ordinal scale" (you can say which states are higher and lower, but you can't say they have equal distance).

What I claim here is that—at any given moment, awake or asleep, and regardless of the sensory and emotional content of one's experience—the organism is in one of these subjective states. I also claim that these subjective states are extremely volatile; that they can shift very dramatically from one instant to another. The higher states often last only brief moments, even split seconds. Right here, right now, your overall experience can be described in one of these states. All of your life has occurred, is occurring and will occur under some kind of subjective state, some higher, some lower—although there may be subjective states, yet lower or higher ones, that you never have experienced and never will.[129]

The advantage of the scale is that it is intuitive to many of us and helps us to effectively compare the subjective states of different organisms. The American philosopher Thomas Nagel famously asked "what it is like to be a bat?" His purpose was simply to see subjectivity as anything that can meaningfully be described as an experience. With this scale we take it a little farther; we begin to ask what it is like to be a sick and frightened bat, or one that flies for the first time into the soundscape of the open night. So while we are by no means claiming to have an exhaustive list of subjective states, we are at least closing in on something important.

Can then the subjective states really be described in discrete steps (whole numbers, like stages)? Perhaps not; maybe a continuous spectrum would be better. But whatever precision such a spectrum would add to the theory, it would be deceptive at this early stage. So let us, for convenience and clarity, go with discrete steps.

Beyond Emotions

Seen from a behavioral perspective (where you study the patterns or rules of behaviors of organisms from the outside, without regard to their inner life), states are *more fundamental* than emotions. If you want to predict behaviors of organisms, it seems to be a better idea to simply assume they are optimizing their state rather than seeking emotions. The emotions are seen as secondary expressions of this state optimization. **Organisms don't really seek or avoid certain emotions, but they seek to raise the level of their subjective state and avoid low states.**[130]

Most of the time, most of us live our lives in the medium state ranges, only vaguely aware of the very real possibilities of the higher or lower states. And, what's more, relatively few people have experienced the highest and lowest states at all.

Some examples: The normal adult person in a modern country is at state 7 most often, being "alright", but with a slight, lingering unease. Some lucky few are actually more often at state 8, being well and satisfied. And then you have a larger minority who are most often at lower states, such as the 6, being uneasy and uncomfortable. I don't have data for this, and you are welcome to create such data if you can (or data that contradicts my claims); but this is my experience: based on the lives and accounts of acquaintances, friends, relatives and lovers as well as myself. I think you might recognize the picture.

State is generally developed by positive rewards from your environments (e.g. successfully accomplishing work, relationships, love and sex) and things that benefit health and physiological well-being. But state can also, and often more radically, be developed by means of meditation as well as other practices of body and mind.[131]

As always, remember that this is only one dimension of adult development in humans: High state does not mean high complexity of thought structures and so on (as we will soon discuss more closely). That said, let us take a closer look at what it means to "develop" subjective state.

That's what next chapter is about.

Chapter 13
REACHING HIGHER

First of all, it is important to recognize that, to the extent that the subjective states can be said to "develop", they follow an entirely different logic than stage development as described in the cognitive complexity in Commons' MHC (chapters 8 and 9), or in the discussion of symbol-stages (chapters 10 and 11). **States are not the same as stages.**

A Definition of "Spirituality"

A fundamental difference between states and stages is that each stage transcends and *includes* the earlier stages (as is the case in the stages of cognitive complexity as well as the symbol-stages), whereas states transcend and *exclude* the lower states. As Ken Wilber has noted in one of his talks, you cannot be sober and drunk, or awake and asleep, at the same time—you have to choose. Shifting state truly is a transformation, from one reality to another. The subjective state doesn't just build upon what came earlier; each lived moment genuinely tears down all earlier moments and asserts itself as the full reality of now.

But states are certainly comparable to one another. Many mystics and contemplative traditions have described stage-like patterns in which subjective states are experienced as the spiritual practice progresses: the nine *yanas* (levels of absorption) of Buddhism perhaps being the emblematic example. It has been noted by comparative religion scholars that there seem to be clear parallels between the "the progression of states" identified across continents and over large stretches of time, in different cultures. It appears as though there may be a common blueprint to subjective states—perhaps not a very surprising finding.[132]

Even if progressions of inner experience may be observed (for long-term meditators and other disciplined contemplative practitioners) and arranged into at least partly recognizable and comparable patterns, subjective states should not be mistaken for stages like the ones in the MHC. An organism's cognitive complexity is relatively rigid: You simply have no six-year-olds inventing new stage 14 Paradigmatic theories; the only people who ever do are the ones who have passed through all of the earlier cognitive stages. It's just a fact of the world. And a person that has "installed" the symbol-stage D Postfaustian code simply cannot think postmodern thoughts: There was no Picasso in the middle ages.

Subjective states are much more irregular and volatile than developmental stages. For sure, relatively few people experience the highest states at all; and very few, if any, experience them regularly or most of the time. Our subjective state fluctuates all the time—and it can make leaps into higher and lower states in an instant. It is not uncommon that people have had experiences (often during childhood) in which we knew a heightened state of awareness, or that we have experienced moments of psychosis in which reality seems to break down and all our nightmares come true.

The conventional way of seeing such exceptional states is to give them *lower ontological status* (that they are seen as "less real" than the reality of everyday life). Everyday life is taken to be the "really real" reality, and all else to be dreams, hallucinations or fantasies. What this view tends to miss is that mental life is never a "correct representation" of some objective reality. So giving an "ontological premium" to medium states at the expense of the lower states and the higher ones just doesn't make sense. Our experience of reality is always felt, embodied; this means that the reality we see in a very high state is not any "less real". Of course, if you see gargoyles and angels, it shouldn't be taken at face value. But if reality seems crystal clear and profoundly meaningful to you for a brief moment, that is not any "less real" than your everyday experience.

We see and recognize different aspects of reality depending on which subjective state we are in. Thus we should avoid the conventional view—which downplays the role of all subjective states other than what is taken to be everyday life "normality". There is no reason to not relate to reality as viewed both from a sense of blissful clarity and as dark, screaming confusion. All of this is part of reality.

But I think that the mystics and transpersonal psychologists who have studied the higher stages tended to overemphasize the higher, spiritual states at the expense of low and medium states. They don't sufficiently account for the varieties of everyday life (in the medium range) and how these are unavoidably continuous with both the highest states and the lowest ones.

The way I have defined it, high states are the ones we would count as spiritual or profound life-changing experiences if exposed to them for the first time. The first of these states, and the only one I have personal knowledge of, is a great, open vastness (state 11); a kind of meaningful emptiness that opens up at times when I work with philosophy and meditate, and on rare occasions when I have sociological or psychological insights or make informed life decisions while taking a longer walk.

But from long trusted friends, as well as from teachers and the writings and recordings of mystics and spiritual teachers, I recognize that there must be at least two whole states above what I personally have experienced; whole worlds of feelings, moods and sentiments that I have not tasted. Most probably, these higher states are only present in humans—seeing as they are intimately connected to spirituality, which is a human endeavor. But of course, we can't be certain (and no, it is not a reason to enslave, murder and torture non-human animals).

Probably the highest states, if we are to believe the folks that claim to be "spiritually enlightened", occur when *Sein* (pure being) and *Da-sein* (being-in-the-world) merge into one. What spiritual teachers like Rupert Spira, Eckhart Tolle and Jiddu Krishnamurti will tell you, is that you are "already enlightened": that there is something you can stumble upon and recognize as self-evident. This is called *non-duality*; that you stop feeling separated from everything in the world around you (and even that description is false, the spiritual teachers say, because you can't actually "stop" doing anything). This is not a book about spirituality and existential insights; suffice to say that some people seem to describe heightened states—and that this seems to be a real thing with physiological correlates in the brain.

This leads us to the definition of spirituality, Hanzi-style: **"Spirituality" is a catch-all phrase for those human activities, experiences and practices which concern the three highest categories of subjective states—and the perspectives on life and the world that flow from such states (and the elaboration and teaching of these perspectives).** In this sense, spirituality has little or nothing to do with specific religious content or belief. It is according to this definition that I claim that spirituality is important for society as a whole.

What Everyday Life Feels Like on Average

Let's not over-emphasize spirituality, however. There are also lower states. The way I have defined it, **low states are the ones in which the organism loses its will to live**. In the lower states you are no longer part of "normal life" or existence. Reality is so alien, unreal and unwelcoming that the usual will to live disappears. But the terrible truth is that there are additional layers upon layers of unbelievable suffering beyond that point. Our whole reality can break down and become nothing but a chaos of unspeakable suffering. Speaking with our old pal, the French philosopher Henri Bergson, a second can last for a very, very long time. So these hells, even if they cover relatively little clock time, cover our planet in what seems to be eternities of unfathomable suffering.

To the tormented organism, even suicide may be too difficult: The severity of what grips us in the lower states can make us so frightened and indecisive—or otherwise helpless—that we cannot go through with killing ourselves. The lower states truly are prisons: comfortless expanses of pain, filth and degradation.[133]

The medium states make up all that lies between these higher and lower ones. They are so prevalent in ourselves and the people around us that we can easily forget or live largely oblivious of the highest and lowest states. Still, the medium range of subjective states is no small stretch: **Each "state level" you shift up or down truly is a world of difference**. Let us look again at the medium states:

5. Very uneasy
6. Uneasy, uncomfortable
7. Somewhat uneasy, "okay", full of small faults
8. Satisfied, well
9. Good, lively
10. Joyous, full of light, invigorated

Where would you place yourself on any given Monday, two o'clock in the afternoon? Some people (or other organisms) have higher **average state** than others. The average state would be if we imagine measuring one's state over time and then calculating the average (where, obviously, the subjective states you spend more time in would count affect your score more).

But perhaps a better measure is your **median state**, which is (almost always) simply the state you are in most often. Think about it: What worlds upon worlds of difference there must be between living your life most often in state 5, being very uneasy, the whole of your experience of the world being shaky, insecure and confused—and state 9, being in a light and kind world that continuously engages and stimulates you. A simple way of saying this is that higher median state makes life *lighter*; it makes it easier to get up in the morning. Have you ever fallen happily in love? You may have noticed how your whole world shifted in a subtle but pervasive manner: how the days became easier and lighter. Or you may have had a depression and noticed the direct opposite: a heavier, darker world.

As I mentioned, the most common median state appears to be what I have categorized as 7, to feel "okay" but subtly uneasy. This state still allows for much happiness, fun and comfort, but life is never quite "all that". Imagine what difference it makes to be at median state 8 (satisfied, feeling well). You may have had such periods in your life? This, I believe, often happens early or late in life, and more seldom during active adulthood—and for most modern people it simply doesn't happen.

How much freer and more secure and effective in everyday life must not the person at median state 8 be compared to median state 7, all else equal? Just one state up. The behavioral difference must have massive social and political implications.

But how stable or volatile is your subjective state? How much does it fluctuate? Some people are steady as rocks; their state seems to shift very little. Others seem extremely volatile, making profound shifts many times a day, even from moment to moment. This is your **state variability**: a measure of how easily, to what degree, and how often, your state shifts (for whatever reason: both endogenous and exogenous factors included).

Is it good or bad to have greater state variability? It depends. If your state varies more easily, and your average is high, you will be more likely to experience the highest states, which can be incredibly valuable. But of course, on a lower range, an unstable subjective state can cast us into the deepest angst and hold us back in so many ways. In more creative and artistic vocations, higher state variability may be advantageous because we thereby access more expanded forms of consciousness, more elegant flow states, and can draw upon more savage inner demons. In most roles within the economy however, still today, stability seems to be better, as we can keep up the steam more steadily.

So the subjective state of an organism varies across a range, with a **minimum state** and a **maximum state**. These are simply the lowest and highest states that a certain organism can experience, or has experienced, during any given period.

There are obviously many unanswered questions here: What about animals of different cognitive stages of complexity and different developments of the nervous system; does it make sense to talk about subjective states of insects, or fish? What are the physiological correlates? How do emotions fit in—surely they are not entirely separate from subjective states? What about the distinction between how pleasurable a state is and the degree of its intensity? Are we more selfish (or self-absorbed) in lower states than in higher ones?

Excuse my theoretical tinkering: You are right to point out that this is only half a theory. But before my discussion, I'd wager, you had no corresponding theory. Am I not correct? Are we not better off with half a theory to start from?

What It Means to Develop Your State

And from the vantage point that our half-theory has won us, we can begin to answer the question: What does it mean to develop in state? Here's a definition. To develop the subjective state of an organism means to either:

- Increase the median state.
- Increase the average state.
- Increase the minimum state.
- Increase the maximum state.
- Increase state variability (decrease stability) in an organism—*if* that would be beneficial given its current average state and context.
- Increase state stability (decrease variability) in an organism—*if* that would be beneficial given its current average state and context.

So your average, median, maximum and minimum state can go up or down over a lifetime. We are not talking of a stage development here or "growth" (like someone's height), but of a much more wobbly affair. Still, subjective states can be transformed in ways that persist over periods of time, and in that sense, they can be developed.[134]

It is sometimes said that only the depressed see the world clearly—the French psychoanalyst Jacques Lacan is often credited with the quote. In everyday situations we tend to be over-optimistic about everything from time use to our own abilities and guesses about the future. I would claim that, beyond such rather banal estimations, we see the world much more clearly in the higher states. **The higher one's state, the wider and more relaxed one's perspective: At higher states we see ourselves, the world, and our place in it more clearly.** But—again—this is true only in the sense that we see the world without the distortions of confusion that come with inner brokenness and suffering, not that we are more "correct" about factual matters, or that we think more complexly.

Example of a "High State" Person

What does a higher state person look like? It is someone who simply has a sense of peace within, a natural flow in their everyday activities and their life as a whole. I give you Doctor Ride-High.

Doctor Ride-High is of course the fictional name of a person I know. He is a medical doctor in his mid-thirties who has spent many years working eagerly with physical exercise, yoga, meditation, reading and listening to wisdom teachings, optimizing diet, taking part in psychotherapy, artwork, love relationships and sex to achieve higher subjective states. What drove him was, not surprisingly, a fundamental sense of anxiety that had followed him since his early teens—he just fervently wanted to get rid of that pervasive angst. I knew him as someone who perhaps too readily grasped for spiritual answers and would "buy in" to things to a somewhat worrying extent. But the angst persisted. Just a few years ago, he still insisted that people cannot fundamentally be rid of their angst and said that life must and even *should* include stress and anxiety. This is what most people who have consistent anxieties will say.

But all of that has changed. I interviewed him earlier this week, as I was preparing for this chapter, and found him reporting a positive change of subjective state. He told me about a few months' streak, thus far, of almost zero mental resistance to anything. His life situation hasn't changed: same job, same apartment, same wife. But his life has. Some moments every morning, he is completely "open" and disidentified with himself; he rests in "all that arises", seeing it as part of his own consciousness. He goes to work and performs his job without frustrations and mental fatigue, feeling truly blessed to be able to help so many people and show them love through the medical profession. He practices unconditional love towards his wife and other members of the family and feels very little frustrations towards them. As he tells me his story, his eyes glow with an unmistakable inner peace.

So Doctor Ride-High has exceptionally high states, at least during these last few months, after what must feel like a lifetime worth of dissatisfaction and struggle. The point here is not to idealize this particular person's subjective states—who knows, maybe he'll relapse into lower states again. I simply wish to point out that **prolonged and stable periods of high equilibriums of subjective states are possible and achievable**. Speaking with the scale we have devised here, Doctor Ride-High would probably be described as ranging from 6 (uneasy, uncomfortable) to 12 (blissful, saintly), where the highest state perhaps only shows up for about twenty minutes at a time, but does so relatively frequently, almost every day. But state 6 isn't very prevalent; the median state (the most commonly experienced) would probably be at 9 (good, lively). Just consider what a world of difference there is between feeling this way, and feeling anxious and insecure all or most of the time. It's safe to say that Doctor Ride-High **out-states** a person like myself, meaning that he has a much higher average state (and median and maximum state as well as stability).

Just imagine how differently society would function if many more of us were in higher states a larger portion of the time. Not only does the development of the subjective state seem to be a moral imperative (the right thing to pursue for the sake of people's well-being); it would also, we can assume, create a considerably less dysfunctional society in a far-reaching variety of ways. I would say that Doctor Ride-High has achieved a certain kind of *wellness*, a general well-being that affects all aspects of his life and all of his relationships in mostly positive ways.

Perhaps we would also, in more expanded states of subjective awareness, be able to grasp more universal, visionary and inclusive perspectives of society, life and existence. Hence, the issue is not only to develop the median state of people, but to develop the maximum state as well.

Naturally, the case of Doctor Ride-High is just an anecdotal example. But there is some research to back it up. The most satisfying study I am aware of supporting the claim that there are some people who consistently frequent the higher states is Jeffry A. Martin's 2010 doctoral dissertation.[135] The study surveyed 36 adults who claim to have persistent, in Martin's terms, "non-symbolic" experiences—i.e., having high states of a spiritual or mystical kind on a day-to-day basis. When compared to the stages of "ego-development" (as described by the developmental theory of Susanne Cook-Greuter, "Nine Levels of Increasing Embrace", which I briefly mentioned earlier), all of these people fall into the post-conventional category (being relatively high stage). But there was still a wide spread among them in terms of stage: some being at much higher stages than others. Hence, you cannot reduce the high states to high stages of personal or cognitive development.

State is *related* to personal development, it seems, but it is not the same thing. Stage development does not *predict* state or vice versa. What then was characteristic of these people? Many of them were meditators with years of meditation experience, but not all of them. Ages ranged from 23 to 69, average age was 51. The average age at which they had begun to experience consistently high states was about 40. Fifteen, less than half, reported having used hallucinogenic drugs at some point. Half of them had a postgraduate education. Other than that, they seemed to be just about anyone. Still, these people seem to actually exist in small but significant numbers—which I believe has important implications.

I am *not* claiming that all people (or other living creatures) can have high states. It is clear that some people are much more predisposed for it than others: Some people have strong spiritual, shamanic or oceanic experiences early in life—others go to years of meditation retreats without having such experiences. William James, for instance, the most authoritative writer on the topic in American history, did not have any mystical experiences himself, prevented as he was by his own "constitution". Charles Sanders Peirce, this more mathematical and less psychological philosopher, did have mystical experiences (rather late in life, in a church in New York): "I have never been mystical, but now I am".[136]

What I *am* claiming, however, is that states are more volatile and easier to affect than stages of cognitive complexity—and that this has vast implications for society as a whole and the future of life. It is a moral imperative, I would argue, to organize society in a way that optimizes the likelihood for higher subjective states of living organisms.

Can Lower States Be Good?

What about the lower states; can they never be of any good? We shall return to the topic in the next two chapters—existential depth can be developed through the experience of lower subjective states. At this moment we need only to note two things.

The first point is that greater state variability can at times be beneficial, and this of course implies the experiencing of lower states: It may well be "worth it" for us. More sensitive people will say things like: "The music was so beautiful, I had to break down and cry." Sensitive people tend to be, I would argue, both more vulnerable to the adversities of life *and* more in tune with the profound beauty of existence. In our days there is a growing discussion of HSPs, *Highly Sensitive People*. Unfortunately, these beautiful souls[137] are more prone to depression and anxiety and are generally at a disadvantage in today's late modern society. A saner, more sensitive, society might turn this heightened state variability into a potential.

The second and more crucial point is that there is a kind of dialectic between the lower and the higher states: Lower states can be instrumental to the acquisition of higher ones. You will find similar ideas in the contemplative traditions: Jesus meets the devil while spending forty days in the desert; you have the "dark night of the soul" as a recognized state in contemplative Christianity; and Tibetan Buddhism is full of monsters you must face with equanimity to realize they were really aspects of your own empty, luminous consciousness all along.[138]

That said, the lower states should never-ever be taken lightly. The seriousness and severity of existence is a fact precisely because these horror-show prisons exist; because they are, as far as experiences go, real. Maybe in some deep, spiritual sense you could say that they are only illusions and that Hell always does freeze over in the end. I suppose that's true, but we must still not treat the issue lightly. Worlds of suffering are always possible, and we have no right to wish such enormous suffering upon any living creature. To praise the lower subjective states—to praise universes of suffocation, torture and degradation—simply lands us in untenable ethical positions. So don't do it.

The Credibility Problem of Higher States

Just as people at lower complexity only understand flattened and caricatured versions of ideas, perspectives and behaviors of higher complexity, so are the higher states difficult, if not impossible, to convey to people who don't share the same experiences.

This creates a problem of lacking credibility for all experiencers and communicators of higher states: Other people simply won't believe them. People aren't generally aware of how different the phenomenological experiences of reality really are; we tend to communicate with one another with our subjective states held implicitly. They tend to stay in the background and we generally have no ways of imagining how different the world looks from the eyes of our neighbor, even our husband or wife.

So let's take a high state person, one who lives in a relatively light universe and sometimes drops into the deep, pristine, open emptiness that appears at the highest states. This person tends to want to convey how utterly awe-struck they are. They might want to express the profound significance of spiritual insight to other people. This is what they might sound like:

> "In the hour of vision there is nothing that can be called gratitude, nor properly joy. The Soul raised over passion beholds identity and eternal causation, perceives the self-existence of Truth and Right, and calms itself with knowing that all things go well. Vast spaces of nature, the Atlantic Ocean, the South Sea; long intervals of time, years, centuries, are of no account…"[139]

This is from the US "national poet" of the 19th century, the great Ralph Waldo Emerson. So take a look at what is being said. If we read Emerson as "only a poet", this paragraph appears rather innocent. These are beautiful and soothing words, with an exciting but solemn tinge of wisdom. We might imagine them as a kind of decoration, on par with flowers painted in the ceiling of a nice marble house. And that is of course how genuine spirituality and expressions of such are generally treated: as innocent words, as art deco, pleasant traditions in church, maybe even cute kitsch —something for us to "appreciate" and then go back to our "real" lives where such words about souls, beauties, eternal truths, oceans and ages and of-no-account, are only ever nonsense.

Now imagine if we actually took Emerson seriously, if we read his words literally, as a descriptive statement about reality. Okay, now we're talking. So what you are saying, dear Emerson, is that:

- There are moments in which you see reality more clearly and profoundly and that this is an experience far beyond what we might call "gratitude" and "joy";
- in such moments you recognize that your own soul is identified with all that happens, with all causality in the world;
- you see a self-evident truth and goodness with which you yourself are fully identified;
- and you understand that everything and all that ever was is going to be alright;
- and that whatever vastness or beauty we may conceive of with our normal minds and senses are just pale shadows of this realization.

Okay, Ralphie. If you mean that *seriously*, we are obliged to inquire: What the hell have you been smoking, dude? So you are saying, first of all, that there are profound experiences beyond anything I have ever experienced or could comprehend, but that *you* know about them.

And then you go on to saying something about your soul being "everything". No, stupid. You are you—just Ralphie—not the causal mechanisms of everything. I don't care if you "felt" like that; you are just *one* person, confined to *one* body.

And then you claim that you are in fact truth and goodness itself. And then you even have the insolence to claim that—despite the fact that my life has been an utter mess of pain and chaos—"everything" is alright, while my loved ones are dying of cancer and I struggle with stress and anxieties. Easy for you to say, if you're having such a dandy spiritual time.

And *then* you flat-out claim that the coolest and most awesome things I know, like the vastness and beauty of the seas, are just bullshit compared to what you find when you look at how pretty you are yourself?

All of this lands us in an awkward position: We have to take Emerson's word for it. But he is making statements about reality that simply seem not only foreign, but even insulting and outright preposterous to most of us. Compared to the subjective experience of what everyday life usually feels like, Emerson appears to be fantasizing and exaggerating. Why should we believe him?

We could think of any number of reasons why Emerson (or anybody else who speaks similarly) would say these things: Maybe he wants to comfort himself because he cannot face the harshness of life; maybe he has hallucinated and believes in some kind of sparkly miracle; maybe he is just very stupid and naive to believe that reality is one big candy store; maybe he wants to impress us and appear "special", thus presenting himself as having marvelous inner qualities, which conveniently enough requires no effort on his behalf, no work for the good of others, and that the rest of us cannot verify; or maybe there is even something more sinister going on—it could be a bait to seduce us into blindly admiring and following him, so that he can fool us and... steal our wives.

People will sometimes tell stories of how their hearts open up and overflow in life-changing moments, or how their minds expand to a kind of cosmic view of reality and their place in it, or how they have found profound peace and rest in the non-duality of all-that-arises, or how they have found an intimate lover in the emptiness of all experience, or how a shocking "Kundalini awakening"[140] tortured them with sleeplessness and ecstasy for years before they managed to control it and how they now have ten minute long orgasms when they have tantric sex (yes, that's a thing).[141] And in holy scriptures we find numerous accounts of an inner life, a "kingdom within" or a radiance that reveals itself as "brighter than a thousand suns".[142]

Generally speaking, such claims are not believed or taken seriously, even while many of the people who make the claims are, in terms of subjective experience, telling the truth. It is well established that very high state experiences do exist—see, for instance, the work of neuroscientist Andrew Newberg.[143] The fact that spiritual experiences have clear physiological correlates and are therefore in some sense "real" doesn't necessarily mean that we should believe people's stories about the details of what they experienced. And it certainly doesn't mean we should take their interpretations at face value (when somebody says they met an angel or the like). It's just that the occurrence of higher states should be taken seriously and that they can have great intensity and significance in people's lives. It has been described in many sources that such spiritual states very often have lasting impact on our overall psychological development.[144]

In short, the higher states, because they are subjective experiences rather than intersubjective facts, cannot be communicated or "proven" to those of us who do not experience them for ourselves. When people communicate across too vast distances of subjective state, the ones who talk of higher states necessarily appear frivolous, naive, confusing, insulting—or even deeply dishonest: "Why are you promising me these things that I know are not true? What are you trying to do? What is your secret agenda? I am asking because I know with every fiber of my body that you are not telling the truth."

This is an important reason for why so many wisdom teachers and spiritual writers awaken such deep suspicion, even disgust, in many if not most modern people. Not only are they telling us that we haven't recognized the awesomeness of life; they also seem to be promising us unrealistic and exaggerated things—and these things refer to the *subjective* realm, rather than the *intersubjective* (which is, as we have discussed, the ontological home base of modernity, i.e. what modern people see as the "really real"—hence modern people tend to see subjective experience as "less real"). The wisdom teachers come off as bombastic, out of place, even fraudulent.

Of course, wisdom teachers can also be perceived as exceptionally inspiring and awaken awe or spiritual experiences in their followers. But this is more often true of those who have some spiritual experience themselves, or who otherwise have committed to a spiritual worldview. To most others, they tend to appear creepy.

It is a good thing that such skepticism exists: Otherwise anybody could just claim to be enlightened and receive a following of credulous slaves. But it is also a problem, because it makes us take the development of higher subjective states much less seriously than we ideally should.

All of this creates a great rift between people who have experienced higher spiritual states and those of us who haven't, which can be confusing and frustrating for all parties involved. For all foreseeable future, humanity will be divided into the spiritual and the non-spiritual. It must be so.

We can view the advancement of subjective state either as a direct transformation of experience (a more "romantic" view) or as a matter of optimizing the psycho-physiological state of the organism, regulating its behavioral responses and changing its environment (a more "behavioral" view).[145] I hold that both of these perspectives go hand-in-hand. Society is a collection of organisms each of which are, in every given moment, in some kind of psycho-physiological state equilibrium. Such states can also be described in terms of inner, subjective experiences. That should do for a summary.

Why Spiritual Communities Turn Into Cults

I would like to end this chapter on a word of warning. There are communities with the express purpose of bringing people to higher subjective states: spiritual communities. I am not primarily thinking of the medieval monastic traditions (to which we return in the next book, when we discuss "existential politics"). Monastic life also had many other roles, and such a central place in European society, that it was far from a purely spiritual congregation. The closest thing to truly contemplative communities has historically been the Buddhist monasteries and the Vedic yoga traditions, although these too have had many other societal roles to play.

In its pure form, however, I would claim that spiritual congregation is actually a *modern* phenomenon, showing up in the 19th and 20th centuries—where people freely devote themselves to a guru, master or teacher who is believed to be enlightened. You may have come across one or more such spiritual communities, often populated by hippies and New Age ideas (or New Thought, or variations of theosophy, or contemporary interpretations of Eastern traditions, or mysticism from any religion).

A striking pattern in these communities is the prevalence of abuses of power—financial or sexual exploitation, physical and emotional violence (sometimes even directed outside of the community), clear uses of brainwashing strategies, con-artist yogi miracle-makers, or at the very least false claims and endless intrigues and lawsuits. Looking at teachers like Sri Aurobindo, Osho, Adi Da (Da Free John), Andrew Cohen, Amma ("the hugging mother") and Chögyam Trungpa—even Jiddu Krishnamurti, who didn't even found any organization—their communities have all devolved into abusive or at least commercialized and dysfunctional relationships. Whereas some of these nasty stories may perhaps be explained by deliberate manipulations on behalf of the teachers, the frequency with which these communities show cult-like and deeply oppressive tendencies must have a more general, sociological and structural explanation.

My take on such an explanation is this. Whenever a community is built, there is a hierarchy. Hierarchies of some kind are necessary for people to successfully cooperate, evaluate the efforts of one another: who puts in the most effort, who is reliable, and so forth. Spiritual communities like these are built primarily around a hierarchy of "subjective state". The leader is taken to be one of higher subjective state than other members of the community, which is why people want to follow him or her. To advance within this hierarchy, one should also be able to rest for longer periods in higher subjective states.

The main problem is that subjective state is not something that can easily be measured, and that it changes from moment to moment. Scientific results, athletic achievements, even a dollar bottom line—all these are things that can be intersubjectively confirmed or falsified, which means that you can relatively easily see who is a qualified scientist, athlete or businesswoman. The spiritual communities build a social hierarchy upon something that can only be personally experienced and imagined. Sure, for a brief moment you can check someone's brainwaves with the right equipment, but then again, you never know if someone's subjective state is quite what they say it is, and you can't measure it all the time. You try to build an intersubjective community upon a subjective thing. It's a just a no-go. It's an illogically constructed social structure, and this poor construction leads to some very bad social consequences.

It's often not even easy to recognize what subjective state we are in ourselves; it often takes great effort just to notice. Ever heard a person shouting about how they're "not angry"? This is just one example out of many of when we fail to recognize an obvious inner state or emotion within ourselves. If each person can hardly know her own state, how can we be expected to build a reliable community upon not only our own state, but the states of a whole group of people?

In spiritual communities, social pressure arises to present oneself as being in as high states as possible (both by personal prestige and because people want to hear that you are doing well in order to validate the spiritual enterprise as a whole). So people begin to subtly lie to themselves and to one another about how lightly and profoundly they experience the world at any given moment. Ever noticed that strange hysterical happiness that sect people display? That's what I'm talking about: They insist upon displaying behaviors that indicate high inner states; hence that strange stare. This applies not least to the guru: If he or she is in a bad mood, the students will still interpret them as acting from a very high state.

So there is a social-psychological "spin" on the whole thing, making people pretend to be something they're not. This becomes a closely guarded, dirty secret for almost everyone and people are likely to react quite aggressively whenever it risks surfacing. This is a central reason for why they turn so oppressive and aggressive when the image of harmony is challenged by all the conflicts and issues that necessarily show up in any community.

And all of this is aggravated by the fact that subjective states are deeply personal and emotional phenomena. If a community is built around achieving higher subjective states, it must by necessity involve people sharing a lot of their inner lives. This leaves little or no personal sphere, no hiding away—which means that people get closely tied up to one another in situations that are full of smoke-screens, lies and self-deceit. It couldn't get much more venomous.

But the troubles don't stop there. Traditional monasteries of earlier centuries were not purely spiritual communities; they were also, perhaps primarily, built around work, theology, philosophy and so on. Thus hierarchies could be constructed around things that people could relate to and evaluate intersubjectively. Modern spiritual communes are different. If you build a community around the idea that "this guy", let's say the US guru Adi Da, is "enlightened", not only can you never get any proof of it, but **you overlook all of the other developmental dimensions**.

In other words, even if your guru really *does* frequent high subjective states; he or she can still be low MHC stage, work from defunct cultural codes, and have all manner of psychological issues and problems.

Just listen to a person like Eckhart Tolle, the author of the book *The Power of Now*, who has been featured on Oprah Winfrey and gained great traction. He obviously has high states. But his answers on any social or societal issues, and the theories propounded in his books, are of average complexity (MHC stage 11 Formal, more precisely). He just doesn't have the answers. Which is okay. The only problem is that he makes all sorts of analyses of society, from politics to mental health to gender and sexuality—and many people listen. It should be made perfectly clear that this man, while being both kind and wise, is poorly educated and, truth be told, not very clever. Nothing wrong with it, but it should be recognized.

The same goes for pretty much all the gurus. They have high state perspectives—the ones that are authentic gurus, that is—but they mistake these existential perspectives for authority on all sorts of other issues. As do their followers.

An issue that we haven't really ventured to discuss here, but that should also briefly be mentioned, is **high state pathologies**. Low state pathologies are pretty obvious—you feel like utter crap and this can make you dysfunctional, make you have destructive behaviors and want to lash out against the world. But higher states can also bring all sorts of complications. If you, for instance, suddenly feel extremely enlarged and filled with cosmic love, this can easily translate to grandiose ideas about yourself and your place in the world. To megalomania and unsustainable optimism. And in moments where you feel that everything is intimately interconnected and that all things are one, you are also likely to draw rather questionable conclusions about how things are *causally* interrelated. It has even been shown that people who have just done mindfulness are more likely to have imagined and false memories and that they are somewhat more gullible.[146] For all the good things I have to say about high states, I can hardly overemphasize just how seductive and dangerous they are. I will return to the topic in chapter 17, when I discuss the dangers of magic beliefs—as these show up in a lot of high state people.

Uncritical praise of people in high subjective states is a recipe for being ruled and fooled, for being abused and for very sudden and disappointing dissolutions of formerly very tightly knit communities. This is true even if some of the gurus turn out to be nice (which seems to be the case with only a minority of them, e.g. Eckhart Tolle, Rupert Spira, and perhaps the Jamaican guru Mooji)—indeed, even if they turn out to be intelligent as well (like Shinzen Young). But nice and intelligent teachers don't make the structural issues I brought up go away: You simply can't build a good community with hierarchies derived from subjective states. It doesn't make sense. Because, *mon ami*, communities and their hierarchies are intersubjective and relatively durable structures; inner states are subjective and very transient.

This is not to say that all spiritual communities are a bad thing. Indeed, the places in which people make a common, concentrated and guided effort to develop higher states often have positive effects on people's lives—and that may positively affect other aspects of society. It's just that the endeavor comes with certain risks that have to do with the social-psychological territory; and these risks are pretty big, like all communities which elicit very deep commitment and fervor.

A possible antidote to this social-psychological malady might be to democratize spirituality; to make it more participatory, transparent and based on measurable results. Such attempts are being made in and around the Burning Man festival culture, and notably in the Syntheist ("religious atheist") movement which recently emerged in Stockholm—and some interesting prospects along these lines have been brought up by public intellectuals like Sam Harris (in his 2014 book *Waking Up*, Harris, a renowned critic of all things religious, makes his case for a scientifically supported exploration of spirituality). However, these are difficult matters; thus far, almost all spiritual communities have taken a long walk down Cult Avenue, so it is quite probable that these movements will do likewise. We'll see.

To conclude: Yes, the subjective state of organisms is the most important thing in the world, and yes, it should therefore be made a central goal of society. And yes, it has great significance for the overall development of people and societies. But no, having higher state does not give you all the answers. And no, we should *not* build a society that creates hierarchies based upon vague and unverifiable phenomena such as subjective state. And YES, more research is needed.[147]

But we *must* try to optimize subjective states, as a society as well as single organisms. We are all always-already in some kind of subjective state. It is an inescapable, merciless fact that the universe has us eternally by the balls.

Chapter 14
DEPTH

From here on, we only have the fourth dimension of development left to discuss before we can put them all together into one model. We can call this dimension a measure of a person's inner *depth*.

Whereas subjective states vary from moment to moment (and we can only meaningfully speak of medians and averages if we would seek to develop them), a person's "inner depth" is a more permanent feature of their psychological development—one that may be described in stages, albeit of a different kind than those of cognitive development and code.

But the state and depth are intimately connected. Let's start with a more formal definition:

- **Depth is a person's intimate, *embodied* acquaintance with subjective states.** A person's inner depth increases through her felt, lived and intuitive knowledge of a new subjective state (lower or higher than previously experienced)—*and* when the intimate acquaintance of that state becomes an integrated part of her psychological constitution; a part, if you will, of her personality.

This definition is of course a little too condensed. We might need to unpack it and give examples. Intuitively, what I call "depth" can be thought of as a kind of existential or spiritual *wisdom*. Again, this "wisdom" doesn't mean that you are smart, right about things, or a complex thinker, or even that you have a balanced, healthy personality. But it *does* mean that you relate more profoundly to more fundamental aspects of reality as it is subjectively experienced. So what does *that* mean?

How about an old, Tibetan nun, who has achieved great equanimity and a profound acceptance of her own death and how all things must melt away, while still managing to lead a life in simple appreciation of every day and its small gifts of beauty? She's hardly the person we'd bring in to shorten hospital waiting lists or hire to solve the crisis on the Horn of Africa or ask about Kant's philosophy—but perhaps she is still *wise* in some sense, more so than your average modern PhD in psychology. Or the 30 years old shaman of a rural illiterate tribe in Mongolia, who has gone through hallucinations and crisis, finding a mentor, learning to get into trance and handling its downsides, gone through "the death of self", found an expanded awareness and extended his circle of compassion—isn't he *wise* in some sense that most of us aren't? Or how about a philosopher like Martin Heidegger—how is he different from a scientific genius like the mathematician John von Neumann?

My suggestion for understanding these examples is that they have developed "greater depth", and that they thereby **out-depth** most of us. In this way, spiritual or existential depth is its own dimension of development: It is something quite different from having high cognitive complexity or access to a more updated symbolic code, or even having a high median state.

Agony and Ecstasy

"Great-depth" people are the ones who have experienced **a wider range of subjective states**, who are well acquainted with being in such states and who have learned to handle them. This goes both for lower states and higher ones. For instance, depth by lower states can come to a person like Viktor Frankl. He survived in a Nazi concentration camp by finding meaning. Or it may come to a tortured soul who has made philosophical ninja moves in order to accept his predicament (Kierkegaard, Schopenhauer, Nietzsche), or to a person who, like Mother Teresa, has lived through the "dark night of the soul" (a depression-like period that befalls deeply religious people in the later stages of their spiritual development).

Acquaintance with higher states can come to spiritual and contemplative practitioners, but also to philosophers, talented artists and athletes, perhaps within martial arts and "extreme sports" in particular. Positive near-death experiences (far from all are positive) and even a stroke in the brain can open up such higher states, as in the neurologist Jill Bolte Taylor's famous account of how her stroke triggered an intense spiritual awakening. And of course, "normal" life experiences, such as having children, or great love, or finding inner peace while alone in the forest, or reaching our deeply desired goals, can stretch our awareness of different subjective states.

So "depth" is the stretch between the lowest states that we intimately remember, know and accept, and the highest states that we have tasted and aspire towards. **Depth is the number of states that have become inseparable parts of us; integrated into our memories and personalities.** Note that this means that a person can have a relatively low average *state*, but still have great *depth*, as she has experienced higher states before and holds them in clear memory—she "knows her way around them" and can understand other people living, acting or thinking from such states, even if she herself may never again experience these same states.

Hence, another way of describing the matter is that **depth is a person's innermost recognition of the greatness and/or seriousness of reality**. As with subjective states we don't have the relevant data, which means that we cannot say very much about how depth is distributed in a population. But we can make reasonable and testable hypotheses. One such hypothesis would be that older people generally out-depth young adults—which is not the case when it comes to MHC complexity and code (symbol-stages) and probably not state either. But given that older people have generally experienced more of life and have had more time to process and integrate these experiences as parts of their identities, habits, attitudes and skills, it seems likely that older people will generally out-depth younger adults.[148]

But it is only when such experiences become integral to our ways of seeing the world, of relating to existence, that they can be said to have become part of our depth. Just taking psychedelics and spacing out for a while and then being all "Dude, I *see* things! It's like... awesome sauce!"—is not what we are looking for. A person may well have experienced very profound subjective states but lack any means of integrating them with the rest of her life and everyday understanding. In such case, low states appear only as confusing hell-holes and higher states as strange exceptions, hallucinations or even as supernatural interventions (they're not).

But greater depth doesn't really entail anything other than a psychological property of a person's relation to the universe and existence: It is her remembered, embodied knowledge of agony and ecstasy. Or, more precisely, agony *and/or* ecstasy.

Measuring Depth

An intuitive way of measuring depth might be by asking people—under good circumstances and with plenty of appropriate probing questions—what they think is of "ultimate significance".[149] What is most important to you, in the whole universe? To my knowledge, this methodology is not sufficiently developed, but let's make some introductory remarks just to get an idea.

What is of ultimate significance? People are likely to understand, interpret and answer the question very differently. Regardless of how well we comply to such interview questions, we all have an answer of some kind (given that we are able to speak). We all relate to the world, to the universe, because we have to. As we noted earlier, life has us eternally by the balls and this requires us to relate to the world, one way or another.

If you ask a person in the US, in 2017, a "low-depth" response might be one that entirely misses the philosophical implication of such a question. People might just mention something they are working on at the moment and that he or she thinks is important. Other low-depth answers may involve feelings of happiness, fun, success in life, to be good to one's family, to be a good person, to achieve progress, to experience as much as possible and the like.

Medium-depth answers (again, in a modern setting) involve more universal values such as love, truth and beauty. A more medium-depth adult might answer: "To live a life that serves love in all forms is what is of ultimate significance." You might find people who answer that one or the other principle is what appears most significant in the universe: for instance, to prevent suffering.

A great-depth response involves yet more universal values which do not necessarily correspond to aspects of everyday life: to manifest divinity in the world, to find radical acceptance, to serve the becoming of the most profound possible unity and multiplicity, to surrender fully and without compromise to God or existence, to "be" wordless emptiness and recognize the pristine meaninglessness of the ultimate truth. You may remember the part in chapter 2, in which we discussed if happiness is important or not. As you recall, I argued in favor of the importance of happiness, but I promised that we would deepen this discussion later on. Well, here we are—at greater depth, happiness does indeed appear as a less self-sufficient goal, as less of an "ultimate significance", no longer an end in-and-of-itself.

A tricky part of interpreting great-depth answers is that these answers tend to relate to all of reality in a very direct and sweeping manner—they tend to be *religious* in some sense. Religion, the word, is often interpreted to stem from a Latin term for "binding together", to reconnect all things into a seamless whole. Experiencing very high or low states, or learning any of the wisdom traditions, puts you face-to-face with existence as a whole in a more complete and direct manner. Hence, if you relate more deeply to reality, your answers will tend to sound religious, because they speak of "all things" and some kind of "final truth" and a very general mode of relatedness. And here's the problem: so does any person who lives by a traditional religion (i.e. relying symbol-stage D Postfaustian); they sound quite similar. But most mainstream Catholics are by no means at greater depth than their more atheist or agnostic fellow citizens (even if some few contemplative Catholics definitely are). So whenever you look at this issue, either in research or just when you analyze people individually, you must be careful not to mistake religious beliefs—pertaining to symbol-stage D Postfaustian or below—with high-depth answers.

Unfortunately, anthropologists sometimes make this mistake, and believe that indigenous cultures at symbol-stage B Animistic are per definition at greater depth (however this is construed in their theory) than e.g. modern or Western society. More likely, modern cultures and indigenous ones are at comparable levels of depth in their population averages.

Developing Depth

To understand how depth develops we must again underscore the difference between state and depth. The subjective state of an organism only ever exists in the "now", in any one given moment. Depth is something that develops and accumulates over time. States come and go; depth very rarely decreases (only if you become senile or the like)—once you have reached a level of depth, it tends to stay.

Let us then zoom in on the relationship between subjective state and depth. Basically, we need only hold three concepts in mind: a) state (as defined in the previous two chapters), b) depth, and c) the successful **integration of inner experiences**. Let's start by recalling the thirteen suggested subjective states:

Lower states:
1. Hell
2. Horrific (phenomenological reality breaks down)
3. Tortured
4. Tormented

Medium states:
5. Very uneasy
6. Uneasy, uncomfortable
7. Somewhat uneasy, "okay", full of small faults
8. Satisfied, well
9. Good, lively
10. Joyous, full of light, invigorated

High states:
11. Vast, grand, open
12. Blissful, saintly
13. Enlightened, spiritual unity

Okay. Now imagine a person, Lonny, who is highly functional and has lived all of her life in states 6, 7 and 8. It might sound absurd to only experience such a narrow stretch of states, but think about it: Is it not very often that weeks, months or even years pass in your life—or at least the lives of most people—without any super-strong experiences? Sure, you have emotions and ups and downs, but you weren't really smashed open into an orgasmic fountain of cosmic love lately, were you (or something correspondingly nasty on the low-state end)? This person will be relatively stable, but not necessarily be forced to kneel before the awe-inspiring and terrifying mysteries of existence.

Compare this to another person, Cinderella, who has lived for years in say states 4, 5, 6, 7 and 8. This person must have suffered much more deeply than her more stable fellow citizen above. But Cinderella may also have learned more about life and existence than Lonny. She has seen darker sides of herself, of society, of life and reality itself. And she has tackled and needed to manage greater demons and travelled a much, much longer road of life.

Does Lonny or Cinderella have greater depth? It depends. It depends on whether or not each of them has had the opportunity to successfully **integrate her inner experiences**. Think of the sad life of Cinderella. Maybe she found an outlet in painting and poetry, maybe she learned ways to calm her own mind, maybe she developed inner grit to wade through intense pain and breathe free in the midst of roaring turmoil. One of the fundamental principles of psychotherapy is precisely this: to accommodate the integration of subjective states, to make them part and parcel of our psychological constitution. Usually, of course, such therapy focuses on handling and integrating lower states. In a clinical setting this has been described as "posttraumatic growth", notably in Calhoun and Tedeschi's book with the same title.[150] There is growing empirical evidence that trauma, when successfully dealt with, can lead to positive psychological development. Go Cinderella, go.

In the future, perhaps, we will have greater knowledge and expertise of the integration of higher states as well. This knowledge has thus far belonged chiefly to the spiritual lineages, to different forms of pre-modern yoga and so forth. Let's hope that changes: We have some promising trends in "positive psychology" and research on mindfulness.

What it means to successfully integrate one's experiences is a whole science in its own right. It has to do with learning from a new kind of experience and then rearranging one's whole sense of reality: a sense of self, of ethics and ontology (what you think is "really real"). We can hardly do the discussion any justice here; suffice to point out that successful integration of higher and lower states is necessary for increased depth. For instance, an extremely painful existential anxiety can bring you to develop inner skills through e.g. meditation practice; where such practices make you become acquainted and comfortable with deeper and more vulnerable parts of your inner landscape. Correspondingly, you can find really messed up and confused people who experience higher or lower states that are not yet part of their overall psychological constitution.

So, returning to our two example persons Lonny and Cinderella. Even if Cinderella is *out-stated* (as discussed in the last chapter) by Lonny, she may well *out-depth* Lonny, given that Cinderella's "negative" experiences have been successfully integrated into her overall personality. She can see *more* of reality, and when she relates to the world, she understands the fundamental seriousness of reality much more clearly. She has, in a sense, become a more sensing soul, gazing deeper into reality.

Likewise, of course, depth is developed by the successful integration of high state experiences, so that these are no longer just "festive occasions", but become part of how one sees reality and the universe. One begins to recognize things such as the unfathomable potential of life, the "glory of God", the emptiness of all sensuous experience and—as we saw Ralph Waldo Emerson observe in the last chapter—that everything, in some cosmic last instance, is going to be alright.

The people we like to imagine as "spiritual masters" are the ones that have both high average state *and* great depth. But then again, we should really not deify such folks; first of all, they too have bad days, and second of all, we might be mistaken (and there is no reliable way for us to check). And there is also a host of potential pathologies (sicknesses) that come with the territory of greater depth and higher states (spiritual arrogance, tendencies for holistic visions that lean towards totalitarianism, and other things; these things need not concern us here). And, again, they can be limited in other respects (low complexity, outdated code, etc.). In fact, they usually are.

So, developing depth means to experience new states and to integrate them into one's psychological constitution so that they "permanently" **change one's relatedness to the world and to existence as a whole**. It is sometimes said that the Buddha learned "implicit knowledge" from meditation, visible in the Buddha statues as the calm, secretive hint of a smile. I feel that this phrase catches a lot of what we're getting at here: Depth is not knowledge of any particular fact, it is not "code", or theory or any particular belief. It's just one's wordless relationship to existence itself. It is how one knows reality as nothing but reality in all of its silent meaninglessness. Implicit knowledge.

On a side note, I would like to underscore a problematic situation often occurring in mental health care and psychiatry: when therapists and psychiatrists are out-depthed by their own patients. Some psychiatric patients may have subjective experiences that are fundamentally alien to the people who have medical and sometimes even legal authority over them. The patients can know worlds of suffering, or have spiritual experiences, that are poorly or wrongly interpreted by the therapists and psychiatrists.

As a young man, I remember very clearly the confused eyes of my psychotherapist as I explained what existential angst felt like, and how her questions, hints and suggestions all felt predictable, naive and terribly off mark. In hindsight, I understand that my case out-depthed the inner horizon of my therapist: She was an old, learned lady, but simply hadn't wrestled these kinds of inner demons. But my case wasn't a serious one. People who have trouble with integrating high spiritual states (by a "Kundalini awakening" or similar)—often a very messy affair—can be interpreted as being bipolar by the mental health professionals. Low or medium depth psychiatrists generally have no conception about what these people are going through. Ideally, therapists and psychiatrists should out-depth their patients, but unfortunately that is quite difficult to achieve.

A lot of the less-than-fully-functional people in society tend to out-depth most of us—or at least they have the potential to do so. Broken and crazy people, for all their limitations, often live in greater worlds; they have walked to hell and back. A lot of them just stumbled on their way back.

Beauty, Mystery and Tragedy

I would like to suggest that there are three specific forms of inner depth that a person can develop. These follow the fundamental philosophical form of Plato's "big three": beauty, truth and justice. Although in this context I have found it more appropriate to speak of the three categories beauty, mystery and tragedy.

After all, is there not a profound difference between, for instance, being moved by a perfect starlit night sky, and being absorbed by the suffering of stranger? Is there not an immense divide between the sense of enchanted curiosity that strikes the heart of the analytical philosopher, and the bleeding, broken heart of the saint? Yet, strangely, all of these forms of experience—beauty, tragedy, mystery—converge in that they constitute forms of wordless relatedness to reality: Each is an aspect of existential depth.

DEPTH AS BEAUTY

Let's begin with **beauty**, this relatedness to reality that must always, in the last instance, remain beyond words and other symbolic representations. The experience of beauty is by definition purely subjective—even if it is certainly dependent upon cultural context and so forth. It can, in the last instance, only ever be known from direct experience. Even if I can tell you of the greatness and beauty of existence, you must always experience it for yourself for my words to make any sense. Like strawberry flavor. How would you explain it to someone who never tasted a strawberry?

For some strange reason, this reality, for all its meaningless grinding and torture, is *sublimely beautiful*. Majesty, clarity, serenity, love—where do these qualities come from? How do they emerge? How come you recognize them and know their meaning? You must have known and felt them at some point. And you will sense them and recognize them again, no doubt, before your time is up. To see the beauty of the world is something that is intimately tied up with having subjective awareness: Only living creatures can be assumed to experience the beauty of reality.

What I want to underscore here is that the beauty of existence is intimately known and recognized to varying degrees by different people. Is it not safe to assume that the greatest painters and composers notice aspects of the beauty of the world that most of us are blind to?

What a strange faculty! How can it be, that a human being can look into a deep-space telescope and recognize faraway galaxies as aesthetically pleasing or awe-inspiring? **Beauty, in this sense, is a kind of *recognition*.** We *recognize* things such as harmony, balance, proportionality, contrast, pattern, variation, rhythm, repetition; aspects of the world that we spontaneously seem to appreciate. We appear to be able to deepen our relationship with reality by expanding this recognition.

Some, more than others, will be more moved by the subtleties of the world. This is a kind of lasting relationship to reality: It is depth in its subjective, 1st person aspect. And somehow, we see that beauty, for all its contextual contingencies, for all its dependencies upon the eye of the beholder, is "the truth". Once we have recognized the beauty of Rembrandt, or

Mozart, or indeed of the sea or the cosmos itself, we don't go back to not recognizing it.

Even if we fail sense it in some particular moment (when we are not in high states), we still know of it in a direct and intimate manner (because we still have the depth). Recognizing the beauty of reality is not only a "matter of opinion"—it is a *faculty*, a capability. Seeing beauty somehow strangely seems to be the *correct* way of seeing. It means to gaze deeper into reality.

DEPTH AS MYSTERY

Speaking of truth. There is a form of sublimity of reality that is recognized not by an aesthetic sense, but by a *will to know*, a search for truth for the sake of truth, by recognizing the fundamental **mystery** of reality. Indeed, are not all sciences and scientific paradigms based upon a fundamental mystery, an ability to ask questions and wonder? The sociological eye is born when humans can ask: What is society? Biology is rooted in another mystery: What is life?

What does it feel like to discover a universal, philosophical truth that speaks across time and space? What does it feel like to be Plato, or Newton or Einstein? There is a profound and almost painful sense of meaning in the search of truth for truth's sake. The ability to not just look out the window and see a mundane street with cars and pedestrians, but to see complexity, self-organizing principles, startlingly bizarre social orders, the workings of political power in the life of every child and old woman.

I remember feeling this sense of mystery when encountering the great sociologists as a young man. And I still feel it when the mind clears and clicks and lets me jot down a new insight in my notebook. In other people, I can sometimes recognize what I believe to be the same sense of purity and awe when they speak about their favorite sciences, be it physics or medicine. This is relatedness of the subject (the "I") to reality in 3rd person, to see reality as an "it", and to see the truth that is eternally bound to this "it".

A human being can develop depth, i.e. develop her relatedness to reality—not necessarily by "studying science", but yes, by knowledge itself, through *science* ("knowingness") as an existential and spiritual endeavor. It is not even necessary to be smart, to be correct about stuff or think complex thoughts: We're just talking about a general sense of mystery and awe that grips your heart. The renowned biologist Richard Dawkins has gone to some length to describe this sense of wonder as he makes the case that we don't need the traditional religions. But he is far from the only one. Carl Sagan is another favorite in popular media. The Roman philosopher Seneca and, some time later, the early Catholic philosopher Boethius (in *The Consolation of Philosophy*) write of similar things. In a world of misery and evil, at least there is the truth.

The pre-modern wisdom traditions have been (and still are) quite weak in this regard, despite the rich scholarly traditions of our monasteries. The awe and curiosity that stem from recognizing the open horizons of the mysteries of the elegant universe, of nature, and of reality itself, are not what people will usually learn to cultivate at Zen retreats. In fact, there tends to be lingering pre-modern irrationalities and beliefs that disrespect any honest search for truth, often supported by explicit anti-intellectualism. On the other hand, our scientifically inspired mainstream society tends to instrumentalize science and knowledge to an excessive degree, reframing it as "academic achievement". The spiritual meaning of science, of knowingness, is subdued to grosser human needs, such as acknowledgment, status, accomplishment, material prosperity and survival. That being said, the recognition of mystery may be the most accepted and encouraged form of depth development in modern society. There should probably be better ways to tap into it, in order to cultivate a more existentially mature and transnational civilization.

DEPTH AS TRAGEDY

But for all its blinding beauty and mysterious elegance, the universe is always broken. We have already discussed that our planet is perpetually screaming into the silence of the surrounding cold, empty cosmos. All systems, all living organisms, are always falling apart. A million things always can, and always will, go horribly wrong.

The third form of depth development is the recognition of **tragedy**. It is the sense and realization that we live in a tragic universe. If there is a fundamental divide between the innocence of (healthy) childhood and the maturity of adulthood, it is that children live in blissful unknowing of the utter tragedy of existence, whereas the (spiritually mature) adult lives in full awareness of suffering. To be spiritually mature means both accepting the unavoidability of suffering and being resolved to prevent and mitigate it.

But such maturity doesn't come to us easily. Even as we may be sad and traumatized as children, or be told of wars and other bad stuff, we don't yet quite grasp the tragedy of reality. Even if our childhoods are really hard, we don't yet as children have the capacity to see the universality of suffering and feel that soft, aching heart that grows from the development of inner depth.

Tragedy. It's not only wars, or disease, or even death. It's everything. People I know grew up to suffer from psychiatric illnesses, others were lonely, others insecure, others afraid and manipulative—and then there's always the millions of tortured piglets all over the state of Denmark. So much abuse, self-hatred, so much misery: There is a fundamental and logically necessary brokenness of reality itself. And before you know it, you start falling apart as you get assigned to a crash course for death. All that blooms, including childhood, love relationships and friendships (especially those), must either rot or wither away to be lost and forever forgotten.

Obviously, the sense of tragedy grows from acquaintance with the lower states and their successful psychological integration into our worldviews. Depth grows from recognizing the profound seriousness of the matter: that your own children will be tortured. They will be tortured. It is the truth of the matter. And even if your kids happen to stay in the middle-range of subjective states for most of their lives (or you don't have any), other kids just as valuable and alive will not. This is serious shit. By-the-ballness.

To not recognize this profound seriousness, and to fail to make it into the main engine of one's life, is what I call **the denial of tragedy**. People tend to react against the claim that we should strive towards the happiness of all people in society, because they assume that such an intention implies a denial of tragedy. But, as I argued earlier, to work for the happiness of all is *not* a denial of tragedy.

What grows out of a clear recognition of the tragedy of existence, is not the relishing of pain, or the excusing of misery and injustice. It simply means, as suggested by philosophers of 2nd person relatedness such as Martin Buber and Emmanuel Levinas (and the Judeo-Christian tradition they build upon), a surrender to the primacy of the "thou", the you-ness of reality; the "youniverse", if you like a play on words.

So what does *that* mean? Long story short, it means that I am nothing without you. I am born through you, and I must live, ultimately, in service of you. It is the recognition that, fundamentally, I love you—that love is a fundamental faculty and a *realization* rather than a specific feeling. Just having "compassion" towards you must always be an understatement; indeed an insult. I must live in service of you.

Depth is developed by the recognition of tragedy, by the successful acceptance of such tragedy, and by the resolve to work, as Sisyphus eternally lugging rocks, against it. Resolve in the face of a fundamental hopelessness and utter meaninglessness. This is depth-as-tragedy.

Depth as tragedy is development of the 2nd person relatedness to reality. This is the depth of the saint, the bodhisattva (an Eastern equivalent of the saint) and of what in Western philosophy is called "philosophical pessimism" (perhaps Schopenhauer is the best example). It is the depth that grows from living with a broken heart. Tragedy is necessary for us to mature beyond our current, limited form of "humanity" and begin to take responsibility for all sentient beings in all times. Only a sense of tragedy can drive us to work for the wretched of the earth: loving until it hurts; as medieval nuns of contemplative Christianity, licking the wounds of lepers.

And for this reason—I can say with perfect conviction—that only broken hearts can save the world.

Chapter 15

WISDOM TROUBLES

So I have presented you with what I take to be three aspects of existential depth, of how people become "wiser" and develop a more intimate relationship to reality. Within the multitude of human endeavors, these different forms of depth—relatedness in 1st, 2nd and 3rd person—are emphasized. Different people seem prone to develop the three forms of depth to different degrees. We surrender to the primacy of subjective experience (beauty), to the innocent face we have to serve and protect (tragedy), or to the search for truth (mystery).

But there is one more distinction that I would like to introduce: the one between "light" and "dark" depth. **Light depth is the acquaintance with higher states and dark depth is the acquaintance with lower states.**

Light and Dark Depth

How to compare people who have experienced lower versus higher states? Let's say a person, named Betty, with experience of states 2 through 7 versus a person, named Sue, with equally intimate experience of states 6 through 11. Given that my suggested scale of states makes sense, this would mean that both of them know and have internalized six states. But which one has "greater depth"?

This is where we need the distinction between light and dark depth. Betty certainly has a much more profound knowledge of the meaningless grinding and misery of the universe, even how reality can fall apart and transform into utter horror. And she lived to tell the tale.

Sue knows how great potential and beauty there is to life and the universe, and has developed profound spiritual faculties and wisdoms. Naturally, Sue *out-states* Betty. But she is fundamentally blind to the tragedies of reality that Betty knows first-hand. Sue lives, for all her spirituality, in what must be said to be a grave *denial of tragedy*. She will speak of universal love and sisterhood, but her eyes will glaze over into a blank stare when confronted with any of the real, meaningless terror that is also part of reality: full stop—denial. She has developed a "light depth", as is often the case in today's yoga and spiritual circles, but she really doesn't understand the depressing insights of Schopenhauer, or indeed, some of the central teachings of the Buddha; the ones about suffering. Sue may have experienced lower states (we all have), but she hasn't successfully integrated them. And yet, she is much "wiser" than the vast majority of people; there is a profundity in her relationship to the universe that you simply cannot find in most of us.

On the other hand, a corresponding blindness afflicts the "dark depth" person we called Betty: She simply cannot see or believe that reality can be light, joyful, let alone spiritually inspired. Thinkers like Sigmund Freud come to mind, where the goal of life and existence is to be somewhat less miserable and to manage a not-too-dysfunctional love relationship and to be able to work. If Freud heard about an inner splendor that matched "the radiance of a thousand suns", he simply didn't believe it and reinterpreted it as a soothing fantasy based upon repressed sex-drive. As do most modern people. And I already mentioned Kierkegaard, Schopenhauer and the existentialists (perhaps Sartre in particular): The whole aim of philosophy revolves around the (quite incorrect) notion that prolonged periods of higher subjective states are not possible to achieve. Needless to say, these folks were never trained in any spiritual discipline, let alone serious meditation, which is an important part of the explanation for why their philosophies look so grim. They haven't developed a spiritual practice that would allow them access to the higher states.

What we touch upon here is a bitter conflict that we can assume will be humanity's companion for all foreseeable future: **the double border drawn between people at different levels of depth as well as between different forms of depth**.

Being out-depthed is *not* fun. When someone out-depths us, it means that they see either a seriousness that we fail to recognize, that our personality and expressions in life-goals, taste and arts are all superficial and frivolous—*or* that we have entirely missed out on some greater meaning in life and are in effect experiencing a quite reduced and impoverished existence. These are not things that are easy to swallow—not least because depth can hardly be transferred from one person to another, so we are helpless in face of the greater depth before us. It remains nebulous, vague, scary, strange and meaningless.

Depth is a form of relatedness, always intimate and always personal; when you gaze into the abyss, it also gazes into you. When you are out-depthed, you are suddenly faced with the limits of your own reality; you are dropped into an abyss of terrifying nothingness. To listen to a sage who genuinely embodies a profundity beyond our own often leaves an extremely icky, eerie feeling. At best, it just leaves us indifferent.

On the other hand, when we are stuck in social settings or relationships in which our inner depth—light or dark—are *not* honored and included, we feel that we are unable to act upon our most profound impulses and motives. We are unable to successfully express ourselves and make our everyday lives revolve around the things that we find most significant. Under these circumstances it becomes difficult not to feel very alone and alienated—and not to harbor a subtle anger towards our all-too-shallow social surroundings. And we are likely to eagerly, sometimes hysterically, seek to have our depths met, recognized and included.

This line of conflict, which divides the shallow from the deep and the light from the dark, is simply unavoidable. People will struggle to maintain the consistency of their own universes (self, ideology and ontology) by all means necessary: ignore, self-censor, ridicule, threaten, alarm the inquisition, call the thought-police, burn the heretic.

But most conflicts are avoided in everyday life because we tend to keep most everyday institutions related to shallow aspects of life. It is much easier to create and maintain social settings and institutions that revolve around lower depth: It takes considerably less sensitivity and skill to set up a manual labor team, a movie night or a game of golf, than it does to set up an a successful psychotherapeutic treatment, a genuine talk about the meaning of life or a truly sublime shared spiritual experience. When spiritual communities, sensitive discussions and purpose-filled movements *are* set up, they very often become oppressive and full of painful contradictions. The greater the depth, the more sensitive the social processes involved: More things can go wrong, affecting even softer spots of our souls.

The greater the depth a social setting seeks to accommodate, the more difficult the social situation is to manage smoothly and productively. Traditionally, monastic life has tackled this problem with extreme levels of regulation of everyone's conduct—a strategy that is, naturally, difficult to translate to most other social settings.

The difficulty inherent to creating social settings that manage greater depth in a functional manner means that most of life's everyday institutions—school, work, family life, even church—generally gravitate towards emphasizing lower depth; i.e. towards the more mundane and "shallow" aspects of life. This creates a widespread illusion in the population: the sense that *it's really only me.* A large portion of people in modern society believe that they have tear-drenched, profound inner depths which can only rarely be found in others. But as I said, it's a mirage. The truth is that very many of us harbor greater inner depths than we normally manifest in our lives, or than others normally recognize in us. We are just not offered the social situations to manifest these inner depths. So we keep it to ourselves. There, another meaningless and excruciating tragedy of existence.

Moreover, we are generally only capable of recognizing the forms of depth that we have developed ourselves: The mystery-driven scientist fails to see that her seemingly simple-minded neighbor has developed a much more profound sense of tragedy of the world, and so forth. With "the voice in our heads" (our normal verbalized thinking) we continue long monologues over the years, believing that we are different from the others. And they think that *they* are different in the same way. In a way, we are talking about the opposite problem from the one that shows up in spiritual communities, where everyone pretends to be of higher state than they really are: In mainstream society, we generally pretend to have less depth than we really do.

As a society, we have not admitted to ourselves just how utterly vulnerable, how beautiful and pathetically tragic we are—and in our loneliness we tend to flatter ourselves with unwarranted beliefs of how uniquely profound we are as "individuals", just how different we are from "most other people" (but we're not).

A crucial aspect of the maturation of humanity is that we not only begin to actively and deliberately cultivate depth in all three aspects (beauty, mystery and tragedy) as well as depth in both its light and dark form—but also that we **create institutions and social settings in everyday life that are much more proficient when it comes to accommodating our inner depths**. This includes managing the inescapable and troublesome fact that people are at different levels of depth.

We must even develop our language structures, our ability to speak more clearly about our inner depths. To be sure, spiritual linages, humanistic psychology and continental philosophy have labored to provide such languages. But in mainstream society such forms of our language are still lacking. This book may provide a little help towards this end, but it is mostly a topic that lies beyond our current scope.

Wisdom Is Overrated

Like concerning high states, I would like to share a cautionary remark. It has to do with the concept of "wisdom" and the related idea of "higher consciousness".

At the time of writing, there is a growing emphasis on "wisdom" within academia and elsewhere, where people are arguing for the promotion of the term and its importance in society. A lot of this stuff is interesting and promising. The best source of information at the time of writing is the website *Evidence Based Wisdom*, which is run by the mathematician Charles Cassidy.

Among the proponents of wisdom you can find philosophers, theologians, psychologists, sociologists, educational scientists, mindfulness instructors, business leaders and quite a few spiritually inclined authors—often employing terms such as "transformational learning" and "self-leadership". The adult development researchers tend to shout with the best of them (my own teacher Michael Commons being an exception to this rule).

Within these settings, wisdom has been defined in many different ways—the three most prominent definitions perhaps being the so-called *Berlin Wisdom Paradigm*, the *Balance Theory of Wisdom* and the *Three-Dimensional Wisdom Scale.*

Wisdom is always defined as something entirely beneficial and unproblematic. It is argued by more people than I could name, that "wisdom" is what humanity needs to solve its multifaceted crisis. Given all the emphasis that I have put in this book on discussing adult development (and the existential aspects thereof) I might be expected to enthusiastically support this trend. Yet, over the years, I have increasingly taken a skeptical position.

The reason for this skepticism is rather simple: I have yet to see a credible attempt to "operationalize" the concept; to make it workable. If wisdom is such a serious matter, how come all its proponents only ever come up with vague and indirect ways of seeing it and measuring it? And what exactly is it that wisdom "does"—exactly *how* does it solve all manner of problems and "wicked issues"? People say that "higher consciousness" is necessary for humanity to solve the great problems we are facing. What exactly is it that people with all this wisdom and "higher consciousness" can do, that others cannot? These questions have been answered, but not quite convincingly.

The proponents of wisdom are certainly on to something. Surely, it makes sense to say that higher consciousness is what humanity needs. As I see it, what the wisdom people are sensing is the importance of seeing inner dimensions of people and society and the possibility of an active and deliberate development of these.

But the problem is that the wisdom people haven't done their analytical homework. In other words, the researchers of this field—and other proponents—haven't figured out exactly what they're talking about. And the result is anything but productive. I should say, anything but "wise".

Do you think I am exaggerating and being unfair? Andreas Fischer, a psychology professor at Heidelberg University, recently published a paper in *The International Journal of Humanities and Social Science*, titled "Wisdom—The Answer to All the Questions Really Worth Asking."[151] As far as I can tell, the title is not ironically meant, and it's not very different from others in the field. This is a scholar who has read through many of the different definitions in ancient teachers and modern researchers alike; he is perfectly up-to-date. His paper is well-written and quite interesting—as are many others in the field—but does its very title not underscore that people take wisdom to be a magic bullet?

Fischer's own suggestion is to see wisdom as fundamental and general insights about how to live a good life. But this definition more or less just says that wisdom is good, and lack of wisdom is bad. Fischer brings up some universally occurring insights in wisdom teachers, such as treating others well, going beyond materialism and selfishness, the importance of being goodhearted rather than successful, and so forth. He also shows that there is research supporting such claims (that following these guidelines tends to lead to happiness and mental health). Such advice *can* be useful, but it takes little account of people's different developmental capabilities and personalities, let alone what society they live in and how this wisdom can ever evolve and change. How come so few of the classical wisdom teachers taught us about sustainability (with some North American exceptions) or animal rights (with some Eastern exceptions)?[152]

Making arguments for "wisdom" and "higher consciousness" without knowing exactly what you are talking about can easily get out of hand. The researchers all *try* to be specific. But the problem persists—because it has to do with the concept of wisdom itself. It's just not a very high-quality variable, simply because it is taken to be unambiguously good. My mentor Michael Commons would have said: "It's a crap variable".

Our search for the wise person easily becomes a search for the perfect person. Should it then surprise us that most people considered "wise" tend to be semi-mythic figures such as Jesus, the Buddha, Lao-Tze or Confucius? The real people always run up against their equally real limitations.

Belief in "wisdom" is the belief that there is a variable that is always good, and the more of it, the better. Has there ever been such a variable?

Not in the world I live in, at least. Where I come from, many variables always work together to create patterns and equilibriums Too much of one single variable always has downsides.

So the proponents of wisdom are in fact defending a project that must by necessity be a fantasy. If they can't say in which context this wisdom is good and when it is not, it's just not a real variable. And if they can't say *how* wisdom grows, through which mechanisms, and how it works, and what its limitations are, it is apparently an imagined magic bullet. It is fond hopes and dreams, not much more.

Of Wisdom and Wise-Guys

The proponents of wisdom fail to differentiate between pretty much all of the dimensions we have explored in these chapters: cognitive complexity, IQ, symbolic code, subjective state, existential depth (and the lightness or darkness of that depth), mental health and having a well-integrated personality, Eriksonian life phases—the list goes on. Especially, people tend to have an irresistible urge for blending in those Eriksonian life phases, which messes up their theories.

For certain, people who study wisdom generally have several components in their models (being both smart, patient, humble, emotionally stable, and so forth—see for instance Stephen Hall's 2010 book *Wisdom: From Philosophy to Neuroscience*), but in turn all of these variables tend to be taken as unambiguously good and there is no serious consideration of what happens when people develop in one such variable but not another.

Without analytical distinctions like the ones in this book, it becomes quite difficult to know what you are talking about. Try this out:

- Is Nelly, a low-complexity (MHC stage 10 Abstract), great-depth, low-state, old and experienced, psychologically stable person who has "installed" the symbol-stage E Modern, "wise" or not?
- Is Eckhart Tolle wise (a New Age wisdom teacher with high state and great depth) or is he plain stupid (believing that flowers are "enlightened plants" and that a wave of New Age mindlessness will save humanity from impending destruction and that he is leading the fray by giving often lousy therapeutic advice to people who actually need psychiatric care)? Does he have "high consciousness"?
- Or how about the great ruler of northern India in the 3rd century BCE, Ashoka? After times of conquest and war, he turned to Buddhism and

pacifism.[153] In his great compassion he decided, among other things, to let all his prisoners out for fresh air once a year.

In these examples, the answer depends on how wisdom is defined. Which brings us to the third problem. With sloppy variables, no reliable measurements and no stringent definitions (even if the researchers do *attempt* to be stringent), the field is wide open for people to have just about anything in mind when they talk about "wisdom". And people always seem to assume that they themselves possess wisdom, and that people who they don't like don't. The wisdom movement goes: "Yeah man! You like wisdom too? Me too! Let's do it, y'all!"

Think about it. The concept of wisdom becomes a projection screen, upon which we can project pretty, wishful images. We can paint anything that feels good onto this "super-duper-variable". The problem is that it would break down into a giant slugfest of disappointment and conflict if operationalized in society: People would have to start arguing about who is wise, really, and why, and what that means. And a lot of people would force a lot of low quality "wisdom" down other people's throats. Or sell it to them by means of expensive consulting and motivational speeches. Wisdom, after all, is most often just taken to mean: "you folks should be more like me". This way, wisdom is simply the speaker's received wisdom.

So here's my take on a narrower, stricter, definition. **Wisdom is great depth, plain and simple.** Nothing more, nothing less. So, the way I use the term, wisdom has to do with things like spirituality and transcendence but not really with being smart or "proficient at living a good life". With this definition the answer is: yes, Eckhart Tolle is wise. To a highly complex but low-depth thinker like Richard Dawkins, Eckhart Tolle simply appears to be a fraud; to his enthused followership, he appears to be a sage. The truth is, quite simply, he has high state, great depth and relatively low complexity.

The first example person, Nelly (great depth, low state, low complexity), is also wise, even if she lives in a darker subjective world than Eckhart Tolle. They are both wise, but perhaps not very clever. What can I say?

With this stricter definition, the rural Mongol shaman we described early in the previous chapter can be viewed as wiser than an average modern person. The same goes for the Tibetan nun. With the definition I propose, they can be called "wiser" simply by virtue of having greater depth. We are being specific about what we mean. And a psychologically healthy, complex thinker, who is of old age and at peace with herself is *not* wise, unless she *also* has great depth—even if the clichés hold that she "should" be wise.

All this lets wisdom be specific, measurable, and just one piece in the puzzle (rather than being a universal fix-it-all). What we might lose by making the term more narrow, we regain manifold by clarifying what we are actually talking about.

We might try another definition if you like, a more inclusive one: Wisdom is the combination of mental health, high complexity and great depth. This might let Ashoka qualify as wise (assuming that he, as a successful ruler, was also a complex thinker). With this definition, people can be "wise" regardless of which symbolic code they have (so you can have a wise person in ancient India, even if he's hardly progressive by modern standards). With this definition it becomes more difficult to answer the question of who is wise, but strictly speaking neither Nelly nor Eckart Tolle would be categorized as such. Ashoka might.

The devil isn't just in the details. He's in the definitions. And, most of all, he's in the *analytical distinctions*: in the ability to tell one thing apart from another. To not mix things up. So before you preach the gospel of wisdom, please consult the devil. It would be wise.

An Example from Bertrand Russell

Let's close this presentation with an example from the autobiography of one of the greatest Western philosophers of the 20th century: Bertrand Russell (1872-1970).

His quote touches quite clearly upon the themes brought up in the previous chapter, and his writing has an elegance that brings the insights to life. Notice how he claims to have offered his life to at least two forms of depth, two forms of relatedness to reality itself. This is from the prologue of his autobiography, written in 1956:

> "What have I lived for? Three passions, simple but overwhelmingly strong, have governed my life: the longing for love, the search for knowledge, and unbearable pity for the suffering of mankind. These passions, like great winds, have blown me hither and thither, in a wayward course, over a deep ocean of anguish, reaching to the very verge of despair.
>
> I have sought love, first, because it brings ecstasy—ecstasy so great that I would often have sacrificed all the rest of life for a few hours of this joy. I have sought it, next, because it relieves loneliness—that terrible loneliness in which one shivering consciousness looks over the rim of the world into the cold unfathomable lifeless abyss. I have sought it, finally, because in the union of love I have seen, in a mystic miniature, the prefiguring vision of the heaven that saints and poets have imagined. This is what I sought, and

> though it might seem too good for human life, this is what—at last—I have found.
>
> With equal passion I have sought knowledge. I have wished to understand the hearts of men. I have wished to know why the stars shine. And I have tried to apprehend the Pythagorean power by which number holds sway above the flux. A little of this, but not much, I have achieved.
>
> Love and knowledge, so far as they were possible, led upward toward the heavens. But always pity brought me back to earth. Echoes of cries of pain reverberate in my heart. Children in famine, victims tortured by oppressors, helpless old people a hated burden to their sons, and the whole world of loneliness, poverty, and pain make a mockery of what human life should be. I long to alleviate the evil, but I cannot, and I too suffer. This has been my life. I have found it worth living, and would gladly live it again if the chance were offered me."

When reflecting upon his own life, Russell explicitly mentions two of the aspects of depth discussed in the last chapter. Instead of beauty he names love, specifically as an ecstatic experience.[154] This should perhaps not surprise us; after all, Russell was a philosopher and activist above all; less a mystic and artist.

Still, two out of three. Not bad, old Bertie.

Chapter 16

EFFECTIVE VALUE MEME

Finally, we have arrived. We can now put the four developmental dimensions of complexity, code, state and depth together into one model: the **effective value meme** of a person. Aren't you excited?

The theory of effective value meme has an "awkward uncle"—one from whom I have learned, but I would not like to rely upon or be closely associated with.

The Awkward Uncle

By yet an ironic twist of fate, one of the best models of human and societal development has been invented and proposed by some of the least intelligent and intellectually honest people of the field.

I am referring of course to the Spiral Dynamics model of Don Beck and Chris Cowan (the latter of whom, to my knowledge, has since disowned the model).[155] Spiral Dynamics, which builds upon the work of the late psychologist Clare Graves, postulates that people develop through a clear, recognizable sequence of value memes (or "vMemes"), which largely determine the overall pattern of their values, logics, personalities and behaviors.

As I said in the prologue, it sometimes takes a charlatan to speak the truth. And with the transpersonal perspective we've discussed, it should perhaps not surprise us that the best ideas can grow from the strangest places. Not to mention the dialectical view of knowledge and the non-linear development of society: Things always emerge in the strangest orders and patterns. All of these insights speak loudly and clearly against intellectual puritanism. Sometimes, the weed, the *pensée sauvage*, is just more stunning than the tended garden rose.

For some strange reason that eludes me, the originators of this model managed to catch a simple but elegant pattern in the psychological and societal development of humans, and described it with a precision and clarity that I have yet to see elsewhere: Even as great sociologists like

Jürgen Habermas and Günter Dux make attempts at similar theories, they all fall short. For instance, when Habermas formulates his theory of "communicative action" he considers Kohlberg's stages of moral development, but fails to see how the different value memes must by necessity be limited in their ability to communicate with one another and find common grounds on a "rational" basis—how difficult it is, for instance, to reconcile a traditional Christian with a postmodern queer-feminist perspective. The same weakness is apparent in his later work on deliberative democracy (and even in the theories of his critic, Iris Marion Young)[156]. How could Spiral Dynamics teach us things that the greatest of sociologists cannot? 'Tis a tale of weeds and roses.

Strange as it may be, this model struck gold. It just needs to be seriously revised, and some parts of it scrapped. Luckily, that's what we have done in the chapters leading up to this one.

So let us bring our awkward uncle, Spiral Dynamics, back in for a beer. Don't worry; we'll throw him out when we're done.

Why "Spiral Dynamics" Doesn't Work

The Spiral Dynamics model squeezes all development into *one single* framework and calls it "the stages of development". These stages are presented as vividly described color codes (often depicted as a colorful spiral that looks like a popsicle) written with CAPITAL LETTERS (not sure why):

- PURPLE (tribal folk people),
- RED (gang members),
- BLUE (traditionally religious people),
- ORANGE (modern mainstream people),
- GREEN (postmodern people),
- YELLOW (metamodern people) and
- TURQUOISE (new-agey "holistic" or "integral" people).[157]

This crude and ahistoric formulation of stages causes a lot of problems.[158] Besides some awkward mistakes, an apparent lack of basic education on behalf of its creators and poor taste (all three of which are, after all, forgivable), the model really cannot answer rather simple questions. For instance, who is higher value meme, a contemporary fourteen-year-old with modern schooling, or a medieval genius like Thomas of Aquinas (to reuse an earlier example)?

With my own model, it becomes clear: The kid *out-codes* Thomas of Aquinas (although Aquinas of course has more "horizontal" code, i.e. he is more of an expert on medieval thinking than the kid is on modern thinking), but Thomas of Aquinas both *out-complexes* and *out-depths* the kid. Aquinas probably also *out-states* the kid, at least in the sense that he has higher maximum state (if not necessarily average state). If we were stuck with Spiral Dynamic we'd have to assume that the kid was of "higher vMeme": She is ORANGE and Thomas of Aquinas is BLUE.

The Spiral Dynamics model also makes a lot of different claims about their respective psychologies, for instance, that the kid has to be "achievement oriented" just because she's from a modern "ORANGE" culture. This is another unfortunate effect of cramming many different things into one single developmental sequence.

Should we perhaps just give up the idea of vMemes, and simply stick with the four dimensions I have presented (complexity, code, state and depth), as well as other psychometric variables (IQ, mental health, etc.) in our quest to understand the political psychology of the world and its developmental demographics? After all, the four dimensions seem quite independent from one another. There is little about being at high MHC stage that would grant you greater existential depth, and there is little about great existential depth that would give you access to an advanced symbol-stage. Obviously, most scientific and social breakthroughs are not made by Zen masters or the like, nor are most inspired spiritual revelations written by theoretical physicists. If complexity, code, state and depth are at all interrelated, they are probably still largely independent, and their interrelation is anything but straightforward. Again, we lack the data, so we can't know exactly, even if we can make some qualified guesses. Since vMeme doesn't seem to tackle even the simple problem of the medieval philosopher versus the modern kid, what good is it?

But still: Once you see the vMemes in Spiral Dynamics it's certainly hard to look away. There really is something about people being Christian and Muslim traditionalists (BLUE), or scientifically- and business minded mainstream Westerners (ORANGE), or post-1968 hippies or radical environmentalist ultra-liberal feminists who love animal rights (GREEN). At least in the world I have grown up in, this makes a whole lot of sense.

And there really does seem to be a developmental *sequence* to this thing: A few hundred years ago, most people were BLUE or below, then people in the richest countries started becoming ORANGE (starting with the Enlightenment and the American and French revolutions), and when that had gone on for a long while, you had a surge of GREEN people in

California, the liberal urban centers on the East Coast and lately in the Nordic countries.

These vMemes seem to develop as people become more well-off, not just materially, but socially as well. If you look at the Middle East, or Africa, there seem to be a lot more people who correspond to Christian fundamentalists in the southern US states (BLUE) than in say Sweden. And if you look at newly rich countries like South Korea, the populations here seem to quite ostensibly manifest the ORANGE vMeme. And when people are threatened, they seem to display lower vMemes, like in Israel, where a highly educated population generally roots for tradition and nationalism—or why not the recent surge of nationalism in Europe, as migration and globalization have together undermined the interests and security of working class and lower middle class populations.

For all its weaknesses, the Spiral Dynamics model catches something vital. Its main insight is far from self-evident; indeed it has been entirely missed by almost all of social science, and the world suffers as a result.

Don't believe me? None of the sociologists prior to 1968 predicted the social revolution that was underway; there was just no clear understanding that the value meme demographic was shifting around the economic centers of the world. So many other people are deeply confused because they fail to see and recognize the value memes. Examples:

- The "humanists" and "New Atheists" (critics of traditional religion and superstition) don't understand why so many people are still religious (because they're at the BLUE vMeme; it's not theology or lack of scientific rigor—it's the development, stupid!);
- the eco-feminists and critical sociologists don't see why mainstream society is so blindly capitalist, anthropocentric and materialist (because they're ORANGE; it's not capitalism or its ideology—it's the development, stupid!),
- and the critics of immigration in Europe tell us that Arab culture is not compatible with Western culture (even if culture matters, the crux is not differences in culture, the modernized Arabs are doing very well—it's the development, stupid!).

There really *is* something going on here. There really *is* an overall pattern of development. We just need to address the weaknesses of Spiral Dynamics and do some updating. So let's take it to the next level. Let's go from vMeme, to effective value meme. How about we throw out the bathwater, but keep the baby? After all, babies are cute.

From vMeme to Effective Value Meme

I would like to propose the following list of effective value memes. When naming the effective value memes, I will use the same titles as I used for symbol-stages in chapters 10 and 11.

- Archaic (corresponds to BEIGE)
- Animistic (or post-archaic) (corresponds to PURPLE)
- Faustian (corresponds to RED)
- Postfaustian (corresponds to BLUE)
- Modern (corresponds to ORANGE)
- Postmodern (corresponds to GREEN)
- Metamodern (corresponds to YELLOW)

The effective value meme is an overall pattern of the mind; it is an equilibrium upon which one's values and worldview tend to stabilize, setting the framework for the political behavior of a citizen. The effective value meme is usually not an explicitly held body of thought—it's more like the water a fish swims in; how your whole reality appears to you, even *before* you notice anything that dwells within that reality.

A population always has a **developmental demographic** of some kind, with some people at earlier and others at later effective value memes. Later value memes are more logically and functionally in tune with larger and more complex societies. A large host of the problems of today's world are of this nature; they are **developmental imbalances**.

The world is a terrible mess *because* the world-system we live in corresponds to a very high effective value meme, while almost all of the world's population is still left at earlier effective value memes.

We live, essentially, in a **retarded world**. Our value systems do not correspond to the society we live in. Our ways of seeing, sensing, feeling, acting and understanding do not correspond to the very society that we ourselves have created. This glitch is lethal. And this is the issue of our age: to develop the political psychology of the world population. Unfortunately, stimulating such political-psychological development is an enormously tricky matter.

So developing the effective value meme of the general population is one of the most important things in the world right now. But a higher effective value meme is not always good: Each stage of development has its own risks and its own pathologies—there are new things that can (and sooner or later always do) go horribly, horribly wrong.

Your effective value meme is a kind of average between your complexity, code, state and depth. It is called "effective" value meme because people tend to have an overall pattern of how they function in society even if they cannot easily be squeezed into one of Beck and Cowan's vMemes; hence they are "in effect" at one value meme, even if they may differ in one or more regards (for instance having lower complexity or greater depth).

The Dimensions of Development Come Together

There are some tricky parts of this, but by and large the picture is relatively straightforward: **Development in each of the four dimensions I have presented adds to your overall effective value meme**.

- Complexity, or MHC stage, adds to your effective value meme because it helps you see and relate to more abstract layers of the world. Simple societies don't require as complex thinking as larger, more complex ones (even if they of course often require you to develop more practical skills and perform more difficult tasks).
- Having "installed" a more advanced symbol-stage, having access to a more advanced symbolic toolkit, adds to your effective value meme. This is because the later symbolic codes are developed specifically to suit the realities we face in larger and more complex societies.
- Higher state (average, median, minimum and maximum) adds to your effective value meme because it means that you live in a lighter world, which gives you the emotional fuel to accept a more universalistic and less selfish view of society. This is necessary in larger and more complex societies.
- Greater depth adds to your effective value meme, because it makes you relate to more profound and universal aspects of reality and existence, which is also increasingly necessary in a globalized internet age.

Whereas I focus mainly on vertical development, it should be noted that horizontal development—width—also plays an important role. **Each of the four dimensions has its kind of width.** Stage has IQ and other measures of cognitive capacity. In code, it's how much and how high quality knowledge you have. For state, width means the length of the time period you manage to stay within different (higher) states. For depth it is the time you have spent at states and the variety of different experiences you have successfully integrated from these experiences.

Now let's compare the different kinds of development to the effective value memes. Looking at how MHC stage and symbol-stages correspond to the effective value memes is pretty easy: They unfold in a linear, parallel pattern.

Effective value meme	Corresponding MHC stage of cognitive complexity	Corresponding symbol-stage
Archaic	Stage 7 Pre-Operational	Symbol-stage A Archaic
Animistic	Stage 8 Primary	Symbol-stage B Animistic
Faustian	Stage 9 Concrete	Symbol-stage C Faustian
Postfaustian	Stage 10 Abstract	Symbol-stage D Postfaustian
Modern	Stage 11 Formal	Symbol-stage E Modern
Postmodern	Stage 12 Systematic	Symbol-stage F Postmodern
Metamodern	Stage 13 Metasystematic	Symbol-stage G Metamodern

I hope that I have thus far convinced you of two things. The first thing is that value memes are really important and that they help us understand the world, including the main challenges of our time. The second thing is that we need to leave behind the simplistic model of vMemes, and instead rely upon the concept of effective value meme. The difference between vMeme and effective value memes is that the latter theory allows for four kinds of comparison.

- You can **out-complex** someone else, or be out-complexed by someone of higher cognitive stage.
- You can **out-code** someone else, or be out-coded by someone who has installed a more advanced symbol-stage.
- You can **out-state** someone else, or be out-stated by someone who has greater wellness and/or more spiritual experiences.

- You can **out-depth** someone else, or be out-depthed by someone who has successfully internalized a wider range of subjective states than you have.

Note that your effective value meme is very often "skewed". For instance, a stage 13 Metasystematic thinker, who has installed the symbol-stage E Modern code, will tend to have higher effective value meme than a stage 10 Abstract thinker who has installed the same code. This is because she will be more prone to thinking about complex and abstract issues, thereby taking a wider perspective on reality, even if the overall ideas about reality are roughly the same. Or you can have a person at stage 10 Abstract who installs the symbol-stage 12 Postmodern code; she will then use a flattened and simplified version of that code.

Alright, so let's bring in state and depth. How do they fit into this scheme of effective value meme? My suggestion is that **both state and depth offer hefty premiums or penalties to our effective value meme**.

Every society has a kind of **gravity point**, depending on its overall development: an effective value meme towards which the members of that society tend to gravitate. As a society develops more complex structures, its gravity can shift to higher value memes. If a society falls apart or suffers major setbacks, its point of gravity generally sets to a lower value meme. Typically, today's societies have their point of gravity at the Postfaustian value meme (India, Iran, etc.) or the Modern value meme (France, the US, etc.).

High state and great depth often lead people to break with the conventions of their society. Take a person like Jesus. He grows up in Roman times and as such only has access to faustian and some postfaustian symbols. Nevertheless, he goes on a spree and formulates some very universal and generally applicable ethics, clearly expressing views that are far ahead of his time. He must have had both great depth and a long streak of high states (lasting for months, at least), as well as high MHC stage (stage 13 Paradigmatic, most probably). So Jesus—and other saints and sages of the Axial Age—expressed views that were certainly beyond the normal traditionalist religions of their time. Their view of the world became universal, loving and optimistic. They wrestled with very fundamental issues of life and existence. Of course, they did not magically gain access to the symbolic codes of future civilizations, but their "implicit knowledge" about reality impelled them to take up very radical and progressive views: Buddhist non-violence and gender equality, Christian class consciousness, Taoist sexual self-development and postmaterialism, Jain animal rights, Muslim social reformism, and so forth. These ideas were brought by folks who, for reasons of depth and state, were of higher effective value memes than their contemporaries.

Or how about a modern person growing up in say Sweden, who learns the modern code in school, but lives a very harsh life and is continuously in low states (feeling afraid, dissatisfied and tormented) and never develops a sense of tragedy, or a sense that the world is grand and beautiful? Can we really expect this person to function fully at the Modern effective value meme, being a fair, democratic citizen who respects merits and scientific truth? Not really—this person is likely to develop a lower effective value meme. Here is the mobster; he or she may, despite being a normally complex thinker in a modern society, manifest the Faustian effective value meme. This corresponds to the social logic of e.g. a Viking society: machismo, honor codes, killing, family feuds, and a rather narrow circle of solidarity.

In criminology you will find plenty examples of this: *the convict code*, described in 1988 by Lawrence D. Wieder, and the positive self-image of criminal felons described by the Swedish sociologist Malin Åkerström in her 1983 interview study *Crooks and Squares*. Long story short, there is an honor among thieves, and they explicitly describe themselves as stronger and more ferocious than those boring, law-abiding squares. In our terminology, they are actively and deliberately upholding their Faustian effective value meme.

So here is my rough hypothesis for you:

- Lower state and lesser depth tend to affect you to develop lower effective value meme than the surrounding society's "point of gravity".
- Medium state and depth tend to let you stay with the average effective value meme of your society, like most "mainstream" people today are at the Modern effective value meme.
- Profound experiences of higher states and the development of great inner depth (of the "light" or "dark" kind), tend to let you see beyond the confines of your own society, pointing you towards more universal issues, which can in effect help you manifest higher value memes than the people around you.

In modern Western society, it is undeniably true that people with higher states and greater depths are the ones that most often tend towards the Postmodern and Metamodern value memes. This makes it tempting to try to align different altitudes of state and depth with certain value memes. But that would lead us down quite strange and illogical paths. After all—would you seriously claim that Stone Age or animistic people were consistently at lower states than modern people? Looking at present-day hunter-gatherers, there is nothing that would support such a claim. Indeed, neither could we say that the medieval person was consistently at lower level of depth—even if the average state may have been *somewhat* lower, as life was simply harder and social life more unforgiving.

We should thus be careful to assign states and depths to specific effective value memes—it's just a trickier affair, so it seems, than stages of cognitive complexity and symbolic code.

Before we continue with a presentation of the effective value memes I should also address the difference between these and the symbol-stages. No doubt, you will notice that there are similarities between how they are described. This is not very surprising, given that the symbol-stages are the most *observable* part of people's overall development; they give us the words and templates we use to relate to the world. Whereas state, depth and even stage are all difficult to observe directly, the symbol-stage is relatively manifest.

But symbol-stages and effective value memes are *not* the same. The symbol-stages are the abstract logics inherent to the symbols, whereas effective value meme are descriptions of *embodied behaviors*. So even people with earlier symbol-stages can behave at higher value memes, if they have high stage, high average state and great depth. Likewise, you can live in a modern society and still have a pre-modern effective value meme.

Zooming In on the Effective Value Memes

With all the "ifs" and "buts" in place it should be possible to present you with descriptions of the different value memes. Remember, remember: The effective value meme is only a "master pattern" in your four dimensions of development. So people within the different effective value memes can look *very* different from one another.

In my book on historical development, *The 6 Hidden Patterns of World History*, I present so-called **metamemes**, which have the same names as these value memes (and the symbol-stages). The difference between metamemes and value memes is that the former is about patterns in the development of society, whereas the latter is about the psychology of a single person or small social setting. It is true that the metamemes and value memes correspond and interact in interesting ways, but for now, let's just stick with trying to understand the value memes.

ARCHAIC VALUE MEME

This effective value meme shows up in early hominid cultures, likely as early as two million years ago with *Homo erectus*. There are no systematized value systems really, and you mostly relate only to bodily and survival-oriented things (but, you still communicate and have a symbolically constructed world). In modern humans, you can find this value meme in the mentally disabled, some of the severely mentally challenged, in *enfants sauvages* (kids who grow up in feral environments with stray dogs and the like), in children under the age of five, in some very unprivileged people living on the streets in India and some mentally ill "street bums" in affluent countries. In other words: No surviving societies today have this value meme; it only shows up in the few people who for different reasons cannot partake in the culture that surrounds them.

ANIMISTIC VALUE MEME

This value meme appears to have been born about 40 000 years ago, when artwork, pictures of imaginary realities, and more advanced tools began appearing and spreading around the world. You partake in a world of spirits and magic, where humanity is not differentiated from nature, and nature, in turn, is extremely anthropomorphized (seen as filled with human-like intentionality and feelings). In today's world, this value meme still of course shows up in hunter-gatherer cultures, but it is also represented by a minority in modern societies. You have all kinds of "healers" and psychics, and beliefs in astrology, and ghost hunters (a modern form of ancestral worship), and casting of spells, and clairvoyants—and all the folks who believe in these things. The same people will tend to anthropomorphize their pets and prefer alternative medicine to Western medicine. I'll return to the subject when discussing the **astrology precariat** in Book Two.

I have used the division into 1st, 2nd and 3rd person views many times in this book. When it comes to worldview, the 1st person view corresponds to our idea of a "self" (how I view the "I" in the world), the 2nd person view to our ideas about right and wrong, what you might call ethics or ideology (because it is about how I treat *you*), and the 3rd person view corresponds to our ontology, how we view the world itself (what we believe is "really real").

One way of overviewing what it means for a person to be at the Animistic value meme is to look at general patterns of their self, ideology and ontology.

- **Animistic self:** Your social identity is not fully differentiated from either the social or the natural surroundings, and your self is closely tied to the direct, visceral experience of your body. And you *are* your relationships. This means that your ideas of self are centered around the very direct and bodily relations between yourself and others: giving food, warmth, protection and comfort, producing something useful to the other people, and so forth.
- **Animistic ideology:** You tend to include your closest group of people—and often pets—and be very concerned that social taboos are not transgressed. The interests of the small group overshadow the individual. Of course, a lot of indigenous cultures can have all of nature within their circle of concern, but it is also common that their word for human is synonymous with their word for the members of their own small tribe. There is a tendency to romanticize this aspect of the Animistic value meme. However, we should remember that the closeness to nature is of a non-differentiated kind. Also, we should be aware that most of the world's large land animals, "megafauna", were in fact driven to extinction by people at this value meme. (This happened before recorded history, as discussed in the Hanzi book on history.)
- **Animistic ontology:** Since your semantic world (world of words) is not differentiated from the natural world, you think that your words are the same as the objects themselves. Hence objects in the natural world can be related to one another just because they sound alike or share a certain number (as in astrology). This is apparent in ethnomedicine (the study of medical practices of indigenous populations), where things are used as medicine because of what the words for those objects *sound* like (in some way that connects to curing the disease). Because you don't differentiate between the natural and the human world, you believe that all things have spirits, and that animals have humanlike inner lives and motives. These spirits can be talked to—i.e. you can use magic, or rain dances or the like. Because this value meme corresponds to MHC stage 8 Primary (which can coordinate groups of paragraphs, but not different such paragraph groups into larger coherent narratives), your explanations about the world tend to be only few paragraph long and the different stories can contradict one another.

FAUSTIAN VALUE MEME

This value meme shows up first in the Neolithic age, when society begins to become agricultural. It is a kind of "declaration of independence" from nature and its spirits. You go from spirits to ambivalent gods who represent different functions in society, and you can defy these gods to rise above and beyond both society and nature. This is of course when the first warlords and armies appear. A system of honor and displays of *social* strength comes into being.

Let's take the 10th century Vikings: These people were, prior to their conversion to Christianity, generally at the Faustian effective value meme. There was no clear rule of law, there were family feuds and people struggled to deem themselves worthy warriors in the eyes of the gods, and killing outsiders was considered quite kosher, not to mention pillaging and capturing Slavic people as thralls. Recent archeological evidence implies that Birka, the largest Viking settlement close to present-day Stockholm, was *de facto* something similar to a forced labor camp. But of course, most of everyday life still revolved around farming.

Roughly, this effective value meme corresponds to today's Mafioso social structures. In the modern world you can find equivalents of the Faustian value meme here and there: in failed states (Somalia and Afghanistan[159]) and the warlord entities that rule these areas, in Maoist rebel groups, in organized crime around the world, in street gangs, in Hells Angels and the like. In modern religions, you might look at congregations such as The Church of Satan, *Dragon Rouge* and some of the West African magic, Wiccan and Pagan and Voodoo practices. These religious practices are, tellingly enough, overrepresented in Western adolescents. This is because, psychologically speaking, such ideas are more in tune with the developmental stage of adolescents.[160] In popular culture you might find corresponding themes in hip-hop music and heavy metal.

- **Faustian self:** The self is part of a larger idea-world, related to gods (or present day equivalents, such as honor codes) and a generalized society. The self must find its destiny, i.e. which place the self has in the social hierarchy. Actions reveal your destiny. You can strive towards power in society and aspire towards supremacy over others. The human self is no longer the same as nature. Your self is part of larger clan, an imagined community, but it can ascend above normal life. Through acts of heroism.
- **Faustian ideology:** The power and interests of the clan (or other community) is the ethical basis: honor identity, to keep an imagined identity of power visible to a larger group. To survive, you need to appease (or intimidate and control) other people rather than nature; hence gods (and other symbols of human roles) take precedence over spirits. The "eye for an eye" morality emerges at this stage: You shouldn't kill the

whole family of an enemy if they poked out your brother's eye. Just poke out one of theirs and you're square.

- **Faustian ontology**: In terms of cognitive complexity, this value meme corresponds to MHC stage 9 Concrete; this means that you have stories or narratives of gods, monsters and heroes—and that these stories connect many paragraphs and coordinate themes. The earliest paragraphs of the Bible don't do this (the first few paragraphs in Genesis directly contradict one another); later on they do. When it comes to Homer you have a coherent epic. But there are no abstract principles spelled out. These stories can tell you about the world, but not really about the abstract principles that govern it. The human and non-human worlds are seen as separate.

POSTFAUSTIAN VALUE MEME

This value meme came online with larger, ordered societies, blooming fully with the Axial Age some 2500 years ago—after which it conquered the world. All of the major religions are direct manifestations of this value meme. Unlike the Faustian value meme, the Postfaustian is against things like war, killing, slavery, oppression of the weak and arbitrary use of power (in theory, if not always in practice). This value meme has been dominant during a large part of recorded human history.

In today's world, you can find the Postfaustian value meme in people who are traditionally religious: from Amish and Christian fundamentalists to orthodox Jews to Sri Lankan Buddhist zealots to most people in India. And, of course, a whole lot of Muslims. But you might also count many of the nationalists and ethnocentric conservatives around Europe and elsewhere as postfaustian—perhaps notably the traditionalist values in rural Russia and the ruling party in Russia. Even if these groups live within modern societies, know about modern science, and can hardly be compared to medieval Christians, they seek to reestablish a more ethnocentric order and generally root for a society more like the monolithic and hierarchically ordered societies of the past. Think of the traditionalist movement in Turkey under its current leadership: Would you say that these folks embody a scientific worldview and follow the Enlightenment paradigm?[161]

A lot of how you understand effective value memes has to do with where you draw the boundaries and how you make the definitions. When it comes to doctrine (symbolic code), you find the purest forms of postfaustianism quite late in history, right before it was dialectically overturned and became modernism. In the 17th century you have all these religious wars as Protestant movements are casting out all saints and magic rituals from the Catholic faith. And in the same century you have the establishment of Divine Right in France, of absolute monarchy, where the monarch is seen as servant of the people (in theory, at least).

- **Postfaustian self:** The typical postfaustian self is based around the belief in a soul that has moral properties that go beyond your skills and capabilities. There is a universal idea that you can be good or evil, that there is an essence within you that relates to the truth You "become someone" by serving the higher truth (either defined in religious or ethnic/nationalist terms), which is the same as finding and keeping your place in the social order: to be king or peasant, but to play your part in the greater whole. Hence, your soul can be pure or not. The soul is an early form of the modern conception of the individual.
- **Postfaustian ideology:** This is where a generalized morality enters the picture. Up until this point, the interests of the group or tribe have been the basis of morality. But in postfaustianism all people who serve the true faith will have their souls salvaged. Slavery, unwarranted aggression and exploitation are seen as unethical. All power must be earned by the moral qualities and virtues of your character.
- **Postfaustian ontology:** This world is second to the eternal world of God or spirit. Society should be ordered in relation to the eternal world. Humanity is imperfect but can approach the perfect or Absolute. Our connection to the universal goes not via the body, but by the abstracted soul and its ethical essence. The ultimate existence of God is the abstraction upon which all mythology rests—hence you can study theology, reason about it: "What is the ultimate abstraction?"

MODERN VALUE MEME

As I said, this value meme is dominant in modern society. It begins, of course, with the French Enlightenment, but you can sense it already in the Italian Renaissance, and to some extent even in ancient Greece, albeit in a very vague, proto- form.

The modern value meme encapsulates what mainstream Westerners are like: They believe in human rights, progress, science, democracy, civil liberties, fair competition, rule of law. They may or may not be religious, but their faith is kept as a more private concern and generally not relied upon as a source of authority in politics and debates. Family life is still important, but it is no longer everything: It's okay to have your own career, to date who you want, to have casual sexual encounters, to have your own opinion—to be an individual. And you have sports: fair competitions where merits are valued and you have to compete by the rules. You tend to only accept explanations that make sense, not relying upon the authority of the Bible or similar.

The mainstream modern mind still lives in a vehemently anthropocentric world, where everything in reality is more or less about people and their needs. So you have no problem with mass-killing and torturing animals for the most trivial of human concerns, such as sausage or profit. Nor do you see anything wrong with overexploiting ecosystems, destroying all life on the planet if it translates to gains for humans—even if you may give lip service to ecology, spirituality, animals and foreign cultures in conversations or Hollywood movie productions. But you tend to believe (in theory, at least) that all humans are of equal value and that not only people of your own clan or faith are real people.

Liberalism, (classical) conservatism and socialism are all expressions of the modern value meme—the idea of a rational social order in which humans are free. Only in the last few decades have a majority of socialists taken up the postmodern value meme.

- **Modern self:** Humans are individuals and have the right to express their individuality, not just in the next world (their moral soul), but in this life, hence moving within the social order to a place that they merit. This individual has inalienable human rights that go beyond even her nation and creed. One of the main faculties of humans is that they can think rationally. Since humans are the sole source of this rationality in the world, they are viewed as being at the center of reality.
- **Modern ideology:** Modernists view themselves as harbingers of death to all myths and irrational beliefs. No kings can call upon gods to justify their power; only democracy can be justified. Humans are not only individuals but also *citizens*. This is an extremely powerful idea. Even all of the 20th century dictatorships used it: claiming to be by citizens, for citizens. Satisfaction of all human needs can be attained by use of scientific perspective on the material world, by the generation of economic growth, and the fair distribution of spoils among equal and deserving citizens. To the greatest possible extent, science should be used to organize society. You have meritocracy, sports; life is a game. You need to know the rules and win. The best individual is whoever knows the truth the best.
- **Modern ontology:** The universe consists of its material constituents and the space between them. They present an absolute truth and people can know this truth by reason and science. But knowing the truth dep-

ends on intersubjective verification; otherwise it might be an illusion of the senses or a delusion of the mind.

POSTMODERN VALUE MEME

The Postmodern value meme is to be found in the many critics that have arisen within modern society in its later and more mature forms. I suppose you can say that proto- forms of Postmodernism have existed since around the beginning of the 19th century, where you first had Immanuel Kant's critique of pure reason, then German Romanticism (which questioned French and British emphasis on the rational mind), and from then on as a growing undercurrent in modern society, voices of dissent and protest. But it only became a true part of mainstream society after 1968, when postmodern values began to reach greater segments of the population. As you may know, critical sociology, anthropology and literature studies led the fray as students attempted to overthrow modern society, notably in Paris.

In today's world you have some societies, like the Nordic countries, where the Postmodern value meme has taken a stronger hold. Most Swedish people are of course not at this value meme themselves, but the entire political and media landscape is dominated by such things as anti-racism, gender equality issues, criticism of norms, general political correctness, environmentalism, multiculturalism, displays of postmaterialist values (at least in the superficial sense that you can brag about eco-vacations and whatnot). People praise themselves for being critical thinkers, for not being mainstream, for being unique. Even animal rights seem to be coming online—according to some sources, 4% are vegans (probably exaggerated, given that these are the new norms of society, and such studies are based on self-reports).

The Postmodern value meme generally doesn't believe in "progress", but rather that societies change over time. After all, can you say that today's society is really "better" than medieval times, given all the environmental degradation, materialist over-consumption, loneliness and anxiety? The postmodern mind focuses on questioning, criticizing and picking apart the things that are generally taken for granted.

- **Postmodern self:** The individual can question the categories of modern society and is defined in *opposition* to these, how she becomes a unique individual, how she is different, an irregularity, an exception. No longer humanity in creative opposition to nature, but rather, in creative opposition to culture. You cannot be an individual unless you somehow oppose society—Erich Fromm and others at this value meme have written about how normal modern people are "robots" or "automatons". Authenticity becomes important: The great humanities scholar Walter Benjamin argues that there is an authenticity in art, one that is not thought to be found in mainstream modern society. You have the same notion in Heidegger's *das Man*. The need for a sense of uniqueness grows from alienation. Alienation makes you miserable so you have a pervasive sense that there must be something wrong: Is it the world, or me? Because we all need to maintain a positive self-image, we must conclude that the world is at fault rather than ourselves, and that we are somehow an exception from the world, hence not partaking in its badness. Thus it becomes very important to prove that we are an authentic exception; unique. As the first proto-postmodern philosopher, Rousseau, quipped: "If I am not better, at least I am different."

- **Postmodern ideology:** Modern society has gone terribly wrong. *Grandes histoires* are totalitarian. Postmodern people emphasize multiplicity, detail, nuance, exception, resistance, critique. You lean towards cultural relativism, in order to avoid the oppression of minority cultures. A central issue is to include the excluded. Another is to fight power structures. There is something real and authentic beyond the structures of modern society. All sentient beings in all times must ultimately be included and their interests taken into account. As we discuss in the following chapter, the "light" pomos (non-intellectual yoga-people etc.) don't necessarily explicitly share all of these *ideas*, but they share in the *sentiments*: postmaterialism, relativism, solidarity with all sentients, environmentalism, praise of authenticity (primarily of emotions) and the striving to being inclusive.
- **Postmodern ontology:** Symbols, structure and culture are, for all practical purposes, the ultimate reality—beyond that, we really don't know. Even phenomenology (one's direct 1st person experience) is steeped in symbolic meaning-making. The universe is social and interactive. All knowledge is contextual. Even natural science is just another perspective and is based upon scientific communities, cultures, practices. We cannot access an ultimate reality.

METAMODERN VALUE MEME

The Metamodern value meme is only being born as we speak, so we can't really give a historical example and a current one. The only historical example *is* the current one.

The primary characteristic of people of this value meme is that they value qualitative development of human beings: that people go up in stage, that psychological development is supported and that you work to create a new society beyond the modern one. Because they have a more developmental perspective, they also **accept, learn from and try to include all of the former value memes**. This is quite unlike any of the other value memes, all of whom believe that they alone have the right path. The Metamodern value meme is less judgmental; it seeks to integrate elements from all the former ones; it sees partial truths in all of them; it wants to integrate them in one grand synergistic scheme, and seeks to accommodate them—to create a society in which traditional, modern and postmodern people live together harmoniously.

And in that vein, the Metamodern value meme is less ostensibly oriented towards a political Right or Left. People of other value memes, like the exploitative boards of major corporations, even folks like the fundamentalist terrorists, are not seen as evil. They are, to put it bluntly, developmentally challenged. Retarded. This means that you need to understand these people and why things couldn't be any different, and why they bear no guilt. It is a sociological-developmental view of life. Of course, the risk with seeing development instead of moral responsibility, is that you can be condescending. It is simply part of the challenge; if you are seen as condescending, it simply means that you have failed to successfully take the perspective of others and adjust your communication accordingly.

But the metamodern mind also realizes that an inclusive and harmonious society cannot be achieved within the confines of modern life or by means of a postmodern critique thereof. Hence, a new society must be created from the modern one, which means that the metamodernist must ultimately be against modern society.

The second characteristic is that they value inner dimensions much more. So you will find that people of this value meme seek to create more authenticity and intimacy in work organization, to democratize institutions with clever social innovations, to promulgate mindfulness and meditation practices, to emphasize more philosophical and existential issues in their work. They will tend to be very process-oriented, trying to involve people in interactive processes a lot more.

- **Metamodern self:** The self is a "dividual", as described by Deleuze, a transpersonal self. I am not the voice in my head, I am all that arises; you create me as I create you, we are not sealed containers, we are often more transparent to one another and controlled by one another than we are to/by ourselves. We co-emerge, we are just bodies and fictional stories; consciousness is transformable and all stories can be developed.

- **Metamodern ideology:** The mission is to help humanity and other creatures develop in a harmonious and sustainable manner. You strive for solidarity with all beings and their perspectives. This means that you don't judge people because of their opinions. The metamodern mind is trying to stimulate development into higher stages *and* manage the ongoing relations between existing stages. All creatures have the right to be who they are. But for the sake of all sentient beings, long-term transformation towards higher stages should be supported in nicest and least painful manner possible. Avoid both "game denial" and "game acceptance", work for "game change" (this is discussed in Book Two). Create a proto-synthesis serving all perspectives by managing their interrelations and helping them evolve together in the most harmonious manner possible.
- **Metamodern ontology:** Potentials and potentiality, rather than facts and actualities, constitute the most fundamental or "more real" reality. What we usually call reality is only "actuality", one slice of an infinitely larger, hypercomplex pie. Actuality is only a "case of" a deeper reality, called "absolute totality". *Realdialektik*: History develops in certain directions for logical reasons. Perspective, physics and consciousness are inextricably intertwined, neither one of them constitutes the ground of reality.

Since the Metamodern value meme almost doesn't exist yet, you may have to look for it in the one place where a value meme always shows up first: the arts. I have briefly mentioned the work of arts scholars like Timotheus Vermeulen and Robin van der Akker, who study art and architecture (see the appendix). But we needn't go into details about their work. Let's just take some very simple examples.

Metamodern artists will go beyond the postmodern irony and critique and instead focus on things like authenticity and existential growth (I discuss the relationship between authenticity and postmodern irony in my history book).

In the movies, you may have seen Darren Aronofski's *The Fountain* (from 2006), a film about death, bereavement, acceptance of the inevitable, the limits of science and the importance of having multiple perspectives. Or maybe you saw Spike Jones' *Her* (2013), which deals with how our love is socially constructed and the fact that love relations across too vast developmental differences may be tragically impossible. It also playfully highlights some sociological trends in society, what the near future might look like. If these movies play with irony, they also bring in some profound vulnerability through the back door.

By and large, you can spot the Metamodern value meme in people who have successfully internalized all of the postmodern values and thinking, but *also* add a developmental perspective and begin to value inner growth and authenticity to a much higher degree. They also have a transpersonal perspective, seeing that root causes of social problems are generally to be found in the great fabric of relationships that constitute society and that this is inseparable from the depths of our inner selves. **The Metamodern value meme also accepts the importance of elites and hierarchies—something to which the postmoderns are deeply allergic—and it accepts the fact that not all people can be included in all settings: for instance, that not all people can become metamodernists.**

And, most of all, metamodernists don't judge the perspectives of others. The postmodern mind seeks to include all voices, but only insofar as those voices say things that are acceptable to the postmodernists themselves. The clarion call heard by all metamodernists is: solidarity with all sentient beings also requires solidarity with their perspectives.

Chapter 17

MAJOR IMPLICATIONS

I hope you didn't stop reading the book after the last chapter, feeling that you had got all the answers you needed. That would be bad. Really bad. Time and again, I have tried to warn you that careless or sloppy use of these theories is extremely dangerous. It can produce sects, oppression, justifications of injustice, marathons of self-deceit, manipulations, totalitarianism and even genocide.

Again, *because* the theory is good—because it is powerful—it is also dangerous. So let's get down to discussing some very, very important things you need to understand about it. And only then should we draw implications for society, and for ourselves.

DEATH TO TURQUOISE

We concluded last chapter with a brief presentation of the Metamodern value meme. This brings us to the issue about the highest value memes—is there really nothing beyond effective value meme Metamodern? After all, Beck and Cowan themselves suggest that there is a TURQUOISE vMeme, and other authors, from Ken Wilber to Susanne Cook-Greuter and others, work with corresponding concepts for very high stages. These very high stages are generally described as being extraordinarily wise, balanced, mature and spiritual.

My answer is no. At this point in history, there are no higher effective value memes, for all practical purposes, than the Metamodern (and even that one almost doesn't exist, as we shall see). There are three main reasons for this.

The first and most important reason is that there is no symbolic code available that seems to cancel and radically overturn the metamodern code, in a way corresponding to the way that the metamodern code overturns the postmodern one. All of these theorists, who claim that there are several stages beyond the postmodern, basically describe the same values and ideas: to adopt a radically holistic, accepting and developmental perspective of reality, as presented also in this book. In other words they all display the metamodern code themselves, and spend a lot of time criticizing postmodernism but never metamodernism itself. **But if there would *truly* be a value meme beyond the metamodern, there would be a murderous critique of the metamodern code—which is nowhere to be found.** For a value meme to manifest in society, it needs a code and language with which to program society and its institutions. At this point in history, there is simply no code with which to build a value meme higher than Metamodern.

The second reason is *rarity*. Even if we disregard the fact that a proper value meme requires a code, there is another problem. We have seen that the symbol-stage G Metamodern can only be *properly* understood by thinkers at the stage 13 Metasystematic, which is probably less than 2% of a normal adult population. If you want to go up one symbol-stage, you would also need to go up one stage of complexity, to stage 14 Paradigmatic. Imagine a symbolic code that would require stage 14 Paradigmatic to operate successfully; that would be only one or two in a thousand adults (and the writers of the code need to be at stage 15 Crossparadigmatic, which is even rarer).

And *then* consider that the depth and state required to fully grasp the philosophical and spiritual underpinnings of such a value meme. Given that depth and state seem to develop relatively independently of one another, and that people with strong spiritual experiences appear to be quite rare, we might be down to *one in a hundred thousand* (or even a million) that could be considered to be stably at this effective value meme. With such a thin slice of the population, how could this new form of culture possibly take form in a believable and stable manner?

Which brings us to the third argument. For a value meme to exist in any substantial sense, it has to have a social setting, i.e. it has to define different institutions, organizations or communities. How could you possibly believe that there is anywhere in the world a community that gathers this highly complex thinkers who are all of great depth and high state? No, the TURQUOISE vMeme (or corresponding) is simply not real. It's an immature fantasy.

What certainly *does* exist, however, and is far from rare, are developments in one or several dimensions that go beyond the requirements for effectively partaking in the Metamodern value meme. For instance, there are plenty of people who are at much greater depth and/or state than what is required to function at this value meme. Some few percent of the population habitually experience very high states, and some develop great depth; you can often find them around Zen retreats and the like. And within the scientific community you can find quite a few thinkers at stage 14 Paradigmatic.

The relative commonness of high state and great depth people is, I believe, what has lead many theorists to believe that there are indeed higher effective value memes. This is also why they generally paint these stages of development in very rosy, spiritual colors. But in reality, all these purportedly TURQUOISE people are seldom even complex enough thinkers to stably operate at the Metamodern value meme. They are usually at postmodern or below. You have here an endless array of mirages and self-deceit, people boasting and exaggerating. But all of this has a rather innocent origin: bad theory. The cure to this madness is good theory.

Developmental imbalances (when e.g. depth and state develop far ahead of complexity and code), unfortunately, often bring with them pathologies, different social diseases. I have already discussed why spiritual communities very often turn into cults, which is partly due to such imbalances. To develop a spiritual depth and very high states, but lacking the code and complexity to match it, very often makes for some pretty sick stuff, which often leads to some deeply regressive and harmful behavioral outcomes I will get back to it in a bit.

To be very clear: If you identify yourself with the TURQUOISE vMeme or above, you are probably sick with harmful self-deceit. You should stop flattering yourself and seriously reconsider. **Just because you have high state and great depth, it doesn't mean that you are also a complex thinker and that you have access to advanced symbolic code; i.e. that you are of high effective value meme.**

But even Metamodern value meme almost doesn't exist. According to Beck and Cowan, as much as 4% of a normal adult Western population are at YELLOW, which is their idea of a counterpart to the Metamodern value meme. If you would count all people who are at stage 13 Metasystematic, and add all people who have strong spiritual experiences, and then add the folks who have greater "dark depth", and then add all the people who have downloaded at least some part of the symbol-stage G Metamodern (complexity scientists, adult development theorists, posthumanists, enactivists, Wilberian integralists, and the like), then yes, that might account for about 4%. But then again, to find the people who are safely and stably at the effective value meme Metamodern, you have to look for the sub-section of people who display *all* of these properties! That would land us somewhere far below half a percent. If we look globally, we're down to much less than a tenth of a percent of the population at metamodern.

In a world where, even in the most affluent and developed societies like Sweden, the Metamodern value meme accounts for less than half a percent of the population, and this value meme and the society it corresponds to are still being born, can you see how ludicrous it is to believe in an even higher value meme?

What happens if you ignore the fact that this value meme doesn't exist and still build a community based on highly enlightened, emotionally mature and cognitively complex people? It becomes an abusive cult, full of very infected conflicts; that's what happens. Because it's based on a lie—on an incorrect assessment of people's development, and on a hysterical attempt to make true what is not. Cults. It has happened many times before. And it will, no doubt, happen again.

So, death to TURQUOISE (and its equally unrealistic counterparts in other theories). Long live the Metamodern effective value meme. Even if it is still being born, it can and will change the world. There will of course be value memes beyond the Metamodern, but the time just hasn't come, not by far. The "post-metamodern" value meme can only show up once a Metamodern society has manifested and can be criticized on its own premises.

Up until that point, the belief in higher value memes is fool's gold.

Higher Secularism Rising

The increases in effective value meme can be understood as a kind of increase in the degree of secularism. Of course, secularism, as we usually think of the term, simply means the shift from the Postfaustian to the Modern value meme (from the Bible to science). But that's not the whole story, far from.

You could say that the Animistic value meme is more secular than the Archaic one because it doesn't take what is present to the senses as the only reality; it looks for how spirits, ancestors, intentions or otherwise invisible factors may have influenced the occurring events. As such it abstracts from the direct experience and takes the perceived world less at face value. This is secularism.

But the Faustian value meme goes beyond that: It points out that humans can use their will to force nature into submission, and they can live to tell the tale. And humans can recreate society itself; create orders of their own. The question is no longer who has the best spirit, but who has the biggest army. It no longer sees spirits as the fundamental essences. Secularism.

But the Postfaustian value meme points out that there really is a universal order beyond all human affairs, and that you can't rely upon patron gods, but only upon the truth itself. This truth cannot follow the whims of rulers or the ebbs and flows of political power, but must have a higher, eternal origin. If you go against the truth, you will be punished. This is also, relatively speaking, a kind of secularism.

And then there's the Modern value meme and what we classically think of as secularism, which points out that there can be no universal truths other than what is universally verifiable by a community of equals. You must also take into consideration the *method* of inquiry. As I said, Protestantism—both in Luther, Calvin and later developments—can either be seen as the pinnacle of postfaustianism, or, as an early form of modernism: The Bible is translated into German and each individual is allowed to check the interpretations of church authorities for themselves. The Church itself is stripped of a lot of its colorful robes, its gold and its many saints. These saints are in fact a kind of lingering spirit worship.

By and large, the Modern value meme explains problems in society as result of people acting irrationally or of their failures to take responsibility. Problems show up because people make the wrong choices. So it's not because you're a bad person and broke the commandments of God, but because you did something unintelligent or unethical, that things went bad.

And then there's the Postmodern value meme, which is where things begin to get really interesting. The postmodern mind doesn't believe in the purported rationality of modern society and "modern man"—there are just too many cracks in the wall. Postmodernism sees that knowledge and rationality always seem to follow certain perspectives and power structures. And science is subject to any number of biases and blind spots. Indeed, our entire universe is only experienced through symbolic representation; through social constructions. Besides, there seems to be much more to life than what science manages to catch in its many journal articles. So it can hardly be that modern society is nearly as rational as it thinks. You no longer believe in the myth of the rational human, creating a rational order. Instead, you see the huge social machinery behind the curtains, which determines what people do—including, to a large extent, the thing called science. Secularism. More secular than the modern mind.

Which brings us to the Metamodern value meme. The postmodern mind believes in there being such things as "power structures", "ideology", "postcolonialism", "patriarchy" and "discourses". The metamodern mind sees beyond these explanations; it understands that the postmodern mind is still being essentialist, i.e. that it believes in essences which are inherent to these invisible forces. The postmodern mind thinks that there is some kind of metaphysical evil called "power structures" and that you can remove this evil by invoking its opposite: emancipating critique, deconstruction, inclusion, more soft and relativist values and so forth. But that means you still believe in there being some evil "out there" and you being the "good guy": No longer the bad intentions of others, but certainly a collective and sociological evil that must be destroyed. The Metamodern value meme doesn't believe in anything like that. It sees that all of these things only emerge by necessity, as emergent properties of complex systems. It sees the world as more mechanical, and less good or evil—all things are explainable, and there are no evil patriarchy spirits or ghosts of colonialism past. These are illusions, just interpretations of effects of self-organizing systems. And the way to solve these problems is not by "crushing patriarchy", but by genuinely understanding the ideas, perspectives and behaviors of all stakeholders, and by finding ways to develop them and otherwise affect their behaviors and interactions. More secular than the postmodern mind.

So step by step, the belief in a "ground of reality", in "true essences", is pushed farther into the periphery. Step by step, people acquire a worldview in which larger parts of reality can be questioned, and thereby explained, and thereby governed. The spirits and ghosts are exorcized again and again. The main takeaway from this is, as I have indicated several times already, that we shouldn't see people at the Modern value meme as "secular". They believe all sorts of deeply irrational and crazy things, and they cannot be trusted to act rationally in matters of societal development. This is because they will tend to rely upon much too rigid an unquestioned assumptions about reality. Only the Metamodern value meme can see the world with a sufficient sobriety. **Secularism isn't really about religion vs. non-religion, or spirituality vs. non-spirituality; it is about expanding the ability to question and recreate reality.**

To achieve a secular world is not about making people not believe in Jesus or Allah anymore; that's just a speck on the larger map. A secular world must be governed by metamodern principles. That's what it's about. Anything less than that will still be a world governed by crazy, irrational and outdated ideas. You go from spirits to gods to a universal God, to reductionist science, to critique and sociology of knowledge, to an understanding of transpersonalism and complexity. At every step, you kill the spirits and gods of yesteryear. The metamodern creed is, at its core, married to an atheism so pervasive and radical that even the modern and postmodern gods are exposed as illusions.

All of the value memes claim to be secular. All claim to speak of universal truth. The problem is that they can only see as far as their own value meme; hence they all believe that they have dispelled the myths and reached "reality". They are all wrong. Even metamodernism is wrong. But unlike all the others, we know it ourselves.

A higher form of secularism is rising. And lagging terribly.

Why Bother with Just a Baby?

It is very important not to be naive here; the Metamodern value meme is only still being born. So no, you won't find one single truly metamodern movement or organization anywhere in the world at this point. Don't kid yourself.

Even if I suggested that The Alternative in Denmark (the political party I described chapter 5) is an interesting place to look, almost all members of that party are in effect still manifesting the Postmodern value meme. It's just that *some* of its leaderships display *some* metamodern values. It's not more than that.

If the Metamodern value meme is so tiny, why should we bother? It's just a baby. There are two reasons. The first is that it is important for the successful development of a sustainable, equitable and non-alienated global society capable of handling the great challenges and opportunities coming our way. Without the Metamodern value meme it's difficult to see how we could make it, because only metamodernists can handle the relationships between all the other value memes productively.

The second reason is the wind; the direction in which it is blowing. Metamodernism has all the structures of the development of the world on its side: Everything points to metamodernism, as these values are the most efficient ones in a global postindustrial, internet society where people of all value memes suddenly meet eye to eye. Not only that; the technological, economic and social structures of our time automatically foster more metamodern ideas and values. The younger you are and the better you are doing in life, and the more central your position in the new global society, the more likely you are to pick up metamodern values. Conversely, the more metamodern values you pick up, the more powerful you are likely to become.

Luckily for us, a value meme can form from many different pieces of a greater puzzle. This is apparent if you apply a transpersonal perspective. **The Metamodern value meme can develop in a *transpersonal* space**; you don't necessarily need that many folks who see clearly what is going on. What you *do* need is a large quantity of people who contribute to the overall shift of pattern in society, each with their own piece of the puzzle.

So, for a society to begin to manifest some metamodern characteristics, it is enough that there are some people around with the code, some with the cognitive complexity, some expressing metamodern aesthetics, some with extra existential depth, some in high states, some creating more metamodern organizations, some doing research on complexity economics, and some creating metamodern economic structures (as I will discuss in another book, titled *Outcompeting Capitalism*). The Metamodern value meme is forming, slowly but surely, from the structures of the emerging global society.

It forms "by itself", through the self-organization of the world-system. Or, rather: from the patterns that emerge through the interactions of many independently acting people and circumstances. But there is a group that is consciously aware of the Metamodern value meme and is actively pursuing its emergence. We know them from chapter 5: **the metamodern aristocracy**. The main difference between the aristocracy and all others is exactly that: The aristocracy has a systemic and clear picture of what is going on—and they have the resources to act upon their understanding.

So why bother with just a baby? Because they grow up fast, that's why.

Danger, Danger Cliché

The most vital flaw of the theory of value memes is that it, like many theories about society, can make us simplify the world too much; it easily lends itself to vague and dull caricatures.

Such caricatures are often evoked. The Faustian value meme becomes a warrior, the Postfaustian a priest, the Modern a shrewd businessman, the Postmodern a Greenpeace activist. Need I point out how useless the theory would be if that was all it offered? Unfortunately, a large majority of all adherents to Spiral Dynamics and similar theories only ever reach this stage of understanding—usually adding the cliché that the highest stage is a New Age person. Sigh.

I'm not just making this up; in 2010, the Harvard researchers Zak Stein and Katie Heikkinen undertook a study of the so-called "integral community" (within which a lot of people subscribe to stage theories like the ones I have discussed). They found—surprise, surprise—that most people only understood the developmental theories from a relatively low stage of complexity. Most people only grasped the developmental stages as a kind of stereotypes.[162] Indeed, such "flattened" theory does more to feed prejudice than to elucidate the social world and our place in it. But none of this should surprise us; after all, I have noted that successfully installing and operating the metamodern symbolic code requires a cognitive complexity at stage 13 Metasystematic, which only less than 2% of the adult population seem to have.

So first of all, we need to simply note that people who are part of the different effective value memes can and do look very different from one another: What unites a village psychic in modern Ukraine (let's say she also has schizotypal tendencies, a psychiatric condition often associated with unconventional beliefs) with a member of a rural San tribe (bushmen) hunter-gatherer in southern Africa? They are both of the Animistic effective value meme. As such, their effective value meme helps us to understand certain aspects of their thinking and ways of seeing the world, but other than that, they are not the same, not at all.

People of the Faustian value meme can be Aztec townsfolk, macho Sumerians with huge beards and long spears, or just a really tough lady from harsh conditions in the Bronx. People at the Postfaustian value meme can be a teenage Russian nationalist, or intellectual and spiritual traditionalists and critics of modernity (like Frithjof Schoun and René Guenon, both of whom out-depth and out-complex most of us), or just your random present-day Egyptian housewife. The Modern value meme can be anyone from Robespierre to Ayn Rand to Richard Dawkins to Frank Sinatra. The Postmodern value meme is Judith Butler (the queer-feminist theorist), Arne Næss (the deep-ecologist), Lady Gaga and Lisa Simpson (yes, the cartoon).

Point being: You need to understand *the pattern and logic* of the value memes; simple clichés will do more harm than good. Nevertheless, this is real stuff; a postmodern world full of Judith Butlers and Lisa Simpsons is just very, very different from a modern world full of Richard Dawkins and Frank Sinatras.

Some Very Well-Needed Nuance

I would now like to offer you two very well-needed nuances to this theory, nuances that follow directly from seeing the four dimensions I have discussed. These are, in order of appearance: **light vs. dark** value memes; and **progressive vs. regressive and retarded** value memes.

Light vs. dark value memes: As I have indicated you can reach a certain value meme by means of complexity, code, depth and state. But do people with great depth and high state manifest value memes in the same way as people with high complexity and good access to complex code? Nay. There is a great qualitative difference between the two. Hence, you can have "light postmodernists" and "dark postmodernists" and so forth. Light pomos are more like hippies: They like environmentalism, self-development, organic food, community, Taoism and the like. And they don't like academic stuff very much or cynical theories about the world. Dark pomos are more like academics, anarchists, critical sociologists, literary critics, queer theorists and neo-Marxists. They like theories, criticism and finding new ways to expose the injustices and madness of the modern condition. They despise the stupid and naive light pomos, who they feel are inauthentic, hysterical cop-outs. The dark pomos take plenty of anti-depressants. And there are the hipsters: people in creative, designer and artsy digital industries, who understand the postmodern condition, steeped in irony and self-distance, retro styles, thick glasses, and refined secondhand fashion, producing indie computer games, underground electro music and participatory museums.

The light pomos build those dome green houses and do lots of yoga and eat fruit-only diets. And the dark pomos smoke and drink and discuss, often with great intellectual talent, the predicament of modern life. And the light pomos secretly dislike them for being unproductive and negative snobs. You get the picture. Yet, these two groups of people will have *a whole lot* in common: they are very liberal, they are anti-racist, they are pro-environment, they prefer soft values over toughness, they don't like commercialism, they tend towards multiculturalism and relativism—the list goes on! In short; they are both of the same value meme. They have just reached it by virtue of different characteristics. Here's a sketch.

"Light" version of value meme	"Dark" version of value meme
* High state * Great depth, "light" depth * Lower complexity * Imperfect code	* High complexity * Well-developed code * Low state * "Dark" depth (i.e. depth derived from acquaintance with lower states)

So, light pomos are higher in state and/or depth, which allows them to take on a more universalistic and solidaric perspective than most mainstream modern people, whereas dark pomos become who they are by being complex thinkers, wrestling with painful experiences and feeling terribly alienated in modern society, and then finding their way to critical humanities. A lot of the light pomos won't really be able to criticize the modern code; they only instinctively feel drawn towards more postmodern values.

You can do the same with pretty much all of the value memes, but we need not go too deep into the discussion. Suffice to say that Richard Dawkins is dark modernism and Frank Sinatra is light: One knows the code super-well and spends his life criticizing the Postfaustian value meme, the other just lives an individualist life and achieves what modern life has to offer, singing *I did it my way*. Likewise, you have dark metamodernists—more like myself and other scholars—and light metamodernists, who are more like spiritually inclined Spiral Dynamics people.

I don't have the data to prove it, but as far as I can tell, the light versions of every value meme seem to outnumber the dark ones. It just seems like most normal people are not that complex or obsessed with symbolic codes; it is more common to just have higher states and greater depth.

Progressive vs. the regressive and the retarded: The second nuance has to do with how your value meme compares to the gravity of our society and to the political, technological and economic structures of which you are part. For instance, consider the "founding father" Thomas Jefferson. Was he progressive? He did more than maybe any person in history for the development and proliferation of democratic governance. And he had slaves. Compare this to Donald Trump. Trump doesn't have slaves. He'd probably find the idea appalling, as most present-day modern people do. Nevertheless, Jefferson defended values that were deeply universalistic and democratic. Trump goes on about building walls, setting up trade barriers, rounding up and expelling Mexicans and Muslims, using torture, killing the families of terrorists, ignoring climate change—you know the drill. Which one would you say has the highest effective value meme? The issue here is to compare the manifestation of value memes to the societies in which they emerge. People who are of high complexity, state and depth, will tend to be progressive in comparison to their own societies. Low complexity, state and depth people will tend to be regressive in comparison to their society's general value meme (and the value meme that their society requires to be sustainable at systemic level).

When a society evolves and the economic systems, technological applications and social relations become more complex, this always produces winners and losers. The people who have lower complexity, who haven't had the opportunity to install the more complex code, and who are disadvantaged (thereby getting lower well-being, lower states) will of course not like where society is going. They have every right in the world to defend their own earlier value meme. But in the long run, the battle is always lost. The value meme retards will try to defend and promulgate values that simply do not match the systemic realities of their own society. For instance, you will hear people in the US saying that "Only through belief in Jesus can we make America great again; let's bring God back to America!" But of course, bringing God back and going on about Jesus won't do much to stop the onslaught of globalization and postindustrial internet society; it will only put you at a further disadvantage in the new global economic environment. Postmodern and metamodern values are the most efficient ones if you want to do well and solve the problems of globalization.

When societies, for any number of reasons, produce large segments of populations that are lagging behind when it comes to value meme development, you get value meme retardation. The word retardation means "being too late", which is what we're talking about here. It is important to understand that this is indeed what is going on.

Excuse the controversial term; I know it sounds as if I am being disrespectful against those of my fellow world citizens who live with disabilities. But that is not the case; I follow the whole critical discourse on "crip is hip" in sociology and anthropology with great enthusiasm and I am deeply opposed to this kind of discrimination. So if you or somebody in your family lives with disabilities, please don't take offence; please allow me to use the word. What I want with the term is simply to point out that we, as a global society, are falling behind in our *developmental* psychology.

I also did it for effect. We live, essentially, in a retarded world. Not then, an evil world, a fallen world, a world of greed and capitalism, a world out of touch with Mother Nature, a crude materialist world—but a retarded world.

"Regressive" political movements can be defined as the ones that draw society towards earlier value memes, often by allying with the value meme retards. So when light-modern Trump draws on postfaustian ethnocentric values he is being regressive; when Jesus did a postfaustian critique of Roman oppression, he was being progressive. And when Jefferson was planning the modern US constitution, the gods held their breath as humanity took a great leap forward. Same value memes—*very* different meanings.

When it comes to ISIS and al-Qaeda and Nazism, go figure. These movements manifest the Faustian value meme with a very thin post-faustian veneer. To a lot of people around the world their "Viking" way of life just makes more sense (where you live under a warrior code and pillage and capture slaves and whatnot) and these movements offer an outlet for living from the Faustian value meme. They are of course deeply regressive in today's world where we need to worry about managing complexity and finding ways to support psychological growth (in order to create a sustainable, equitable and non-alienated civilization capable of ending global inequality and animal slavery) rather than looking out for our honor and killing the heathens.

Even within nationalist parties around Europe you will find a similar pattern: The same movements that host the strictest upholders of justice, proponents of severe punishment and defenders of the honest virtues of old, are filled with criminal records, beaten wives, corruption scandals, street violence and purchases of prostitution. For some reason, you just don't have these problems in and around the Green parties.

But value meme retardation doesn't stop at Trumpism and obvious things like Nazi and terrorist organizations. It's everywhere. The Modern value meme has been retarded for some time already; and nowadays even the Postmodern value meme is becoming a form of retardation. I say this because neither of them can successfully take responsibility for our runaway world. Only metamodernism can.

Developmental Imbalances Make You Sick

The world never develops smoothly. It is always eternally broken, always striving for an impossible balance that is never achieved. Things always develop out of pace with one another, and this always causes troubles of all imaginable kinds. Our economic systems develop in ways that outpace our psychologies, one civilization develops in a way that destroys others, one species develops in ways that are cancerous to the ecosystems and the whole biosphere. The glory of the world and its greatest sorrows have the same source: **developmental imbalances**—the fact that some things develop ahead of others and that some parts are always lagging behind. And it is these strange glitches and paradoxes that propel the world in its non-linear, dialectical journey towards greater beauty, tragedy and mystery. **To understand the world, you must not only understand development, but**

the fundamental role that developmental imbalances play in the universe.

So people can out-depth and out-complex one another. But can we out-depth and out-complex ourselves? Yes. When we develop far in one aspect but not another, we tend to display developmental imbalances of different kinds. I would like to highlight two such developmental imbalances: **the magic residual** and **reductionism**.

Ever noticed that there are prickly people and soft-edged people? Some folks, for some reason, consistently seem to like "harder" explanations, to see the clear and tough mechanical aspects of reality. Others seem more inclined towards soft, holistic images of reality: How everything is interconnected and forms a part of a greater whole. Ideally, the metamodern mind seeks marry these two aspects of life to one another. But in reality, most of us are skewed towards one side or the other.

Generally speaking, the soft-edged folks—who prefer vagueness over certainty, openness over boundary-making, and wholeness over parts—are the ones who **out-depth and/or out-state their *own* complexity and code**. Why are all the expressions of New Age culture and yoga parlors of this kind? Where are all the hardliner, analytical, materialist yoga-people? These are perhaps the most emblematic example of this tendency: It is visible in the demeanors of such people, in their aesthetics, in the very structure of their thoughts.

So where do "magic beliefs" come from? Of course, in an animistic society, it is normal to believe in magic. But strangely, you can find all kinds of magic beliefs in modern people as well—even among the educated and intelligent ones. For instance, I have encountered any number of successful modern people who think that fate has something in stall for them, that the world around them conspired to reveal that they were special, that they can "sense" what is going to happen, that there is such a thing as "synchronicity" (the idea that very improbable things happen because the world supports you in your spiritual journey), that a loving heart can literally heal somebody at a distance, that really advanced Zen masters can walk through walls or levitate (float above the ground)—the list goes on. Of course, none of this is true. It's all make-believe and nonsense or there are perfectly natural explanations (for instance, the experience of "synchronicity" can be explained by a combination of selective memory, self-deceit, narcissism, probability theory and network or cluster effects). We live in a magical and miraculous world, but there is no magic and there are no miracles.

What we are dealing with in these many cases is the occurrence of **the magic residual**, i.e. that people have seen greater depth, mystery and beauty in the world than their cognitive minds—and their available symbolic codes—can handle. Thus, there is a *glitch*, a developmental imbalance, through which magical beliefs and other superstitions can sneak in.

The way we conventionally think about it is that intelligent and complex thinkers are the ones that are resistant to magical beliefs. There is of course a lot of research to support this claim. But I hold that this is only half-true. The researchers didn't ask the right question. What you should look for is how depth, state, complexity and code relate to one another. You find magic beliefs in people who are of greater depth and higher state *in comparison to* their complexity and symbolic code. Magic can be reintroduced again and again in smaller doses at the higher stages of complexity. Whereas kids believe in snarks and magic tricks, above average complex adults can believe in "synchronicity", reincarnation, the astral plane, flows of subtle energy, spiritual family constellation work, telepathy, the Maya calendar, that you can "manifest" things in your life by way of thoughts and wishes, or even just that God hears your prayers (again, it's all utter bogus).

I have heard any number of serious psychotherapists and PhDs (even within the natural sciences) go on about this stuff. It is not because these folks are more stupid than your average modern Joe—on the contrary, they are above average intelligence—but because **they out-depth and out-state themselves**.

This creates a rather strange matter of affairs: The people at the highest value memes—like Metamodern—are *more* likely, rather than less, to believe in preposterous and magical things. The magic residual has snuck in. The exact same openness towards the beauty and mystery of the universe, that sense of grand wholeness and awe, also cracks your head open so that the most dim-witted of ideas can sneak in and stick.

If you ever heard the debates between the New Age writer Deepak Chopra and New Atheists like Sam Harris or Richard Dawkins (critics of religion), you may have noticed how they fail to reach common ground. There can be little doubt that Deepak out-depths the New Atheists; but this is precisely also the reason that he, an otherwise intelligent person, out-depths his own complexity and code. As his mind grasps to express the heights spiritual experience, all kinds magic beliefs sneak in through the backdoor: He tries to use quantum mechanics to save his spiritual worldview. Harris expresses only vague experiences of the spiritual, and Dawkins none. Nevertheless, whenever any of them confront Deepak's claims and reasoning, his arguments fall flat on the ground. They are exposed as magic residuals—even as Deepak himself claims to represent a thinking that lies beyond traditional religions and is purportedly based firmly upon science.

This imbalance between your depth/state and code/complexity occurs especially in periods of your life when you have had profound spiritual experiences or existential changes. For instance, people who have gone on a long and very profound LSD-trip will, despite a long and sturdy education in computer engineering, go magical for a while—at least until their development of code and complexity catch up (or the memory of their experience fades). Or, going through a profound Kundalini awakening, a middle class rationalist can start believing that there actually is a gargoyle in their living room. There's not.

So what you have is this ironic twist: Magical beliefs, albeit often of more complex nature, are *drastically overrepresented* in people who close in on the Metamodern value meme. This explains why intelligent folks like Ken Wilber will believe the most stupefyingly preposterous things (Wilber believes in miracles, in a love-force called Eros that propels evolution and in Lamarckist evolutionary theory). They out-depth and out-state their own cognitive and symbolic stage.

Hey, I told you development wasn't an easy, straightforward matter. I told you higher value memes aren't always better. But then again, is it so bad if these folks believe in a little magic? Has it ever done any harm?

Yes. It is deeply, severely harmful. In today's global capitalist, post-industrial internet society, magical beliefs are a social pathology, a disease of the mind. Why? Because they open up the door for any number of misuses of power. If there is magic in the world, anyone who you believe has more contact with this magic than you do, gains arbitrary power over you. You surrender your own mental faculties to them, and from there on, very bad things can and will happen. It is the royal road to totalitarianism.

Also, all magic beliefs make you waste time and energy doing things that simply don't work. These faulty towers of thought can cause all kinds of nasty hang-ups that make your life miserable. And given the state of the world, we just don't have the time for your "subtle energy purification" and magic spells. Not even for your prayers—unless you mean contemplative prayer, the purpose of which is to develop your own psychology. Most of all, this kind of fuzzy thinking makes it difficult to think correct, complex, analytical thoughts: It can *hinder* your successful management of complexity.

But there is another kind of developmental imbalance that is just as harmful: **reductionism**. The prickly people. It is when you **out-complex and out-code your own depth and state**. Whereas the harm in magic beliefs is quite obvious, reductionism is harmful in a more subtle way. It is when your mind picks everything apart and uses its intellect in a much-too-instrumental manner. The world appears too dead, too meaningless, too mechanical for you to really care about it.

At a subtle level, the reductionist feels a vague aggression towards reality and existence: "Was this all?" You gain a sense of satisfaction, a faint feeling of revenge, from exposing reality for the meaningless, dead piece of indifferent shit that it really is. You pick it apart and see that there is always hardness beneath the softness, selfishness beneath the love, mechanics beneath the wonder, and so forth. The reductionist mind is blind to the greater whole, blind to serving a deeper principle of life. It becomes a cancer: Thinking, thinking, serving small and selfish desires by turning all of existence into an extraction project. And why not? Reality is dead, meaningless dirt. And I will use my hard, effective reason to show that all that glitters is only ever grime. But at least I will get what I want.

Need I point out—together with so many deep ecologists, Heideggerians, even Catholic popes—that this is what is going on a global level with the environmental crisis and with so many aspects of our social reality? Our reductionist, manipulative minds have gone haywire. Nothing is sacred or divine. And this process of reducing the world to dead parts hinders holistic insight: it hinders higher states and the development of greater depth.

Because the Metamodern value meme is often an expression of high complexity, severe reductionism is *also* overrepresented in people with high value memes. Nobody said the development of a sane civilization would be easy. Ideally speaking, the metamodern mind marries sense and soul—avoiding both magic beliefs and reductionism. Of course, that is what everybody will say, a cliché anybody can agree to. But it is easier said than done. The world strives for an always-impossible balance. Reality is always in a perturbed state, always far from equilibrium; indeed, always broken. And so are we.

But such developmental imbalances do not pertain only to the psychology of the single person. They are, of course, also prevalent in society at large. What happens if you have a modern state, with all of its power, bureaucracy and technology—and you rule it with the mental framework of Genghis Khan? Nazism, that's what happens. Nazism isn't pure evil; it is a value meme retardation, a developmental imbalance. Nothing more.

What happens if you have free information in a super-efficient, self-organizing global network of computers (i.e. the internet) and some people use it for holy war, following the Faustian value meme so that its warriors can go to Valhalla? You get Al-Qaeda and ISIS.

What happens if you have nanotechnology and biological hacking readily available, and millions of people use these super-technologies in a narrowly profit-maximizing capitalist manner? What happens when an authoritarian Chinese government gets its hands on metamodern theory (or an equivalent) and starts using it in a non-democratic, manipulative way? I guess we'll find out pretty soon.

Can you see now that development matters? That inner dimensions matter? Can you see that we need to balance science and cognitive complexity with inner growth—and vice versa?

The Philosopher's Stone

On a short side-note, I would like to offer you an idea about the role of exceptional people in history. Most of what I talk about has to do with wider issues: transpersonal things, clusters and structures, deep shifts within our common reality—the results of interactions between many different people across vast networks and many different contexts. But it should *also* be noted that relatively few people actually re-write the code, actually change our faiths, worldviews and so on. These are most often the people with exceptional developmental qualities.

Our intellectual history, at least until the mid-20th century, has revolved around philosophers. The sociologist Randall Collins has described it quite well in his network analysis of the great philosophers and their interrelations: The great philosophers form a center or core of culture itself; they connect the dots, at least intellectually speaking.[163] Aristotle taught the guy who conquered his way to India and connected western and eastern Eurasia (Alexander the Great), Augustine informed the Catholic church, Voltaire advised Frederic the Great and inspired the French Revolution, philosophers formulated the principles upon which the US was founded, Marx informed the greatest political movement of the 20th century, the Vienna Circle and Anglo-Saxon analytical philosophers laid the foundations for computation and information technology and Foucault created the framework today used by queer feminist and postcolonial movements around the world. And so on.

But the philosophers are also exceptional people. As Randall Collins has remarked, the people around major philosophers—their mentors, more specifically, who are also philosophers—can often guess in advance that they will play a major role, the emblematic example perhaps being when Bertrand Russell said to the sister of the young Wittgenstein that he and his colleagues expected the next major step in philosophy to be taken by Ludwig. Jürgen Habermas heard similar comments.

Type of exceptional person	Great scientist or inventor	Mystic or saint	Philosopher
Characteristics that create the genius	* High MHC stage and intelligence	* High state * Great depth	* Great depth *and* * High MHC complexity * Depth can be "light" or "dark"

What, then, are the characteristics of the philosopher? For all their different flavors and personalities and historical epochs and symbolic codes, all the major philosophers clearly share two things: high cognitive complexity *and* great depth. This separates them from mystics, yogis, sages, saints and prophets, who have great depth and high states (but not complexity)—*and* from major scientists and inventors who have high complexity (but not necessarily great depth). **The philosopher's stone is simply the cross-section of great depth and very high complexity (stage 14 Paradigmatic and above).** Of course, some philosophers are more on the depth-side, like Plotinus or Schelling, and some are more on the complexity side, like Kant or Hume.

The "hue" of the philosopher's depth can be light or dark; i.e. the philosophers don't necessarily need to have high states: The inner lives of Kierkegaard, Nietzsche, Schopenhauer, Adorno and Sartre were no festivals. People like Plotinus and Schelling quite obviously did experience very high states.

The depth-side of philosophy is generally overlooked in the mainstream academic rendering of the philosophers. For instance, how come Plato and Aristotle talk of "God" when they live in a polytheistic society? Is there not clearly a mystical tinge to the allegory of the cave, or the eternal God whose only activity is to think of himself? Where do they get this stuff?

Clearly, these philosophers are expressing complex thoughts about *mystical, spiritual* experiences. Indeed, a vibrant mystical undercurrent is present already at the birth of philosophy, when Thales asks what the ultimate essence is, and when Protagoras states that "Man is the measure of all things: of the things that are, that they are, of the things that are not, that they are not."

Is he not talking of pure being, an experience beyond the conceptual mind? Who had Hegel been without great depth? Or even Marx? They would have been scientists, but not philosophers. And without high MHC stage, they may have been spiritual, but not philosophical.

Studying philosophy at the university unfortunately doesn't give you either great depth or complexity. Just like studying the history of art doesn't make you into Rembrandt. This is why there is such a great difference between philosophy professors and philosophers. Academic philosophy is good for all manner of things, but it's not where you find the philosopher's stone.

Rip Them Apart. Spare No One

We don't really have to bother with going through the other theories of adult development; I should only briefly point out that they don't really work—despite that they each have good points and merits. I am of course grateful to all of them, and there are certainly things to be learned from them. But they all fall on the same rope: the failure to differentiate between stage, code, state and depth.

Take Harvard psychologist Robert Kegan's theory of the development of the self. He says there are five stages that the "self" evolves through—first becoming socialized and conventional, then some folks becoming self-authoring individualists, then some folks (fewer yet) becoming self-transforming people who see themselves as part of a greater dialectical development of reality as a whole, and must always be in flux, always transforming.

His theory is useful and has some merits. But think about it—does he mean that people can *think* more abstractly about their selves because they are of higher complexity, or does he mean that they gain access to better code, which grants them more advanced language to discuss themselves (with ideas such as "identity", "gender structures" and "the unconscious"), or does he mean that some people are in more whole and fulfilled subjective states in which our sense of self seems more self-evident (as described by Emerson's spiritual poem) or does he mean that a greater depth is internalized through posttraumatic growth or psychedelic experience? Or any combination of the four? What exactly is he talking about?

Kegan's theory doesn't give us very specific or reliable ideas about people and their development. And Kegan himself suffers as a result of the cracks in his theory. For instance, it has led him to believe—as he presented during a recent seminar—that "the reason" that humanity is aging (that people live longer than they did a few decades ago) is that the world "wants" us to become wise so that we transition to a wiser, ecological civilization. This is exactly the kind of teleological thinking I warned you about in chapter 10. It is utterly ludicrous and an unforgivable intellectual sell-out to magic beliefs. According to my own theory, it is a result of Kegan out-depthing his own complexity. This is the magic residual in action—magic beliefs sneaking in through the backdoor. As you can see, this is a real thing; it doesn't exclude Harvard professors.

All of the other theories, like that of Susanne Cook-Greuter, or Gerald Young, or even Larry Kohlberg himself—even those of the very intelligent Theo Dawson and spiritually insightful Terri O'Fallon—you can rip apart with the same simple scheme: how they fail to differentiate between the four dimensions of stage, code, state and depth. Enjoy.

We are left with Michael Commons' stages of complexity and my own reconstruction of Spiral Dynamics. Michael's theory still holds. It's just that we need to add the three other dimensions I have suggested as well as a general discussion of value memes. And in a way, our awkward uncle Spiral Dynamics still holds. We picked him apart, it's true, but we then put him back together. All according to the metamodern dictum: **after deconstruction must follow reconstruction**.

Let's also take stock of some things that we have *not* discussed in this theory. First of all we haven't touched upon skill theory, which some of the mentioned authors elaborate upon. Strictly speaking, it is difficult to imagine how the development I have discussed is possible without the learning of skills. Secondly, we haven't really discussed other aspects of psychology, such as personality types, interests, degree of emotional self-knowledge, the occurrence of self-deceit and other biases, general psychological health and so forth. Hence, there is plenty of room for people to have psychologies that are quite different from one another, even if they are of comparable complexity, code, state and depth (and thus value meme). Neither have we discussed things such as life-phases: An old person nearing her death is of course different from a 20-year old, even if they happen to have the same value meme. Nor culture: how Japanese people are different from Swedes. And we haven't touched upon psychiatric disorders and how they may interact with the value memes. Or how sociological things like privilege, capital and exclusion might affect them (although I discuss these matters in my other book, *Outcompeting Capitalism*).

I guess I am saying: The value memes are good at explaining the world, and for understanding society, politics and people around us. But they obviously don't answer all of your questions. So when you go out and apply these insights in your life, please keep in mind that there is much more to psychology, sociology and politics.

Still though, it is my honest belief that you have just been equipped with one of the best and most powerful theories around. Use it well.

Implications for a Global Society

Can it really be this easy? Can you really understand so much about the world and its development by means of value memes and its four dimensions? Yes. But isn't the world much more fussy and complex? Of course it is. However, there are underlying patterns in this chaos. Much like our eyes only really see three colors, and we can taste relatively few flavors, but we still manage to have a wide array of sense experiences. In physics you study the simple, clear underlying principles that create all the astonishing complexity around us. And the laws are always surprisingly simple.

So it is with psychological and sociological development. The reason that the world seems so fussy is simply that you haven't yet discovered and understood the patterns through which it is ordered. This includes the social world. Even if there are many things we have not explained with this theory, it still helps you see a simplicity around you—a pattern that connects, a "second simplicity".

I once met a young American during a flight; we were crossing the Atlantic as I was going to visit Michael Commons. This 21-year-old, I think his name was Andrew, had just spent the summer in Rome to study with some pretty well-known theologians. He made a lasting impression on me.

Andrew had a Bachelor's degree in philosophy and one in classical languages, finishing top of his class, and had now decided to not become a monk after all, but to be a medical doctor and have a family. So this was a smart young man. But what made an impression was his story about himself, his faith, how he defended his beliefs—and his kind, glowing eyes. Apparently he had already gone through severe crises during his teens and found guidance in a Catholic priest and in the faith. He had been guided through contemplative prayer and his life had changed completely: his heart breaking open, and his soul being filled with light and humility. There was an unmistakable softness in his eyes, a glow, an idealism, a kind of love—or wisdom, perhaps. I have never seen anything like it in a non-spiritual non-believer—not even in the most idealistic animal rights activist.

This young man had grown up in a modern culture. Nevertheless he believed in transubstantiation (that wine literally becomes the blood of Christ, etc.), free will, sin, heaven, the soul, that Jesus is literally speaking the son of God and all kinds of other preposterous Catholic things. Politically, he rooted for the Republicans, and he saw a problem in all the "leeches" sucking blood off society by not working and living on welfare. But he himself did much charity work for the poor. When I explained that welfare was better than charity because it avoided some of the social degradation and power relations implicit to the latter, his kind eyes lit up—he just hadn't thought about it that way.

Come to think of it, I did meet somebody else with the same softly glowing eyes, also a beautiful young man. His name was Jonas, an environmental science student from Stockholm. I last met him the day before he turned 25 and we walked through Stockholm, a clear day in May, talked about metamodernism and the future of society. As we parted Jonas looked at me with those intimate, kind eyes and said he had found new hope. He killed himself a few months later.

I can't help but to think that our emerging global society needs more people like Andrew—but who are *also* politically progressive, complex thinkers and who don't rely upon mythologies derived from symbol-stage D Postfaustian. Is it too much to ask for? Can we create a society in which people can have that depth and inner glow without relying on things like traditional Catholicism?

And more people like Jonas—but whose inner depths are met and whose kind, soft souls are allowed to productively manifest in the world.

The technological and economic development of the world (and the multi-dimensional crisis-revolution) requires of us that we grow within all four dimensions: complexity, code, state and depth.

But if I had to choose one, I would go with state. We need to, above all, improve the subjective states of all humans. It is the only dimension that is ethically unproblematic to wish for people. If we want to make them "more complex" or the like, it implies we want to change them to suit the needs and demands of others. But higher state just means we wish each other well. And it is more volatile; hence easier to affect. A happier world is probably a saner world. It should be possible, I believe, to let high states and loving embraces of life encompass many more of us, more of the time.

But for that to be possible, we need to begin to take a metamodern perspective on reality and on politics. We need a group of people—a metamodern aristocracy—who are complex thinkers, who never resort to magic beliefs *or* reductionism, and who are moved by a profound inner depth, who can work transnationally and work to create a more listening society, and who can treat all of the other value memes with kindness and respect.

A lot is at stake.

In case you still don't get it

DEVELOPMENT MATTERS

> "Ground Control to Major Tom
> Ground Control to Major Tom
> Take your protein pills and put your helmet on
> Ground Control to Major Tom (ten, nine, eight, seven, six)
> Commencing countdown, engines on (five, four, three)
> Check ignition and may God's love be with you (two, one, liftoff)"

Am I getting through to you? Or are you lost to outer space like David Bowie's Major Tom? Here's my message: **Development is real and it matters**. Humans develop through a series of stages—albeit in a tricky, complex and often seemingly contradictory manner. But underneath the confusion is a relatively simple set of progressions, an elegant simplicity.

Our ability as a society to support the growth into higher stages is not only an ethical imperative—as our current societies are full of inexcusable suffering—but a requirement for our emerging global society to thrive and survive.

The main idea of metamodern politics is to create **a listening society** that mitigates the suffering of "normal" life and uses a wide range of social technologies and political strategies to support the psychological growth of all citizens.

It is not a simple thing to do. But why aren't we even starting a conversation about how it can be done? As a society, we do all sorts of difficult things: vaccinating everybody, guaranteeing schooling, keeping the airplanes flying, inventing new ways to use the internet. Is it really beyond our ability to create institutions that support our happiness and development?

Higher Stage Populations

The reason that the Nordic countries have developed in a progressive direction is simply that Nordic people have had better opportunities to do so. As my friends discuss in another book, *The Nordic Secret*, this was *the explicit plan* of the founder of Swedish Social Democracy, Hjalmar Branting. But the Nordic countries are only now beginning to show significant percentages of populations at the Postmodern and Metamodern value memes. And the postmoderns still vastly outnumber the metamoderns, which is a problem. If things go poorly, the countries might lose their unique position and stagnate—or even regress.

What then is the difference between having a developed population and not having one? On an individual level, it doesn't really make much difference: A person can be happy and productive at any value meme. The issue here is that bigger, more complex civilizations with access to more powerful technology require people to be at higher effective value memes in order to be sustainable. Just consider the difference between a modern, a postmodern and a metamodern population as presented in the table below.

Modern	Postmodern	Metamodern
* Doesn't care that much about the environment	* Cares a lot about the environment	* Has sustainability as an integrated part of their thinking in all matters of life
* Thinks of all pre-modern people as stupid and superstitious	* Takes a relativist stance and embraces multiculturalism	* Thinks that you must integrate the perspectives of all earlier stages, but not let the earlier stages gain power
* Has no real conception of animal rights, focuses only on humans	* Includes all animals in the circle of solidarity	* Includes both animals and the perspectives of those who don't believe in animal rights
* Is meritocratic	* Thinks that power structures oppress people and hold them back	* Thinks that you have to improve the quality of human relationships
* Thinks that society will be fine if we continue along our current path and develop further	* Thinks that society is rotten and must be morally purified	* Thinks that society is under-developed and that steps must be taken to help us develop psychologically

Think about it. How do you imagine a global society of some seven billion will do best, if a majority of people are modern (or pre-modern), or if they are post- and metamodern? Consider these issues:

- Which population would create more stable markets?
- Which would be best at ending animal slavery (the worst crime in the history of our planet)?
- Which one would create a softer, more inclusive society for people of all cultures and value memes?
- Which would be best at ecological sustainability?
- Which would be likely to use its economic resources most efficiently, if the goal is to create human and animal happiness?
- Which population is most likely to use the incredible forces of nanotech, AI and bioengineering responsibly?
- Which one would be most efficient at combating inequality and poverty, both relative and absolute?

These are the major issues of our time. And they simply cannot be solved by people working from the modern value meme. The modern value meme didn't evolve for the purpose of maintaining a super-productive, environmentally monstrous, hyper-connected, hyper-mobile mega-civilization of seven-going-on-nine billion people, spanning across all world cultures and across all value memes. It just didn't, and it just can't. None of the modern positions—being leftwing or libertarian or conservative—make much difference. It's like having a rotten-egg sandwich, but you get to choose the bread. As things are looking today, dear Major Tom, I'm afraid we're going for a global crash landing.

We need to stimulate psychological development in millions of our fellow citizens. That's one of the main reasons we need a listening society. Whereas we cannot know exactly how to spur the growth into higher value memes of a population, we *can* know for certain that it is doable.

Otherwise—how could Sweden's population have much higher average effective value meme than the US population, which is in turn much higher than India's average population? And how come the value memes of these populations emerged in historical sequence—from traditional, to modern, to postmodern, to metamodern? Why were there no queer feminist vegans in the 1800s?

It is quite apparent that a safe, efficient and technologically advanced society which takes care of its citizens seems to spur growth into higher value memes. But the goals of society are *themselves* cast in terms of value memes. People of the former value meme are unlikely to share the goals of people of a later value meme. And increasing the average value meme only becomes a societal goal if you are at metamodern yourself.

The postfaustian mind doesn't *want* society to become a modern, rational and borderless marketplace. The modern mind doesn't *want* queer feminism, bike paths, animal rights, lower material consumption, decoupling of work and money, basic income or yoga and mindfulness. And the postmodern mind doesn't *want* a society in which postfaustians and moderns feel welcome and that is deliberately geared towards supporting people's growth into the metamodern stage.

Development always sneaks up on you. It always comes non-linearly. The postfaustian societies of the past didn't expect to be overtaken by moderns. In fact, they fought fiercely to defend their symbolic universe against modernity. The moderns didn't expect to be taken over by pomos, who suddenly seem to control all the universities and large parts of the arts and media. And the pomos don't like it *one bit* when metamodernism shows up and tells them that they're not being anywhere nearly as inclusive, critical and multiperspectival as they thought they were.

The mainstream modernists can't really tell the difference between the postmodern and the metamodern. But the metamodernists are still a bit less annoying than those postmodern hipster snobs and creepy yoga hippies (because the metamodernists have solidarity with the modern perspective).

The same goes for postfaustians—they don't like moderns or postmoderns (and can't really tell the difference between them), whereas the metamodernists can talk about religion, nationality and spirituality on their terms (without antagonizing them too much). So the metamoderns are somewhat preferable even to the postfaustians.

By and large, the metamodern position is closer to all of the others than they are to one another. This makes it a quite powerful position.

Why the Postmoderns Cannot Save the World

To the pomos, the metamodern revolution looks like something that crawled straight out of hell. Suddenly, it's all back: hierarchies and developmental models and *grandes histories* and social engineering—even spirituality.

Except this time, you keep losing the arguments. Every time you attack this obvious evil, *you* end up being the bad guy. When you say that they are hierarchical, they admit it and say that if you *don't* accept hierarchies, you are being judgmental yourself. When you tell them they are accommodating hillbilly racists, they say that hillbilly perspectives cannot be excluded and that you are attacking them from a position of greater cultural capital, a position of privilege. (Besides, if you despise hillbillies and mainstream whites but not the same positions within other communities, you are implicitly downgrading other ethnicities, as whites are seen as more morally responsible than minorities.) When you accuse them of excusing capitalism, they point out that they are better at creating an alternative than you have been (see my other book, *Outcompeting Capitalism*). When you say that they are deterministic, crude developmentalists, they answer with empirical evidence and note that if you're *not* a developmentalist you can't say why feminism and animals rights would be better than mainstream capitalism. When you say that they are being mystical and "new agey", they point out that your own position is based upon beliefs that cannot be proven, and that you are excluding and degrading minorities if you devalue all their spiritual experiences. When you tell them that their developmental view is elitist, they point out that a vast majority of the population feels extremely alienated by your own values, but that metamoderns at least allow for a developmental path that leads to their own position. When you say they don't oppose patriarchy, they point out that patriarchy is context dependent and so you cannot categorically hate it. When you rage against the machine and neoliberalism, they point out that you are being essentialist, ascribing inherent qualities to complex phenomena that couldn't possibly have an "inner essence". When you say that they are not egalitarian enough, they point out that you have an elitist, narrow conception of equality. When you say that they think they have the one truth, they say that their developmental model implies that there are yet higher value memes, which your own model does not. When you say they are obsessed with development, they point out that development is always messy, context bound and problematic and that your only alternative seems to be moralism.

Being confronted with metamodernism is an extremely frustrating experience for the postmodern mind. People so much want to believe that they themselves are the good guys. But when faced with a higher effective value meme, you are beaten on your own terms.

It is, admittedly, tempting to gloat at the painful confusion that this can cause people who hold opinions and perspectives differing from our own. Postmodernists have shown very little mercy against the modern mainstream people these last few decades: Using all manner of judgmental shaming strategies and political correctness to make people comply with moral causes like gender equality, anti-racism and animal rights.

Note, however, that the real difference between postmodernists and metamodernists is that the latter have solidarity with the perspectives of others. Hence, unlike the postmodernists, the metamodernists don't judge people for their opinions. And so, they will understand that a normal postmodern person has struggled all her life to find some meaning and a moral compass in this dark world. And now that she has finally found it, and uses it to serve her conscience, some strange person shows up and takes it away from her—leaving her alone and confused in a world of darkness, where evil can and will reign. (Or that's what it feels like.)

And *because* the metamodern mind can see that, because she takes responsibility for and cares about people working from all perspectives, she is superior to the postmodern mind. She doesn't judge capitalist society, or conservative Christians, or even the terrorist bombers. She sees that only by understanding their perspectives—and synthesizing them so that they can work together, or at least find less destructive outlets—can you affect their behaviors. And she doesn't judge the postmodern, but has solidarity with her.

Because the fact is, for global society to become genuinely peaceful, non-exploitative, sustainable and free from animal slavery, you would need a solid majority of the world population at the Postmodern value meme. Since that isn't going to happen anytime soon—perhaps not for another century—**our society can and will crash if people don't actively and consciously manage all of the existing value memes: from animistic to metamodern**.

And since the Postmodern value meme doesn't admit the existence of value memes—and believes that all will be fine if you go on "fighting patriarchy" and "explaining abolitionist animal rights" and "curbing racism" or "crushing global capitalism" or "creating a movement of protestors" or "criticizing society's power structures" or making more casual words and expressions taboo—they simply cannot productively manage the other value memes.

The postmoderns end up alienating a vast majority of normal modern people, making them feel confused, insulted and frustrated. And once that has gone on for a long while, the majority revolts and begins voting with Trump and the nationalists. Non-postmodern people begin to feel a subtle sense of revenge when somebody speaks out against political correctness.

The Metamodern value meme can and will manage people of lower value memes, finding ways to include them in more productive manners. This is what the postmoderns cannot do. Nor can they devise a plan for increasing the effective value meme over a few decades.

So the Metamodern value meme is here to stay. It is just a fact of life that the different value memes cannot really be friends. After all, each value meme is defined precisely opposing its predecessor.

But again—why can't we just stay at postmodern? After all, things were so nice. We were the good guys; anarchists, communitarians, multiculturalists, environmentalists, vegans, queer feminists, inter-faith dialogue people, volunteering activists, creative industries workers who gave much of our income to charity. Why can't we just keep doing our thing?

Because it doesn't work, that's why. Most people are of other value memes, and they really don't want what you want. And because you cannot get most people on board, because you confuse, alienate and even disgust them, they won't cooperate. They won't buy your framework. Did you ever notice that most people just don't care about your activism? They really don't care about you.

Postmoderns cannot save the world. Certainly not Noam Chomsky. The poor old man, for all his intelligence and kindness, is profoundly deluded. Noam Chomsky is profoundly deluded. The world doesn't work the way he says it does. Not even Bono can save us.

What can? The metamodern value meme. And how? By means of creating a listening society; one that can bring a majority of people to the Postmodern value meme, and a solid percentage to the Metamodern value meme—perhaps even more than two percent of the population. We can develop both code, state and depth. It remains to be seen to what extent cognitive complexity can be extended in a human population.

But since there are currently no metamodern governments in the world, nobody's expending time and resources to find out. Which might be a problem.

The Great Stretching Out

The new game of life looks a lot like this: Whoever has mastered the most perspectives when she dies, wins.

Just looking at the world today, the great stretching out in terms of value memes is apparent. As more people become modern, more become postmodern, and more become metamodern. You have a greater variety of value memes—interacting through the global markets, across cultural and linguistic barriers, often through the internet—than ever before in history.

You have postmodern young Western women, walking down the streets of Calcutta, wondering why the postfaustian and poverty-stricken

Indian men stare at them. (Because, in their social universe, the freely moving young woman makes very little sense and it creates a both intensely alluring and deeply frustrating feeling, one that nags their very sense of reality.) You have internet organizations gathering young men—who would rather have lived Viking lives—into dangerous rebel and terrorist groups. You have modern South Koreans who try to brag with how hardworking and materialist they have become to Westerners who have already begun to take up post-materialist values, and find their own wealth and privilege embarrassing. Walking down the same street, passing one another, is the Roma old woman with three years of schooling, the materialist-reductionist modern businesswoman, the postmodern linguistics professor who views reality as deeply tied up with meanings, and the metamodern hacker, who sees the world as potentials of evolving perspectives in an increasingly virtual reality.

We are living in the age of **the great stretching out**. Never before has there been such intense and close contact between so many different value memes. Not only that: The interactions work across all stages of complexity, symbolic codes, inner states and levels of depth.

Do you really think that a modern perspective, just defending science and the individual, will cut it? Will it successfully manage all of these different lived experiences and their interactions?

And will an endless onslaught of postmodern political correctness make all of these perspectives function well together? Modernism and postmodernism might take us some way along the road. But neither can lead us all the way to the next stage of our society—to one where the major problems of modern life have largely been resolved.

The great stretching out means that the different value memes begin to compete more openly. The metamodernists may be outnumbered, for obvious reasons, but they are also the most developed and privileged group. Hence, their values are likely to win out in the long run.

There is a clear tendency towards increased cooperation for each value meme you climb. If you look at the faustians, these tend to not cooperate with one another beyond clans and gangs. Postfaustians cooperate with other postfaustians who share their own faith, but view postfaustians of other faiths with suspicion (e.g. traditional Christians vs. Muslims). Moderns tend to overlook religious differences but can't get along across different ideologies (being Left or Right, etc.). Postmodernists seem to get along more, but they are always divided into the light pomos (yoga bourgeoisie and so on) and dark pomos (critical intelligentsia), which means that they have problems organizing themselves. The anarchist Left is always split into so many fractions and factions.

Metamodernists define themselves through the struggle of value memes against value memes: It's not if you're Right or Left that matters the most, but how complex your thinking is. Hence they can work across religions, political ideologies and different developmental profiles (light vs. dark) as long as their interests are defended against the interests of the other value memes. And they are less appalling to all the other value memes than these are to one another (i.e postfaustians despise metamodernists a little less than they do postmodernists, etc.).

So what you get is a tendency towards a deliberate organization of the Metamodern value meme. The metamodern forces in the world are likely to have more influence than their share of the population would suggest. And in "the great stretching out", the world needs metamodernists to find one another and organize—so that they can work for the creation of a more metamodern world, a listening society in which everyone is seen and heard.

The paradox is just that people of the other value memes really don't want a metamodern society. We will have to start living by such paradoxes. Value memes cannot be friends.

Development Matters

This lands us back in the idea of a metamodern aristocracy. If the map I have proposed is indeed functional—and it is—the people who navigate the world with its help can and will gain great competitive advantages over others.

But of course, there are many pieces of the puzzle. One such piece is the process oriented party, like The Alternative in Denmark and some other interesting movements around Europe. Another piece is the fundamental shifts within the political landscape of the Nordic countries—and perhaps corresponding developments in other countries—where the old political paradigms are losing their meaning. These are transpersonal developments; many pieces that come together in creating new patterns in the world.

We have developments within the arts, radical new technological possibilities, and progressive business hubs around the world that are hooking up in a giant global network that works transnationally according to logics and interests that lie far beyond the modern nation state. We are approaching a new stage of society where new rules apply. The people who understand these new rules first will play central parts in shaping society in the coming period.

A lot of people won't believe in the map and get along fine without it. But these people will, on average and over time, be outcompeted by the ones who do recognize its usefulness. The ones who use the map will much more accurately predict the behaviors of others, spot the developmental trends of society, and identify the key issues and problems of the world. They will gain power.

We do not need to convince anyone. If you protect yourself from understanding for whatever reason, we will just outcompete you in the many games of politics and life.

So here we are. We're not asking nicely, because we don't have to. We just have to find one another and work together towards creating a metamodern society.

We can go ahead to create a Green Social Liberalism 2.0, working nonlinearly, co-developing ourselves towards a listening society. We go ahead with pragmatic idealism, with magical realism and informed naivety. At the crossroads of fact and fiction, we work and play with religious fervor, keeping an ironic smile at our own self-importance.

In case you still don't get it: Development matters.

Appendix

METAMODERNISM

This book has given us a brief taste of what metamodern politics might look like. In this appendix we should deepen this understanding somewhat, primarily by looking at the word "metamodernism". We are taking a look at the philosophical engine of the book.

But just to start us off *very* roughly: First you have **pre-modern** society, like in medieval Europe. Then you have **modern** society. Then you have a **postmodern** criticism of modern society. Then you have the **metamodern** society, which takes the best from modern society and postmodernism. So, remember: 1. modern, 2. postmodern, 3. metamodern. That's basically it. But for fun, let's flesh it out a bit, shall we?

Three Meanings of "Metamodernism"

The word metamodernism is basically a term that describes that which comes after modern society (and after the "postmodern" critique of it), a point in history when people begin to *see through* modern society, as well as *beyond* it; hence the word "meta". There are three versions of metamodernism, three different meanings of the term, all three of which are employed here. A smart person will sometimes use one of the three meanings distinctively, and sometimes let the meaning of the word slide somewhat, so that you can cover more than one meaning at once. Either way, there is a profound interrelatedness between the three meanings.

Meaning 1: a cultural phase. The first meaning, the most commonly used in other sources thus far, is metamodernism as a certain *cultural phase* in matters such as art, architecture, media, philosophy and politics. In this sense, metamodernism is a certain kind of "mood" or *Zeitgeist* (spirit-of-the-time). In that sense "metamodernism" is comparable to things such as the Romantic period, the Baroque, *fin de siècle*, the Enlightenment, realism or naturalism or cubism and postmodernism. If you ever studied arts, philosophy or literature you are familiar with this way of thinking in cultural phases. Each epoch has its own mood, its own vibe based on a certain cultural logic that responds to circumstances and events of the period.

Meaning 2: a developmental stage. The second meaning, which is the one primarily used in this book, is metamodernism as a *developmental stage*. This is very different from a cultural phase. The idea of a phase, like Romanticism, which came after the Enlightenment, does not say anything about which one is "more advanced" or "more developed". It simply states that this phase came after that one (for instance, because the German idealists wanted to distance themselves from French rationalism). Stage theories are different. They claim, for instance, that adulthood comes after childhood, which in turn comes after infancy, which comes after life in the womb—these stages are well theorized and empirically supported in developmental psychology. Or that industrial civilization comes after traditional, agricultural civilization, which comes after warrior societies, which come after tribal hunter-gatherer societies—each with their own corresponding form of information technology.

Stage theories make greater claims than phase theories. They hold that there is a much deeper qualitative shift between each stage and that there is a certain pattern or logic that describes the relationship between all of the studied stages, what I call a ***Realdialektik*** in chapter 10. Phases cannot be "ranked" as higher or lower, only as earlier or later. For instance, "old age" is of course a later phase than "adulthood"—but it is usually not a higher stage. There is a huge developmental stage difference between a newborn and a ten-year-old—but the same difference is not there between a 70- and an 80-year-old. In fact, in the latter case the developmental difference is more likely to be a negative one: The 80-year-old is likely to be on a lower developmental stage due to the burdens of aging.

Meaning 3: a philosophical paradigm. The third meaning is one that is not yet established, but we are trying to establish in this and later Hanzi books. It is simply a term to describe the thinking of Hanzi Freinacht and related philosophers—and the worldview and politics that come along with that philosophy. To be clear, our claim is that Hanzi's line of thinking represents a high developmental stage *and* a certain *Zeitgeist* of a new form of society that is being born. Because this line of thinking is both sophisticated and intimately connected with a wide and deep understanding of the dynamics of the new era, it is very useful for all manner of things. In this sense, metamodernism is a *paradigm*. A paradigm, as the word is used here, is a fundamental worldview with its own form of science, politics, market, culture and self-knowledge—just as the Enlightenment thinking is connected to the modern liberal democracy, capitalism (and state socialism), the individual person and modern science.

THE METAMODERN PARADIGM, CONDENSED

To give some general notes on what the metamodern paradigm entails, we can mention a list of things, here enumerated in six categories (life, science, reality, spirituality, society and the human being) and summarized somewhat pell-mell.

At the time of writing, I only expect very few people in the world to look down the following list and nod in intimate agreement. For the rest of you, feel free to bookmark these pages and come back to it in a few years. I guarantee that you will find more things on the list, see new meanings—like when you reread a book and say "I'm pretty sure this sentence wasn't here last time". But here it is; a brief outline of the metamodern paradigm. This is the conceptual engine that drives this book and where Hanzi gets his analytical edge.

METAMODERN STANCE TOWARDS LIFE

- To be exquisitely ironic *and* sincere, both at once.
- To be both extremely idealistic *and* extremely Machiavellian.
- To see that God is dead and humanism dying (humanism is the humanity-centered worldview originating in the Renaissance) and to accept and celebrate this by taking meaning-creation into one's own hands.
- To intellectually see, and intuitively sense, the intimate interconnectedness of all things: "The universe in a grain of sand."
- To accept and thrive in the paradoxical, self-contradictory, always incomplete and broken nature of society, culture, and reality itself.
- To have a general **both-and perspective**. But note that it is not *either* "both-and" *or* "either-or"—rather, it is *both* "both-and" *and* "either-or". In each case, it is still possible to have well-argued preferences:
  - both political Left *and* Right (*and* neither one!);
  - both top-down *and* bottom-up governance;
  - both historical individuals *and* social structures;
  - both objective science *and* subjective experience;
  - both cooperation *and* competition;
  - both extreme secularism *and* sincere spirituality.
- To accept and thrive in both manifesting, systematizing philosophy (like Plato or natural science) and non-manifesting, process oriented, open-ended philosophy (like Nietzsche or critical social science).

- To recognize the impermanence of all things, that life and existence are always in a flow, a process of becoming, of emergence, immanence and ever-present death.
- To see normal, bourgeois life and its associated normality and professional identity as insufficiently manifesting the greatness and beauty of existence.
- To assume a genuinely playful stance towards life and existence, a playfulness that demands of us the gravest seriousness, given the ever-present potentials for unimaginable suffering and bliss.

METAMODERN VIEW OF SCIENCE

- To respect science as an indispensable form of knowing.
- To see that science is always contextual and truth always tentative; that reality always holds deeper truths. All that we think is real will one day melt away as snow in the sun.
- To understand that different sciences and paradigms are simultaneously true; that many of their apparent contradictions are superficial and based on misperceptions or failures of translation or integration.
- To see that there are substantial insights and relevant knowledge in all stages of human and societal development, including tribal life, polytheism, traditional theology, modern industrialism and postmodern critique. In another book, I call this the evolution of "**meta-memes**".
- To celebrate and embody **non-linearity** in all non-mechanical matters, such as society and culture. Non-linearity, in its simplest definition, means that the output of a system is not proportional to its input.
- To harbor a case sensitive suspicion against mechanical models and linear causation.
- To have "a systems view" of life, to see that things form parts of self-organizing bottom-up systems: from sub-atomic units to atomic particles to molecules to cells to organisms.[164]
- To see that things are alive and self-organizing *because* they are falling apart, that life is always a whirlwind of destruction: The only way to create and maintain an ordered pattern is to create a corresponding disorder. These are the principles of **autopoiesis**: entropy (that things degrade and fall apart) and "negative entropy" (the falling apart is what makes life possible).
- To accept that all humans and other organisms have a connecting, overarching worldview, a great story or grand narrative (a *religion*, in what is often interpreted as being the literal sense of the word: something that connects all things) and therefore accept the necessity of a

grande histoire, an overarching story about the world.[165] The metamodernist has her own unapologetically held grand narrative, synthesizing her available understanding. But it is held lightly, as one recognizes that it is always partly fictional—a **protosynthesis**.

- To take ontological questions very seriously, i.e. to let questions about "what is really real" guide us in science and politics. This is called *the ontological turn*.

METAMODERN VIEW OF REALITY

- To see the **fractal** nature of reality and of the development and applicability of ideas, that all understanding consists of reused elements taken from other forms of understanding.
- To be **anti-essentialist**, not believing in "ultimate essences" such as matter, consciousness, goodness, evil, masculinity, femininity or the like—but rather that all these things are contextual and interpretations made from relations and comparisons. Even the today so praised "relationality" is not an essence of the universe.
- To no longer believe in an atomistic, mechanical universe where the ultimate stuff is matter, but rather to view the ultimate nature of reality as a great unknown that we must metaphorically capture in our symbols, words and stories. To accept the view of a world being newly born again and again.
- To see that the world is radically, unyieldingly and completely socially constructed, always relative and context bound.
- To see that the world emerges through complex interactions of its parts and that our intuitive understandings tend to be much too static and mono-causal. This is called **complexity**. It is the fundamental principle of not only meteorology but also of social psychology, where patterns (such as the "self") emerge through the interactions of interrelated, interdependent **dividuals**.
- To accept the necessity of **developmental hierarchies**—but to be very critical and careful with how they are described and used. Hierarchies are studied empirically, not arbitrarily assumed.
- To see that language and thereby our whole worldviews travel through a much greater space of possible, never-conceptualized worlds; that language is evolving.
- To look at the world holistically, where things such as scientific facts, perspectives, culture and emotions interact (this form of interactivity is called **hypercomplexity**, because it involves not only many interacting

units, but interacting perspectives and qualitatively different dimensions of reality, such as subjective vs. objective reality).[166]

- To see that information and management of information is fundamental to all aspects of reality and society: from genes to memes to money and science and political revolutions.
- To accept an informational-Darwinian view of both genes (organisms) and memes (cultural patterns) competing to survive through a process of developmental evolution that involves negative selection (that disfavored genes and memes go extinct, but continue to exist as potentials).
- To see that Darwinian evolution depends equally on mutual cooperation and competition; that competition and cooperation are always intertwined.
- To see the dynamic interplay of the universal and the particular, where for instance humans in more complex societies become more individualized, which in turn drives the development of more complex societies where people are more interdependent and more universal values are needed to avoid collapse.
- To see that the world runs on **dialectic logic**, where things are always broken, always "stumbling backwards" as it were; that things are always striving for an impossible balance and in that accidental movement create the whole dance that we experience as reality. So the development of reality does have directionality, it's just that we are always blind to this direction; hence the metaphor of "stumbling backwards".
- To see that reality is fundamentally open-ended, broken, as it were, even in its mathematical and physical structure, as shown in Gödel's incompleteness theorem and in some of the core findings of modern physics.
- To recognize that potentials and **potentiality**, rather than facts and actualities, constitute the most fundamental or "more real" reality. What we usually call reality is only "actuality", one slice of an infinitely larger, hypercomplex pie. Actuality is only a "case of" a deeper reality, called "absolute totality".
- To explore visions of **panpsychism**, i.e. that consciousness is everywhere in the universe and "as real" as matter and space. But panpsychism should not be confused with animistic visions of all things having "spirits".

METAMODERN SPIRITUALITY, EXISTENCE AND AESTHETICS

- To take existential and spiritual matters very seriously; to view humanity, intelligence and consciousness as expressions of higher principles inherent to the universe.
- To recognize that the esoteric, spiritual disciplines and wisdom traditions East and West relate to real insights of great significance—a recognition of the importance of mysticism.
- To have a careful, unknowing and explorative mindset in matters of spirituality and existence.
- To understand that elevated, expanded subjective states relate to higher existential and spiritual truths than do most of the experiences of everyday life.
- To see that inner experience—and the direct development of the subjectivity of organisms—is crucial to all things, and is perhaps the main ingredient lacking in the perspective of the modern world; acknowledging inner experience is often the golden key to managing society's problems.
- To take philosophical, cultural and aesthetic matters very seriously, as they are seen as inherent dimensions of reality, not just "additional woo-woo" on top of physics.
- To create art and architecture that allude to the depth and mystery of existence, without putting it "in your face" or trying to tell you what to think or what is real.
- To support a democratic, intersubjective, participatory, scientifically supported, peer-to-peer created spirituality, rather than traditional paths, teachers, gurus or authorities.
- To see that both a spiritual and non-spiritual life experience and worldview are fundamentally okay. Spirituality and non-spirituality: Neither is inherently better than the other.
- To understand that people are fundamentally crazy, that our everyday consciousness is not a sane reflection of reality, but a bizarre, psychotic hallucination that is utterly contingent, made up and arbitrary.
- To intuit that the central spiritual and existential insight is the perfection of absolute totality as it always-already is; that there is a pristine, serene clarity underneath all the chaos and contradiction; that there is an underlying elegance even in the often tragic, hell-like experience of life; hidden, as it were, in plain sight. This can be called the recognition of "basic goodness".

METAMODERN VIEW OF SOCIETY

- To see no fundamental divide between nature and culture.
- To see that we live in a new technological era (the information age), and that human societies evolve through different developmental stages for better or worse.
- To believe that history has some kind of directionality based on logic, but that this directionality can never be certainly known, only metaphorically and told as a story—playfully and purposefully.
- To believe that we can always synthesize the knowledge we have about society to some kind of overarching narrative, a **meta-narrative**, but that this metanarrative is never taken to be a complete synthesis, but rather always a self-critically held, but necessary **protosynthesis**.
- To have a **nomadic** view of social life; knowing that our "self" is part of a social flow, a journey—and that we are becoming more tribal and nomadic in the internet age with our virtual identities.
- To celebrate participatory culture and co-creation of society through non-linear, interactive *processes* where the whole is more than the sum of its parts.
- To see the importance of **collective intelligence** (not to be confused, as it unfortunately often is, with collective consciousness, often associated with Carl Jung, etc., which is not part of the metamodern paradigm). Collective intelligence is simply the ability of a group or society to solve problems and respond to collective challenges.
- To understand that technology is not neutral, not just "a tool in our hands", but that it adopts its own agenda and logic, shaping and steering history.
- To see sustainability and resilience as fundamental questions to all social life.
- To see that sexuality and sexual development are a widely overlooked centerpiece in the mainstream understanding of all human societies. Sexuality has extraordinary explanatory, behavioral and predictive power.
- To see "everyday life" as something that humanity can and should transcend in favor of a more actual and authentic form of life and community.
- To take the rights and lived experience of *all* animals very seriously, human and non-human. Human society is just a cognitive category, and this category can just as well include all cultures, all deep-ecological entities (ecosystems, biotopes) and all sentient beings.

METAMODERN VIEW OF THE HUMAN BEING

- To see that humans are behavioral, organic "robots", controlled by our responses to the environment, *and* that we are simultaneously subjective, self-organizing and alive—beings of great existential depth.
- To see that my identity and "self" are not ultimately my body or the voice speaking in my head; or at least that my fundamental identity is *not exhausted* by that everyday conception of a self (my body plus the voice talking in my head), what is sometimes called "the ego". The ego is just an idea, an object of awareness as any other created category that describes an object.
- To adopt a **depth psychology** stance towards humanity, seeing that her consciousness is transformable by changing her fundamental sense of self and sense of reality. This is achievable through psychoanalysis (or "schizoanalysis") and love relationships as well as athletic, aesthetic, erotic, intellectual and spiritual practices—where contemplative mysticism stands out as a very valuable path.
- To see that every person has a three-dimensional view of reality of her own, consisting of an **ontology** (a strong sense of what is real), an **ideology** (a strong sense what is right) and a **self** (a strong sense of one's own place in reality)—and that these three dimensions can be described in a pattern of sequentially unfolding developmental stages.
- To see that different human organisms are at fundamentally different developmental stages and therefore display very different behavioral patterns.
- To understand the **transpersonal** view of the human being, where her deepest inner depths are intrinsically intertwined with the seemingly rigid structures of society. She is not an individual—her deeper identity reaches through and beyond the individual, the person. The "person" is just a mask, or a role, dependent on context. It is not inherent to the individual—even if the human organism can of course be described with behavioral science.
- To see that in the transpersonal perspective, individual people cannot really be blamed for anything. All moralism is meaningless. This translates to a radical acceptance of people as they are; a radical non-judgment that can also be described as a civic, impersonal and secular bid to love thy neighbor.
- To see that the human **dividual** has many layers, that she is both animal, "human" in a multiplicity of roles, and that she has higher potentials within herself—and that she is born through the interactions,

(or even **intra-actions**) of such layers within different people.[167] This has some important implications:

- The multi-layered psyche has both subconscious, conscious and supraconscious processes (where the supraconscious processes constitute higher and more subtle intelligence than our normal thoughts, such as universal love, philosophical insight, deep artistic inspiration and the like).
- The higher layers of the psyche follow more general, abstract and universal logics, whereas the lower layers follow cruder, more selfish and concrete logics. But they operate simultaneously and interact with one another.
- The multilayered nature of the dividual psyche means that we can often see unconscious and supraconscious layers in one another; we can often understand one another better than we understand ourselves. This is what makes practices such as psychoanalysis or psychiatry possible. It also means that my agency can originate from you and vice versa.
- This transpersonal perspective holds that our selves, even our bodies, are not "sealed" or "autonomous"; we develop together in one great, multidimensional network. This network follows a logic that is often largely alien to our individual thought processes and agencies.

- To acknowledge the inalienable right of every creature to be who she is.
- To have a **non-anthropocentric** view of reality, where human experience is not seen as the measure of all things.
- To accept the idea that humanity's biology and fundamental life experience can and will change through science and technology, what is called **transhumanism**.
- To stretch solidarity towards the highest possible universality: Love and care for **all sentient beings**, in all times, from all perspectives, from the greatest possible depths of our hearts.

Phew, that's a mouthful. Seventy-one bullet points and some subpoints. If you don't already know what we're talking about, it most probably sounds like a bunch of buzzwords. Some of it gives you hefty allergic reactions too, no doubt.

But it is not just buzz, as time will tell. Those who think that these are just empty phrases will be outcompeted, in so many subtle ways, by the ones who can understand their meaning and act accordingly.

ORIGINS OF THE TERM "METAMODERNISM"

Oh, where were we? Right, we said that metamodernism has three meanings: **phase**, **developmental stage** and **paradigm**. We discuss developmental stage throughout this book and the next. When it comes to the paradigm, I have chosen not to write a philosophy book, but a book about political psychology. In a way, we're doing a "show it don't tell it", by revealing some of the muscle that this new paradigm has. We're showing that metamodernism can help us solve the very real problems of society. Later on, if you are curious, we can write about the philosophy itself, expanding on the bullet points above.

Let's stay with the first meaning, then, discussing metamodernism as a cultural phase. The notion of metamodernism as a cultural phase began to seriously show up in art, architecture and academia sometime after 2000 —although the term was coined already in 1975 by Mas'ud Zavarzadeh, a critical theorist in literature and film studies.

The American writer and cultural theorist Seth Abramson (who is a bit of a friend of mine) claims that Zavarzadeh is the most important and foundational source when it comes to seeing metamodernism as a cultural phase.[168] In an academic paper, Zavarzadeh discussed a novel based on a true story. But what happens if the story is so unbelievable, yet honestly told, that it becomes fiction to the reader? Somehow, you are being ironic and sincere both at once; you have entered a new kind of literary territory. Quoting Zavarzadeh himself, as he coins the term in 1975:

> "The fusion of fact and fiction blurs the dichotomy between 'life' and 'art' and indeed such a sharp division between the two does not exist in the emerging aesthetics which I shall, for lack of a better term, call 'Metamodernist.' [In literature, metamodernism]... combines such allegedly antithetical elements as the 'fictional' and the 'factual,' 'critical' and the 'creative,' 'art' and 'life.'"[169]

So Zarvarzadeh thought of metamodernism as a kind of fusion between opposing categories of literature. Did this herald a new cultural phase?

THE DIFFERENCE BETWEEN POST- AND METAMODERNISM

As the word is used by scholars nowadays, the basic premise of metamodernism is that it comes after and completes an earlier cultural phase, called **postmodernism**. Postmodernism in turn means "that which comes after modern society". Modern society is based around beliefs in science, progress, an objective and independent reality, the individual, and so forth. "Modernism", in this sense, is the standard worldview we get in secular Western societies today (unless we happen to attend very religious schools or get liberal arts degrees at the universities, where other paradigms are dominant).

Postmodernism is a catch-all term for the ideas and cultural currents that have increasingly challenged the standard modern worldview, at least from the late sixties and onwards. But postmodernism isn't really an academic school of thought—usually when people speak of postmodernism they have in mind the French *poststructuralist* thinkers. These include Michel Foucault, Jean Baudrillard, Jacques Derrida, Roland Barthes, Jean-François Lyotard—and perhaps Americans like Richard Rorty, Daniel Bell or Frederic Jameson and Judith Butler. I am not going to try to describe postmodernism in any detail; suffice to say that postmodernism does not believe in "progress", is suspicious of grand narratives for our day and age, likes to focus on details, exceptions and peripheries, and is critical of the power and prestige that science wields in modern life.

Postmodern art (to make matters more complicated this is what people usually call "modern art")[170] can give us an intuitive sense of what postmodernism is. It is perhaps best described with the image of Andy Warhol—who, in the sense I use the term here, can be called a postmodern artist. Warhol shows us that fine art and popular culture are not so different from one another: Surfaces and appearances within contexts are all that really matter. His triptychs and paintings indicate that mundane and popular things such as images of canned tomato soup or Marilyn Monroe repeatedly drowned in shrieking colors can also be fine art—because there is really nothing behind the curtains, no depth or secret to reveal, nothing "special" about the artist and his artwork. Postmodernism sees through all such illusions. There is only surface. And you can play with these surfaces in irreverent ways: Pablo Picasso squeezes several dimensions and multiple perspectives into the same two-dimensional frame—and the *pastiche* becomes increasingly popular. Pastiche is the mixing of different styles, fashions or epochs in surprising and often ironic ways.

In early forms, postmodern thought first showed up in late 19th century literature: You may remember the wizard of Oz, who, upon being revealed as a fraud, points out to Dorothy that he's not a bad man—only a bad wizard. Or Lewis Carroll's *Alice in Wonderland*, in which the stupefying dialogues reveal the absurd and contingent nature of speech and language. Surface, context, absurdity.

Postmodernism is closely related to such things as relativism, social constructivism and a kind of cynicism that comes from seeing many different perspectives, with no longer being a naive believer in religious, political or even scientific movements. Postmodernism is interested not so much in what is true, in what should be done, but rather in questioning everything, in picking things apart, *deconstructing* them, to make us think again, to make us less sure, to make life harder for those who would control or manipulate others: the politicians, the media moguls, the scientists and the medical professionals. To the postmodern mind, the goal is to reach an *anti-thesis*—the critique or criticism of the existing is what counts as a real result; not to give answers but to refute old answers and dwell on new questions.

Whereas postmodernism, in some vague proto- form, appeared in arts and philosophy already during the 19th century, and prospered in the arts and literature in the early 20th century, it was clearly formulated only in the 1960s and 70s—and it became a powerful academic trend in the 80s and 90s. Sociologists remarked, however, that the rest of society was hardly "postmodern" in the ways that the French theorists had described—which is why other epoch labels such as "late modernity" and "second modernity" were tried out to describe the period.[171] Only now, in the age of internet and social media, are we approaching a time which can truly be described as postmodern—where surface truly is everything, and where everything becomes a cut-and-paste collage, an endless pastiche.

But history is always on its way—we never seem to catch it. So while society in the rich parts of the world is finally becoming postmodern, the philosophers and cultural theorists are already spotting the next tendency: metamodernism.[172]

Metamodernism, the word, is a silly adaptation in a way. "Meta" means "after" in old Greek, just like "post" does in Latin—so it's the same word as postmodernism, basically. But the connotations are different. The "meta" prefix brings to mind such things as "meta-discussion", i.e. a discussion about the discussion and "meta-theory", which is theory about theories. So the metamodern cultural phase somehow brings with it a bird's eye on modern life and it begins to reflect more deliberately upon it, to try to shape it.

Meta is often taken to mean *above*, or *beyond*—and sometimes both of these. Metamodernism as a cultural phase is what comes after postmodernism, but it does so by being *more* postmodern than postmodernism itself—just as the postmodernism of the 1980s was more secular and disenchanted than the modernist mindset itself.

In a now famous 2010 paper, the two Dutch art theorists Timotheus Vermeulen and Robin van der Akker described a trend in art and architecture they had spotted in recent years—a trend they called metamodernism. Art, architecture and to some extent popular culture, are coming out of their cynical, ironic, critical postmodern phase with manifestations of abstract art and comedy such as *The Simpsons*, *Family Guy* and *South Park*. Postmodernism was antithetical to a lot of what the modern age had brought; it was concerned with being an *antithesis*, with questioning what we take for granted.

Metamodernism instead sees itself as a synthesis of modernism and postmodernism—or rather, a *protosynthesis*, (a "proto"-synthesis because it acknowledges that whatever story we tell ourselves, it must be inconsistent and temporary).[173] As Vermeulen and van der Akker write, metamodernism "oscillates" between modernism and postmodernism. To oscillate means to move back and forth like a wave—you may remember the word from physics class. I'd best quote Vermeulen and van der Akker (it's a bit academic):

> "Ontologically, metamodernism oscillates between the modern and the postmodern. It oscillates between a modern enthusiasm and a postmodern irony, between hope and melancholy, between naïveté and knowingness, empathy and apathy, unity and plurality, totality and fragmentation, purity and ambiguity."[174]

Ontology is a word for what you believe about reality, about what is "really real". So when Vermeulen and van der Akker claim that metamodernism oscillates "ontologically", they mean to say that the metamodernist artists adopt a new view of reality itself. In this view you are both a modern believer in science and progress, and a skeptical, ironic critic of your own naive belief.

We will not go farther into the analysis of art and architecture that these authors present with a rich array of examples. Basically, metamodernism is keeping the postmodern suspicion of progress and "grand narratives" (science, socialism, etc.) but bringing in the modern hope and sense of direction through the backdoor, as vaguely suggested open potentials.

Vermeulen and van der Akker are chiefly leftwing intellectuals like most people of their brand, and they link this new trend to a wider hope in political renewal, critique of capitalism (or neoliberalism), etc. Their paper spurred considerable attention and there is a blog named after it, *Notes on Metamodernism*, with many different intellectual contributors. We should mention one: Luke Turner, an art scholar, who had the Hollywood star and scandalous polymath artist, Shia Laboef (of the *Transformers* movie, you know those giant robots, and dancer in Sia's music video for *Elastic Heart*), figuring as author of the 2011 *Metamodern Manifesto*. This text outlines some of the principles of this artistic and cultural current. The manifesto proposes such ideas as **informed naivety**, **magical realism** and **pragmatic romanticism**—all of which you can probably see traces of in this book.

When we speak of metamodernism as a cultural phase, as a *Zeitgeist*, it is possible to make the argument that it shows up in all manner of present day contexts—that many of the current day events are "metamodern phenomena". Note, again, that this is not how the term is mostly used in this book.

But note also that what we said about postmodernism holds true of metamodernism: The fact that there were some French theorists writing about it did not mean that society as a whole was suddenly "postmodern". These people were ahead of their time, and their analyses were certainly rushing things. In a corresponding manner people who think we today live in a metamodern age, are precocious and ahead of their time. If they study today's society instead of working out the philosophy inherent to a metamodern perspective, they risk mistaking late or extreme forms of postmodernism for metamodernism. But metamodernism is qualitatively very, very different from postmodernism: It accepts progress, hierarchy, sincerity, spirituality, development, grand narratives, party politics, both-and thinking and much else. It puts forward dreams and makes suggestions. And it is still being born.

Some societal phenomena of our day and age *could* be described as metamodern ones, because they require a metamodern mindset to understand and respond correctly towards. Take ISIS (the Islamic State). Can it be seen as part of the metamodern *Zeitgeist*? To really understand what is going on with ISIS, why it emerged with such force, you must be able to understand the logic of a globalized information society in which sincerity and irony merge.

Although ISIS is hardly run by people at the metamodern stage of development, its very occurrence is, in a way, a metamodern phenomenon—its rise pertains to the logic of a globalized, online society and its *developmental* pathologies. Viewed from this perspective metamodernism is, as Seth Abramson has observed, the dominant, underlying cultural logic of the internet age. But that cultural logic has yet to come fully into play.

Bringing a New Metamodernism into Being

What I am doing in this book (and its sequel) is something that is closely related to cultural theory, but still quite different. I share much of the analysis of these different scholars of metamodernism (whose works, to be fair, I have presented in a simplified manner). But I also add a few things that I believe they would hardly appreciate. I think these scholars are right in their analysis, by and large, and I share their spirit. But they fall short; their project doesn't really land us in hope and pragmatic idealism. It doesn't really take modern society into its hands and look beyond it, towards what comes after.

I commend these thinkers as scholars, but I denounce them as small spirits and yellow cowards. They are too careful, too critical of themselves, too afraid of putting forward visions of progress and development. They are too wary of evoking existential or spiritual faith. They are, in a sentence, not sufficiently sincere in their sincerity—or, indeed, ironic enough in their irony. This lands them in late or extreme forms of postmodernism, rather than making them authentically metamodern.

In Hanzi Freinacht's version of metamodernism, we are not contented with viewing metamodernism as a cultural phase. There is also the developmental stage dimension (that people and societies develop to a metamodern stage, according to adult development psychology, etc.), a general philosophical dimension (the paradigm I outlined above) and, which is the main focus of this book, a *political* dimension—a certain analysis of our time which points to how society is evolving and how we as a society can and should reasonably proceed, a vision of what politics we need.

I am hereby stealing the term "metamodernism" from its original context, and adding *more* meaning to it. Like all wild things, information must be free. And one of the most metamodern phenomena, if we use the term as a cultural phase again, is the piracy of symbols for idealistic purposes. Metamodernism is being shanghaied.

When I found it, the thing called "metamodernism" was a cute little obsession for academic conferences and art expositions, perhaps a source of inspiration for architects and filmmakers. When I am done with it, you have a powerful, effective ideology that can save societies from collapse and dramatically improve the lives of millions—a stream of thought that can outcompete and replace liberal democracy and capitalism.

If you believe me when I'm saying that, you are either a naive fool, or you may be starting to finally get a hang of this "magical realism" thing.

Notes

[1] For a thorough discussion about the ethics and complications of sex with students, see Bruce, M. & Steward, R. M., 2010: *College Sex: Philosophers With Benefits.* Oxford: Wiley-Blackwell.

For a discussion concerning psychedelic drugs, see Harris, S., 2011: *The Moral Landscape: How Science Can Determine Human Values.* New York: Free Press.

[2] See Foster, J. G., Rzhetsky, A. & Evans, J. A., 2015: Tradition and innovation in scientists. *American Sociological Review,* Volume 80, pp. 875-908.

[3] It is also a fact that "scientific credibility" is socially constructed; that appearances matter very much when it comes to what we believe in. During the last years, we have increasingly seen a scientific critique of science itself. For instance, it has become apparent from one study that less than half of the psychology papers published in major academic journals rely upon replicable results (Open Science Collaboration, 2015: Estimating the reproducibility of psychological science. Science, 349(6251), pp. 943-53)

Except that study was *also* shown to have major flaws by an even more recent article in *Science*; see Gilbert, D., et al., 2016: Comment on "Estimating the reproducibility of psychological science". *Science,* 351 (6277), pp. 1037-38.

Similar critiques have surfaced within medical science; see: Begley, C. G. & Ellis, M. L., 2012. Drug development: Raise standards for preclinical cancer research. *Nature,* Volume 483, pp. 531-33.

[4] No, I don't believe in the existence of souls. I use the word mainly metaphorically. Read the rest of the book and you'll get the hang of it.

[5] This is according to the Human Rights Watch World Report 2015, see under Egypt.

[6] Yes, the Nordic countries seem to be the most stable societies to date. See *The Fragile State Index 2016*, a report published by the non-profit *Fund For Peace.*

[7] No, I don't believe in the existence of gods. I use the word mainly metaphorically. Read the rest of the book and you'll get the hang of it.

[8] According to the 2016 Global Peace Index Report, Sweden is the 14th most peaceful country in the world. Iceland is number one and Denmark number two.

[9] Or actually it is not quite the whole story. There were also small elites, corresponding to what I in this book call "the metamodern aristocracy", such as the founder of the social democratic party Hjalmar Branting, who was deeply influenced by the German romantic idealists. My friends Lene Andersen and Tomas Björkman are writing a book about it, titled *The Nordic Secret.*

[10] I have also elaborated upon the concept of post-materialism (here meaning that people in developed economies tend to adopt more emphasis on cultural, non-material political issues), criticizing Inglehart for confounding pre-materialism (in

religious, traditional countries) with post-materialism (in secular, rich, liberal postindustrial countries).

[11] For now, we're just using the word "modern"—but as you will see, we are really talking about a progression from traditional, to modern, to postmodern, to metamodern values.

[12] Easterlin, R. A., 1974: Does economic growth improve the human lot? some empirical evidence. In: P. A. David & M. W. Reder, eds. *Nations and Households in Economic Growth: Essays in Honor of Moses Abramovitz.* New York: Academic Press.

[13] Stevenson, B. & Wolfers, J., 2008: Economic growth and subjective well-being: reassessing the Easterlin Paradox. *Brookings Papers on Economic Activity,* pp. 1-87.

[14] Post-materialism meaning that people value lovemaking more that cars, not to be confused with "postmaterialism" as a strand of philosophical thought connected to posthumanism, postconstructivism, Bruno Latour and the like.

[15] In fact, this narrative of post-materialism offers a good answer to the old 20th century debate between Left intellectuals, who believed economic demand would be saturated as the economy grew, and (libertarian) Right economists, like Friedrich von Hayek, who believed this was nonsense and that demand would keep growing with economic output. So far it has appeared as though the latter group were right, but now we have reason to reconsider, at least in part; rising post-materialism means that the market demand changes *qualitatively* (meaning, people want other things, such as yoga courses and organic food) with the evolving values and psychological needs of the consumers and citizens. And that, in turn, changes the nature of the market itself.

[16] See an interesting suggestion for a reinterpretation of Maslow's model in Harrigan W. J. & Commons M. L., 2015: Replacing Maslow's hierarchy of needs with an account based on stage and value. *Behavioral Development Bulletin,* Volume 20(1), pp. 24-31.

Another discussion, and suggestions for revisiting the model, can be found in Young, G., 2015. *Development and Causality: Neo-Piagetian Perspectives.* New York: Springer, pp. 447-56.

[17] Bauman, Z., 1997. *Postmodernity and Its Discontents.* New York: New York University Press.

[18] Bauman, Z., 2000. *Liquid Modernity.* Malden, MA: Polity Press.

[19] Giddens, A., 1991. *The Consequences of Modernity.* Stanford, CA: Stanford University Press.

[20] Excuse my speceist French—bulls should not be defined by our uses of them: be tamed or "taken by the horns". They have value in and of themselves, as dividuals with their own interests.

[21] Florida, R., 2011/2014. *The Rise of the Creative Class, Revisited.* New York: Basic Books.

[22] Taub, A. "The rise of American authoritarianism". *Vox.* March 1st 2016.

[23] "Vast majority of Swedish MPs support Hillary Clinton". *The Local.* October 19th 2016. And: "Here's how many Swedes would vote for Clinton". *The Local.* October 10th 2016.

See also: "From Thailand to Denmark, Saudi Arabia to Vietnam, the world wants President Clinton". *YouGov*. November 6th 2016.

[24] Laloux, F., 2014. Reinventing Organizations: A Guide to Creating Organizations Inspired by the Next Stage of Human Consciousness. Brussels: Belgium.

[25] A good place to start is Schwab, K., 2016. *The Fourth Industrial Revolution.* Cologny/Geneva: World Economic Forum.

[26] What about conservatism? Yes, it is also included. You will get the answer in the next book, *The Nordic Ideology.*

[27] Rodriguez, T., Negative Emotions Are Key to Well-Being. *Scientific American Mind*, May 1st 2013.

[28] I realize that I am doing a straw man; few people would explicitly argue along these lines. But since many, if not most, people habitually question the idea that one should try to make society substantially happier and kindlier, often with a peculiarly intense resentment, I think that this may be how many people unconsciously feel. Remember, I sometimes speak to the rider, and sometimes to the elephant. So often people will let their elephant argue for them, only to let the rider be offended when confronted with a summary of their own positions.

[29] Calhoun, L. G., Tedeschi, R. G., 2013. *Posttraumatic Growth in Clinical Practice.* London: Routledge.

[30] Feldman Barrett, L., 2017. *How Emotions Are Made: The Secret Life of the Brain.* Boston: Houghton Mifflin Harcourt.

[31] See Fowler, J. H. & Christakis, N. A., 2008. Dynamic spread of happiness in a large social network: longitudinal analysis over 20 years in the Framingham Heart Study. *British Medical Journal*—a study in which 4739 individuals were followed from 1983 to 2003.

[32] Stineman, M. G. & Streim, J. E., 2010. The biopsycho-ecological paradigm: a foundational theory for medicine. *PM&R: The Journal of Injury, Function and Rehabilitation*, pp. 1035-45.

[33] Cripps, E., 2011. Climate change, collective harm and legitimate coercion. *Critical Review of International Social and Political Philosophy*, XIV(2), pp. 171-93.

[34] Smith, A., 1759. *Theory of Moral Sentiment.* London: A. Millar: paragraph VI.II.42 (Available at http://www.econlib.org/library/).

[35] Thaler, R. H. & Sunstein, C. R., 2009. *Nudge. Imporving Decisions About Health, Wealth and Happiness.* New York: Penguin Press.
Sunstein, C. R., 2014. Why Nudge? The Politics of Libertarian Paternalism (The Storrs Lectures). New Haven: Yale University Press.

[36] See for instance Heckman, J. J., 2006. Skill formation and the economics of investing in disadvantaged children. *Science Magazine*, 30 June, pp. 1900-1902—investments in preschoolers seem to have much greater return than e.g. job training.

[37] Kegan, R., 1994. *In Over Our Heads: The Mental Demands of Modern Life.* Cambridge, MA: Harvard University Press.

[38] This is the main issue discussed in a future Hanzi-book, a metamodern guide to the economy.

[39] Kok, B. E., Singer, T., 2016. Phenomenological fingerprints of four meditations: Differential state changes in affect, mind-wandering, meta-cognition and interoception before and after daily practice across nine months of training. *Mindfulness*, August 2016.
[40] You can find very compelling evidence presented by the British Education Endowment Foundation. Reducing class size makes some difference, but is very expensive. There are other strategies towards which we should direct our resources and attention: meta-cognition (learning to learn), feedback to students (detailed accounts about their work efforts), reading comprehension strategies, peer tutoring, collaborative group learning, homework, and more.
See www.educationendowmentfoundation.org.uk.
[41] Machado, A., 2014. Should Schools Teach Kids to Meditate? *The Atlantic*, January 27th.
[42] This is according to AMRA, the American Mindfulness Research Association.
See: https://goamra.org/resources/ (homepage viewed November 2016).
[43] Wänköö, U., 2015. Happarandas unga mår bättre. *SVT Nyheter Norrbotten*, November 27th. ["Happaranda's young are feeling better" *Swedish Television News Network.*]
[44] Nelis, D., Quoidbach, J., Mikolajczak, M., Hansenne, M., 2009. Increasing emotional intelligence: (How) is it possible? *Personality and Individual Differences*, Vol. 47, Issue 1, July 2009, pp. 36-41 .
[45] For an excellent review of the research see: Williams Woolley, A., Aggarwal, I., Malone, T. W., 2015. Collective Intelligence and Group Performance. *Current Directions in Psychological Science*, vol. 24(6) 420-24.
[46] Standing, G., 2011. *The Precariat: The New Dangerous Class.* Kindle edition: Bloomsbury Publishing Plc.
See also: Standing, G., 2014. *A Precariat Charter: From Denizens to Citizens.* New York: Bloomsbury Publishing Plc.
[47] Bourdieu, P., 1979/1992. Distinction: A Social Critique of the Judgment of Taste. London: Routledge.
[48] Beck, U. & Levy, D., 2013. Cosmopolitanized nations: re-imagining collectivity in world risk society. *Theory, Culture and Society,* Volume 30(2), pp. 3-31.
[49] According to Schubart, A major is a key suitable for "declarations of innocent love, [...] hope of seeing one's beloved again when parting; youthful cheerfulness and trust in God." Steblin, R., 2007. *A History of Key Characteristics in the Eighteenth and Early Nineteenth Century.* Rochester: University of Rochester Press: p. 127)
[50] Now, make no mistake, Vladimir Lenin was a bad guy—his actions and doctrines clearly reveal an authoritarian diversion from the libertarian and leftwing Marxism of his day (Rosa Luxemburg and others). But he was also incredibly intelligent and the Soviet Union remains, together with the USA and the first French Republic, one of the few states that were really shaped by a political-philosophical genius. "He never wrote a sentence that has any interest in itself," the American poet Ezra Pound said of Lenin, "but he evolved almost a new medium, a sort of expression halfway between writing and action." (quoted in Robin,

C.: "How intellectuals create a public". *The Chronicle of Higher Education*. January 22nd 2016).

We need something in that direction. We need to talk our way to new forms of business, new existential insights, and we need to "hack" the political discourses of different key countries so that people start acting more according to metamodern principles and ideas.

[51] As we shall discuss later, this definition of oppression is a more superficial version of a deeper argument—the informational perspective on oppression, in which oppression is defined as any short-circuited feedback process of information, hindering a self-organizing system from adjusting, going into "shooting messengers"-mode.

[52] Bard, A. & Söderqvist, J., 2012. *The Futurica Triology*. Stockholm: Stockholm Text.

[53] Urry, J., 2002. *Global Complexity*. Cambridge, UK: Polity Press.

[54] See their excellent introductory courses on www.complexityexplorer.org.

[55] Reiner, R., 1992. *The Politics of the Police*. London: Wheatsheaf.

[56] Haidt, J., 2013. *The Righteous Mind: Why Good People Are Divided by Politics and Religion*. New York: Random House.

[57] Giddens, A., 1994. *Beyond Left and Right: The Future of Radical Politics*. Stanford, CA: Stanford University Press.

[58] See the discussion about the light and dark sides of the civil sphere in Alexander, J. C., 2006. *The Civil Sphere*. New York/Oxford: Oxford University Press.

[59] Habermas, J., 1962/1992. *The Structural Transformation of the Public Sphere: Inquiry into a Category of Bourgeois Society*. Cambrige, UK: Polity Press.

[60] This could be compared to what Habermas calls "communicative action" which is discussed in Habermas, J., 1981/1984. *The Theory of Communicative Action. Volume One: Reason and The Rationalization of Society*. Boston: Beacon Press.

[61] And by the way, drug liberalization facilitates state regulation, reduces negative feedback cycles due to stigmatization and makes damage reduction easier, thereby reducing overall death tolls and psychiatric harm—but still, yes, some people that would otherwise have not used drugs, will, and while some of them may benefit, it is unavoidable that some of them will be harmed.

[62] Not literally, stupid. Be nice and non-violent.

[63] In our days, there is a growing criticism of "humanism", the dominant strands of thought that take humans and humanity as the measure of all things. People are increasingly questioning the anthropocentrism inherent to all institutions of society. Part by part, we are coming out of this prolonged period of unhealthy fixation with "humans" and "humanity". You may have come across Gary Francione's abolitionist animal rights, Corey Lee Wrenn's sociological (feminist, intersectional) development of these, or one of the many streams of posthumanist thought, perhaps Manuel DeLanda's "flat ontology", which seeks to challenge received assumptions about humanity as being "above and beyond" the rest of creation, or perhaps some of the ideas of deep ecology, from Arne Næss and Sigmund Kvaløy to people like Gary Snyder and his eco-Buddhism.

An important part of challenging humanism is to write history books that are less anthropocentric, which is the business of the discipline called "big history".

But unfortunately, even this fascinating field suffers the same destructive self-fixation. Consider Yuval Noah Harari's 2012 book on big history. Even as it includes critical perspectives on the treatment of animals, it has the title *Sapiens*.

Once the primacy of human beings and humanity has been challenged, we still need to resolve crucial issues such as prioritizing conflicting interests, choosing one path over another, and giving ethical value to different living creatures: say an amoeba and a two year old human child. When dealing with such cases, it is important to remember that the developmental hierarchies don't necessarily answer the question. As I said, they are not in themselves indicative of a moral order.

[64] The "three Ns" is an idea taken from Melanie Joy's social psychology of "carnism", i.e. the dominant ideology that legitimizes the killing and exploitation of animals.

[65] Note that we are of course speaking of humility in the face of truth and knowledge, an "epistemological humility" rather than humility as a character trait. Humility as a character trait very often translates to being subservient towards the existing dominator hierarchies. On this note, I hold that the world needs less "humility", not more. But that's another discussion entirely.

[66] The best definition of stages I have found is in a paper by a Portuguese psychologist: Lourenço, O. M., 2016. Developmental stages, Piagetian stages in particular: a critical review. *New Ideas in Psychology,* Volume 40, pp. 123-37.

Lourenço presents five properties: *hierarchy* (that stages are hierarchically ordered), *integration* (that the higher stage transcends and includes the lower one), *consolidation* (that it takes time and effort for an emerging stage to stabilize), *structuration* (that higher stages organize operations from lower ones), and *equilibration* (that the stage gravitates towards an equilibrium). This is what Lourenço defends as "strong" stage theories, where stages are clearly defined, no stage can be skipped and they logically build upon one another.

[67] Gilligan, C., 1982. *In a Different Voice—Psychological Theory and Development in Women*. Cambridge, MA: Harvard Univerity Press.

Note that Gilligan's argument can itself be challenged in different ways, notably concerning how universal reasoning her feminine stages really have in comparison to the male ones seen from a moral philosophical perspective, and concerning how ridigly people can be said to follow the gender stereotypes she suggests.

[68] There are about 22 schools of learning—which says something about why we can't delve into the field. These are: situated learning, organizational learning, experiential learning, learning styles (horrible theory, by the way), de-schooling, homeschooling/unschooling, critical pedagogy, Montessori education (overrated), experiential education, constructivism (where we should probably count as different, separate schools expressive constructionism, radical constructivism, social constructionism, Piagetian constructionism, and connectivism) expansive learning, meaningful learning, multiple intelligences (overrated), mastery learning, radical behaviorism and theological instructivism. To this list we should probably add a couple of schools that are still being established: posthumanism, integral education and Roth's integrative learning—and perhaps Deleuzian education.

And that's not mentioning the new brand of studies that are beginning to consider the practical techniques employed by good teachers in classrooms. For all its bad reputation, educational science has a glorious future.

[69] Fischer, K. & Yan, Z., 2002. The development of dynamic skill theory. In: D. Lewkowicz & R. Lickliter, eds. *Conceptions of Development: Lessons from the Laboratory*. Hove: Psychology Press, pp. 279-312.

[70] For the best comparison available between the developmental stages Fischer and others, see Tuladhar, C. H. & Commons, M. L., 2014. Correspondence between some life-span, stage theory developmental sequences of stages and level. *Behavioral Development Bulletin,* Volume 19(3), pp. 24-27.

[71] The four stages were: sensorimotor (0-2), preoperational (2-7), concrete operational (7-11) and formal operational (11-), with some substages described. Since these stages are better known in later theories, notably the MHC as described in this book.

[72] The Piagetian paradigm has had a much more profound impact on developmental psychology than most realize. As Lourenço, 2016, p. 133, writes: "There are: (a) *Piagetian* theories (e.g., Kohlberg's moral theory); (b) *neo-Piagetian* theories (e.g., Case's theory of intellectual development); (c) *post-Piagetian* theories (e.g., Commons et al.'s model of cognitive development beyond Piagetian formal operations); (d) *anti-Piagetian* theories (e.g., Perner's approach to children's theories of mind); and (e) even *neo-neo-Piagetian* theories (e.g., Bickhard's interactive model of development). We do not know of any other psychological theory that has received all five prefixes."

[73] To further complicate things, these Spiral Dynamics color codes are often used within some communities to designate different *layers* within the psyche: from grosser, animal drives of the subconscious, to the conscious processes of the thinking mind, to supraconscious layers of spiritual and existential experience. Although such layers have not been scientifically verified beyond the fact that we seem to have three major layers of the brain (reptilian brain, the limbic system and the neocortex), they have been avidly theorized throughout the history of psychology: from Freud's unconscious, ego and superego, to Kohut's three-part self-psychology, to yet more esoteric versions such as Timothy Leary's eight circuit model of consciousness. Similar models are also to be found in older esoteric traditions such as the Jewish Kabala, the yogic chakras of the Vedic mystic tradition and in present day attempts at systematizing spiritual practice, such as so-called "chaos magick". I hold that such layers are interesting, and that there is good reason to relate to them, but that they should not be confused with stages of development, even if useful parallels may exist.

[74] I owe more to Wilber than I perhaps give him credit for in this book. However, being a metamodern thinker who believes more in ideas under development than in individuals, I do not feel I owe anything to any of my inspirations. As I have said, metamodernism is idealistic piracy. Because of some of Wilber's more questionable esoteric work—and his very problematic involvements with sectarian groups and due to other issues revolving around his persona—I do not want to associate my work too closely with his. That being said, I am in some ways more Wilberian than Wilber himself, as the four dimensions of development (cognitive

development, code, state and depth) are based on a fractal application of his "four quadrant" model. I have used Wilber's thoughts more stringently than he did himself, and that is precisely what allowed me to tease out the four dimensions of development.

For those of you familiar with the Wilberian framework, my developmental model is based on a fractal re-application of the four quadrants to an individual's behavior seen in the Upper Right quadrant. Once you zoom in on the development of one individual organism, and you break the Upper Right into four new quadrants, a counter-intuitive pattern is revealed: Cognitive development becomes the Lower Right (because it's how you put behaviors into a coherent system); cultural code becomes the Upper Right (because it's the symbolic behavior that you actually display); subjective state becomes the Upper Left (because it's the subjective experience of that organism): and "existential depth" becomes the Lower Left, as it is how the organisms relates its subjective experience to a 2nd person, a "you". Again, this is counter-intuitive, which is probably why the other theorists, Wilber himself included, missed it. Don't hurry past to say I'm wrong; think it through and you will see that I am absolutely correct.

[75] The exception to this 30-year-genius rule are philosophers who generally mature in their fifties or later—although they tend to "have known" of their own genius decades in advance; it's just that developing a philosophy tends to take time. But then again, there are plenty of exceptions to the exception, from Blaise Pascal to Ludwig Wittgenstein to Simone Weil.

For all the bad things I may have to say about Gary Young's own theoretical construct and how he fundamentally misinterprets the Model of Hierarchical Complexity and squeezes cognitive stages into the same framework as the Eriksonian phases, I would still warmly recommend his authoritative textbook on adult development *Development and Causality* from 2015 (Springer Press). It is the most comprehensive and inclusive textbook to date, and his attempts to deal with both emotional and cognitive development must be seen as commendable.

[76] Yes, even income correlates with MHC stage. But this in itself does not justify income inequality—more on this in my book on the metamodern economy.

See: Miller, P. M. et al., 2015. Stage of pricing strategy predicts earnings: a study of informal economics. *Behavioral Bulletin,* p. 20(1). See also: Goodheart, E. A., Commons, M. L. & Chen, S. J., 2015. Stage of development and million dollar earnings from sales per year. *Behavioral Development Bulletin,* Volume 20(1), pp. 93-105.

[77] Gerontophilia: the (sexual) preference for the elderly.

[78] Okay, I realize the gerontophilia charges are a bit mean. It is a sympathetic and valuable part of adult development research to find out how aging can be made more psychologically productive and less painful—especially from a deeper welfare and "listening society" perspective. But the need for solace and care in the face of aging must not bring us to make sloppy analyses of developmental stages and their relationship to age. With the right distinctions made between the different dimensions of development, you will see how this problem dissolves: yes, older people are generally more mature and "wiser", but no, they are not of much higher cognitive stage, nor do they have access to more "advanced" ideas about the

world. They are of later Eriksonian phases, yes, and they have more skill and knowledge, so called "crystallized intelligence", but that is not the same as having higher stage overall.

79 If you are a meditator, you may have gone to one of S. N. Goenka's ten day *Vipassana* retreats and heard the recording of Goenka when he tells the story of a super smart Nobel Prize-winning scientist who became utterly miserable and had to go through a really tough time in his meditation training in Burma, screaming on the floor. Well, this is him, Alvarez, the inventor of the bubble chamber. Just a funny detail.

80 Most of the neo-Piagetians themselves fail to understand the vast consequences of their theory for understanding society and the world at large. Many tend to be relatively narrow researchers who don't fully take stock of the social implications of their own theoretical framework—Michael Commons and his followers being an extraordinary exception. Other, more holistic, theorists of adult development such as Cook-Greuter, Wilber and the proponents of Spiral Dynamics tend to be better at seeing how their theories impact the understanding of society. But then again, these theorists in turn tend to be lousy political sociologists. That is just another reason we need Hanzi.

81 Well, that's the long story short. There is also the phenomenon of *décalage*, i.e. the spread of an individual's performance between and even within different domains—see Bond, T., 2010. Comparing décalage and development with cognitive developmental tests. *Journal of Applied Measurement,* Volume 11, pp. 158-71.

Generally speaking, I would argue, the observed décalage is reduced when the quality of the theory and research methods are increased and important distinctions are made between different factors such as IQ, working memory, attention capacity, mental stamina, previous exposure to the task and MHC stage. The MHC tests generally show low levels of décalage, which is part of why the theory is so good.

82 Commons, M. L. & Jiang, T. R., 2014. Introducing a new stage for the model of hierarchical complexity: A new stage for reflex conditioning. *Behavioral Development Bulletin,* Volume 19 (3), pp. 1-8.
This stage was described first in 2014, pushing the numbering of all subsequent stages up by one.

83 The animal stages are from Commons, M. L. & Miller, P. M., 2003. Development of behavioral stages in animals.

The paper is available at www.dareassociation.com. Michael Commons has said, in 2016, that there are a few errors in this paper. Thus I have presented some detail differently.

84 Pepperberg, I., 1992. Proficient performance of a conjunctive, recursive task by an African gray parrot (Psittacus erithacus). *Journal of Comparative Psychology,* Volume 106(3), pp. 295-305.

85 de Waal, F. B. M. & Lanting, F., 1997. *Bonobo: The Forgotten Ape.* Berkeley: California University Press.

86 "Standard deviation" is a statistical term: the average deviation from the average (or, in the case of a function, from the function line).

[87] If you want to know, this is the stage Hanzi is at. Hanzi has high stage but is within the normal IQ range. This means that I can come up with more novel theory than almost anyone you'll ever meet, but my keen little nephew still beats me at chess.
[88] There have been speculative attempts to formulate a seventeenth stage called "Meta-Crossparadigmatic", but frankly I am not convinced, as the stage has yet to be clearly formulated and exemplified. But in theory, sure, since every stage seems to build hierarchically upon the former, there should be higher stages.
[89] Enard, W. & al, e., 2009. A humanized version of foxp2 affects cortico-basal ganglia circuits in mice. *Cell,* Volume 137(5), p. 961–971.
[90] And, yes, it is okay to speak of "psychology" in animals. If we humans have something we could loosely call psyches or "souls", so do non-human animals.
[91] The MHC stage of organisms (once they have become adults) generally follows a power function of the number of neurons, see Harrigan & Commons, 2014. This does seem to present us with a conundrum, however: how come that adult humans vary over a span of no less than seven stages? Surely, one person does not have a million times more neurons than another. Without having addressed this issue directly, Gary Young may have an interesting suggestion—namely that all of the postformal stages (the ones after stage 11 Formal) are in fact substeps of one single stage. Sara Nora Ross has suggested that stage transitions follows a fractal pattern which might support such a claim, that the human cognitive stages are somehow "packed" within a fractal of stages in a way that the MHC does not account for.

See: Ross, S. N., 2008. Fractal transition steps to fractal stages: the dynamics of evolution. *World Futures,* Volume 64, p. 361–374.

See also: Ross, S. N., 2014. Fractal model of nonlinear hierarchical complexity: measuring transition dynamics as fractals of themselves. *Behavioral Development Bulletin,* Volume 19(3), pp. 28-32.
[92] Featherston, K. G. et al., 2016. An analysis of the Verbal Comprehension Index of the Wechsler Adult Intelligence Scale—Fourth Edition (WAIS-IV) using the Model of Hierarchical Complexity (MHC): why might stage be a better measure of 'smarts' than verbal IQ?. *Behavioral Development Bulletin,* Volume 21(1).

Kyle Featherson himself (first author of above paper), however, notes in an email correspondence that the research is far from conclusive. More research needed.
[93] The first two rules were already present in Piaget. Commons added the third one (and, more recently, two more rules).
[94] Although there are, of course, neuroscientists who work from other developmental perspectives. See for instance Churchland, P., 2011. *Braintrust: What Neuroscience Tells Us About Morality.* Princeton: Princeton University Press.

And: Gazzaniga, M., 2005. The Ethical Brain: The Science of Our Moral Dilemmas. New York: Harper Perennial.

And: Damasio, A., 1999. *The Feeling of What Happens.* London: Heineman.
[95] See: Leite, S. & Barber, C. D., 2016. The neural correlates of postformal stages of reasoning: the biological determinants of behavior. *Behavioral Development Bulletin* (in print).

Leite and Barber argue "…that cognitive neuroscience studies of human intelligence should shift from the general laws that govern development and brain maturation to focusing on inter-individual differences across development, so as to complete the picture of human cognition".

[96] Barry, B. 2005. *Why Social Justice Matters*. Cambridge: Polity Press, pp. 122-24.

[97] Some readers would remark, no doubt, that I am not relating to multiple intelligences (Howard Gardner) and emotional and social intelligence (Daniel Goleman). I would here simply like to claim that MHC stage is a more solid and important model which can, if used correctly, be combined with Kurt Fischer's skill theory. Gardner's theory may still have value but has less logical coherence and certainly explains less than does the MHC.

[98] Katz, J. 1999/2001. *How Emotions Work*. Chicago: University of Chicago Press.

[99] Some readers might think that it seems unlikely that only 20% of adults could properly understand Darwin's theory when we all learn it in school. First of all, this is not my claim. Again, we are only looking at Darwinism as an example of a systematic form of understanding that emerged in the history of science. We could also have picked Adam Smith's political economy from 1776, or Marxism, for that matter.

But secondly, you might be surprised how gravely Darwin's theory is often misunderstood. Ask around and you might be surprised.

Note also, of course, that inventing the theory of evolution is a stage 15 Cross-paradigmatic task.

[100] Here is an intuitive graphic illustration of how the stages relate to one another: as going from lines to squares to cubes to 4-dimensional "hyper-cubes" to 5-dimensional "hyper-cubes" (this end note continues next page).

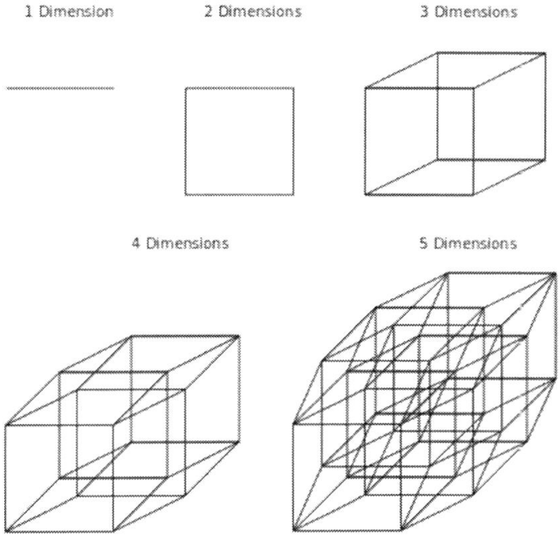

Oftentimes developmental stages are simply illustrated as a line, on which later stages are higher up. This communicates a somewhat clumsy understanding of what the different stages are like. Two markings on a straight line hardly give us any idea about just how qualitatively different each stage is from the former. It gives the false impression that a higher stage is simply "more of the same" or "farther in the same direction" as a lower one. It creates an impression that stage development is a *linear* and predictable matter (when it is in fact a matter of different equilibriums, each equilibrium creating a whole self-perpetuating eco-system of its own).

Commons himself likes to use a pyramid of interlinked boxes to illustrate how the higher stages non-arbitrarily coordinate elements from the lower ones. So the boxes all end up looking alike, which is a problem.

One attempt to solve this is by plotting the stages on an upwards expanding spiral and coloring the different parts of the spiral to symbolize that the higher stages are "wider" and have another quality to them—this is the illustration used in Beck and Cowan's Spiral Dynamics (discussed in chapter 16). This image is also problematic. First of all, you end up with something looking like a popsicle you'd feed to a five-year-old (a very colorful spiral, you can look online). Secondly, and more importantly, the model makes you **over-essentialize** the stages, as if each of them had a particular color, mood or glow.

A better illustration is to be found in space dimensions—a metaphor famously used in Edwin A. Abbott's 1884 novel *Flatland: A Romance of Many Dimensions*. The inhabitants of Flatland (the flatlanders) live unaware of the third dimension; they just can't see it. To them a sphere is only a circle. If flatlanders see a sphere passing through the plane they live on, they only see a circle that grows, then shrinks, and finally pops out of existence. To flatlanders, that is the only correct and relevant description of the sphere. But the flatlanders think linelanders are silly who don't understand squares and circles, never realizing that there is a higher dimension than theirs. In a corresponding manner, we are all flatlanders—there are always more abstract ways of seeing reality, in which our own under-standing seems to lack depth.

The point is that the earlier stages cannot see what the later stages see; they see only caricature, flattened versions of what's going on. And, what's more, they will arduously insist that their flatter version of reality is the real deal, whereas the more complex picture is unnecessarily complicated, false, mistaken—or just plain weird. For this simple reason, we seldom realize when we are being **out-com-plexed**, i.e. that someone thinks and acts with higher complexity than we do.

In more than one way, the stages discussed correspond to seeing additional dimensions in the world. It is not purely metaphorical to claim that:

- stage 9 Concrete thinking corresponds to a line;
- stage 10 Abstract to a square;
- stage 11 Formal to a cube;
- stage 12 Systematic to a 4-dimensional hypercube; and
- stage 13 Metasystematic to a 5-dimensional hypercube.

For instance, stage 11 Formal operations are required to understand Newtonian physics in 3D space, and stage 12 Systematic operations are required to be able to break away from that imagined space and understand that it is just a perspective among others.

You can see how each stage produces complexity that the earlier stage is simply unable to see or grasp. The higher stage lives in other dimensions, as it were; it works through time and space in unseen ways. For instance, with a 4D cube or "tesseract", you can always pull a new cube out of its center (as projected on a 3D "surface")—which feels quite counter-intuitive to us.

Humans tend to be able to visualize only three dimensions, which affects our understanding of all kinds of complex phenomena. And even worse—on paper sheets and screens we tend to develop theories in only two-dimensional diagrams, which simplifies and "flattens" more complex issues. In this example, only the line and the square are correctly represented on the page; all the rest is in our heads: *there is no cube*. Yet, because you understand the third dimension, you can see the cube, and turn it around before your inner gaze.

If you have seen the movie *The Matrix*, you may remember the scene where one monk-like child bends a spoon with his mind, and explains to the protagonist: *there is no spoon*. Likewise, you can see a cube on the paper, where there is none. And you can bend a cube through the fourth dimension, because "there is no cube".

The higher dimension shapes generally look weird and counter-intuitive as seen from the lower ones; they are simply not recognized for what they are. But to see them you must leave the world that feels concrete and directly present to you and travel the universe through your faculties of abstraction. Can you find the cube? You'll get a reward.

[101] Now you know the major stages. But I suppose you are still curious about the two highest ones? There are a couple of reasons that I focus less on them: they are rare, as I said, and we don't have as good research on them. Also, they fall above the range of what is relevant for us to analyze in this book, where the aim is after all to produce a useful theory for metamodern politics.

But generally speaking, most of the major theorists within different sciences tend to be at stage 14 Paradigmatic, meaning that they can put together different "metasystems" into new paradigms, entire new ways of seeing reality. How do you recognize this stage? One thing is that you, if you know a science, can study the major pioneers of your field, and how their thoughts qualitatively differ from those of others: what is special about a physicist like Richard Feynman? But here's a hint: whereas the stage 13 Metasystematic thinker produces insightful comparisons and interactions between e.g. ecosystems and the economy, her insights are only applicable at the studied level; they are not generally applicable. The insights of the stage 14 Paradigmatic thinker are of a much more **fractal** nature—you can apply them to anything and they will work again and again on ever new phenomena. That's why the stage is "paradigmatic"; it creates whole new perspectives from which you can view pretty much anything in reality, whole new paradigms. Another, perhaps simpler, way of recognizing a person at this stage is to look closely at their biography: if their life story is a long streak of inventions, original insights and discoveries, it's probably stage 14 Paradigmatic (obviously, you need reliable biographic sources; not make-believe stories about Kim Yong Il or L. Ron Hubbard). This is simply because of the large comparative advantage that people at this rare stage have over others.

When it comes to Crossparadigmatic, we already discussed John von Neumann and mentioned Isaac Newton. Here you can see theorizing that redefines reality itself. Other folks clearly at this stage are Leonardo da Vinci, Charles Darwin and Albert Einstein. But all of these also happen to be exceptional in other ways. You can be at stage 15 Crossparadigmatic without necessarily having other "super-powers"—I would suggest the contemporary physicist Max Tegmark. His work and ways of reasoning clearly reveal a stage 15 Crossparadigmatic mind, but his attempts at philosophy (a universe consisting of "mathematics") or takes on consciousness and existence are comparatively trivial (likely because he lacks a corresponding existential depth).

Why so many guys at the highest stages? Where are the girls? I'm not sure, frankly. One part might be explained by institutional sexism—that exceptionally talented women are given less attention and thereby are less known. Or maybe *I'm* just sexist, having excluded obvious examples due to my prejudices? I really can't be sure, but I'm open for suggestions. Another part might be that there really *is* a difference, with more guys represented at the highest cognitive stages for some yet unknown reason—research needed.

[102] Or why not step it up, to the professors of academia? These are most often at stages 11 Formal and 12 Systematic—whereas the concepts they operate generally come from stages 13 Metasystematic and 14 Paradigmatic theorists. So you will find all sorts of subtle but pervasive downward assimilations, where professors will spend a lifetime under the wing of a theory they reduce and misrepresent to an extent that they never quite grasp themselves.

[103] The transitional steps are:

- Reinforcement of thesis decreases
- Antithesis: Negation or complementation
- Relativism: Alternation of thesis and antithesis
- Smash: Synthesis begins
- Random hits, false alarms, and misses, low correct rejections (Smash1)
- More hits, excess false alarms (Smash2)
- Correct rejections and excess misses, low hits and false alarms (Smash3)
- Synthesis and new thesis: New temporary equilibrium.

So basically you go from one insight, to "smashing" it together with a conflicting insight, until you finally learn how to coordinate them successfully—and that's when you've advanced to a higher stage.

See: Commons, M. L. & Richards, F. A., 2002. Organizing components in combinations: how stage transition works. *Journal of Adult Development*, Volume 9(3), pp. 159-177.

See also: Ross, S. N., 2008. Fractal transition steps to fractal stages: the dynamics of evolution. *World Futures*, Volume 64, p. 361–374.

And: Ross, S. N., 2014. Fractal model of nonlinear hierarchical complexity: measuring transition dynamics as fractals of themselves. *Behavioral Development Bulletin,* Volume 19(3), pp. 28-32.

[104] Erdynast, A. & Chen, W., 2014. Relations between adult developmental conceptions of the beautiful and moral development. *Behavioral Development Bulletin,* Volume 19(4), pp. 62-75.

[105] If you read Danish, there is an interesting discussion on the topic in my friend Jesper Knallhatt's work. In his impressive series of books *Both And* named after weekdays, metamemes are discussed in "Wednesday".

[106] We mean here the grammatical categories, where 3rd person relates to he-she-it (reality, ontology), 2nd person to "you" (ideology, ethics), and 1st person to "I" (a sense of self).

[107] Cole, M., Levetin, K. & Luria, A., 1979/2010. *The Autobiography of Alexander Luria. A Dialogue With the Making of Mind.* New York: Psychology Press, pp. 79-80.

[108] Either way, if you read up on complexity theory and quantum physics, it becomes difficult to maintain a fully mechanistic determinism when it comes to complex systems like the brain and society, but that's another discussion.

[109] Note that the notion of Laplace's demon has since been more or less disproven by information theory: because the manipulation of information itself expends energy, the exact computation of all things would generate greater entropy (heat) which would render those same computations irrelevant. Hence Laplace's demon is not even possible in theory.

[110] Although they probably do not feel pain in a manner directly translatable to human experience, at least judging from research into their nervous systems.

See: Rose, J. D., Arlinghaus, R., Cooke, S. J., Diggles, B. K., Sawynok W., Stevens, E. D., Wynne C. D. L. 2012. Can fish really feel pain?" *Fish and Fisheries.*

[111] Or how about Ludwig Wittgenstein? When modern philosophy had reached the end of its rope in Bertrand Russell, who hoped to found a "scientific philosophy", he found the promising young Austrian genius engineer Ludwig Wittgenstein. This young man, an eager follower of Russell's, would soon turn this very thinking on its head. In his *Tractatus Logico-Philosophicus,* published in 1921 (but written earlier), he laid the analytical foundations for the postmodern revolt. This offers the perhaps clearest example of how advanced modern thinking pushes itself into postmodernism.

Even mathematics follows a similar pattern, as Euler and Gauss redeemed the "imaginary numbers" during the 18th century. When mathematics speaks of numbers that are entirely a product of the interrelations of symbols, you could argue, that it has taken a "postmodern" turn. Who knows, maybe there are other goldmines in mathematics that hint towards future developments of our overall symbol-stage?

[112] Derrida, J., 1993. *Spectres of Marx.* New York: Routledge, p. 85.

[113] Noam Chomsky, who of course knows a lot of philosophy, but, as you may know, despises "French theory" and tends to criticize US foreign policy without much philosophical commentary.

[114] Examples may be the adult development theorist, the Wilberian integralist, the metatheorist, the "theory U" consultant, the complexity theorist, the syntheist, the speculative realist, the postcapitalist peer-to-peer network economist, to some extent the Habermasian and the posthumanist.
[115] By the way, "pomo" means postmodernist, here used in a wide sense including not only those few who call themselves postmodernists, but all people who explicitly or implicitly subscribe to the critical, relativist, constructivist vision presented above.
[116] Friedrich Nietzsche in *Man Alone with Himself.*
[117] Some interesting developments have been made in this direction (looking at altered states) by the Canadian psychologist Terri O'Fallon, but as you shall see, I follow another path which I find to be more advantageous and to have greater explanatory power.

See O'Fallon, T., 2013. *The Senses: Demystifying Awakening.* San Fransisco, Integral Theory Conference July 2013, Pacific Integral, LLC.

O'Fallon is, to my knowledge, the only theorist who has made explicit the relationship between subjective states and stages of depth development. But there are some issues that render her perspective quite dysfunctional for the purposes of a political sociology. The three major problems with O'Fallon's approach are: 1. she greatly overemphasizes the importance of spiritual experience at the expense of cognitive and symbolic development; 2. she reduces human growth to depth and state development; and 3. she fails to catch the variance and richness of subjective states in everyday life, focusing too much on static stages.
[118] For the purposes of this book we can leave aside the philosophical question about whether or not it is a good idea to "split" reality into two parts: an objective and subjective one. Even if there is ultimately just one reality, we can still benefit from a distinction, at least in this context, between studied behaviors (as viewed by means of intersubjectively verifiable/falsifiable science) and experienced states (the experience you have right here, right now). So *no*, the following argument does not rely upon Cartesian dualism (a soul and a mechanical body, as Descartes proposed), and *no*, I am not a Cartesian dualist. If you want to discuss this further, we can write another Hanzi-book on philosophy. But let's focus on what's important for the moment.
[119] When do such inner horizons occur? Inner landscapes are developed and created when the material world self-organizes in specific ways—a discussion we can omit in this book, but which is fruitfully discussed in (excuse the name-dropping) Søren Brier's cybersemiotics, Karen Barad's agential realism, in systems scientists like Maturana and Varela or Fritjof Capra, and, more speculatively perhaps, in the physicist Sir Roger Penrose's work (the one known for the Penrose-Hawking singularity theorems and many other things).

I am a prudent, not entirely convinced, supporter of quantum mind theory, which suggests that there may be quantum-mechanical explanations for biology and nervous systems. As you may know, the renowned physicist Roger Penrose and medical researcher Stuart Hameroff champion this position, much to detriment of their good names. But their critics, notably Max Tegmark, have pointed out that the scale difference between bio-chemical and quantum phenomena is simply too great for any interaction to realistically occur. Penrose and Hameroff have not been able to produce an explanation for why such interaction should occur. But quantum choice theorists (like Dierderik Aerts and pals) have in turn pointed out that quantum mechanical mathematical modeling seems to fit real behaviors very well, "resolving" some of the "paradoxes" of choice theory in psychology, presented by Daniel Kahneman and earlier by Daniel Ellsberg. This lends some support to the quantum mind theory—as the astonishing results of researchers like Zheng Joyce Wang seem to lend support to there being an intrinsic connection between things quantum and mental processes.

I risk getting out of my depth here. Sticking with social scientists and philosophers like myself, I would recommend the political scientist Alexander Wendt's 2015 book *Quantum Mind*, whose exposé is lucid and diligently made, but whose own theories I would distance myself from (he speculates about collective consciousness, a position I feel is profoundly mistaken). I would also recommend the chapter on ontology and quantum physics in Slavoj Žižek's 2012 book *Less Than Nothing*.

But none of this is actually relevant to the main argument: that subjective experience matters and that it constitutes an inherent part of reality. In our days, in a modern society where everything is evaluated according to its closeness to physics and "objective" reality, it is not surprising that people want to "bolster" the societal value attached to subjective experience by means of "objective" science, often quantum physics. But the whole premise underlying such projects is mistaken: it takes the preeminence of objective science for granted, devaluing the subjective realm in the first place. If this devaluation is avoided to begin with, the need to "prove" consciousness fades away.

More *dualistic* visions (seeing subjectivity and objectivity as separate aspects of reality), like that of David Chalmers, avoid this problem. Quite unfortunately, Chalmers, like Alexander Wendt, also flirts with ideas of collective consciousness, which is something that complicates his theory. I don't support theories about collective consciousness.

[120] Interesting advances have been made in the field of neurophenomenology (looking at how subjective experience and the brain correlate, etc.). The best theory advanced thus far, in my view and to my knowledge, is neuroscientist Christof Koch's *Integrated Information Theory* (IIT).

See: Tononi, G., Koch, C., 2015. Consciousness: here, there and everywhere? *Phil. Trans. R. Soc. B* 370. I can hardly laud this paper enough; these writers have the rare gift of being able to combine neuroscience with philosophy.

[121] I should say something more about the method of this chapter and the following ones. I am presenting a theory about different subjective states that organisms can experience. This necessitates an unconventional methodological move; one that I hold is nevertheless fully valid.

During the cognitive development discussion I had the luxury of relying upon existing empirical research; in the last about "symbol-stages" I employed a kind of interpretative method (a tweaked form of "hermeneutics"). In this chapter and the next one, I rely upon a method that is not, to my knowledge, fully established in the literature on methodology (but is still fairly widely used), a method I call

subjective-deductive. Basically, I use my own subjective experience of life and existence, as well as what I can glean from others through friends, family, lovers, films and literature—and then I *reason* as coherently and stringently as possible to find (or *deduce*) general patterns of the inner landscapes of organisms, and knowledge about the contours of such patterns.

I suppose that the Baltic-German biologist Jakob von Uexküll did something similar when he tried to describe, in his theoretical biology from the early 20th century, the *Umwelt* of different animal species: how they each felt and saw the world. An English term for *Umwelt* might be the "phenomenological environment" of a species. We are looking for the inner horizons of organisms, but now we are not looking at specific species, only at subjective experience in general. We are also avoiding the specific form or content of subjective experience (emotions, sensations, moods, thoughts and so on), and looking at experience as a totality, as the overall pattern of your inner horizons at any given moment—quite simply, which subjective state you are in.

Whereas I believe that the subjective-deductive method is valid, I don't think it is *sufficient* for a scientific theory. It's just a useful crutch for us to think about these things. Hence, neurophenomenological research should be conducted to flesh out (and eventually scrap) my theorizing. The point here, however, is that I cannot seem to find any other theory that I think is more useful than what I propose. So if I am *less wrong* and *more useful* than your default understanding and the prevalent theories in psychology, then my theory is good.

[122] Not in practice; but with the right common efforts subjective states can be affected, which is one of the main points of this book

[123] A theory of emotion that discusses happiness, anger, sadness, surprise, fear, disgust and mixes thereof (which, by the way, is what theories of emotions look like these days, Paul Ekman's "basic emotions" and Robert Plutchik's "wheel of emotions" being the most famous ones, a tradition going back to Darwin's work on emotions) couldn't quite account for most of these words, or for what their common denominator might be. Neither could behavioral science, which looks at behavioral responses to "punishments" and "rewards". Maybe we could go some way by studying the brain, looking at things like the balance of dopamine, noradrenalin and serotonin (as in the "Lövheim cube of emotion") or the different brain wave patterns (so-called "neural oscillation": usually people speak of Alpha, Theta, Beta-waves and the like, but of course, as always with the brain, there is more to the story).

[124] See: Segerstrom, S. C. & Nes, L. S., 2007. Heart rate variability reflects self-regulatory strength, effort and fatigue. *Psychological Science,* Volume 18, pp. 275-81.

See also: Geisler, F. C. M. & Kubiak, T., 2009. Heart rate variability predicts self-control in goal pursuit. *European Journal of Personality,* Volume 23, pp. 623-33.

And: Thayer, J. F., Hansen, A. L., Saus-Rose, E. & Johnsen, B. H., 2009. Heart rate variability, prefrontal neural function, and cognitive performance: the neurovisceral integration perspective on self-regulation, adaptation and health. *Annals of Behavioral Medicine,* Volume 37, pp. 141-53.

[125] German: *Amklötenheit*. Also, excuse the male-centrism. Let's come up with a gender-neutral version, shall we?
[126] Heidegger, M., 1927/1996. *Being and Time*. Albany: State of New York University Press. Translation by Joan Stambaugh.
[127] In conventional happiness research the methodology is usually surveys, i.e. asking people about how well they are doing on e.g. a scale from one to ten, then checking if there is any connection between this answer and other factors, such as age, sex, health, background and so forth.

As happiness research has shown, following Daniel Kahneman's work, there is a difference between the "remembered self" (when you are asked how you've been doing over a period) and the "experienced self" (when you are asked how you are doing a few times a day). They only correlate about 50%, which is comparable to an identical twin.
[128] Perhaps, even, Daniel Kahneman (see previous endnote) brings too much baggage of Western philosophy in through his research question: maybe we should start by asking what experience is, and what forms it may take, prior to any interpretation of a "self". I don't mean to score cheap points off Kahneman's seminal work; only to direct our attention towards *experience proper*.
[129] Even if my scale isn't "proven", it is certainly testable: you would need to device a way of measuring physiological correlates and perhaps people's self-described experiences.
[130] This would explain a lot of the fuss about whether or not humans and other animals act to seek out "happiness" or "pleasure" and "avoid pain". Emotion and sensation are secondary to states. The answer, then, is that organisms sometimes seek "negative" sensations or emotions when this is part of their attempts to self-organize into higher subjective states.
[131] Drugs can also regulate state—although to be frank I am no enthusiast. The comment about LSD in the prologue was mostly to provoke you a bit. It is true that drugs can cause sudden high state experiences, but it is a risky and unreliable path ahead, and—as I will discuss later—it can create unbalanced and thereby pathological (sick) forms of development. Most of all, they can cause very low states and in some cases activate permanent psychiatric disorders. This is not the place to discuss the matter; unfortunately the deeper medical literature on this topic is generally both expensive and rather dense. But sure, sometimes, for some people, consumption of narcotics or medically prescribed drugs may be useful: either to regulate the lower states or to have a "peak experience" and get an idea of the higher ones. As a society, we should probably try to make the taking of drugs legal and regulated under medical expertise and consultation. The work of British neuroscientist Robin Carhart-Harris and his international network of colleagues suggest there may be important therapeutic uses of psychedelics.

See: Carhart-Harris, R. L., Leech, R., Hellyer, P. J. Shanahan, M., Feilding, A., Tagliazucchi, E., Chialvo, D. R., Nutt, D,. The entropic brain: a theory of conscious states informed by neuroimaging research with psychedelic drugs. *Frontiers in Human Neuroscience*, 8: 20. 2014.
[132] Similar claims are made in transpersonal psychologies, notably in the classical American psychologist William James' 1902 published lectures *The Varieties of*

Religious Experience (in which James works implicitly from this assumption), the English Christian mystic Evelyn Underhill's 1911 book *Mysticism* (in which she explicitly speaks of stages of mystical experience) and perhaps, more systematically but less ingeniously, in Daniel Goleman's 1977 work, *The Varieties of Meditative Experience* (in which several mystical traditions are compared). A more recent scholar is the Harvard Medical School professor Daniel P. Brown, whose work of comparative religious psychology has shown that the traditions seem to describe corresponding kinds of progression. I suppose this list of Anglo-Saxon transpersonal psychology would be incomplete without an honorable mention of Ken Wilber and Terri O'Fallon.

[133] I personally know only the first of these lower states, not the more extreme ones—mainly as I suffered from severe anxieties for a period of about seven years during my early adulthood. It is a state in which the heart is darkened, empty, filthy and tormented, and life has no joy or meaning; a helpless and desperate state (what we have categorized here as state 4). I may have nudged upon a yet lower state once during a psychedelic experience: a kind of formless, utter terror—in which I felt almost unimaginably exposed and vulnerable. Other than that, I have only heard and read accounts of psychosis and very negative psychedelic experiences and seen the suffering of others—loved ones as well as people I met when I did studies with the police and saw some very broken human beings.

[134] Note that median state can only be given a discrete number (6, 7, 8, etc.), whereas average can very well be calculated in fractions. Using myself as an example, I went up about two "state levels" of average state after the age of 25, when I had learned meditation through a few hundred hours of guided practice, adjusted my worldview and life goals, worked through some knots and feelings of emptiness in my heart, gotten some routines in on physical exercise, got love relations to work (somewhat), and started being recognized as a philosophical talent by a number of people in authoritative positions. For a long while I had only experienced states ranging from 4 to 7 on the scale; state 6 probably being the most common one—but the average was much lower; I was very often in states 4 and 5. After a period of about seven years, life shifted dramatically: I have never since felt what could be described as genuine angst, even amidst rather challenging periods and adversities. My state now, in its current equilibrium, ranges from a 6 (uneasy, uncomfortable) to an 11 (vast, grand, open), where the 11 is relatively frequent but only lasts for brief moments. My median (most common) state is 7, and my average state is a bit above that that, perhaps at 7.5, meaning that I am more often above 7 than below—so I am probably relatively "normal" in this regard.

[135] Martin, J. A., 2010. *Ego Development Stage Does Not Predict Persistent Non-Symbolic Experience*. San Francisco: UMI Dissertation Publishing.

[136] It has long been established that depression may have genetic components (and, more recent research adds, epigenetic ones). So low states certainly come with certain hardwiring: it should be obvious, for instance, that some organisms have healthier and less painful existences than others. But even the higher states may depend upon genes; the geneticist and HIV-researcher Dean Hamer

published a book in 2004 called *The God Gene*, in which he claims that certain genetic variations may strongly influence our openness to spiritual experience.

[137] Note that I here use the expression "beautiful soul" without any spite or sarcasm. When Hegel discusses the "beautiful soul", he means people who will reject responding productively to political actualities in order to flatter themselves with moralism; this is closer to what I call the "liberal innocent".

[138] Speaking for myself, seven years of severe anxieties motivated me to put in the effort that eventually shifted my state to a point where I began to have deeply existential and spiritual experiences. Even before my shift of median state at the age of 25, there would be rare brief moments in which my angst would fade away and I would feel a kind of enormous clarity and love. It is as if my anxieties are what forced my perspective towards the universality and depth that allowed for the philosophical and spiritual subjective experience to emerge. The same could be said of our friend Doctor Ride-High.

[139] Emerson, R. W., 1909-1914/1969. *Ralph Waldo Emerson—Selected Prose and Poetry*. Ed. R. Cook. San Francisco: Rinehart, p. 97.

[140] Naturally, it is difficult to know exactly what people are talking about when they report Kundalini awakenings and related experiences. But there are some stubs here and there with research on the topic. Not exactly what big pharma like to fund (or governments, for that matter).

See: Arambula, P., E., P., Kawakami, M. & Hughes Gibney, K., 2001. The physiological correlates of Kundalini yoga meditation: a study of a yoga master. *Applied Psychophysiology and Biofeedback*, 26(2), pp. 147-153.

See also: Modestino, E. J., 2016. Neurophenomenology of an altered state of consciousness: an fMRI case study. *Explore: The Journal of Science and Healing*, 12(2), p. 128–35.

[141] Within tantric communities such reports are not uncommon—even men report having prolonged orgasms. Again, the scientific literature is meager, which is a shame.

See: Lousada, M., Angel, E., 2011. Tantric Orgasm: Beyond Masters and Johnson. *Sexual Relationship and Therapy*, 26(4), 389-402.

[142] That last part is of course from the Bhagavad Gita. "As the radiance of a thousand suns, such is the splendor of the mighty one. I am become death, the destroyer of worlds."

Maybe that is a bit over the top? Surely they are making this up? But then again—should it really surprise us if Hindu sages found a thousand suns within, given that we live in a universe where the brightest supernova explosion observed in modern times, ASSASN-15lh, lit up like 600 billion? Just a thought. All I am saying is: it's an awesome world, so why should there not be awesome aspects within ourselves?

[143] Through his brain-scan studies on Brazilian psychic mediums, Sufi mystics, Buddhist meditators, Franciscan nuns, Pentecostals, and participants in secular spirituality rituals, Newberg claims to have found the specific neurological mechanisms responsible for an "enlightenment" experience.

See Newberg, A. & Waldman, M.R., 2006: *How Enlightenment Changes Your Brain: The New Science of Transformation*. New York, Penguin Random House.

[144] A wonderful overview can be found in Jonathan Rowson's RSA report. See: Rowson, J., 2014. *Spiritualise: Revitalising Spirituality to Address 21st Century Challenges*. RSA (Royal Society for the Encouragement of Arts, Manufactures and Commerce).

[145] For a number of reasons, this theory about **the scale of subjective states** is very difficult to understand for most people. A normal person is simply relatively limited in their scope of which subjective states they have experienced. There are generally only a few states that we are consciously aware of, and therefore see as real. If you haven't experienced and have clear memories of very high or low states, you simply have a more difficult time to wrap your head around them.

But the main reason that so few people grasp the "scale of states" is that it requires the coordination of two very different kinds of thinking: a **1st person** view of reality and a **3rd person** view. On the one hand, you must be able to think in terms of phenomenological, subjective experience, being comfortable with using such categories as "being", "awareness", "consciousness", "spirituality", "inner transformation" and so on. Basically, you need to be a romantic and existential kind of person. This is the 1st person view: a view from the inside of your own subjective awareness—looking through your own eyes, smelling with your own nose, and so forth. It is so called because, in grammar, 1st person is that which categorizes "me" and "I".

On the other hand, you must be able to see human beings as *organisms*; indeed as physical and behavioral robots—this is the 3rd person view; in grammar covering the he/she/it/they categories. You view the human organism "from the outside", without any regard to her inner experience: its behaviors, its biochemistry, its brain and nervous system. When seen from this perspective, it becomes apparent that human societies are a set of organisms whose bodies are in some kind of physiological states. These states can be changed by means of exercise, nutrition, social interactions, relaxation and play, contemplation, medical care and pharmacy, fresh air—and, above all, by means of changing the reward/punishment mechanisms that guide behaviors.

In classical Skinnerian (as in B. F. Skinner) behaviorism humans and other organisms are assumed to repeat behaviors which give us rewards, and avoid behaviors that give us punishments (what is called "operant conditioning"). You may remember Pavlov's dogs, who drool when the bell rings, because they know that ringing bell means dinnertime. There are actually four kinds of such mechanisms: positive or negative reward, and positive or negative punishment.

- Positive reward means gaining something you like.
- Negative reward means getting rid of something you don't like, shedding something that hurts.
- Positive punishment means getting hurt.
- Negative punishment means losing something you like.

What we do in this chapter, when seeing human organisms as always being in higher or lower subjective states, is that we connect this relatively mechanical view of psychology to an unyieldingly romantic one. Humans will try to manifest higher states (positive reward), try to get rid of the things that lower their state (negative reward), avoid things which lower their state (positive punishment), and avoid losing things that maintain higher states (negative punishment). An important implication of this is that society is always driven by all four mechanisms, and that all four play a part in maintaining high subjective states in organisms.

What behavioral psychology has not been good at is to see how the state that an organism is *already* in affects how their behavior plays out. For instance, a person who is in a lower state will be more desperate and tend to look for negative rewards very eagerly (getting rid of the pain). A person in a higher state will be able to look for more long-term and sustainable results. But this requires that we have an idea about which subjective states people are in. Come experimental psychology, help us out, will you?

I have already mentioned "pragmatic romanticism" as being an integral part of the metamodern paradigm. Now I would like to suggest a small expansion of this philosophy. This way of thinking connects romantic, existential and spiritual psychology to more scientifically rigid studies of behavior. It is a kind of **romantic behaviorism**. Because these two ways of thinking (romanticism and behaviorism) generally attract very different kinds of people, the combination of the two is rare. More romantically inclined people will shy away from any suggestions that the deeply held, tear-drenched angst of the human condition can be changed by means of jogging, cutting down on sugar, meditating twenty minutes a day, getting better at scoring sexual partners and adjusting the difficulty level of whatever work tasks you have so that you get in a positive flow more often. No!—they will cry with Kierkegaard and Schopenhauer—it is only by facing the deep authentic suffering within yourself, and accepting its inevitability, that you will truly learn! (and so on).

On the other hand, the more scientifically minded folks will vehemently deny the importance of inner growth and subjective experience and will want to return to their "precise metrics" and get away from existential and spiritual searching as quickly as possible: "Decide important matters on basis mere opinion, experience and wishful thinking? Bah, humbug!" Because that stuff just creeps them out—it appears both ineffective and inauthentic.

But reality is made up of both ends: we must look deep within ourselves, *and* understand that this inner life is nothing but the state of an organism. The only true measure of a society, indeed of a world, is which subjective states the organisms are in. That is, by definition, the difference between heaven and hell. And these subjective states are very possible to affect: there is a scale of higher and lower subjective states; and it is perfectly possible to let most people live most of their time in much, much higher subjective states than what is the case in today's world. And in higher states, people would think, act, live and love differently than we do today.

Subjective state is hence a kind of fuel for behaviors. Different kinds of behaviors may require different kinds of subjective states. I would suggest that the more complex and creative behaviors required of us in the new world economy and the internet age run a more refined kind of "fuel": on higher states. Whereas farming and factory work, even administrative office work, can be upheld under conditions of relatively low state drudgery, being creative, curious, tenacious and responsive may require higher subjective states. **The new global knowledge economy requires higher average states to function properly.**

In Stanford psychologist Kelly McGonigal's 2012 book *The Willpower Instinct*, there is plenty of support for such an assumption—she cites examples from more experimental studies than I could name. When people feel bad and exhausted, they tend to act more short-term, giving in to all sorts of temptations and losing self-control more easily. To sustain attention, willpower and flow—or even just keeping an open mind in a world full of contradicting claims—might require greater "wellness" of some sort. In our terminology, it can be said that creativity and independence require higher subjective states.

[146] Wilson, B. M., Mickes, L., Stolarz-Fantino, S., Evrard, M., Fantino, E., 2015. Increased False-Memory Susceptibility After Mindfulness Meditation. *Psychological Science*. September 4, 1-7.

[147] A very promising research program is to be found around the young British neuroscientist Robin Carhart-Harris.

See: Carhart-Harris, R. L., Leech, R., Hellyer, P. J. Shanahan, M., Feilding, A., Tagliazucchi, E., Chialvo, D. R., Nutt, D, 2014. The entropic brain: a theory of conscious states informed by neuroimaging research with psychedelic drugs. *Frontiers in Human Neuroscience*. 8: 20.

[148] Rather than a straightforward linear relationship, some research suggests that "wisdom" does vary with age, but has a different profile than expected. Gisela Labouvie-Vief, a psychologist at the University of Geneva, found that wisdom increases from adolescence to adulthood, peaking in the 30s or 40s, and then trails off in later adulthood.

All of this depends, of course, on how wisdom is defined. I largely dispute Labouvie-Vief's definition, which focuses on how cognition, self-reflexivity and feelings develop together. As you will see in this chapter, I focus on existential depth—for the sake of creating a good model of "effective value meme".

[149] In effect, this corresponds to asking someone about their take on "the meaning of life". It just avoids some of the silliness of that question.

[150] Calhoun, L. G., Tedeschi, R. G., 2013. *Posttraumatic Growth in Clinical Practice*. London: Routledge.

[151] Fischer, A. 2015. Wisdom—the answer to all the questions really worth asking. *The International Journal of Humanities and Social Science*, 5: 9.

[152] Hanzi Freinacht has his own brand of wisdom teaching. It only has three tenets. If you're good, you might read about it in a future book. The three tenets are:

1) It's not about me. Life is not about me.
2) I love you. This is a realization, not a feeling: life is about you, not me.
3) And yes, dear Ralph Waldo Emerson, everything *is* going to be okay. In fact, it always-already is.

[153] The history of Ashoka's reign is partly disputed, but please bear with me for sake of the example.

[154] Then again—*what about* love? Are not love relationships the main source of depth in many people's lives? And what about the body? Some readers, no doubt,

think I have not sufficiently addressed the bodily, sensational aspects of relating to reality. Is not a Tai Chi master or a tantric yogi developed in depth? While I cannot offer an exhaustive discussion in this book, I would like to point out that such practices help us reach states and integrate them; hence they can be conductive to the development of depth.

[155] Beck, D. E., Cowan, C. C., 1996/2005. *Spiral Dynamics: Mastering Values, Leadership and Change*. Malden, MA: Wiley-Blackwell.

[156] Young, I. M., 1996. "Communication and the Other: Beyond Deliberative Democracy" in *Democracy and Difference: Contesting the Boundaries of the Political* ed. Seyla Benhabib; Princeton, Princeton University Press.

[157] Here is a more detailed presentation of the Spiral Dynamics vMemes:

vMeme "color" and name	Historic Period	Society	Psychology
BEIGE "SurvivalSense"	Prehistoric: 100 000 years ago (note that this is an obviously incorrect figure).	Loose bands struggling to survive, fire, tools and burial. No larger clan structures. No contemporary equivalent, not counting *enfants sauvages*.	Impulse-driven, instincts, fulfill basic physiological needs.
PURPLE "KinSpirits"	Stone age: circa 50 000 years ago, including Neolithic age.	Clans and tribal culture. Artwork, imaginary worlds, animistic religion, magic, shamanism, spirits, totem and taboo.	Views oneself as part of nature and the environment, makes no clear distinction between inner and outer world.
RED "PowerGods"	Imperial, agricultural age: circa 10000 years ago.	Organized society with a ruler, slavery and gods. Based around military power and conquest.	Power, glory, status, revenge, rage—defy the gods and gain mastery over the world.
BLUE "TruthForce"	Traditional, religious society: 5000 years ago.	States with organized religions, rule of law under "divine right".	Find meaning by serving a greater good. Obedience, harmony.
ORANGE "StriveDrive"	Modern age: circa 300 years ago.	Capitalist democracies, modern science.	Achieve, compete in fair market, use the best possible information.

GREEN "HumanBond"	Postmodern age: first appeared circa 150 years ago, grew big post-1968.	Social democracies, social movements, critique of modern society.	Sensitive, soft values, inclusion, multiplicity, relativism, care, collective values.
YELLOW "FlexFlow"	Systemic and cybernetic thinking. Only about 50 years.	World-centric values, trying to synthesize and defend all former vMemes. No society described.	Process-oriented and system-sensitive thinking. Dynamic, dialectical, open-ended.
TURQUOISE "GlobalView"	Holistic thinking. Identified with the emergence of Spiral Dynamics itself, the 1990s.	New Age communities (my choice of words, not theirs) where people are both deeply individualized and connected to a sense of universal spirituality.	Experience the wholeness of existence through spirit and mind. Wrestle profound, eternal questions, in solidarity with all sentient beings.

[158] Let's specify my claims about the model's weaknesses and its lack of almost any basic scientific rigor, perhaps even what must be seen as the intellectual dishonesty of its originator and main proponent Don Beck. The first and foremost weakness of the model is that it squeezes all developmental dimensions into one single framework: there is only really one single sequence of development, and it takes no account of which culture a person lives in, in which time, of psychological health or anything else. But to be fair, this is a mistake shared by most of the field of adult stage development.

It furthermore bases these very strong claims upon a weak empirical method, simply asking folks to fill in a rather simple questionaire. From there, it makes quite strong empirical claims about how many people in the world belong to each value meme and how much power they hold globally (without even defining "power"). And then it opens the door to a series of scholars who can only be described as very poor intellectuals, claiming to be able to explain political systems and economic policies with its help (they cannot), who are actively supported by Don Beck himself.

Other than that, the model flatters and glorifies the higher value memes, and defines them largely as adhering to the Spiral Dynamics model itself (making higher stage people "spiral wizards" and whatnot)—so all you need to do in order to be a super-duper person is to believe in everything that Don Beck says and try to use his model to explain pretty much everything. And, of course, it paints these rosy higher value memes in very spiritual terms, so that all the New Age folks can safely assume that they themselves are the highest and most developed people in history. And whenever anybody disagrees with you for whatever reason, Spiral

Dynamics lets you pat your own shoulder: surely, they are of a lower value meme than yourself.

[159] No joke. Contemporary Afghan society manifests many Faustian properties. I once taught a course about the historical emergence of the "self" (social psychology) and used the Icelandic sagas as an example of writing which did not include speculations upon the inner lives of the characters (because Faustian culture corresponds to MHC stage 9 Concrete). As you may know, these stories give earthy and detailed depictions of endless family feuds. A bright young student from Afghanistan noted: "This is exactly what things are like back home".

[160] Note that I am not saying that Pagan or Voodoo practitioners are mobsters, juvenile or anything of the sort. The same value meme can find many different expressions, and most religions can, in practice, span across several value memes.

[161] I am not claiming, of course, that all people who are against the EU or opposed to immigration into Western countries are necessarily of this effective value meme, but there certainly is a correlation.

[162] I can hardly give enough praise to Stein's work here. It really is an excellent piece of work.

Stein, Z., (2010). Now you get it, now you don't: developmental differences in the understanding of integral theory and practice. In Esbjörn-Hargens (Ed.) *Integral theory in action: applied, theoretical, and practical applications of the AQAL model.* (pp. 175-203). SUNY University Press (the paper is available at www.zakstein.org).

See also: Stein, Z. & Hiekkinen, K., (2010). Developmental differences in the understanding of Integral Theory and Practice: Preliminary results from the iTEACH project. Paper presented at Biannual Integral Theory Conference, John F. Kennedy University. Pleasant Hill, CA (www.zakstein.org).

[163] Collins, R., 2002/1998. The Sociology of Philosophies: A Global Theory of Intellectual Change. Cambridge, MA: Harvard University Press.

[164] Capra, F. & Luisi, P. L., 2014. *The Systems View of Life: A Unifying Vision.* New York: Cambridge University Press.

[165] The *grande histoire* of metamodernism is described in the history book of this series.

[166] Brier, S., 2008. *Cybersemiotics: Why Information Is Not Enough!* Toronto: University of Toronto Press.

[167] Barad, K., 2007. Meeting the Universe Halfway. Quantum Physics and the Entanglement of Matter and Meaning. London: Duke University Press.

[168] Published April 2015 by Seth Abramson on www.metamoderna.org.

[169] Zavarzadeh, M., 1975. The apocalyptic fact and the eclipse of fiction in recent American prose narratives. *Journal of American Studies,* IX(1), pp. 69-83.

[170] Please see the discussion in another Hanzi-book: *The 6 Hidden Patterns of World History.*

[171] Beck, U., Bonss, W. & Lau, C., 2003. The theory of reflexive modernization: problematic, hypothesis and research programme. *Theory, Culture and Society,* Volume 20(2), pp. 1-33.

See also Giddens, A., 1991. *The Consequences of Modernity.* Stanford, CA: Stanford University Press.

[172] I return to discussing postmodernism at length in another book, *The 6 Hidden Patterns of World History*, in which I discuss historical "meta-memes".
[173] Note that this "protosythesis" thing is my wording, not Vermeulen and van der Akker's.
[174] Vermeulen, T. & van der Akker, R., 2010. Notes on Metamodernism. *Journal of Aesthetics and Culture,* Volume II, pp. 1-14.

Printed by Amazon Italia Logistica S.r.l.
Torrazza Piemonte (TO), Italy

28949350R00237